Understanding Language Series

Series Editors: Bernard Comrie and Greville Corbett

Understanding Morphology

Martin Haspelmath

Max Planck Institute for Evolutionary Anthropology, Leipzig

A member of the Hodder Headline Group
LONDON

Distributed in the United States of America by
Oxford University Press Inc., New York

First published in Great Britain in 2002 by
Arnold, a member of the Hodder Headline Group,
338 Euston Road, London NW1 3BH

http://www.arnoldpublishers.com

Distributed in the United States of America by
Oxford University Press Inc.,
198 Madison Avenue, New York, NY10016

British Library Cataloguing in Publication Data
A catalogue record for this book is available from the British Library

Library of Congress Cataloging-in-Publication Data
A catalog record for this book is available from the Library.of Congress

ISBN 0 340 76025 7 (hb)
ISBN 0 340 76026 5 (pb)

4 5 6 7 8 9 10

Typeset in 10/12pt Palatino by Phoenix Photosetting, Chatham, Kent
Printed and bound by Replika Press Pvt. Ltd., India.

Contents

Preface

This book provides an introduction to the field of linguistic morphology. It gives an overview of the basic notions and the most important theoretical issues, emphasizing throughout the diversity of morphological patterns in human languages. Readers who are primarily interested in understanding English morphology should not be deterred by this, however, because an individual language can be understood in much greater depth when viewed against the cross-linguistic background.

The focus of this book is on morphological phenomena and on broad issues that have occupied morphologists of various persuasions for a long time. No attempt is made to trace the history of linguists' thinking about these issues, and references to the theoretical literature are mostly confined to the 'Further reading' sections. I have not adopted any particular theoretical framework, although I did have to opt for one particular descriptive format for morphological rules (see Section 3.2.2). Readers should be warned that this format is no more 'standard' than any other format, and not particularly widespread either. But I have found it useful, and the advanced student will soon realize how it can be translated into other formats.

Although it is often said that beginning students are likely to be confused by the presentation of alternative views in textbooks, this book does not pretend that there is one single coherent and authoritative view of morphology. Debates and opposing viewpoints are so much part of science that omitting them completely from a textbook would convey a wrong impression of what linguistic research is like. And I did not intend to remain neutral in these debates, not only because it would have been virtually impossible anyway, but also because a text that argues for a particular view is invariably more interesting than one that just presents alternative views.

A number of people have helped me in writing this book. My greatest thanks go to the series editors, Bernard Comrie and Greville Corbett, who provided countless suggestions for improving the book.

I also thank Renate Raffelsiefen for her expert advice on phonological questions, as well as Tomasz Bak and Agnieszka Reid for help with Polish examples, and Claudia Schmidt for help with the indexes.

Finally, I thank Susanne Michaelis for all kinds of help, both in very specific and in very general ways. This book is dedicated to our son, Gabriel.

Leipzig
December 2001

Abbreviations

ABL	ablative	EXCL	exclusive
ABS	absolutive	FOC	focus
ACC	accusative	F	feminine
AG	agent	FUT	future
ADJ	adjective	G	gender (e.g. G1 = gender 1)
ADV	adverb(ial)	GEN	genitive
AFF	affirmative	HYP	hypothetical
AGR	agreement	IMP	imperative
ALL	allative	IMPF	imperfect(ive)
ANTIC	anticausative	IMPV	imperative
ANTIP	antipassive	INCL	inclusive
AOR	aorist	INESS	inessive
ART	article	INF	infinitive
ASP	aspect	INSTR	instrumental
AUX	auxiliary	INTF	interfix
CAUS	causative	INTR/intr.	intransitive
CLF	classifier	LOC	locative
COMP	complementizer	M	masculine
COMPL	completive	N	noun
COND	conditional	N	neuter
CONT	continuative	NEG	negation, negative
CONV	converb	NP	noun phrase
DAT	dative	NOM	nominative
DECL	declarative	OBJ	object
DEF	definite	OBL	oblique
DEM	demonstrative	OED	*Oxford English Dictionary*
DET	determiner	PASS	passive
DO	direct object	PAT	patient
DU	dual	PERF	perfect
DUR	durative	PFV	perfective
ERG	ergative	PL	plural

POSS	possessive	REFL	reflexive
PP	prepositional phrase	REL	relative clause marker
PRED	predicate	SG	singular
PREF	prefix	SS	same-subject
PRES	present	SUBJ	subject
PRET	preterite	SUBORD	subordinator
PRIV	privative	SUF	suffix
PROG	progressive	TOP	topic
PROPR	proprietive	TR/tr.	transitive
PTCP	participle	V	verb
RECIP	reciprocal	VP	verb phrase

Introduction

1.1 What is morphology?

Morphology is the study of the **internal structure of words**. Somewhat paradoxically, morphology is both the oldest and one of the youngest sub-disciplines of grammar. It is the oldest because, as far as we know, the first linguists were primarily morphologists. The earliest extant grammatical texts are well-structured lists of morphological forms of Sumerian words, some of which are shown in (1.1). They are attested on clay tablets from Ancient Mesopotamia and date from around 1600 BCE.

(1.1) *badu*   'he goes away'   *inǧen*   'he went'
      baduun   'I go away'   *inǧenen*   'I went'
      bašidu   'he goes away to him'   *inšiǧen*   'he went to him'
      bašiduun   'I go away to him'   *inšiǧenen*   'I went to him'
                                                              (Jacobsen 1974: 53–4)

Sumerian was the traditional literary language of Mesopotamia, but by the second millennium BCE, it was no longer spoken as a medium of everyday communication (having been replaced by the Semitic language Akkadian), so it needed to be recorded in grammatical texts. Morphology was also prominent in the writings of the greatest grammarian of Antiquity, the Indian Pāṇini (fifth century BCE), and in the Greek and Roman grammatical tradition. Until the nineteenth century, Western linguists often thought of grammar as consisting primarily of word structure, perhaps because the classical languages Greek and Latin had fairly rich morphological patterns that were difficult for speakers of the modern European languages.

This is also the reason why it was only in the second half of the nine-teenth century that the term *morphology* was invented and became current. Earlier there was no need for a special term, because the term *grammar* mostly evoked word structure, i.e. morphology. The terms *phonology* (for sound structure) and *syntax* (for sentence structure) had existed for centuries when the term *morphology* was introduced. Thus, in this sense morphology is a young discipline.

Our initial definition of morphology, as the study of the internal structure of words, needs some qualification, because words have internal structure in two very different senses. On the one hand, they are made up of sequences of sounds (or gestures in sign language), i.e. they have internal **phonological structure**. Thus, the English word *nuts* consists of the four sounds (or, as we will say, *phonological segments*) [nʌts]. In general, phonological segments such as [n] or [t] cannot be assigned a specific meaning – they have a purely contrastive value (so that, for instance, *nuts* can be distinguished from *cuts, guts, shuts*, from *nets, notes, nights*, and so on).

But often formal variations in the shapes of words correlate systematically with semantic changes. For instance, the words *nuts, nights, necks, backs, taps* (and so on) share not only a phonological segment (the final [s]), but also a semantic component: they all refer to a multiplicity of entities from the same class. And, if the final [s] is lacking (*nut, night, neck, back, tap*), reference is made consistently to only one such entity. By contrast, the words *blitz, box, lapse* do not refer to a multiplicity of entities, and there are no semantically related words **blit, *bok, *lap*.[1] We will call words like *nuts* '(morphologically) **complex words**'.

In a morphological analysis, we would say that the final [s] of *nuts* expresses plural meaning when it occurs at the end of a noun. But the final [s] in *lapse* does not have any meaning, and *lapse* does not have morphological structure. Thus, morphological structure exists if there are groups of words that show identical partial resemblances in both form and meaning. Morphology can be defined as in Definition 1.

Definition 1
Morphology is the study of systematic covariation in the form and meaning of words.

It is important that this form–meaning covariation occurs systematically in groups of words. When there are just two words with partial form–meaning resemblances, these may be merely accidental. Thus, one would not say that the word *hear* is morphologically structured and related to *ear*. Conceivably, *h* could mean 'use', so *h-ear* would be 'use one's ear', i.e. 'hear'. But this is the only pair of words of this kind (there is no **heye* 'use one's eye', **helbow* 'use one's elbow', etc.), and everyone agrees that the resemblances are accidental in this case.

---

[1] The asterisk symbol (*) is used to mark nonexistent or impossible expressions.

Morphological analysis typically consists of the identification of parts of words, or, more technically, **constituents** of words. We can say that the word *nuts* consists of two constituents: the element *nut* and the element *s*. In accordance with a widespread typographical convention, we will often separate word constituents by a hyphen: *nut-s*. It is often suggested that morphological analysis primarily consists in breaking up words into their parts and establishing the rules that govern the co-occurrence of these parts. The smallest meaningful constituents of words that can be identified are called **morphemes**. In *nut-s*, both the suffix *-s* and the stem *nut* represent a morpheme. Other examples of words consisting of two morphemes would be *break-ing, hope-less, re-write, cheese-board*; words consisting of three morphemes are *re-writ-ing, hope-less-ness, ear-plug-s*; and so on. Thus, morphology could alternatively be defined as in Definition 2.

Definition 2
Morphology is the study of the combination of morphemes to yield words.

This definition looks simpler and more concrete than Definition 1. It would make morphology quite similar to syntax, which is usually defined as 'the study of the combination of words to yield sentences'. However, we will see later that Definition 2 does not work in all cases, so that we should stick to the somewhat more abstract Definition 1 (see especially Section 3.2.2 and Chapter 9).

In addition to its main sense, where morphology refers to a subdiscipline of linguistics, it is also often used in a closely related sense, to denote a part of the language system. Thus, we can speak of 'the morphology of Spanish' (meaning Spanish word structures) or of 'morphology in the 1980s' (meaning a subdiscipline of linguistics). The term *morphology* shares this ambiguity with other terms such as *syntax*, *phonology* and *grammar*, which may also refer either to a part of the language or to the study of that part of the language. This book is about morphology in both senses. It is hoped that it will help the reader to understand morphology both as a part of the language system and as a part of linguistics.

One important limitation of the present book should be mentioned right at the beginning: it deals only with spoken languages. Sign languages of course have morphology as well, and the only justification for leaving them out of consideration here is the author's limited competence. As more and more research is done on sign languages, it can be expected that these studies will have a major impact on our views of morphology and language structure in general.

1.2 Morphology in different languages

Morphology is not equally prominent in all (spoken) languages. What one language expresses morphologically may be expressed by a separate word or left implicit in another language. For example, English expresses the plural of nouns by means of morphology (*nut/nuts, night/nights*, and so on), but Yoruba (a language of south-western Nigeria) uses a separate word for expressing the same meaning. Thus, *ọkùnrin* means '(the) man', and the word *àwọn* can be used to express the plural: *àwọn ọkùnrin* 'the men'. But in many cases where several entities are referred to, this word is not used and plurality is simply left implicit.

Quite generally, we can say that English makes more use of morphology than Yoruba. But there are many languages that make more use of morphology than English. For instance, as we saw in (1.1), Sumerian uses morphology to distinguish between 'he went' and 'I went', and between 'he went' and 'he went to him', where English must use separate words. In Classical Greek, there is a dual form for referring to two items, e.g. *adelphṓ* 'two brothers'. In English it is possible to use the separate word 'two' to render this form, but most of the time one would simply use the plural form and leave the precise number of items implicit.

Linguists sometimes use the terms **analytic** and **synthetic** to describe the degree to which morphology is made use of in a language. Languages like Yoruba, Vietnamese or English, where morphology plays a relatively modest role, are called **analytic**. Consider the following example sentences.[2]

(1.2) Yoruba
> *Nwọn ó   maa gbà   pọ́nùn   mẹ́wǎ   lọ́sọ̀ọ̀sẹ̀.*
> they FUT PROG get   pound   ten   weekly
> 'They will be getting £10 a week.'

(Rowlands 1969:93)

(1.3) Vietnamese
> *Hai đú.a   bo⁷   nhau   là   tại   gia-đình thằng chông.*
> two individual leave each.other be because.of family   guy   husband
> 'They divorced because of his family.'

(Nguyen 1997:223)

When a language has almost no morphology and thus exhibits an extreme degree of analyticity, it is also called **isolating**. Yoruba and Vietnamese, but not English, are usually qualified as isolating. Languages like Sumerian, Swahili (a language of East Africa) or Lezgian (an eastern

---

[2] For each example sentence from an unfamiliar language, not only an idiomatic translation is provided, but also a literal ('morpheme-by-morpheme') translation. The abbreviations are found on pp. xii–xiii, and further notational conventions are explained in the Appendix to Chapter 2.

Caucasian language), where morphology plays a more important role, would be called **synthetic**. Let us again look at two example sentences.

(1.4) Swahili

Ndovu	*wa-wili*	*wa-ki-song-ana*		*zi-umia-zo*	*ni*	*nyika.*
elephants	PL-two	3PL-SUBORD-jostle-RECIP		3SG-hurt-REL	is	grass

'When two elephants jostle, what is hurt is the grass.'

(Ashton 1947:114)

(1.5) Lezgian

Marf-adi	*wiči-n*	*qalin*	*st'al-ra-ldi*	*qaw*	*gata-zwa-j.*
rain-ERG	self-GEN	dense	drop-PL-INSTR	roof	hit-IMPF-PAST

'The rain was hitting the roof with its dense drops.'

(Haspelmath 1993:140)

When a language has an extraordinary amount of morphology and perhaps many compound words, it is called **polysynthetic**. An example is Greenlandic Eskimo.

(1.6) Greenlandic Eskimo

Paasi-nngil-luinnar-para	*ilaa-juma-sutit.*
understand-not-completely-1SG.SUBJ.3SG.OBJ.INDIC	come-want-2SG.PTCP

'I didn't understand at all that you wanted to come along.'

(Fortescue 1984:36)

The distinction between analytic and (poly)synthetic languages is not a bipartition or a tripartition, but a continuum, ranging from the most radically isolating to the most highly polysynthetic languages. We can determine the position of a language on this continuum by computing its degree of synthesis, i.e. the ratio of morphemes per word in a random text sample of the language. Table 1.1 gives the degree of synthesis for a small selection of languages.

Language	Ratio of morphemes per word
Greenlandic Eskimo	3.72
Sanskrit	2.59
Swahili	2.55
Old English	2.12
Lezgian	1.93
German	1.92
Modern English	1.68
Vietnamese	1.06

Table 1.1 The degree of synthesis of some languages

Source: based on Greenberg (1959), except for Lezgian.

Although English has much more morphology than isolating languages like Yoruba and Vietnamese, it still has a lot less than many other languages. For this reason, it will be necessary to refer extensively to languages other than English in this book.

1.3 The goals of morphological research

Morphological research aims to describe and explain the morphological patterns of human languages. It is useful to distinguish four more specific sub-goals of this endeavour: elegant description, cognitively realistic description, system-external explanation and a restrictive architecture for description.

(i) **Elegant description**. All linguists agree that morphological patterns (just like other linguistic patterns) should be described in an elegant and intuitively satisfactory way. Thus, morphological descriptions should contain a rule saying that English nouns form their plural by adding -s, rather than simply listing the plural forms for each noun in the dictionary (*abbot, abbots; ability, abilities; abyss, abysses; accent, accents; ...*). In a computer program that simulates human language, it may in fact be more practical to adopt the listing solution, but linguists would find this inelegant. The main criterion for elegance is **generality**. Scientific descriptions should, of course, reflect generalizations in the data and should not merely list all known individual facts. But generalizations can be formulated in various ways, and linguists often disagree in their judgements of what is the most elegant description. It is therefore useful to have a further objective criterion that makes reference to the speakers' knowledge of their language.

(ii) **Cognitively realistic description**. Most linguists would say that their descriptions should not only be elegant and general, but they should also be cognitively realistic. In other words, they should express the same generalizations about grammatical systems that the speakers' cognitive apparatus has unconsciously arrived at. We know that the speakers' knowledge of English does not only consist of lists of singulars and plurals, but comprises a general rule of the type 'add -s to a singular form to get a plural noun'. Otherwise speakers would be unable to form the plural of nouns they have never encountered before. But they do have this ability: if you tell an English speaker that a certain musical instrument is called a *duduk*, they know that the plural is (or can be) *duduks*. The dumb computer program that contains only lists of singulars and plurals would fail miserably here. Of course, cognitively realistic description is a much more ambitious goal than merely elegant description, and we would really have to be able to look inside people's heads for a full understanding of the cognitive machinery. So this is mainly a programmatic goal at present, but it often affects the way linguists work. Sometimes they reject proposed descriptions because they seem cognitively implausible, and sometimes they collaborate with psychologists and neurologists and take their research results into account.

(iii) **System-external explanation**. Once a satisfactory description of morphological patterns has been obtained, many linguists ask an even more ambitious question: why are the patterns the way they are? In other words, they ask for explanations. But we have to be careful: most facts about linguistic patterns are historical accidents and as such cannot be explained. The fact that the English plural is formed by adding -s is a good example of such a historical accident. There is nothing necessary about plural -s: Hungarian plurals are formed by adding -k, Swedish plurals add -r, Hebrew plurals add -im or -ot, and so on. Only non-accidental facts, i.e. universals of human language, can be explained, so, before asking why-questions, we must find out which morphological patterns are universal. Clearly, the s-plural is not universal, and, as we saw in the preceding section, not even the morphological expression of the plural is universal – Yoruba is an example of a language that lacks morphological plurals. So even the fact that English nouns have plurals is not more than a historical accident. But there is something about plurals that is not accidental: nouns denoting people are quite generally more likely to have plurals than nouns denoting things. For instance, in Tzutujil (a Mayan language of Guatemala), only human nouns have regular morphological plural forms (Dayley 1985: 139). We can formulate the universal statement in (1.7).

(1.7) *A universal statement:*
If a language has morphological plural forms of nouns at all, it will have plurals of nouns denoting people.

(Corbett 2000: ch. 3)

Because of its 'if ... then' form, this statement is true also of languages like English (where most nouns have plurals) and Yoruba (where nouns do not have a morphological plural). Since it is (apparently) true of all languages, it is in all likelihood not a historical accident, but reflects something deeper, a general property of human language that can perhaps be explained with reference to system-external considerations. For instance, one might propose that (1.7) is the case because, when the referents of nouns are people, it makes a greater difference how many they are than when the referents are things. Thus, plurals of people-denoting nouns are more useful, and languages across the world are thus more likely to have them. This explanation (whatever its merits) is an example of a system-external explanation in the sense that it refers to facts outside the language system: the usefulness of number distinctions in speech is such a system-external fact, because it concerns exclusively the sphere of language use.

(iv) **A restrictive architecture for description**. Many linguists see an important goal of grammatical research in formulating some general design principles of grammatical systems that all languages seem to adhere to. In other words, linguists try to construct an architecture for description (also called **grammatical theory**) that all language-particular descriptions must conform to. For instance, it has been observed that rules by which constituents are fronted to the beginning of a sentence can affect syntactic constituents (such as whole words or phrases), but not morphological constituents (i.e. morphemes that are parts of larger words). Thus, (1.8b) is a possible sentence (it can be derived from a structure like 1.8a), but (1.9b) is impossible (it cannot be derived from 1.9a). (The subscript line ___ stands for the position that the question word *what* would occupy if it had not been moved to the front.)

(1.8) a. *We can buy cheese.*
 b. *What can we buy ___ ?*

(1.9) a. *We can buy a cheeseboard.*
 b. **What can we buy a ___-board?*

This restriction on fronting (which seems to hold for all languages that have such a fronting rule) follows automatically if fronting rules (such as *what*-fronting) and morpheme-combination rules (such as compounding, which yields *cheeseboard* from *cheese* and *board*) are separated from each other in the descriptive architecture. A possible architecture for grammar is shown in Figure 1.1, where the boxes around the grammatical components 'syntax', 'morphology' and 'phonology' symbolize the separateness of each of the components.

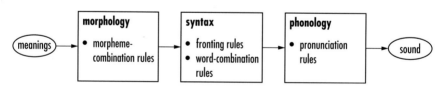

Figure 1.1 A possible descriptive architecture for grammar

This architecture is restrictive because it automatically disallows certain logically possible interactions of rules (see Section 8.5 for more discussion). Many linguists assume that the architecture of grammar is innate – it is the same for all languages because it is genetically fixed for the human species. The innate part of speakers' grammatical knowledge is also called **Universal Grammar**. To sum up, one goal of morphological research is to discover those principles of the innate Universal Grammar that are relevant for word structure.

The goals (iii) and (iv) are similar in that both ask deeper, **theoretical** questions, and both exclusively concern universal aspects of morphology. And both are more ambitious than (i) and (ii) in that they involve explanation in some sense. Thus, one might say that Universal Grammar-oriented research asks questions such as 'Why cannot constituents of words be fronted to the beginning of the sentence?' and answers them with reference to a hypothesis about the innate architecture of grammar ('Because fronting rules are part of the syntactic component, and morpheme-combinations are part of morphology, and syntax and morphology are separate'). However, explanations of this kind are strictly system-internal, whereas explanations of the kind we saw earlier are even more general in that they link universal properties of grammars to general facts about human beings that are external to the grammatical system.

It is a curious observation on the sociology of science that currently most linguists seem to be concerned either with system-external explanation or with formulating an architecture for grammatical description, but not with both goals simultaneously. There are thus two primary orientations in contemporary theoretical morphological research: the **functionalist** orientation, which aims at system-external explanation, and the **generative** (or **formalist**) orientation, which seeks to discover the principles of the innate grammatical architecture. However, it does not seem wise to divide the labour of morphological research in this way, because neither system-external factors nor innate principles can explain the whole range of morphological patterns. Accordingly, both goals will be simultaneously pursued in the more theoretically oriented parts of this book.

1.4 A brief user's guide to this book

Sources of data

In this book I give examples from many different languages. When they are from well-known and widely studied languages such as Modern English, Russian, Standard Arabic or Old English, I do not give a reference because the data can easily be obtained from any standard reference book. But for examples from less widely known languages, the reference is given after the example.

Sources of ideas

In this book, I focus on morphological data and problems of analysis, not on the history of thinking about these issues in linguistics. Thus, I rarely mention names of particular authors in the text, and references to sources of ideas are given only in a few very specific cases (as in Table 1.1 and ex. (1.7)). In general, the reader is referred to the section 'Further reading', where all the most important works on theoretical morphology are mentioned.

Glossary

The glossary contains the technical terms relating to morphology that are used in this book. In addition to giving a brief definition, the glossary also refers the reader to the most important places where the term is discussed in the text.

Language index

Many languages mentioned in this book will be unfamiliar to the reader. The language index simultaneously serves to give information on each language, in particular about its genealogical affiliation and the place where it is spoken.

Spelling and transcription

Morphology of spoken languages deals with spoken words, so ideally all the examples should be in phonetic transcription in this book. But since many languages have a conventional spelling that renders the pronunciation more or less faithfully, it was more practical and less confusing to adopt that spelling for the examples here. (Although English spelling is not particularly close to the pronunciation, English examples will usually be given in the spelling, because it is assumed that the readers know their pronunciation.) Examples cited in the spelling (or conventional transcription) are always printed in italics, whereas examples cited in phonetic transcription are printed in ordinary typeface and are usually included in square brackets.

Abbreviations

A list of abbreviations (especially abbreviations of grammatical terms) is found on pp. xii–xiii.

Summary of Chapter 1

Morphology is most simply defined as the study of the combination of morphemes to yield words, but a somewhat more abstract definition (as the study of systematic covariation in the form and meaning of words) will turn out to be more satisfactory. Different languages vary strikingly in the extent to which they make use of morphology. The goals of morphological research are (on the descriptive level) elegant and cognitively realistic description of morphological structures, plus (on the theoretical level) system-external explanation and the discovery of a restrictive architecture for description (perhaps based on innate knowledge).

Further reading

For an elementary introduction to morphology, see Coates (1999).

Other morphology textbooks that are somewhat similar in scope to the present book are Bauer (1988) and Bubenik (1999) (as well as Scalise (1994), in Italian, and Plungian (2000), in Russian). Spencer (1991) is a very thorough introduction that concentrates on the generative orientation in morphology. Matthews (1991) puts particular emphasis on the definition of morphological concepts. Carstairs-McCarthy (1991) gives an excellent overview of the theoretical debates in the 1970s and 1980s.

The most comprehensive work on morphology that has ever been written by a single author is Mel'čuk (1993–2000) (five volumes, in French). Although its style is somewhat unusual, it is very readable.

Reference works that are devoted exclusively to morphology are Spencer and Zwicky (1998) and Booij, Lehmann and Mugdan (2000–2). A bibliography is Beard and Szymanek (1988).

The complementarity of the functionalist and the generative approaches to morphology is explained and emphasized in the introductory chapter of Hall (1992).

An introduction to a sign language that also discusses morphology is Sutton-Spence and Woll (1999).

A note on the history of the term *morphology*: in the biological sense ('the study of the form of animals and plants'), the term was coined by Johann Wolfgang von Goethe (1749–1832), and, in the linguistic sense, it was first used by August Schleicher (1859).

Exercises

1. Which of the following English words are morphologically complex? For each complex word, list at least two other words that provide evidence for your decision (i.e. words that are both semantically and formally related to it).

    nights, owl, playing, affordable, indecent, reprimand, indolent, bubble, during, searched, hopeful, redo

2. Identify the morphological constituents and describe their meanings in the following Standard Chinese nouns.

chàngcí	'libretto'	*dǐngdēng*	'top light'
chàngjī	'gramophone'	*diànchē*	'streetcar, tram'
chuánwěi	'stern'	*diàndēng*	'electric lamp'
cíwěi	'suffix'	*diànjī*	'electrical machine'

diànlì	'electric power'	*qìchē*	'car'
diànshì	'television'	*qìchuán*	'steamship'
dòngwùxué	'zoology'	*shāndǐng*	'summit'
dòngwùyóu	'animal oil'	*shìchàng*	'sightsinging'
dòngwùyuán	'zoo'	*shìlì*	'eyesight'
fángdǐng	'roof'	*shùcí*	'number word'
fángkè	'tenant'	*shuǐchē*	'watercart'
fēichuán	'airship'	*shuǐlì*	'waterpower'
fēijī	'aeroplane'	*shùxué*	'mathematics'
fēiyú	'flying fish'	*wěidēng*	'tail light'
huāchē	'festooned vehicle'	*wěishuǐ*	'tail water'
huāyuán	'flower garden'	*yóudēng*	'oil lamp'
jīchē	'locomotive'	*yóuzhǐ*	'oil paper'
jiǎolì	'strength of one's legs'	*yúyóu*	'fishoil'
kèfáng	'guest house'	*zhǐhuā*	'paper flower'

3. Identify the morphological constituents and their meanings in the following Tzutujil verbs (Dayley 1985:87) (A note on Tzutujil spelling: *x* is pronounced [ʃ], and 7 is pronounced [ʔ].)

xinwari	'I slept'	*xoqeeli*	'we left'
neeli	'he or she leaves'	*ninwari*	'I sleep'
ne7eeli	'they leave'	*xixwari*	'you(PL) slept'
nixwari	'you(PL) sleep'	*xe7eeli*	'they left'
xateeli	'you(SG) left'	*xwari*	'he or she slept'
natwari	'you(SG) sleep'		

How would you say 'I left', 'he or she sleeps', 'we sleep'?

4. In the following list of Hebrew words, find at least three sets of word pairs whose two members covary formally and semantically, so that a morphological relationship can be assumed. For each set of word pairs, describe the formal and semantic differences.

kimut	'wrinkling'	*maħšev*	'computer'
diber	'he spoke'	*masger*	'lock'
ħašav	'he thought'	*dibra*	'she spoke'
sagra	'she shut'	*milmel*	'he muttered'
ħašav	'she thought'	*kimta*	'she wrinkled'
kalat	'he received'	*milmla*	'she muttered'
maklet	'radio receiver'	*sagar*	'he shut'
kalta	'she received'	*dibur*	'speech'
kimet	'he wrinkled'		

Basic concepts

2

2.1 Lexemes and word-forms

The most basic concept of morphology is of course the concept 'word'. The possibility of singling out words from the stream of speech is basic to our writing system, and for the moment let us assume that a word is whatever corresponds to a contiguous sequence of letters (a more sophisticated approach to this problem will be deferred to Chapter 8). Thus, the first sentence of this chapter consists of twelve words, each separated by a blank space from the neighbouring word(s). But when a dictionary is made, not every sequence of letters is given its own entry. For instance, the words *live, lives, lived* and *living* are pronounced and written differently and are different words in that sense. But a dictionary would contain only a single entry LIVE. The dictionary user is expected to know that *live, lives, lived* and *living* are different instantiations of the 'same' word LIVE.

Thus, there are two rather different notions of 'word': the 'dictionary word' and the 'text word'. Since this distinction is central to morphology, we need special technical terms for the two notions, **lexeme** and **word-form**.

(2.1) Definitions of *lexeme* and *word-form*

> **Lexeme:** A 'dictionary word' is called a *lexeme* (this is because the mental dictionary in our heads is called the *lexicon* by linguists). Lexemes are abstract entities and can be thought of as sets of word-forms. Sometimes we will use the convention of writing lexemes in small capitals (e.g. LIVE is a lexeme).

> **Word-form:** A 'text word' (i.e. whatever is separated by spaces in writing) is called a *word-form*. Word-forms are concrete in that they can be pronounced and used in texts. Every word-form belongs to one lexeme, e.g. the word-form *lived* belongs to the lexeme LIVE.

In the most interesting case, lexemes consist of a fair number of word-forms. The set of word-forms that belongs to a lexeme is often called a **paradigm**. As an example, the paradigm of the Latin noun lexeme INSULA 'island' is given in (2.2). (Earlier we saw a partial paradigm of two Sumerian verb lexemes (see Section 1.1).)

(2.2) The paradigm of INSULA

	singular	plural
nominative	*insula*	*insulae*
accusative	*insulam*	*insulas*
genitive	*insulae*	*insularum*
dative	*insulae*	*insulis*
ablative	*insula*	*insulis*

Latin nouns have at least ten different word-forms and express notions of number (singular, plural) and case (nominative, accusative, etc.). By contrast, English nouns generally have only two or three word-forms (e.g. ISLAND: *island*, *islands* and perhaps *island's*), but the notional distinction between lexemes and word-forms is no less important when the paradigm is small. In fact, for the sake of consistency we have to make the distinction even when a lexeme has just a single word-form, as in the case of many English adjectives (e.g. the adjective SOLID, which has only the word-form *solid*). Since the lexeme is an abstract entity, its name is quite arbitrary. Usually a particularly frequent word-form is selected from the paradigm to represent the lexeme. Thus, in Latin dictionaries, verbs are listed in the first person singular present form, so SCRIBO stands for the lexeme that means 'write' (*scribo* 'I write', *scribis* 'you write', etc.). In Arabic, by contrast, the third person singular perfect is used in dictionaries, so KATABA stands for the lexeme 'write' (*kataba* 'he wrote', *katabtu* 'I wrote', etc.). This form is called the **citation form**, and it is a purely practical convention with no theoretical significance.

Not all morphological relationships are of the type illustrated in (2.2). Different lexemes may also be related to each other, and a set of related lexemes is sometimes called a **word family** (though it should more properly be called a *lexeme family*):

(2.3) Two English word families
a. READ, READABLE, UNREADABLE, READER, READABILITY, REREAD
b. LOGIC, LOGICIAN, LOGICAL, ILLOGICAL, ILLOGICALITY

Although everyone recognizes that these words are related, they are given their own dictionary entries. Thus, the difference between word-forms and lexemes, and between paradigms and word families, is well established in the practice of dictionary-makers, which is known to all educated language users.

At this point we have to ask: why is it that dictionaries treat different morphological relationships in different ways? And why should linguists recognize the distinction between paradigms and word families? After all, linguists cannot base their theoretical decisions on the practice of dictionary-makers – it ought to be the other way round: lexicographers ought to be informed by linguists' analyses. The nature of the difference between lexemes and word-forms will be the topic of Chapter 4, but the most important points will be anticipated here.

(i) Complex lexemes (such as READER or LOGICIAN) generally denote new concepts that are different from the concepts of the corresponding simple lexemes, whereas word-forms often exist primarily to satisfy a formal requirement of the syntactic machinery of the language. Thus, word-forms like *reads* or *reading* do not stand for concepts different from *read*, but they are needed in certain syntactic contexts (e.g. *the girl reads a magazine; reading magazines is fun*).

(ii) Complex lexemes must be listed separately in dictionaries because they are less predictable than word-forms. For instance, one cannot predict that the lexeme *illogicality* exists, because by no means all adjectives have a corresponding -*ity* lexeme (cf. nonexistent words like **naturality, *logicality*). It is impossible to predict that a specialist in logic should be called a *logician* (rather than, say, a **logicist*), and the meaning of complex lexemes is often unpredictable, too: a *reader* can denote not just any person who reads, but also a specific academic position (in the British system) or even a kind of book. By contrast, the properties of word-forms are mostly predictable and hence do not need to be listed separately for each lexeme.

Thus, there are two rather different kinds of morphological relationship among words, for which two technical terms are commonly used:

(2.4) Kinds of morphological relationship
       inflection   (= inflectional morphology)
                the relationship between word-forms of a lexeme
       derivation (= derivational morphology)
                the relationship between lexemes of a word family

Morphologists also use the corresponding verbs *inflect* and *derive*. For instance, one would say that the Latin lexeme INSULA is inflected (or inflects) for case and number, and that the lexeme READER is derived from the lexeme READ. A derived lexeme is also called a **derivative**.

It is not always easy to tell how word-forms are grouped into lexemes. For instance, does the word-form *nicely* belong to the lexeme NICE, or does it represent a lexeme of its own (NICELY), which is in the same word family as NICE? Issues of this sort will be discussed in some detail in Chapter 4. Whenever it is unclear or irrelevant whether two words are inflectionally or derivationally related, the term *word* will be used in this book instead of *lexeme* or *word-form*. And for the same reason even the most technical writings on morphology often continue to use the term *word*.

Some morphologically complex words belong to two (or more) word families simultaneously. For instance, the lexeme FIREWOOD belongs both in the family of FIRE and in the family of WOOD. Such relationships are called

compounding, and lexemes like FIREWOOD are called **compound lexemes.** Compounding is often grouped together with derivation under the category of **word formation** (i.e. lexeme formation). The various conceptual distinctions that we have seen so far are summarized in Figure 2.1.

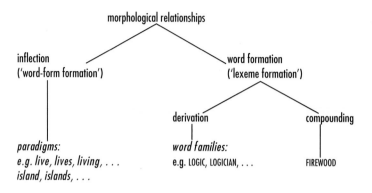

Figure 2.1 Subdivisions of morphology

2.2 Morphemes

We have seen that morphological structure exists if a group of words shows partial form–meaning resemblances. In most cases, the relation between form and meaning is quite straightforward: parts of word-forms bear different meanings. Consider the examples in (2.5).

(2.5) *read*   *read-s*   *read-er*   *read-able*
      wash   *wash-es*   *wash-er*   *wash-able*
      write   *write-s*   *writ-er*   *writ-able*

      kind   *kind-ness*   *un-kind*
      happy   *happi-ness* *un-happy*
      friendly *friendli-ness* *un-friendly*

The words in (2.5) are easily **segmented**, i.e. broken up into individually meaningful parts: *read* + *s*, *read* + *er*, *kind* + *ness*, *un* + *happy*, and so on. These parts are called **morphemes.** Words may of course consist of more than two morphemes, e.g. *un-happi-ness, read-abil-ity, un-friend-ly, un-friend-li-ness.*

Morphemes can be defined as the **smallest meaningful constituents** of a linguistic expression. When we have a sentence such as *Camilla met an unfriendly chameleon,* we can divide it into meaningful parts in various ways, e.g. *Camilla/met an unfriendly chameleon,* or *Camilla/met/an/unfriendly/ chameleon,* or *Camilla/met/an/un/friend/ly/chameleon.* But further division is not possible. When we try to divide *chameleon* further (e.g. *cha/meleon*), we do not obtain parts that can be said to be meaningful, either because they are not found in any other words (as seems to be the case with *meleon*), or because the other words in which they occur do not share any aspect of meaning with *chameleon* (cf. *charisma, Canadian, caboodle, capacity*, in which it would be theoretically possible to identify a word part *cha/ca-*). Thus, *chameleon* cannot be segmented into several morphemes, it is **mono-morphemic**. Morphemes are the ultimate elements of morphological analysis; they are, so to speak, **morphological atoms**.

Morphemes can have various kinds of meanings. Some meanings are very concrete and can be described easily (e.g. the meanings of the morphemes *wash, logic, chameleon, un-*), but other meanings are abstract and more difficult to describe. For instance, the morpheme *-al* in *logic-al* can perhaps be said to mean 'relating to' (cf. *logic-al, mathematic-al, physic-al, natur-al*), *-able* in *read-able* can be said to mean 'capable of undergoing a process', and the meaning of *-ity* is 'quality' (e.g. *readability* is 'the quality of being readable'). Some meanings are so abstract that they can hardly be called meanings. For example, the Latin morpheme *-m* in *insula-m* (see (2.2)) serves to mark the direct object, but it is difficult to say what its meaning is. And English *-s* in *read-s* is required when the subject is a third person singular NP, but again it is unclear whether it can be said to have meaning. In such cases, linguists are more comfortable saying that these morphemes have certain **grammatical functions**. But, since the ultimate purpose of grammatical constructions is to express meaning, we will continue to say that morphemes bear meaning, even when that meaning is very abstract and can be identified only in the larger grammatical context.

Equipped with the notion of morpheme, we can now say that morphologically complex words consist of a string of morphemes, in much the same way as sentences consist of a string of words, and morphemes themselves consist of a string of phonemes. This apparent parallelism between sentences, morphemes and phonemes is shown in Figure 2.2.

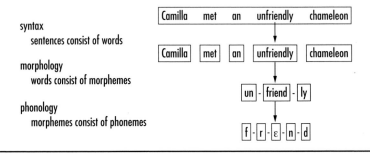

Figure 2.2 A simple picture

However, seductive as the neat picture in Figure 2.2 may be, reality turns out to be more complicated. These complications will occupy us on several occasions later in this book (see especially Section 3.2 and Chapter 9).

For the moment, consider just one example of such a complication. In German, one way of forming the plural of a noun is by replacing a back vowel of the singular form (e.g. [ʊ], [a:], [ɔ]) by a front vowel (e.g. [ʏ], [e:], [œ], spelled *ü, ä, ö*). Some examples are given in (2.6).

(2.6) | singular | plural | |
|---|---|---|
| *Mutter* | *Mütter* | 'mother(s)' |
| *Vater* | *Väter* | 'father(s)' |
| *Tochter* | *Töchter* | 'daughter(s)' |
| *Garten* | *Gärten* | 'garden(s)' |
| *Nagel* | *Nägel* | 'nail(s)' |

Here we have a clear-cut example of morphological structure in that a recurrent meaning ('plural') corresponds to a recurrent aspect of form (the front vowel), but the plural word-forms cannot be segmented. There is no segmental part of *Mütter* that could be assigned the meaning 'plural'. Thus, morphology is more than the concatenation of morphemes to form words.

Still, most kinds of morphological structuring can be described in terms of morphemes, and in practical terms the notion of morpheme is very important in morphology.

2.3 Affixes, bases and roots

Word-forms in an inflectional paradigm generally share (at least) one longer morpheme with a concrete meaning and are distinguished from each other in that they in addition contain different shorter morphemes with an abstract meaning. Such short morphemes with an abstract meaning are called **affixes**. For instance, Russian nouns have different case affixes in the paradigm in (2.7) (*-a* for nominative, *-u* for accusative, etc.), and Classical Nahuatl nouns have different possessor prefixes in the paradigm in (2.8) (*no-* for 'my', *mo-* for 'your', etc.).

(2.7) Russian case inflection

nominative	*ruk-a*	'hand'
accusative	*ruk-u*	
genitive	*ruk-i*	
dative	*ruk-e*	
locative	*ruk-e*	
instrumental	*ruk-oj*	

(2.8) Nahuatl possessor inflection

1SG	*no-cal*	'my house'
2SG	*mo-cal*	'your (SG) house'
3SG	*i-cal*	'his/her house'

1PL	*to-cal*	'our house'
2PL	*amo-cal*	'your (PL) house'
3PL	*in-cal*	'their house'

(Sullivan 1988: 26)

Morphologists often use special terms for different kinds of affixes, depending on their position within the word. Affixes that follow the main part of the word are called **suffixes** (e.g. the Russian case suffixes in (2.7)), and affixes that precede it are called **prefixes** (e.g. the Classical Nahuatl possessor prefixes in (2.8)). There are still other kinds of affixes, which are briefly described and illustrated in Table 2.1.

Types of affixes		Examples
suffix:	follows the base	Russian *-a* in *ruk-a* 'hand'
		English *-ful* in *event-ful*
prefix:	precedes the base	Classical Nahuatl *no-cal* 'my house'
		English *un-* in *unhappy*
infix:	occurs inside the base	Arabic *-t-* in *iš-t-aġala* 'be occupied'
		Tagalog *-um-* in *s-um-ulat* 'write'
circumfix:	occurs on both sides of the base	German *ge-...-en*, e.g. *ge-geb-en* 'given'

Table 2.1 Types of affixes

The part of the word that an affix is attached to is called the **base**, e.g. *ruk-* in Russian, or *-cal* in Classical Nahuatl. Affixes and bases can, of course, be identified both in inflected word-forms and in derived lexemes. For instance, in *read-er, read-able* and *re-read*, *read* is the base, *-er* and *-able* are suffixes, and *re-* is a prefix. In inflected word-forms, a base is also called a **stem**, and occasionally this term is also used for bases of derived lexemes.

Bases or stems can be complex themselves. For instance, in *activity, -ity* is a suffix that combines with the base *active*, which itself consists of the suffix *-ive* and the base *act*. A base that cannot be analysed any further into constituent morphemes is called a **root**. Thus, in *readability, read* is the root (and the base for *readable*), and *readable* is the base for *readability*, but it is not a root. Thus, the base is a relative notion that is defined with respect to the notion 'affix' (but we will propose a revised definition of 'base' in the next section). Affixes are similar to roots in that they are primitive elements.

It should be noted that, here and in the following, we are making a terminological simplification: we are talking about lexemes as if they could be broken up into morphemes just like word-forms. But in fact, a lexeme is an abstract entity (see (2.1)), and the lexeme itself cannot be segmented. What we mean when we say that a derived lexeme consists of an affix and a base is that the **stem** of the derived lexeme consists of an affix and a base. In

English, this does not make a big difference, because the stem is always identical to the citation form. In languages such as Russian, this need not be the case. For instance, the (stem of the) derived lexeme MOLČALIVOST' ('taciturnness') can be broken up into the suffix -ost' ('-ness') and the adjectival stem *molčaliv-*, which is not identical to the citation form MOLČALIVYJ ('taciturn'). This in turn consists of the suffix -liv ('prone') and the verbal lexeme stem *molča-* (citation form MOLČAT' 'be silent'). If this terminological simplification is kept in mind, we can say even for Russian that the suffix -liv(yj) combines with the lexeme MOLČAT' to yield the lexeme MOLČALIVYJ, and that the suffix -ost' combines with the lexeme MOLČALIVYJ to yield the lexeme MOLČALIVOST'.

Roots and affixes can generally be distinguished quite easily, but sometimes there are problems. For example, the Salishan language Bella Coola has a number of suffix-like elements that do not seem to have an abstract meaning at all (see 2.9)). In (2.10), we see two examples of how these elements are used.

(2.9) -*us* 'face' -*lik* 'body'
    -*an* 'ear' -*altwa* 'sky, weather'
    -*uc* 'mouth' -*lt* 'child'
    -*ał* 'foot' -*lst* 'rock'
    -*ak* 'hand' -*lx̩s* 'nose'

(2.10) a. *quć-ał-ic*
      wash-foot-I.him
      'I am going to wash his foot' (lit.: 'foot-wash him')
    b. *kma-lx̩s-c*
      hurt-nose-I
      'my nose hurts' (lit.: 'I nose-hurt')

                                         (Mithun 1998: 300–5)

In these cases, it is not immediately clear whether we are dealing with suffix–root combinations or with root–root combinations, i.e. compounds. The elements in (2.9) do not occur as lexemes by themselves but must always be combined with other roots. In this respect they are like affixes, and scholars of Salishan languages have generally regarded them as such. However, if affixes are defined as 'short morphemes with an abstract meaning', then these elements are very atypical affixes, to say the least.

English has a number of morphemes that are similarly difficult to classify as roots or affixes. Some examples are given in (2.11).

(2.11) *biogeography*   *aristocrat*
       bioethics   *autocrat*
       bioengineering   *democrat*
       biorhythm   *Eurocrat*
       bioterrorism   *plutocrat*
       biomedicine   *technocrat*
       biochip   *theocrat*

The elements *bio-* and *-crat* could be regarded as affixes because they do not occur as independent lexemes, but their very concrete meaning and also their (not particularly short) form suggests that they should be regarded as roots that have the special property of occurring only in compounds (often called **bound roots**). For English elements like *bio-* and *-crat* (and other similar elements such as *socio-, psycho-, geo-, -graph, -path, -scope*), the term **combining form** is often used, and this term might also be applied to the morphemes in (2.9).

2.4 Formal operations

So far we have talked mostly about morphological structure in purely **static terms**: words 'have' affixes or 'share' parts, they 'exhibit' resemblances and they 'consist of' a base and an affix. However, it is often convenient to describe morphological patterns as if these were the results of events. Thus, we said that affixes 'are attached' to the base or that they 'combine' with it. Linguists use such **process terms** very often. They talk about elements 'being affixed' to bases, about a complex word 'being **derived**'[1] from (i.e. built on the basis of) a simpler one, or about one affix 'replacing' another one. It is important to keep in mind that these process terms are purely metaphorical, and that they do not refer to any actual events or processes. A linguist who describes linguistic structure in process terms is much like an art historian who describes a church by means of an imagined walk around and through the building.

Of course, human language is used in real time, and many of the metaphorical terms can also be used in a literal sense. For example, the adjective READABLE is (metaphorically) described as derived from the verb READ, i.e. standing in a synchronic derivational relation to it, and it was also literally derived from it (i.e. created on its basis) at some point in history. The verb READ has always existed in the English language (the first attestation in the *OED* is from King Aelfred's writings in 888), but the adjective READABLE was first recorded only in 1570. When it was first coined, a speaker took READ as her model, added *-able* to it and thereby created a new lexeme. Often such real-time (or **diachronic**) processes correspond closely to the virtual (or **synchronic**) processes that linguists talk about. The word READABLE was diachronically derived from READ, and synchronically it can best be described as derived from READ as well.

Most of the examples of morphologically complex words that we have seen so far can be neatly segmented into roots and affixes; or, in process

---

[1] It should be noted that the use of the term *derive* in linguistics is somewhat confusing because it is also commonly applied to inflectional morphology, not just to derivational morphology. Thus, one would say that the comparative form *warmer* is derived from the positive form *warm*, or that the past-tense form *played* is derived from the present-tense form *play*.

terms, they can be described as derived by **affixation** (suffixation, prefixation, etc.) and **compounding**. But we have already seen that the simple
picture of words consisting of strings of morphemes is too simple. Besides
affixation and compounding, there are quite a few other **formal operations**
by which complex words can be derived from bases, and these will be
described in this section. These operations are called **non-concatenative** (as
opposed to affixation and compounding, which are concatenative operations). Morphologically complex words derived by non-concatenative
operations cannot be easily segmented into morphemes, and they are most
conveniently described in process terms.

One important class of non-concatenative operations is called **base modification** or **alternation** (or *stem modification/alternation*). This means that a
part of the base is modified by a phonological change of some kind. For
example, in Albanian the plural of nouns can be formed by **palatalizing** the
last consonant of the base, so that [k] becomes [c], [g] becomes [ɟ], and [ɫ]
becomes [j]:

(2.12) SINGULAR   PLURAL
    armik [-k]   *armiq* [-c]   'enemy/enemies'
    fik [-k]   *fiq* [-c]   'fig(s)'
    frëng [-g]   *frëngj* [-ɟ]   'Frenchman/-men'
    murg [-g]   *murgj* [-ɟ]   'monk(s)'
    papagall [-ɫ]   *papagaj* [-j]   'parrot(s)'
    portokall [-ɫ]   *portokaj* [-j]   'orange(s)'
                              (Buchholz and Fiedler 1987: 264–5)

English has a few cases where a verb is derived from a noun by **voicing**
the last consonant of the root (e.g. *hou*[s]*e*$_N$ → *hou*[z]*e*$_V$, *thie*[f]$_N$ → *thie*[v]*e*$_V$,
wrea[θ]$_N$ → *wrea*[ð]*e*$_V$).[2] In Arabic, a causative verb is formed by **geminating**
the second root consonant (e.g. *darasa* 'learn' → *darrasa* 'teach', *waqafa* 'stop
(intr.)' → *waqqafa* 'stop (tr.)', *damara* 'perish' → *dammara* 'annihilate'). In
Huallaga Quechua, the first person singular of verbs is formed by
lengthening the final stem vowel, as indicated by the colon:

(2.13) 2ND SINGULAR   1ST SINGULAR
    aywa-nki   'you go'   *aywa:*   'I go'
    aywa-pti-ki   'when you went'   *aywa-pti:*   'when I went'
    aywa-shka-nki 'you have gone'   *aywa-shka:* 'I have gone'
                              (Weber 1989: 99, 118)

In Hindi/Urdu, intransitive verbs are formed from transitive verbs by **shortening** the stem vowel (e.g. *maar-* 'kill' → *mar-* 'die', *khool-* 'open (tr.)' → *khul-*
'open (intr.)', *pheer-* 'turn (tr.)' → *phir-* 'turn (intr.)'). In German, **fronting** of
the stem vowel may express the plural, as we saw in Section 2.2, ex. (2.6).

---

[2] The arrow symbol (→) is used to express a relationship of derivation: 'A → B' means that B is
    derived from A (synchronically).

Base modification may also take the form of a **tonal change**. For example, in Chalcatongo Mixtec denominal adjectives are formed by changing the tone pattern of the base to a high–high pattern (indicated by two acute accents):

(2.14)

NOUN		ADJECTIVE	
káʔba	'filth'	káʔbá	'dirty'
žuù	'rock'	žúú	'solid, hard'
xaʔà	'foot'	xáʔá	'standing'

(Macaulay 1996: 64)

We have used various terms from phonology for describing these base modifications (palatalizing, voicing, fronting, etc.). These represent common diachronic phonological changes, and ultimately most morphological base modifications have their origin in phonological changes. For example, the English verb *house* used to have a voiceless [s], like the noun *house*, but at some point it underwent a voicing change that did not affect the noun because of different phonological conditions (the verb used to have a vowel suffix until Middle English times, whereas in the noun the *s* was word final already in Old English).

Sometimes there are doubts whether we are dealing with base modification or affixation. For instance, the English pattern in (2.15) is normally described as modification: the past tense is formed by replacing the stem vowel with [ʌ].

(2.15)

BASIC STEM	PAST TENSE	
win	*won*	[wʌn]
dig	*dug*	[dʌg]
strike	*struck*	[strʌk]
hang	*hung*	[hʌŋ]

An alternative description would say that the past-tense form is marked by an infix [ʌ], and that the base vowel is somehow deleted. Such a description is often adopted for Semitic languages such as Standard Arabic. For example, in the Standard Arabic perfect, the passive is formed by replacing the two stem vowels by *u* and *i*, respectively:

(2.16)

ACTIVE PERFECT		PASSIVE PERFECT	
kataba	'wrote'	*kutiba*	'was written'
ħalaqa	'shaved'	*ħuliqa*	'was shaved'
faraḍa	'decided'	*furiḍa*	'was decided'

Here most linguists would adopt an analysis whereby the base consists of the three root consonants (*k-t-b*, *ħ-l-q*, *f-r-ḍ*), the stem vowels *a-a* express the active perfect, the stem vowels *u-i* express the passive perfect. Such cases of interdigitation of vowel and consonant morphemes have come to be known as **transfixation**. There is no strict dividing line between base vowel modification and infixation or transfixation, and, if one wanted, one could analyse English as being of the Arabic type.

Another very common morphological operation is **reduplication**, whereby part of the base or the complete base is copied and attached to the base. Depending on whether the reduplicant (i.e. the copied element) precedes or follows the base, we may distinguish prereduplication and postreduplication. Some examples are given in (2.17)–(2.18).

(2.17) Prereduplication of a CV sequence: Ponapean

duhp	'dive'	*du-duhp*	'be diving'
mihk	'suck'	*mi-mihk*	'be sucking'
wehk	'confess'	*we-wehk*	'be confessing'

(Rehg 1981: 78)

(2.18) Postreduplication of a VC sequence: Mangap-Mbula

kuk	'bark'	*kuk-uk*	'be barking'
kel	'dig'	*kel-el*	'be digging'
kan	'eat'	*kan-an*	'be eating'

(Bugenhagen 1995: 53)

The element that is attached to the base often consists of both copied segments and fixed segments, so that a kind of mixture between affix and reduplicant results. Such elements may be called **duplifixes**.

(2.19) Somali plurals: duplifix -aC

buug	'book'	*buug-ag*	'books'
fool	'face'	*fool-al*	'faces'
koob	'cup'	*koob-ab*	'cups'
jid	'street'	*jid-ad*	'streets'

(Berchem 1991: 102)

(2.20) Tzutujil 'sort of' adjectives: duplifix -Coj

saq	'white'	*saq-soj*	'whitish'
rax	'green'	*rax-roj*	'greenish'
q'eq	'black'	*q'eq-q'oj*	'blackish'
tz'iil	'dirty'	*tz'il-tz'oj*	'dirtyish'

(Dayley 1985: 213)

A further operation that is occasionally attested is **subtraction**, i.e. the signalling of a morphological relationship by deleting a segment (or more) from the base. For example, one way of forming the plural in Murle is by subtracting the last consonant:

(2.21)
nyoon	'lamb'	*nyoo*	'lambs'
wawoc	'white heron'	*wawo*	'white herons'
onyiit	'rib'	*onyii*	'ribs'
rottin	'warrior'	*rotti*	'warriors'

(Arensen 1982: 40–1)

Finally, the limiting case of a morphological operation is **conversion**, in which the form of the base remains unaltered. A standard example is the derivation of verbs from nouns in English (*hammer*$_N$ → *hammer*$_V$, *book*$_N$ → *book*$_V$, *ship*$_N$ → *ship*$_V$, and countless others). Since we defined morphological patterns as partial resemblances in form and meaning among groups of words, conversion can be regarded as morphological in nature only if this definition is somewhat relaxed, because the resemblance in form is total here. Conversion is generally invoked only for derivational morphology, and primarily for relating two lexemes that differ in word-class only. However, in languages that have a richer inflectional system than English, there is a broader range of cases that might be subsumed under conversion – for instance, pairs of lexemes that share the same stem and differ only in their inflectional behaviour. Thus, one might say that Latin derives female nouns by changing from the *-us*-class to the *-a*-class (e.g. *fili-us* 'son-NOMINATIVE' → *fili-a* 'daughter-NOMINATIVE'), and that German forms transitive verbs by changing from the irregular vowel-modifying class (*erschrecken* 'startle (intr.)', past tense *erschrak*) to the regular suffixing class (*erschrecken* 'startle (tr.)', past tense *erschreckte*).

Sometimes a number of additional types are given under the heading of morphological operations, such as alphabet-based abbreviations (**acronyms** such as *NATO*, and **alphabetisms** such as *CD* (pronounced [siːˈdiː]), *Ph.D.* (pronounced [piːeitʃˈdiː]), **clippings** (e.g. *fridge* from *refrigerator*, *pram* from *perambulator*) and **blends** (e.g. *smog* from *smoke* and *fog*, *infotainment* from *information* and *entertainment*). However, while these are clearly operations that can be used to **create** new words (like morphological operations), they do not fall under morphology, because the resulting new words do not show systematic meaning–sound resemblances of the sort that speakers would recognize. If we know that *CD* is an abbreviation of *compact disc*, we do not know it as a result of unconscious language acquisition, but because we were explicitly told so. Thus, not all processes of word-creation fall under word-formation, and abbreviations and clippings will play no role in this book.

The fact that there exist a whole range of morphological operations different from affixation means that our original definition of *base* ('the part of a word that an affix is attached to' (Section 2.3)) becomes questionable. We want to say that Albanian *armik* is the base for *armiq* (see 2.12), Ponapean *duhp* is the base for *duduhp* (see 2.17), English *ship*$_N$ is the base for *ship*$_V$, and so on. Thus, (2.22) is a better definition of *base*.

(2.22) The **base** of a morphologically complex word is the element to which a morphological operation applies.

This subsumes the earlier definition and gives us the right results for non-concatenative operations.

For the functioning of the language system, the non-concatenative processes work just as well as the more straightforward concatenative processes (affixation and compounding), and some linguists have attempted to extend the morpheme concept to these processes as well.

Thus, one might speak of 'replacive morphemes' in the base of base modification, where a phonological property of the base is replaced by another one. In this book, in line with most current practice, we will restrict the term 'morpheme' to segmentable parts of words. As a more general concept comprising both the results of concatenative processes and the results of non-concatenative processes, we will use the term **morphological pattern**. For instance, we will say that Albanian has several patterns for the plural of nouns: suffixation of -a (e.g. *automobil/automobila* 'car(s)'), suffixation of -ra (e.g. *bisht/bishtra* 'tail(s)'), base vowel fronting (e.g. *dash/desh* 'wether(s)'), base consonant palatalization (e.g. *murg/murgj* 'monk(s)') and conversion or zero (e.g. *lule/lule* 'flower(s)'). In this terminology, a morpheme is thus merely a special kind of morphological pattern. However, since concatenative operations are far more common than non-concatenative operations, the morpheme still has a prominent role in practice.

2.5 Morphemes and allomorphs

One of the most common complications of the simple picture that we saw in Figure 2.2 is that morphemes may have different shapes under different circumstances. For instance, the plural morpheme in English is sometimes pronounced [s] (as in *cats* [kæts]), sometimes [z] (as in *dogs* [dɒgz]), and sometimes [-əz] (as in *faces* [feisəz]). For such cases, linguists use the term **allomorph** (or **morpheme alternant**). Affixes very often have different allomorphs – two further cases from other languages are given in (2.23).

(2.23) a. Korean accusative suffix (marker of direct object): two allomorphs

-ul:	ton	'money'	ton-ul	'money-ACC'
	chayk	'book'	chayk-ul	'book-ACC'
-lul:	tali	'leg'	tali-lul	'leg-ACC'
	sakwa	'apple'	sakwa-lul	'apple-ACC'

b. Turkish first person possessive suffix: five allomorphs

-im:	ev	'house'	ev-im	'my house'
	dil	'language'	dil-im	'my language'
-üm:	köy	'village'	köy-üm	'my village'
	gün	'day'	gün-üm	'my day'
-um:	yol	'way'	yol-um	'my way'
	tuz	'salt'	tuz-um	'my salt'
-ım:	ad	'name'	ad-ım	'my name'
	kız	'girl'	kız-ım	'my daughter'
-m:	baba	'father'	baba-m	'my father'

But not only affixes, also roots and stems may have different allomorphs (or, as linguists often say, 'exhibit allomorphy'). For instance, English verbs such as *sleep, keep, deal, feel, mean,* whose root has the long vowel [i:] in the present-tense forms, show a root allomorph with short [e] in the past-tense forms (*slept, kept, dealt, felt, meant*). Cases of stem allomorphy from other languages are given in (2.24).

(2.24) a. German: when the stem is not followed by a vowel-initial suffix, the final obstruent is voiceless

Tag	[ta:k]	'day'	*Tage*	[ta:gə]	'days'
Hund	[hʊnt]	'dog'	*Hunde*	[hʊndə]	'dogs'
Los	[lo:s]	'lot'	*Lose*	[lo:zə]	'lots'

b. Russian: when the stem is followed by a vowel-initial suffix, the vowel *o/e* is dropped

zamok	'castle'	*zamk-i*	'castles'
kamen'	'stone'	*kamn-i*	'stones'
nemec	'German'	*nemc-y*	'Germans'
nogot'	'nail'	*nogt-i*	'nails'

The crucial defining property is that they have the same meaning and occur in different environments in **complementary distribution**.

So far all our examples have shown only fairly small differences in the shapes of morphemes, which can by and large be regarded as mere differences in pronunciation. In other words, the allomorphs considered so far are **phonological allomorphs**. Linguists often describe them with a special set of **phonological** (or **morphophonological**) **rules**, which are originally phonetically motivated and only secondarily affect morphology. Phonological and morphophonological rules and the difference between them will be discussed more extensively in Chapter 10, and we will consider them only briefly here.

In the description of phonological allomorphs, it is often convenient to start out with a fictitious **underlying representation** that is manipulated by (morpho)phonological rules. For instance, the alternations in (2.24a–b) can be described by the underlying representations in (2.25a) and (2.26a), and by the respective rules in (2.25b) and 2.26b).

(2.25) a. underlying: [ta:g] 'day' [ta:g-ə] 'days'
b. rule: a voiced obstruent becomes voiced when syllable-final ([ta:g] → [ta:k])[3]

(2.26) a. underlying: *zamok* 'castle' *zamok-i* 'castles'
b. rule: *o/e* in the final stem syllable disappears when the stem is followed by a vowel-initial suffix (*zamoki* → *zamki*)

---

[3] In this (morpho)phonological context, the arrow has a different meaning: 'X → Y' means that X turns into Y.

That the alternation is produced by the (morpho)phonological rule is made particularly clear in this way: the underlying representation shows no allomorphy at all. In many cases of phonological allomorphy, it is evident that the ultimate reason for the existence of the (morpho)phonological rule and thus for the allomorphy is to facilitate the pronunciation. For instance, if the English plural were uniformly [-z], words such as *cats* and *faces* would be almost unpronounceable (try to pronounce [kætz] and [feisz]!). In Korean, a vowel sequence such as *sakwaul* or *taliul* would be difficult to pronounce, so the Korean alternation in (2.23a) also helps pronunciation. Ease of pronunciation is less evident as a motivating factor in the Russian example (*zamok/zamki*, etc.), because the rules of Russian pronunciation would clearly permit *zamk* or *zamoki*. Still, phonologists agree that consonant sequences are generally more difficult in syllable-final position than in intervocalic position (i.e. between vowels), so that this case, too, can be subsumed under the generalization that phonological allomorphs exist to facilitate pronunciation. Since this is a textbook on morphology, we cannot go into greater phonological detail here, but phonological allomorphs will be taken up again in Chapter 10.

Besides phonological allomorphs, languages may also exhibit allomorphs that are not at all similar in pronunciation. These are called **suppletive allomorphs** here. An example is the suffix of the English past participle, which is *-ed* with some verbs (actually, most verbs, e.g. *pave/paved, cry/cried, call/called, stop/stopped, pat/patted*), but *-en* with others (e.g. *give/given, take/taken, shake/shaken, hide/hidden, break/broken*). (Note that *-ed* itself exhibits three different phonological allomorphs, [d], [t], [əd], similar to the plural suffix *-s*, but we will disregard this complication here.) The items *-ed* and *-en* are not similar phonologically, and no amount of (morpho)phonological analysis will make them similar, so they are regarded as suppletive. More examples of suppletive allomorphs are given in (2.27).

(2.27)   a. Martuthunira locative case: disyllabic nouns take *-ngka*, trisyllabic nouns take *-la*

-*ngka*:	*parla*	'stone'	*parla-ngka*	'at stone'
	muyi	'dog'	*muyi-ngka*	'at dog'
-*la*	*kanyara*	'person'	*kanyara-la*	'at person'
	warrirti	'spear'	*warrirti-la*	'at spear'

(Dench 1995: 64)

b. Persian plural marking: human nouns *-an*, non-human nouns *-ha*

-*an*:	*mærd*	'man'	*mærd-an*	'men'
	geda	'beggar'	*geday-an*	'beggars'
-*ha*	*gorbe*	'cat'	*gorbe-ha*	'cats'
	ettefaq	'incident'	*ettefaq-ha*	'incidents'

(Mahootian 1997: 190)

c. Latin singular person marking: 1st singular -o/-m/-i, 2nd singular
  -s/isti (no suppletion in 3rd person)

	PRESENT TENSE	IMPERFECT TENSE	PERFECT TENSE
1SG	laud-o	lauda-ba-m	lauda-v-i
2SG	lauda-s	lauda-ba-s	lauda-v-isti
3SG	lauda-t	lauda-ba-t	lauda-v-it
	'I praise, etc.'	'I was praising, etc.'	'I (have) praised, etc.'

(The Latin example involves some phonological allomorphy as well, e.g. *laudo* instead of *laudao*, *laudavit* instead of *laudavt*.) We also saw examples of suppletive plural allomorphy in Albanian at the end of Section 2.4.

Like phonological allomorphy, suppletive allomorphy may affect root or stem morphemes as well as affix morphemes. For instance, the English verb *go* has the suppletive stem *wen* in the past tense (*wen-t*), and the English adjective *good* has the suppletive stem *bett* in the comparative degree (*better*). The Russian noun *čelovek* 'human being' has the suppletive stem *ljud'* in the plural (*ljud-i* 'people'). The Spanish verb *ir* 'go' has the suppletive stem *va* in the present tense (*vas* 'you go', *va* 'she goes', *vamos* 'we go', etc.).

It is not always easy to decide whether an alternation is phonological or suppletive. For instance, what about English *buy/bought, catch/caught, teach/taught*? The root allomorphs of these verbs ([bai]/[bɔ:], [kætʃ]/[kɔ:], [ti:tʃ]/[tɔ:]) are not as radically different as *go/wen-t*, but they are not similar enough to be described by phonological rules either. In such cases, linguists often speak of **weak suppletion**, as opposed to **strong suppletion** in cases like *go/went, good/better*.

When describing the allomorphy patterns of a language, another important dimension is the **conditioning** of the allomorphy, i.e. the conditions under which different allomorphs are selected. Perhaps the most important factor is **phonological conditioning**. Very often the phonological context determines the choice of allomorphs. For instance, the English plural allomorphs [-z], [-s] and [-əz] are strictly phonologically conditioned: [-əz] appears after a sibilant (i.e. [s], [z], [ʃ] or [ʒ], e.g. *face-s, maze-s, bush-es, badge-s*), [-s] appears after a voiceless non-sibilant obstruent (e.g. *cat-s, book-s, lip-s, cliff-s*) and [-z] appears elsewhere (e.g. *bag-s, bell-s, key-s*). The Korean accusative allomorphs *-ul/-lul* (see (2.23a)) are also phonologically conditioned: *-ul* appears after a consonant, *-lul* after a vowel.

Another possibility is **morphological conditioning**, where the morphological context determines the choice of allomorphs. For example, in Latin (see 2.27c)) the ending of the first person singular indicative is *-o* in the present tense, *-m* in the imperfect tense and *-i* in the perfect tense. Stem suppletion is usually morphologically conditioned (e.g. Spanish *ir* 'go' in the infinitive and future tense, *va-* in the present and imperfective past tense and *fu-* in the perfective past tense). However, it may also be phonologically conditioned: in Italian, the verb *andare* 'go' has the stem *and-* when the stress is on a suffix, but *va-* when the stress is on the stem: *vád-o* 'I go', *va-i* 'you go', *va* 's/he goes', *and-iámo* 'we go', *and-áte* 'you(PL) go', *vá-nno* 'they go'.

And, finally, we find **lexical conditioning**, where the choice of affix allomorphs is dependent on other properties of the base, for instance semantic properties (e.g. the Persian plural in 2.27b), or where the choice of allomorphs cannot be derived from any general rule and must be learned individually for each case. This is the case for the English past participle suffix *-en*: speakers must simply learn which verbs take this suffix and not the more common suffix *-ed*.

Phonological allomorphs are always phonologically conditioned (almost by definition), but suppletive allomorphs may be phonologically, morphologically or lexically conditioned. Table 2.2 gives a summary of types of allomorphy and Table 2.3 of types of conditioning.

Type of allomorphy	Description	Example
Phonological allomorphy	Alternation could be described by a rule of pronunciation	English plural [-z], [-s], [-əz]; Russian *zamok/zamk-*
Weak suppletive allomorphy	Allomorphs exhibit some similarity, but this cannot be described by phonological rules	English *buy/bough-*, *catch/caugh-*, etc.
Strong suppletive allomorphy	Allomorphs exhibit no similarity at all	Latin first person singular *-o/-i*; English *good/bett-*

Table 2.2 Types of allomorphy: summary

Type of conditioning	Description	Example
Phonological conditioning	Choice of allomorphs depends on the phonological context	Martuthunira locative case *-ngka/-la* depends on number of syllables
Morphological conditioning	Choice of allomorphs depends on the morphological context	Latin first person singular *-o/-i* depends on tense
Lexical conditioning	Choice of allomorphs depends on the individual lexical item	English past participle *-en/-ed* is unpredictable and depends on individual verbs

Table 2.3 Types of conditioning: summary

2.6 Some difficulties in morpheme analysis

In the preceding section, we defined an allomorph as one of the possible shapes that a morpheme can have depending on the circumstances. This is straightforward in the case of phonological allomorphs. It sounds reasonable to say that English [s] and [z], or German [ta:k] and [ta:g] represent the 'same' morpheme and are just different manifestations of it. But things get more complicated when suppletive allomorphs come into play. Are English -*ed* and -*en* (as in *called* and *given*) also manifestations of the same morpheme? And English *good* and *bett-* (in *better*)? This would require a very abstract concept of the morpheme: a morpheme would no longer be associated with a particular phonological shape. Indeed, some linguists have proposed that the term *morpheme* should be reserved for this abstract notion. Concrete elements such as -*ed* and -*en*, *good* and *bett-*, [ta:g] and [ta:k] are then called **morphs**, and the relationship between morphs and morphemes is analogous to the relationship between word-forms and lexemes: a morpheme is a set of morphs (which are often but not always formally similar), and only morphs can be pronounced and used in performance.

Many morphology textbooks introduce the distinction between *morph* and *morpheme* in this sense, but in actual practice linguists rarely use the term *morph*, and the term *morpheme* is often used in a concrete sense as well. In line with this practice of morphologists, we will not use the term *morph* in this book. Here the most basic term is the *morphological pattern* (Section 2.4), and the (concrete) *morpheme* is a frequently occurring special type of morphological pattern (namely a pattern in which a morphological mean- ing can be associated with a segmentable part of a word). Occasionally we also use *morpheme* in a more abstract sense (as when we said in Section 2.5 that the English plural morpheme -*s* has three different pronunciations), but this is mostly restricted to cases of straightforward phonological allo- morphy. Thus, the term *morpheme* is used ambiguously as either (concretely) 'a minimal morphological constituent' or (abstractly) 'the set of alternating morphs that have the same meaning and occur in comple- mentary distribution'. (This is, incidentally, similar to the ambiguity of *word*, which can be used for 'word-form' or for 'lexeme'. In most cases, the context makes it clear what is intended.)

In our terminology, we will say that two morphological patterns are allo- morphs if they express the same lexeme or the same inflectional meaning. Since English *good* and *bett* have the same lexical meaning and represent the same lexeme, they are considered allomorphs standing in a suppletive relationship. And English -*ed* and -*en* both express the same inflectional meaning (past participle), so again they are allomorphs. Allomorphs need not be constituents of words: different non-concatenative operations may also express the same inflectional meaning and thus stand in an allo- morphic relationship. For instance, in Ancient Greek the perfect is formed by one of three operations, depending on the phonological context:

		PRESENT TENSE	PERFECT TENSE
(2.28)	a. pre-duplifix *Ce-*	*boúl-omai*	*be-boúlē-mai*
	(stems beginning with *CV-*)	'I want'	'I have wanted'
	b. prefix *e-*	*phthín-omai*	*é-phthi-mai*
	(stems beginning with *CC-*)	'I perish'	'I have perished'
	c. lengthened first vowel	*eá-omai*	*ēa-mai*
	(stems beginning with *V-*)	'I am left'	'I have been left'

Similarly, the Albanian plural (see Section 2.4) is expressed by a variety of patterns, among them different base modifications, different suffixes and conversion.

In the following, we will see three more problems for morphological segmentation: cumulative expression, zero expression and empty morphemes.

When an affix expresses two different morphological meanings simultaneously, we have **cumulative expression** (also called **fusion**). For example, the Serbian/Croatian noun *ovca* 'sheep' has the number and case forms shown in (2.29).

(2.29)	SINGULAR	PLURAL
NOMINATIVE	*ovc-a*	*ovc-e*
ACCUSATIVE	*ovc-u*	*ovc-e*
GENITIVE	*ovc-e*	*ovac-a*
DATIVE	*ovc-i*	*ovc-ama*
INSTRUMENTAL	*ovc-om*	*ovc-ama*
VOCATIVE	*ovc-o*	*ovc-e*

Clearly, it is not possible to isolate separate singular or plural or nominative or accusative (etc.) morphemes. The suffixes that follow the stem *ov(a)c-* express number and case simultaneously, or, in the technical term of morphology, cumulatively. It has been proposed that an element like *-u* (accusative singular) should be analysed as a morph that happens to realize two abstract morphemes, but here we will simply say that the morphological pattern *-u* simultaneously expresses the two inflectional meanings 'accusative' and 'singular'. Cumulative or fused expression is most often illustrated with different inflectional meanings, but it is also possible for an inflectional meaning and a derivational meaning to be expressed cumulatively. In Krongo, the derivational meaning 'agent' and the inflectional meanings 'singular' and 'plural' are expressed in a single affix: *cà-/cò-* denotes 'agent/singular', and *kà-/kò-* denotes 'agent/plural'.

(2.30)	*màlìŋ*	'theft'	*càmàlìŋ*	'thief'	*kàmàlìŋ*	'thieves'
	mòtò	'work'	*còmòtò*	'worker'	*kòmòtò*	'workers'

(Reh 1985: 157)

Finally, a suppletive stem may simultaneously express the base meaning and the grammatical meaning. Thus, English *worse* expresses the lexeme meaning 'bad' and the inflectional meaning 'comparative' in a cumulative way. Affixes and stems that cumulatively express two meanings that would be expected to be expresed separately are also called **portmanteau morphs**.

Another phenomenon that causes problems for segmentation is the existence of words in which a morphological meaning corresponds to no overt formal element; this is generally called **zero expression**. Two examples are given in (2.31) and (2.32).

(2.31) Coptic
       jǒ-i   'my head'
       jǒ-k   'your (M) head'
       jō   'your (F) head'
       jǒ-f   'his head'
       jō-s   'her head'

(2.32) Finnish
       oli-n   'I was'
       oli-t   'you were'
       oli   'he/she was'
       oli-mme   'we were'
       oli-tte   'you(PL) were'
       oli-vat   'they were'

Some morphologists have worked with the requirement that the segmentation of words into morphemes must be exhaustive and all meanings must be assigned to a morpheme. If one adopts this requirement, then one is forced to posit zero morph(eme)s here that have a meaning, but no form (so Finnish *oli* would really have the structure *oli-Ø*, where the morpheme Ø stands for the third person singular). But the requirement is not necessary, and alternatively one could say, for instance, that Finnish has no marker for the third person singular in verbs. To be sure, the conceptual difference between the affixation of an unpronounced element and no affixation at all is not great, but it does seem to be the case that the latter is less far-fetched and cognitively more plausible.

The opposite of zero morphemes can also be found: apparent cases of morphemes that have form but no meaning (also called **empty morphemes**). For example, in Lezgian all nominal case-forms except for the absolutive case (i.e. the most basic case) contain a suffix that follows the noun stem and precedes the case suffix. In (2.33), four of Lezgian's sixteen cases are shown.

(2.33)

ABSOLUTIVE	*sew*	*fil*	*Rahim*
GENITIVE	*sew-re-n*	*fil-di-n*	*Rahim-a-n*
DATIVE	*sew-re-z*	*fil-di-z*	*Rahim-a-z*
SUBESSIVE	*sew-re-k*	*fil-di-k*	*Rahim-a-k*
	'bear'	'elephant'	(male name)

(Haspelmath 1993: 74–5)

This suffix, called the **oblique stem** suffix in Lezgian grammar, has no meaning, but it must be posited if we want to have an elegant description. With the notion of an empty morpheme we can say that different nouns select different suppletive oblique stem suffixes, but that the actual case suffixes that are affixed to the oblique stem are uniform for all nouns. The alternative would be to say that the genitive suffix has several different suppletive allomorphs (*-ren, -din, -an*), the dative case has several different allomorphs (*-rez, -diz, -az*), and so on. But such a description would be inelegant, missing the obvious and exceptionless generalization that the non-absolutive case suffixes share an element. Again, empty morphemes are an embarrassment for the attempt at exhaustive segmentation of words into morphemes.

Thus, there are quite a few problems that face any attempt to make the morpheme (in the sense of minimal morphological constituents) the cornerstone of morphological analysis. The most basic notion of morphology should be the parallelism of form and meaning, as discussed in Chapter 1.

Summary of Chapter 2

Two different notions of word have to be distinguished: the lexeme (or 'dictionary word') and the word-form (or 'text word'). Inflectional morphology describes the relationship between the word-forms in a lexeme's paradigm, and derivational morphology describes the relation between lexemes. Complex words can often be segmented into morphemes, which are called affixes when they are short and have an abstract meaning, and roots when they are longer and have a more concrete meaning. To derive complex words from roots and bases, languages employ not just affixation and compounding, but also other formal operations such as base modification, reduplication and conversion. When several formal operations or (concrete) morphemes express the same meaning and occur in complementary distribution, they are often considered allomorphs. Further problems for segmentation of words into morphemes are cumulative expression, zero expression and empty morphemes.

Appendix. Morpheme-by-morpheme glosses

When presenting longer examples (such as sentences or entire texts) from a language that the reader is unlikely to know, linguists usually add **interlinear morpheme-by-morpheme glosses** to help the reader understand the structure of the examples. We saw instances of such glosses in (1.2–6), and we will see more examples later in this book. Interlinear morpheme-by-morpheme glosses are an important aspect of 'applied morphology', and every syntactician or fieldworker needs them. We will therefore explain the most important principles involved. The following conventions are more or less standard in contemporary linguistics:

(i) **One-to-one correspondence.** Each element of the object language is translated by one element of the metalanguage (in the present context, this is English). Hyphens separate both the word-internal morphemes in the object language and the gloss, e.g.

Japanese
Taroo	*ga*	*hana*	*o*	*migotoni*	*saka-se-ta.*
Taro	NOM	flower	ACC	beautifully	bloom-CAUS-PAST

'Taro made the flowers bloom beautifully.'

(Shibatani 1990: 309)

Object-language words and their translations are left aligned. The interlinear gloss is usually followed by an idiomatic gloss in quotation marks.

(ii) **Grammatical-category abbreviations.** Grammatical elements (both function words and inflectional affixes) are not translated directly, but are rendered by grammatical-category labels, generally in abbreviated form (see the list of abbreviations on pp. xii–xiii). To highlight the difference between the category labels and the ordinary English words, the category labels are usually printed in small capitals, as seen in the above example.

(iii) **Hyphens and periods.** Hyphens are used to separate word-internal morphemes in object-language examples, and each hyphen in an example corresponds to a hyphen in the gloss. Periods are used in the gloss when two gloss elements correspond to one element in the example. This may be when a single example element corresponds to a multi-word expression in the gloss, e.g.

Turkish
çık-mak
come.out-INF
'to come out'

or it may be when a single example element corresponds to several inflectional meanings, as is the case with cumulative expression:

Latin
insul-arum
island-GEN.PL
'of the islands'

or it may be when an inflectional meaning is expressed in a non-concatenative way, e.g.

Albanian
fiq
fig.PL
'figs'

The period is omitted when the two meanings are person and number, e.g.

Tzutujil
x-in-wari
COMPL-1SG-sleep
'I slept'

(Dayley 1985: 87)

Here '1SG' is used instead of '1.SG' (the period is felt to be redundant in these cases).

(iv) Possible simplifications. Sometimes the precise morpheme division is irrelevant or perhaps unknown. Authors may still want to give information on the inflectional meanings, and again periods are used to separate these elements, e.g.

Japanese   Latin
sakaseta   *insularum*
bloom.CAUS.PAST   island.GEN.PL
'made to bloom'   'of the islands'

Sometimes morpheme-by-morpheme glosses are used also when the example is not set off from the running text. In such cases the gloss is enclosed in square brackets, e.g. 'the Japanese verb *saka-se-ta* [bloom-CAUS-PAST] "made to bloom" …'.

A detailed (though somewhat outdated) discussion of issues surrounding interlinear morpheme-by-morpheme glosses is found in Lehmann (1982).

Exercises

1. Somali exhibits a great amount of allomorphy in the plural formation of its nouns. Four different allomorphs are represented in the following examples. Based on these examples, formulate a hypothesis about the phonological conditions for each of the plural allomorphs. (In actual fact, the conditions are more complex, but for this exercise, we have to limit ourselves to a subset of the data and generalizations.)

SINGULAR	PLURAL	
awowe	*awowayaal*	'grandfather'
baabaco	*baabacooyin*	'palm'
beed	*beedad*	'egg'
buug	*buugag*	'book'
cashar	*casharro*	'lesson'
fure	*furayaal*	'key'
ilmo	*ilmooyin*	'tear'
miis	*miisas*	'table'
qado	*qadooyin*	'lunch'
shabeel	*shabeello*	'leopard'
waraabe	*waraabayaal*	'hyena'
xidid	*xididdo*	'eagle'

Based on the generalizations found, form the plural of the following nouns:

tuulo	'village'
tog	'river'
albaab	'door'
buste	'blanket'

(Berchem 1991: 98–117)

2. It was mentioned that the English past participle suffix spelled *-ed* has three different alternants: [d], [t], and [əd]. Are these phonologically or morphologically conditioned? Try to describe the conditioning factors in an approximate way.

3. Which formal operation (or combination of operations) is involved in the following morphological patterns?

a. Mbay (v̀ = low tone, v́ = high tone, v̄ = mid tone)

tétə̀	'break'	*tétā*	'break several times'
ɓìndā	'wrap'	*ɓíndā*	'wrap several times'
rīyā	'split'	*ríyā*	'split several times'
			(Keegan 1997: 40)

b. Yimas

manpa	'crocodile'	*manpawi*	'crocodiles'
kika	'rat'	*kikawi*	'rats'
yaka	'black possum'	*yakawi*	'black possums'
			(Foley 1991: 129)

c. Coptic

kōt	'build'	*kēt*	'be built'
hōp	'hide'	*hēp*	'be hidden'
tōm	'shut'	*tēm*	'be shut'

d. Hausa (v̀ = low tone, v́ = high tone)

búgàa	'beat'	búbbùgáa	'beat many times'
táakàa	'step on'	táttàakáa	'trample'
dánnèe	'oppress'	dáddànnée	'oppress (many (times))'
			(Newman 2000: 424)

e. Tagalog

ibigay	'give'	ibinigay	'gave'
ipaglaba	'wash (for)'	ipinaglaba	'washed (for)'
ipambili	'buy (with)'	ipinambili	'bought (with)'

f. German

finden	'find'	gefunden	'found'
singen	'sing'	gesungen	'sung'
binden	'tie'	gebunden	'tied'

4. In what way is the Tzutujil paradigm of Exercise 3 in Chapter 1 similar to the Finnish paradigm of (2.32)?

5. The distinction between strong suppletion, weak suppletion and non-suppletion is a continuum rather than a clear-cut three-way distinction, as is shown by Italian inhabitant nouns, which exhibit different degrees of similarity to the corresponding city names. Order the following pairs of city names and inhabitant names on a scale from clear suppletion to clear non-suppletion with affixation, depending on the number of segments in which the derivative differs from the base (see Crocco-Galèas 1991).

CITY NAME	INHABITANT NOUN	
Ancona	Anconetano	
Bologna	Petroniano	
Bressanone	Brissinese	
Domodossola	Domossolano	
Gubbio	Eugubino	
Ivrea	Eporediese	
Milano	Milanese	'Milan'
Napoli	Partenopeo	'Naples'
Palermo	Palermitano	
Palestrina	Prenestino	
Piacenza	Piacentino	
Savona	Saonese	
Trento	Trentino	
Treviso	Trevigiano	
Venezia	Veneziano	'Venice'
Volterra	Volaterrano	

Lexicon and rules

3

3.1 Productivity and the lexicon

We have seen that the morphology of a language is (the study of) the knowledge that speakers have of the structure of complex words in their language. Now it turns out that defining and delimiting the set of complex words of a language is not an easy matter. This set contains both words that are familiar to most speakers (such as *mis-represent* and *global-ize* in English) and words that are novel and were perhaps never used before (such as *mis-transliterate* and *bagel-ize*, two words that I have just made up). Morphologists refer to these two types of words as **actual words** and **possible words** (or *usual* and *potential words*). Thus, the set of words in a language is never quite fixed. Speakers have the capacity to create, and hearers can understand, an almost unlimited number of new words. Dictionaries can record only the actual words, but at any time a speaker may use a possible (but non-actual) word, and, if it is picked up by other speakers, it may join the set of actual words (thus, if the number of bagel restaurants in Europe continues to grow, people will perhaps start saying that Europe is being *bagelized*). Attested novel lexemes that were not observed before in the language are called **neologisms**, and neologisms that do not really catch on and are restricted to occasional occurrences are called **occasionalisms**.

Morphological patterns or rules (such as the *mis-* prefixing rule and the *-ize* suffixing rule in English) that can be used to create new words are called **productive**. Not only derivational rules, but also inflectional rules are often productive. Thus, the German pluralization rule that suffixes *-en* (e.g. *Fahrt* 'trip', plural *Fahrt-en* 'trips') can create new word-forms when it is applied to new bases such as loanwords (e.g. *Box* 'loudspeaker unit', borrowed from English *box*, plural *Box-en*). The fact that many morphological rules are productive means that a computer program for natural language processing will not work properly if it just contains a dictionary and a set of syntactic rules. True novel words are far less common than novel sentences, and most of the time we use words that we have used many times before. But, in principle, morphology is like syntax in that its rules may be productive.

From this perspective, what is really remarkable about morphology is that morphological rules may also be **unproductive**. An example of an unproductive derivational rule is the English suffix *-al* that forms action nouns (some of which are listed in (3.1a)). As the hypothetical but unacceptable forms in (3.1b) show, there are many verbs to which this suffix cannot be applied.

(3.1) a. *refusal, revival, dismissal, upheaval, arrival, bestowal, denial, betrayal*
 b. **repairal, *ignoral, *amusal, *belial, *debuggal*

But the crucial point is one that cannot be made by giving examples: the suffix *-al* cannot be used at all to form novel lexemes in English. The list of nouns formed with *-al* is fixed (it contains 35 nouns according to the *OED*), and no new nouns can be added to this list. An example of an unproductive inflectional rule is the plural-forming German suffix *-er*, which occurs with dozens of German nouns (some of which are listed in (3.2a)), but cannot be extended to new nouns such as loanwords or abbreviated words (see (3.2b)).

(3.2) a. *Feld/Felder* 'field(s)', *Kind/Kinder* 'child(ren)', *Kalb/Kälber* 'calf/calves', *Wort/Wörter* 'word(s)', *Mann/Männer* 'man/men'
 b. *Film/*Filmer* 'film(s)', *Skateboard/*Skatebörder* 'skateboard(s)', *ICE/*ICEer* 'Inter-City Express train(s)'

English, too, has unproductive plural formations (*ox/oxen, child/children, man/men, foot/feet*, and others), but these are so idiosyncratic that they can be easily dismissed as 'irregular', i.e. not subject to any rule at all. One could hypothesize that speakers simply memorize both the singular and the plural form and do not establish a morphological relation between them. But not all unproductive formations are irregular or rule-less. It would be much less plausible to claim that German *-er* plurals are irregular in this sense, simply because there are so many of them. And, in fact, the notion of an unproductive rule is widely accepted among morphologists, both for word-formation and for inflection. Unproductive rules are a remarkable property of morphology, because there is no direct analogue to them in syntax.

The reason why languages may have unproductive rules is that complex words, like simple words, may be **listed** in the **lexicon**. The lexicon is the linguists' term for the mental dictionary that language-users must be equipped with, in addition to the grammatical rules of their language. When a linguist says that something is listed in the lexicon, this really means that it must be **stored** in speakers' **memories**, but linguists generally prefer more abstract, less psychological-sounding terminology. The lexicon must contain at least all the information that is not predictable from general rules. For instance, the English lexicon must contain the monomorphemic English verbs *arrive, refuse, deny*, and it must contain words showing semantic peculiarities (e.g. *awful*, which is not the same as 'full of awe'). And, since it cannot be predicted that these verbs have an action noun in *-al*, the lexicon contains the nouns *arrival, refusal, denial* as well.

Thus, morphological rules play a dual role. When they are used to create a new word that is not listed in the lexicon, they have a **creative role**. If the neologism becomes current in the language, it may be added to the lexicon, and morphology thus serves to enrich the lexicon. But the fact that morphologically complex words may be listed in the lexicon means that morphological rules may also have a purely **descriptive role**, helping speakers to memorize and organize words in the lexicon. When English speakers use a noun like *arrival*, in all likelihood they simply retrieve it from their lexicon rather than constructing it on the fly. Thus, the *-al* rule is not needed to make words, but it helps organize the existing words in such a way that they can be used more efficiently. For example, a speaker whose grammatical knowledge includes the *-al* rule will find it easier to learn a new *-al* word never encountered previously.

However, although the existence of unproductive morphological rules with a purely descriptive role is widely assumed by linguists, it is difficult to find hard evidence that such rules are indeed learned by speakers and are cognitively real. Linguists are very eager to find patterns and rules everywhere in language structure, and no linguist would want to miss the generalization that one class of German nouns has an *-er* plural, or that one class of English action nouns ends in *-al*. But we do not really know whether speakers show the same eagerness for rules as linguists. Since they have to remember every word with an *-er* plural and every action noun in *-al* anyway, they might well be content with this information in list format and not abstract a rule from it. Only when a rule is productive and is observed to be extended to new bases can we be sure not only that the rule exists in linguists' descriptions, but that it is also cognitively real.

Even though most morphologists agree that all simple and at least some complex words are listed in speakers' lexicons, it is difficult to say which complex words are listed and which ones are not. One of the reasons for this is that morphological rules do not fall neatly into two types, productive and completely unproductive. Productivity is rather a matter of degree, and there are many rules of intermediate productivity. An example of an English derivational rule with a high degree of productivity is the English quality-noun suffix *-ness*, which can combine freely with almost any adjective that expresses a quality. The prefix *mis-* and the suffix *-ize* seem to be less productive, because many neologisms created with them sound rather awkward at first (cf. *?mis-pay, ?paper-ize*). Another English suffix with limited productivity is *-ee* (as in *employee, invitee*). There are quite a few neologisms with this suffix throughout the twentieth century (e.g. *arrestee,* *offendee, mergee, editee, enrollee, abusee* (see Barker 1998)), but some of them sound peculiar, and, when one encounters such a neologism, it does not go unnoticed (in contrast to *-ness* neologisms, many of which are not even perceived as new). And, finally, there are also suffixes that are almost unproductive, but not completely unproductive, like English *-eer*, which has given rise to fairly recent neologisms such as *Common Marketeer* 'advocate of the Common Market'.

Thus, word-formation patterns in English can be arranged on a scale ranging from the most productive to the least productive. Figure 3.1 shows such a scale with a few examples of affixes and exemplary derivatives. In addition to the affixes mentioned so far in this section, Figure 3.1 also shows the unproductive deadjectival quality-noun suffix *-th* (as in *warmth, width, length*) and the action-noun suffix *-ter*, which occurs only with a single base (*laugh-ter*). Strictly speaking, a scale as in Figure 3.1 of course presupposes that we have a rigorous method for measuring the degree of productivity of a pattern. So far, Figure 3.1 is based only on impressionistic observations, but in Chapter 6 we will see ways of quantifying the productivity of a pattern.

-ness	-ize	mis-	-ee	-eer	-al	-th	-ter
(goodness)	(globalize)	(misrepresent)	(invitee)	(profiteer)	(refusal)	(warmth)	(laughter)

◄——— most productive ————————————————————— least productive ———————►

Figure 3.1 A scale of productivity: Some examples from English

If it is admitted that the productivity of word-formation patterns is not an all-or-nothing question but a matter of degree, the question of which words are listed in the lexicon becomes more difficult to answer. We cannot simply say that all non-productively derived words are listed, and all others are not listed, but we would need to specify some threshold degree of productivity beyond which listing is no longer required. This theoretical problem is completely analogous to the practical problem of deciding which words should be listed in a dictionary. Dictionary-makers seem to find it more urgent to list English words with the suffixes *-th* and *-al* than words with the suffix *-ness*, simply because the latter is much more productive.

One radical solution to this problem that has been adopted by some linguists is the hypothesis that no regular complex words are listed in the lexicon. On this view, the lexicon contains just simple, monomorphemic elements, i.e. roots and affixes, plus idiosyncratic complex words. This hypothesis is associated with an extreme version of the morpheme-combination approach to morphology (see Definition 2 in Section 1.1). The lexicon is a **morpheme lexicon**, and all complex words, whether productively or unproductively derived, are created by rules. In addition to avoiding the decision of which complex words to include in the lexicon, this approach has the advantage of requiring only a minimal lexicon. But the morpheme lexicon must somehow also specify which unproductively formed lexemes are possible and which ones are not. If complex words cannot be listed directly, this information must be associated with the root morphemes by adding **diacritic features** to them, i.e. features that give information beyond the phonological and semantic make-up of the lexical entry. Thus, the root *warm* must bear a diacritic feature '[combines with *-th*]' (because *warmth* is an English word), and the root *arrive* must bear a diacritic feature '[combines with *-al*]' (because *arrival* is an English word). The disadvantage of this solution is that it claims that the existence of words like *warmth* and *arrival* is a property of their respective roots, although intuitively it is a property of the lexemes themselves. Moreover, the problem of the productivity continuum comes back eventually: for the affixes in the middle of the continuum, it is not so clear whether the roots need a diacritic or not.

Another radical solution to the problem of which words are listed in the lexicon takes exactly the opposite view: not just some, but all complex words are listed in the lexicon, whether they are regular or idiosyncratic, whether they are formed productively or unproductively. On this view, the lexicon is a **word-form lexicon**. One strong argument against the most radical version of this view comes from languages with richer inflectional systems than English. In Turkish, every verb can have hundreds of inflected forms, so that it seems completely impossible to memorize all verb forms that a speaker might want to use (Hankamer 1989). However, it is possible to assume a weaker version of the word-form lexicon, according to which a speaker memorizes all word-forms that they have heard, or that they have heard a certain number of times.

Of course, the big disadvantage of this approach is that it seems uneconomical, and thus inelegant. One important goal of linguistics is to provide an elegant description of language structure (see Section 1.2), and lists are inherently inelegant. A general methodological principle of linguistics (as in any other science) is that as many facts as possible should be subsumed under general rules and principles rather than merely stated in the form of a list. Since the rules are needed anyway for the creative role they play, they might as well be exploited for descriptive purposes, so that regularly derived words do not have to be listed. This is particularly true of inflected word-forms. No English dictionary would bother to list all regular third person singular forms and regular past tenses (*call, calls, called; like, likes, liked;* etc.), so why should a linguistic theory do so?

This is a classical case in which different goals lead to a conflict. As we saw in Section 1.2, another important goal of morphology is to provide a cognitively realistic description of morphological structures. The only way that the two goals of economy and cognitive realism would not come into conflict would be if speakers always chose the most economical analysis in their internal grammars. But there are strong indications that this is not the case. Speakers remember a word not only if it is unpredictable, but also if it is very frequent. This is a general feature of animal (including human) cognition: the more often a cognitive stimulus occurs, the more easily it is remembered (for instance, the more often a pianist plays a piece, the sooner she will be able to play it by heart). This applies to words, whether predictable or unpredictable, as to anything else. Thus, it is quite likely that speakers store highly frequent complex words such as *things, goes, wanted, happiness* in their memories (i.e. their mental lexicons), although they are completely predictable and could easily be derived by productive rules from *thing, go, want, happy*. One piece of evidence for this is the fact that regular inflected forms may undergo an idiosyncratic sound change and thus become irregular. For instance, the past-tense forms of *have, say* and *make* used to be perfectly regular in earlier English (*haved, sayed, maked*). Since these are among the most frequently occurring verbs of the English language, they were vulnerable to an idiosyncratic shortening (see Section 12.3), and as a result they are now somewhat irregular (*had, said* [sɛd], *made*). If speakers had never stored these words in their lexicons, if they had stored just the stem and applied the *-ed*-suffixation rule each time the words were used, then it is difficult to see how they could have become irregular in the first place.

Thus, the cognitively most plausible model is probably one in which the mental lexicon consists of all idiosyncratic words (whether simple or complex) and some regular complex words. For regular words, all we can say is that the less productive the morphological rule is and the more frequent they are, the likelier it is that they are stored in the mental lexicon. This statement implies that we would not be able to make a general decision for the language as a whole, because word frequency is a performance phenomenon that is different for different speakers.

3.2 The form of morphological rules

By **morphological rule** (or **pattern**, or **process**), we mean any kind of regularity or generalization that is noticed by speakers and reflected in their unconscious linguistic knowledge. Morphologists try to develop a descriptive apparatus for expressing morphological rules, and the ultimate goal is to mimic the mental organization of speakers' linguistic knowledge in the form of morphological descriptions. There is, of course, a vast number of conceivable possibilities, and, compared to the complexities of human cognition, linguistic models are quite simplistic and probably not very realistic.

On the whole, the emphasis in this book is on questions of substance rather than questions of formal description. But in this section, two representative formalisms for morphological rules will be presented and contrasted, and it will be seen that questions of formalization can be enlightening and help to bring some major issues into clear focus. The two formalisms that will be discussed are variants of the morpheme-based model and of the word-based model.

3.2.1 The morpheme-based model

In the morpheme-based model, morphological rules are thought of as combining morphemes in much the same way as syntactic rules combine words (see Section 2.2). In order to describe the structure of English words like *cheeseboard, bags, unhappier, eventfulness*, one could make use of the word-structure rules in (3.3), which are quite analogous to familiar phrase-structure rules as they might be used in syntax (see (3.4)).[1]

(3.3) Word-structure rules
    a. word-form   = stem (+ inflectional suffix)
    b. stem   = (i) { (deeriv. prefix +) root (+ deriv. suffix)
                              (ii) { stem + stem
    c. inflectional suffix   = -s, -er, . . .
    d. derivational prefix = *un-*, . . .
    e. root   = *bag, event, cheese, board, happy*, . . .
    f. derivational suffix = *-ful, -ness*, . . .

(3.4) Phrase-structure rules
    a. sentence   = noun phrase + verb phrase
    b. noun phrase   = (i) { determiner (+ adjective) + noun
                              (ii) { sentence
    c. verb phrase   = verb (+ noun phrase)
    d. determiner   = *the, a, some*, . . .
    e. noun   = *cat, rat, bat*, . . .
    f. verb   = *chased, thought, slept*, . . .
    g. adjective   = *big, grey*, . . .

We can use the word-structure rules in (3.3) to create complex words by replacing elements in the left-hand column by elements in the right-hand column ('X ⇒ Y' means 'insert Y for X'). In the following, we see the individual steps by which the words *bags, unhappier* and *cheeseboard* can be created using the rules in (3.3).

(3.5) word-form ⇒ stem + inflectional suffix   (by 3.3a)
      stem ⇒ root ⇒ *bag*   (by 3.3bi, 3.3e)
      inflectional suffix ⇒ *-s*   (by 3.3c)
      word-form: *bag-s*

(3.6) word-form ⇒ stem + inflectional suffix   (by 3.3a)
      stem ⇒ derivational prefix + root   (by 3.3bi)

---

[1] Elements in parentheses are optional; curly brackets and commas represent a choice between alternative options.

derivational prefix ⇒ *un-*   (by 3.3d)
root ⇒ *happy*   (by 3.3e)
inflectional suffix ⇒ *-er*   (by 3.3c)
stem: *un-happy*
word-form: *un-happi-er*

(3.7) word-form ⇒ stem   (by 3.3a)
   stem ⇒ stem + stem   (by 3.3bii)
   stem ⇒ root   (by 3.3bi)
   root ⇒ *cheese*   (by 3.3e)
   root ⇒ *board*   (by 3.3e)
   stem: *cheese-board*
   word-form: *cheese-board*

Since this approach assumes a close parallelism between morphology and syntax (and in the extreme case denies the distinction between the two domains altogether), it is sometimes called **word syntax**. The last four 'rules' of (3.3) are of course nothing but lists of morphemes, i.e. a morpheme lexicon. Thus, the word-syntactic approach fits well with the view that the lexicon contains just morphemes.

Many syntacticians have called into question the need for phrase-structure rules like (3.4a–c), on the grounds that the **combinatory potential**[2] of words is already contained in their lexical entry, so that the general rules are a redundant duplication. For example, the verb *chased* must be listed in the lexicon as having the combinatory potential [__ NP],[3] the verb *thought* has the combinatory potential [__ sentence] and the verb *slept* has no com-binatory potential, i.e. it does not need to combine with any other syntactic element within the verb phrase. The verb-phrase rule (3.4c) is thus not really needed.

Similarly, in morphology we can dispense with word-structure rules in (3.3) and put all the relevant information into the lexical entries. Like full words, affixes may be said to have a combinatory potential that contains, among other things, information on the word-class of the base. Thus the comparative suffix *-er* combines with adjectives (combinatory potential [A __]), the suffix *-ful* combines with nouns ([N __]) and the prefix *un-* again combines with adjectives ([__ A]).

When lexical entries of roots and affixes are enriched in this way, mor-phological description seems to reduce largely to the description of the lexical entries of morphemes, illustrated in (3.8). These contain at least information on the pronunciation, on the syntactic properties and on the meaning of the morpheme. In (3.8), the pronunciation is given between

---

[2] Another term for *combinatory potential* that is widely used is the term *subcategorization frame*.
[3] In the formal description of combinatory potentials, a straight line is a variable for the element that is characterized by the combinatory potential (so here '[__ NP]' means that *chased* is followed by an NP).

slashes in phonetic transcription; the syntactic properties consist of the word-class (for roots) or of the combinatory potential (for affixes); and a rough indication of the meaning is given in quotation marks (naturally, a lot more needs to be said on the semantics of morphemes, but the details can be ignored for present purposes; see Section 11.1.1 for some aspects of the semantics that are relevant to morphology).

(3.8) proposed lexical entries for some morphemes:

a. *bag*   b. -s   c. *happy*   d. *un-*

$$\begin{bmatrix} /\text{bæg}/ \\ N \\ \text{'bag'} \end{bmatrix} \quad \begin{bmatrix} /z/ \\ N\_\_ \\ \text{'plural'} \end{bmatrix} \quad \begin{bmatrix} /\text{hæpi}/ \\ A \\ \text{'happy'} \end{bmatrix} \quad \begin{bmatrix} /\text{ʌn}/ \\ \_\_A \\ \text{'not'} \end{bmatrix}$$

Assuming that affixes have lexical entries much like roots (as in (3.8b) and (3.8c)) has the advantage that special rules for combining affixes and roots can be largely dispensed with. Root morphemes and affix morphemes are very similar on this view, differing mainly in that affixes have an obligatory combinatory potential and roots belong to one of the lexical word-classes (in Section 5.3 we will see that affixes, too, have sometimes been assigned word-class features). Moreover, a lexicon that contains only morphemes and no complex words is attractive because it is very economical, as we saw in Section 3.1. For these reasons, the morpheme-based approach to morphological description has been quite popular among theoretically minded morphologists.

3.2.2 The word-based model

In the word-based model, the fundamental significance of the word is emphasized and the relationship between complex words is captured not by splitting them up into parts, but by formulating **word-schemas** that represent the common features of sets of morphologically related words. For instance, the similarities among the English words *bags, keys, gods, ribs, bones, gems* (and of course many others) can be expressed in the word-schema in (3.9b).

(3.9) a. *bags, keys, gods, ribs, bones, gems, ...*

b. $\begin{bmatrix} /Xz/ \\ N \\ \text{'plurality of } xs \text{'} \end{bmatrix}$

A word-schema is like a lexical entry in that it contains information on pronunciation, syntactic properties and meaning, but it may contain variables. In this way, it abstracts away from the differences between the related words and just expresses the common features. The schema in (3.9b) expresses the fact that all words in (3.9a) end in /z/, that they all denote a plurality of things and that they are all nouns. The phonological string preceding the /z/ is quite diverse and is thus replaced by the variable /X/. Likewise, semantically these words share nothing besides the plurality component, so again the semantic part of the schema contains a variable ('*x*'). We will use the terms *match* and *subsume* for the relation between concrete words and the abstract schema: words **match** a schema, and a schema **subsumes** words (for example, the schema in (3.9b) subsumes the nouns in (3.9a) and many others, but not all English plural nouns match it; for instance, the plural *feet* does not match its phonological part).

Crucially, a word-schema stands for complete words, not for individual morphemes. In the word-based model, the lexicon consists of words, not of morphemes, and word-schemas capture the relationships between the words in the lexicon. Now what makes the word-schema in (3.9b) really significant for morphology is the fact that there exists a closely related schema (3.10b) that subsumes a very similar set of words (3.10a).

(3.10) a. *bag, key, god, rib, bone, gem, …*

b. $\begin{bmatrix} /X/ \\ N \\ \text{'}x\text{'} \end{bmatrix}$

The morphological relationship between these sets of words can now be represented in the morphological correspondence in (3.11).

(3.11) $\begin{bmatrix} /X/ \\ N \\ \text{'}x\text{'} \end{bmatrix} \longleftrightarrow \begin{bmatrix} /Xz/ \\ N \\ \text{'plurality of } xs\text{'} \end{bmatrix}$

The double arrow means that, for some words matching the schema on the left, there is a corresponding word matching the schema on the right. (3.11) thus shows what a morphological rule looks like in the word-based model. Unlike the morpheme-based model, the word-based model has no way of dispensing with morphological rules, but it does not require lexical entries that not words (i.e. neither affixes nor bases or roots). In fact, in the word-based model, the notion of morpheme is not necessary at all for the formal description. The rule in (3.11) is the word-based equivalent of the plural morpheme in (3.8b). Just as the morpheme-based model fits with the morpheme-lexicon view of Section 3.1, the word-based model fits with the word-form-lexicon view of Section 3.1. The basic idea is that speakers can form abstract categories or schemas of similar mental entities, and that morphological structure arises when speakers form a schema in which a formal aspect corresponds to a semantic aspect.

A striking advantage of the word-based model is that all kinds of non-concatenative processes can be described with it quite naturally, whereas such phenomena are difficult to accommodate in morpheme-based models.

As an example, (3.12b–c) shows the English rule for noun–verb conversion of nouns denoting instruments.[4]

(3.12) a. *hammer*$_N$/*hammer*$_V$, *saw*$_N$/*saw*$_V$, *spoon*$_N$/*spoon*$_V$, *funnel*$_N$/*funnel*$_V$, ...

b. $\left[\begin{array}{l} /X/ \\ N \\ \text{'}x \text{ (= an instrument)'} \end{array}\right]$ $\leftrightarrow$ $\left[\begin{array}{l} /X/ \\ V \\ \text{'use } x \text{ (= an instrument)'} \end{array}\right]$

c. $\left[\begin{array}{l} /X/_N \\ \text{'}x \text{ (= an instrument)'} \end{array}\right]$ $\leftrightarrow$ $\left[\begin{array}{l} /X/_V \\ \text{'use } x \text{ (= an instrument)'} \end{array}\right]$

Here the word-schema on the right differs from the schema on the left only in word-class and meaning, but not in phonological form. Processes of base modification can be easily described by elaborating the phonological variable somewhat. For instance, shortening in Hindi/Urdu can be represented as in (3.13b), where /V/ stands for any short vowel and /VV/ stands for any long vowel.

(3.13) a. *maar-*/*mar-* 'kill/die'

b. $\left[\begin{array}{l} /XV_1V_1Y/_V \\ \text{'A causes B to happen '} \end{array}\right]$ $\leftrightarrow$ $\left[\begin{array}{l} /XV_1Y/_V \\ \text{'B happens'} \end{array}\right]$

Reduplication is described by copying part of the phonological string in one of the word-schemas. (3.14b) shows the rule for the Somali duplifix *-aC* that we saw in (2.19) in the previous chapter (here /C/ is a variable for an arbitrary consonant).

(3.14) a. *buug*/*buugag* 'book(s)', *fool*/*foolal* 'face(s)', *koob*/*koobab* 'cup(s)', ...

b. $\left[\begin{array}{l} /XC_1/_N \\ \text{'}x' \end{array}\right]$ $\leftrightarrow$ $\left[\begin{array}{l} /XC_1aC_1/_N \\ \text{'plurality of } xs' \end{array}\right]$

Moreover, the word-based model can explain how **back-formations** (like to *babysit* from *babysitter*) are possible. In the morpheme-based model, it is quite puzzling that speakers should be able to create a verb *babysit*, because English does not have a productive rule combining a noun and a verb in this way, and there is no explanation for the fact that *babysit* is semantically closely related to *babysitter*. In the word-based model, this can be readily described. The noun *babysitter* happens to match two word-schemas simultaneously. First, it matches the nominal compound schema in (3.15), and everyone agrees that it was first created using this rule.

(3.15) $\left[\begin{array}{l} /X/_N \\ \text{'}x' \end{array}\right]$ & $\left[\begin{array}{l} /Y/_N \\ \text{'}y' \end{array}\right]$ $\leftrightarrow$ $\left[\begin{array}{l} /XY/_N \\ \text{'a } y \text{ that has to} \\ \text{do with } x' \end{array}\right]$

(Note that, for compounds, the left-hand side of the correspondence must consist of two word-schemas.) And, second, it matches the word-schema of

---

[4] In (3.12c) I give an abbreviated notational variant of (3.12b), in which the word-class information is shown as a subscript. To save space, I will henceforth use only this notation.

non-compound agent nouns given on the right in (3.16). (Here 'do$_x$' represents a variable action meaning.)

(3.16) $\begin{bmatrix} /X/_V \\ \text{'do}_x\text{'} \end{bmatrix}$ $\longleftrightarrow$ $\begin{bmatrix} /X\text{ər}/_N \\ \text{'a person who} \\ \text{(habitually) does}_x\text{'} \end{bmatrix}$

Crucially, the correspondence in (3.16) is not inherently directed, as the bidirectional arrow indicates. In addition to the creation of -er nouns from verbs (like *bak-er, writ-er, sinn-er,* etc.), this rule also allows the creation of verbs lacking the element -er from nouns containing -er that denote an agent of some sort. In fact, back-formation is so natural in this model that one wonders why it does not occur more often: why do we not get **to butch* from *butcher, *to past* from *pastor,* and so on? However, it should be kept in mind that the rule format of our word-based model is neutral with respect to productivity. The arrows do not represent the productivity of the rule; they just record the existence of a correspondence. Clearly, the rule (3.16) is much more productive from left to right than from right to left. Under what sort of circumstances a rule is productive or unproductive is an important question that we return to in Chapter 6 (see also Section 9.2).

Finally, in the word-based model it is possible to describe relations between more than two sets of words. Consider the three sets of English words in (3.17).

(3.17) | | | |
|---|---|---|
| *attract* | *attraction* | *attractive* |
| *suggest* | *suggestion* | *suggestive* |
| *prohibit* | *prohibition* | *prohibitive* |
| *elude* | — | *elusive* |
| *insert* | *insertion* | — |
| *discuss* | *discussion* | — |
| — | *illusion* | *illusive* |
| — | *aggression* | *aggressive* |

In order to describe the relations between these three sets, we minimally need the two rules in (3.18a–b), or in the morpheme-based model the morphemes [/-ion/; N; V__] and [/-ive/; A; V__]. (For the sake of simplicity, we use the spelling rather than the pronunciation in representing the affixes -ion and -ive here.)

(3.18) a. $\begin{bmatrix} /X/_V & \longleftrightarrow & /Xion/_N \\ \text{'do}_x\text{'} & & \text{'action of doing}_x\text{'} \end{bmatrix}$ b. $\begin{bmatrix} /X/_V & \longleftrightarrow & /Xive/_A \\ \text{'do}_x\text{'} & & \text{'prone to doing}_x\text{'} \end{bmatrix}$

But these two rules do not suffice, because there are pairs like *illusion/ illusive, aggression/aggressive* that lack a corresponding verb (**aggress, *illude*). This means that we also need the rule (3.18c).

(3.18) c. $\begin{bmatrix} /Xion/_N \\ \text{'action of doing}_x\text{'} \end{bmatrix}$ $\longleftrightarrow$ $\begin{bmatrix} /Xive/_A \\ \text{'prone to doing}_x\text{'} \end{bmatrix}$

This morphological relationship cannot be described so easily in a pure morpheme-based model. The three rules (3.18a–c) can be collapsed into a single rule with three mutually corresponding word-schemas if we allow the two-dimensional triangular representation shown in (3.19).

(3.19) $\begin{bmatrix} /X/_V \\ \text{'do}_x\text{'} \end{bmatrix} \leftrightarrow \begin{bmatrix} /Xion/_N \\ \text{'action of doing}_x\text{'} \end{bmatrix}$

$\begin{bmatrix} /Xive/_A \\ \text{'prone to doing}_x\text{'} \end{bmatrix}$

Such rules involving more than two corresponding word-schemas will become important again later when we discuss inflectional morphology. We therefore introduce a further notational convention: sets of corresponding word-schemas are enclosed in curly brackets and separated by commas. Thus, (3.20) is a more convenient alternative notation for (3.19).

(3.20) $\left\{ \begin{bmatrix} /X/_V \\ \text{'do}_x\text{'} \end{bmatrix}, \begin{bmatrix} /Xion/_N \\ \text{'action of doing}_x\text{'} \end{bmatrix}, \begin{bmatrix} /Xive/_A \\ \text{'prone to doing}_x\text{'} \end{bmatrix} \right\}$

3.3 Morphological change

This book is primarily about synchronic morphology, the nature of morphological patterns as they function in a particular language at a given time. But, in order to understand synchronic patterns better, it is sometimes useful to consider also the diachronic aspect of morphology, i.e. the way in which morphological patterns change over the centuries. Morphological change will be mentioned at various points later in this book. Here only some basic notions will be introduced. Four main types of morphological change will be distinguished: pattern loss, coalescence, analogical change, and reanalysis.

3.3.1 Pattern loss

When a morphological pattern disappears from the language, sometimes this means that all the words formed by that pattern disappear. Such loss without traces seems to happen primarily in inflection. For instance, in older Ancient Greek a distinction between dual number ('two') and plural number ('more than two') was made in nouns, as illustrated in (3.21).

(3.21)

SINGULAR		DUAL		PLURAL	
adelph-ós	'brother'	adelph-ṓ	'2 brothers'	adelph-oí	'brothers'
ánthrōpos	'human'	anthrṓp-ō	'2 people'	ánthrōp-oi	'people'

This distinction was lost in later Ancient Greek and is, for instance, absent by the time of New Testament Greek (first century CE). After the change, the plural had to be used even if two items were referred to, and no dual-marked noun in -*ō* survived. In Latin, nouns distinguished at least five different case forms (nominative, genitive, dative, accusative, ablative), but all case distinctions have been lost in modern Romance languages such as Italian and Spanish. No genitive, dative or ablative noun has survived. The meaning distinctions that were expressed by cases are now carried by other means (prepositions and syntactic constructions).

Derivational patterns may also be completely lost. This happens when all lexemes formed according to a derivational pattern disappear from the language. Thus, Old English had a quality-noun pattern ending in -*u* (e.g. *menig* 'many'/*menigu* 'multitude', *eald* 'old'/*ieldu* 'old age', *strong*/*strengu* 'strength'). None of these nouns survived into modern English, so the pattern was lost without trace.

But morphological patterns often leave plenty of traces when they die. For example, English used to have a suffix -*t* that formed action nouns from verbs:

(3.22) VERB   ACTION NOUN
       draw   *draft*
       drive   *drift*
       may   *might*
       weigh   *weight*
       freeze   *frost*
       shove   *shift*

In most cases, both the semantic and the formal connection between the two lexemes was lost, as a result of semantic and phonological change that did not affect all words equally. The verb *may* used to mean 'have power', but in its contemporary meaning 'be allowed' it is no longer semantically connected to *might*. Perhaps with the exception of *weigh*/*weight*, the above pairs of words are no longer morphologically related, and the suffix -*t* has ceased to exist in English. However, many of the words that were once derived with -*t* survive, and, although they are no longer morphologically complex, they bear witness to the former existence of a rule of *t*-suffixation.

Pattern loss with lexical traces also occurs in inflection. For instance, older Slavic used to have a singular–dual-plural distinction, much like older Classical Greek (e.g. Old Church Slavonic *rǫka* 'hand', *rǫcě* 'two hands', *rǫky* 'hands'). In modern Polish, the dual was lost as a morphological distinction, and nouns have only a singular and a plural form (e.g. *żona* 'wife', *żony* 'wives'). However, in a few nouns the modern plural form is identical to the former dual (e.g. in *ręka* 'hand', plural *ręce* 'hands'). Thus, although the dual as a pattern disappeared, not all dual word-forms disappeared from the language.

3.3.2 Coalescence

By far the most important way in which new morphological patterns arise is by **coalescence** of several formerly free syntactic elements. When the two elements that coalesce are full, non-auxiliary words, the result of the coalescence is a compound (the process of coalescence that results in a compound is also called **univerbation**). For example, the pattern exemplified by the Swedish compound *kyrkomusik* 'church music' (cf. *kyrka* 'church', *musik* 'music') comes from a syntactic phrase in which the genitive NP precedes the head (*kyrko* was the genitive form of *kyrka* in older Swedish). After the univerbation, this phrase had become a single word. The vowel *-o* is no longer a genitive suffix (all nouns now take the genitive suffix *-s*, so 'church's' is *kyrkas*), but an affix that is peculiar to the compound pattern.

When one of the coalescing elements is a semantically abstract, auxiliary element, the result of the coalescence is an affixed word, and the process by which this happens is called **grammaticalization**. Let us consider an example from Spanish, which has a future tense that is formed by adding the suffix *-r* to the stem, followed by a series of special person–number suffixes:

(3.23)

		PRESENT TENSE		FUTURE TENSE	
1SG		*cant-o*	'I sing'	*canta-r-é*	'I will sing'
2SG		*canta-s*		*canta-r-ás*	
3SG		*canta*		*canta-r-á*	
1PL		*canta-mos*		*canta-r-émos*	
2PL		*cantá-is*		*canta-r-éis*	
3PL		*canta-n*		*canta-r-án*	

In Latin, Spanish's ancestor, there existed a future tense (e.g. *cantabo* 'I will sing'), but this pattern disappeared from the language without trace, and instead a completely new future-tense pattern was created. Originally this was a syntactic pattern, involving the auxiliary verb *habere* 'have' (Spanish *haber*), which was combined with the infinitive to express obligation, as in English: *habeo cantare* or *cantare habeo* 'I have to sing'. Then the meaning shifted from obligation to future, and the verb *haber* lost its freedom of position and came to occur only immediately after the main verb. As a result of phonological reduction, the infinitive lost its final *-e* (*cantare* became *cantar*) and the forms of the verb *haber* were shortened (*he, has, ha, habemos, habéis, han*). Finally, the infinitive and the forms of *haber* were fused together to form a set of single complex words:

(3.24)

cantar	*he*	>	*cantaré*
cantar	*has*	>	*cantarás*
cantar	*ha*	>	*cantará*
cantar	*(hab)emos*	>	*cantarémos*
cantar	*(hab)éis*	>	*cantaréis*
cantar	*han*	>	*cantarán*

Such grammaticalization changes are extremely common in languages, and the vast majority of all (non-compound) morphological patterns seem ultimately to go back to such syntactic phrases with auxiliary words. In most contemporary cases, we cannot tell exactly what happened because the changes occurred in prehistoric times. Thus, it is a quite plausible hypothesis that the English past-tense suffix *-ed* goes back to the form *did* (so *walked* comes from *walk did*, etc.), but, since this change occurred at least 2000 years ago, we will never know for sure. However, there are enough attested cases of grammaticalization like the Spanish future that help us understand the way grammaticalization works.

3.3.3 Analogical change

An analogical change is said to occur when speakers form a new word on the model of (or **by analogy** with) another word. For instance, the English verb *dig* used to have past tense formed with the suffix *-ed* (*digged*), but at some point the past-tense form *dug* was created, clearly on the model of verbs like *sting/stung, stick/stuck*, and so on. In order to show clearly what happens in analogical change, linguists often use **proportional equations** as in (3.25). The two terms on the left-hand side of the equation represent the model, and the X on the right-hand side represents the word that is newly created by analogy.

(3.25) *stick : stuck = dig :* X
$$X = dug$$

Two main types of analogy are distinguished: analogical extension and analogical levelling. The creation of the past-tense form *dug* is an example of **analogical extension**: the *i/u* pattern is extended to a new lexeme. Another example is the Polish plural suffix *-owie*. Originally this occurred only with a few nouns (those belonging to the *u*-declension), e.g. *syn* 'son', plural *synowie* 'sons'. But later it was extended to quite a few other nouns denoting male humans, e.g. *pan* 'lord, sir', plural *panowie*.

(3.26) *syn : synowie = pan :* X
$$X = panowie$$

Analogical extension also occurs in derivational morphology. For instance, on the model of pairs of French loanwords such as *change*$_v$, *changeable*$_A$, adjectives in *-able* were formed from native English words like *wash*:

(3.27) *change : changeable = wash :* X
$$X = washable$$

However, analogical extension in derivation is not usually regarded as analogical 'change', because new lexemes like *washable* simply enrich the lexicon and do not (or not necessarily) oust other forms that are replaced by them.

Analogical levelling occurs when a morphophonological alternation in the stem is eliminated (or 'levelled'). An example comes from French: the verb *trouver* 'find' used to have two different forms of the stem in older French, *trouv-* and *treuv-*. The former occurred in word-forms that were stressed on the suffix, and the latter occurred in word-forms that were stressed on the stem. This alternation resulted from a sound change that treated the original stem vowel differently in different environments. When the old stem vowel *o* was unstressed, it turned into *ou*, but when it was stressed, it turned into *eu* (compare Italian *trovare*, which underwent neither of these sound changes). (In (3.28), a dot below the syllable indicates the position of the stress.)

(3.28)

	older French	modern French
'I find'	*je treuve*	*je trouve*
'you find'	*tu treuves*	*tu trouves*
'he finds'	*il treuve*	*il trouve*
'we find'	*nous trouvons*	*nous trouvons*
'you(PL) find'	*vous trouvez*	*vous trouvez*
'they find'	*ils treuvent*	*ils trouvent*

As (3.28) shows, this stem alternation no longer exists in modern French: all forms of the verb *trouver* have the same stem vowel. This change, too, can be described by a proportional equation. The analogical model might be a verb that never showed a stem alternation because its stem vowel was not subject to stress-sensitive sound changes (e.g. *chercher* 'seek'):

(3.29) *chercher : (je) cherche = trouver : X*

$$X = (je)\ trouve$$

The description of these changes in terms of analogy and proportional equations is widespread in the study of diachronic morphology, but it should be noted that these changes can also be described in different terms. Analogical extension can simply be described as increase in the productivity of a morphological rule. Thus, the English *i/u* alternation (as in *stick/stuck*) became more productive at a certain stage and came to be applied to new words, in this case to words that used to have a different past-tense form. And analogical levelling can be described as a change whereby a phonological allomorph is lost from the language. The notation in terms of proportional equations as in (3.25)–(3.29) suggests that a single word pair served as the model for the change. But, in fact, there is no particular reason to assume that, for instance, French *trouve* was created on the basis of *chercher : cherche*, rather than, say, *chanter : chante* ('sing'), or *penser : pense* ('think'). It seems that the left-hand part of a proportional equation, the model, has to be understood as a general pattern, a word-schema, rather than as a specific word. If that is the case, then a formula such as *chercher : cherche* becomes virtually indistinguishable from word-based rules of the kind we saw in Section 3.2.2 ([/Xer/$_v$ 'infinitive'] ↔ [/Xe/$_v$ 'first person singular']). Thus, the solution of an analogical equation is practically the same as the application of a word-based rule to a novel word.

3.3.4 Reanalysis

Reanalysis is the commonly used term for a change by which a complex word comes to be regarded as matching a different word-schema from the one it was originally created by. For instance, Ancient Greek has a suffix *-ízō* deriving denominal verbs that denote an activity associated with the base noun, e.g. *kithára* 'guitar', *kitharízō* 'play the guitar'. In addition, there is a suffix *-tēs* that derives agent nouns from verbs, e.g. *kitharistēs* 'guitar player' (see 3.30a–b). Although *kitharistēs* was originally derived from *kitharízō*, it could also be seen as related directly to *kithára*. In other words, because of the formal and semantic resemblances between *kitharistēs* and *kithára* (and other similar word pairs), it was possible to set up a new correspondence between the left-hand word-schema in (3.30a) and the right-hand word-schema in (3.30b). The new correspondence or rule is shown in (3.30c).

(3.30) a. $[/X/_N \text{'}x\text{'}] \leftrightarrow [/X\text{í}z\bar{o}/_V \text{ 'do something with } x\text{'}]$
b. $[/X\bar{o}/_V \text{'do}_x\text{'}] \leftrightarrow [/Xt\text{é}s/_N \text{ 'person who does}_x\text{'}]$
c. $[/X/_N \text{'}x\text{'}] \leftrightarrow [/Xist\text{é}s/_N \text{ 'person who does something with } x\text{'}]$

This rule (3.30c) became productive and it was thus possible to create new words in *-istēs* (later pronounced *-istís*) without the existence of a verb in *-ízō*. For example, the Modern Greek word for 'spiritist' is *pnevmatistís*, directly derived from *pnevma(t)* 'spirit' (there is no verb **pnevmatízo*). Put somewhat more simply, we can say that *kitharis-tēs* was **reanalysed** as *kithar-istēs*, and thereby the suffix *-istēs* was created (this is, incidentally, the source of the English suffix *-ist*). This type of reanalysis may be called **affix telescoping**, because two formerly independent affixes are combined into a new compound affix.

By the definition of reanalysis given here, back-formation (discussed in Section 3.2.2) is also a kind of reanalysis, because here, too, a new formation becomes possible after a complex word has been associated with a word-schema that played no role in creating the word.

Another kind of reanalysis is **secretion**, whereby an element that used to be part of a root is turned into an affix. Secretion is in general a rare phenomenon, but it happens to be fairly common in contemporary English. At the beginning usually stands a process of blending, e.g. the word *workaholic*, which is a blend of *alcoholic* and *work*. When more blends of this kind are being created (e.g. *tobaccoholic*, *marihuanaholic*), we can start recognizing a suffix *-aholic* ('person addicted to something'). This suffix did not arise by coalescence, but was, so to speak, 'secreted' from the original word *alcoholic*.

Thus, like coalescence, reanalysis creates new morphological patterns, but, as we noted in Section 3.3.2, new patterns seem to arise much more often by coalescence than by reanalysis.

3.3.5 Other changes

The four main types of change discussed so far in this section do not exhaust the possibilities, and I will mention two more here. Morphological patterns may have their origin in phonological rules that are no longer truly phonologically conditioned and come to be associated with morphological patterns. For instance, the German Umlaut was once phonologically conditioned by a high front vowel in the following syllable (e.g. *Tag* 'day'/*täglich* 'daily', *Gott* 'God'/*göttlich* 'godly, divine'), but the rule has long ceased to be a phonological rule. It is now an operation that accompanies certain morphological patterns and is used productively (e.g. *Revolutiönchen* 'little revolution', *Fäxchen* 'little fax'), and sometimes it can signal the plural on its own (e.g. *Mutter/Mütter* 'mother(s)' (see Section 2.2). The role of phonology in morphology will be discussed further in Chapter 10.

Another kind of change is simply semantic change. The contemporary future-tense form in Lezgian (*-da*) expresses both future and habitual meaning (e.g. *čüxüda* 'will wash; washes habitually'), but it must have expressed the ongoing present tense at an earlier point as well (Haspelmath 1998). Such semantic changes in inflectional categories are common and interesting, but they are not normally discussed under the heading of morphology. This particular change would be discussed in the context of the study of grammatical semantics of tense–aspect systems.

Summary of Chapter 3

In morphology, the relation between listed elements and combinatory rules is more complicated than in syntax because rules vary in productivity and it is difficult to maintain that only simple words and morphemes are listed in the lexicon. The opposite view, that all words (even those formed by the most productive rules) are listed, is not possible either, so the most realistic view is that all idiosyncratic and many regular words are stored in speakers' memories.

Morphological structures can be described by a morpheme-based model, with rules or principles for the combination of morphemes, or by a word-based model in which correspondences between abstract word-schemas are the main formal device. The word-based model naturally accommodates non-concatenative operations, back-formation and relations between more than two sets of words.

There is a wide range of processes of morphological change, the most important of which are pattern loss (with or without traces), coalescence (especially grammaticalization), analogical change (extension and levelling) and reanalysis.

Further reading

For further references on productivity, see Chapter 6.

A morpheme lexicon and the morpheme-based model is advocated by Bloomfield (1933), Selkirk (1982), Di Sciullo and Williams (1987) and Lieber (1992). A word-form lexicon and the word-based model is advocated by Bybee (1988), Becker (1990) and Bochner (1993).

For morphological change in general, see McMahon (1994: ch. 4) and Anderson (1988). For grammaticalization, see Lehmann (1985, 1995), Hopper and Traugott (1993) and Haspelmath (1999). Analogy and its relation to morphological rules are discussed by Becker (1990), and morphological reanalysis is discussed in Haspelmath (1995).

Exercises

1. Which of the following English words are actual, possible and impossible?

   replay, libertarian, itinerance, reknow, fraternitarian, penchance, rebagelize, abundance, happytarian

2. What would be the lexical entries of the following English morphemes (using the formalism of (3.8))?

   hear, -ing (as in *playing, dancing*, etc.), *re-* (as in *replay, rewrite*, etc.), *good, -s* (as in *sells, knows*, etc.)

3. Formulate the morphological rule in the word-based format of (3.11) (i.e. as a correspondence between word-schemas) for the following pairs of words (each standing for a large set of such pairs):

   warm – warmer
   happy – unhappy
   play – replay
   happy – happily

4. Formulate the word-based morphological rule for the six sets of word pairs in Exercise 3 of Chapter 2.

5. The word *edit* (first attested in 1791) is a famous example of a back-formation from the noun *editor* (first attested in 1649). Which morphological rule was used in the reverse direction in this back-formation?

6. Formulate the proportional equations for the following analogical changes:

a. The earlier English vowel alternation in adjectival degree inflection (e.g. *strong/strenger, long/lenger, broad/breader*) underwent analogical levelling on the model of *clean/cleaner*, thus leading to the new comparatives *stronger, longer, broader*.

b. The Greek noun *patír*_{NOM.SG}/*patéra*_{ACC.SG} 'father' acquired a new nominative singular *patéras* by analogical levelling of the stem and analogical extension of the nominative singular suffix *-s* (cf. words such as *neanías*_{NOM.SG}/*neanía*_{ACC.SG} 'young man').

c. The Old English genitive singular suffix *-es* (as in *stan*_{NOM.SG}, *stanes*_{GEN.SG} 'stone('s)') was analogically extended to other nouns such as *modor*_{NOM.SG}, *modor*_{GEN.SG} 'mother' and *sunu*_{NOM.SG}, *suna*_{GEN.SG} 'son' (cf. Modern English *mother's, son's*).

7. Formulate the morphological rule for the following Tagalog lexeme pairs:

búhay	'life'	*buháy*	'alive'
gútom	'hunger'	*gutóm*	'hungry'
tákot	'fear'	*takót*	'afraid'
hába ʔ	'length'	*habá ʔ*	'long'
gálit	'anger'	*galít*	'angry'

8. Go back to the Sumerian example in (1.1) and provide a morphological description.

Inflection and derivation

4

In this chapter, we discuss the nature of (and the difference between) word-forms and lexemes in greater depth. As we saw in Section 2.1, this conceptual distinction is quite basic to most morphological theorizing and terminology, though it is not always easy to determine the relation between two morphologically complex words: is *nicely* a separate lexeme from *nice*, or is it just another word-form in the paradigm of the lexeme *nice*? In other words, is the suffix *-ly* that is attached to *nice* to form *nicely* a **derivational** suffix or an **inflectional** suffix?

We will survey inflectional categories in Section 4.1 and derivational meanings in Section 4.2. In Section 4.3 we will examine a range of properties that have been proposed as distinguishing between inflection and derivation. Finally, Section 4.4 gives an overview of the ways in which the relation between inflection and derivation has been conceptualized by morphologists. The two most important views are the **dichotomy approach**, which assumes that complex words can be neatly divided into two disjoint classes, and the **continuum approach**, which claims that morphological patterns are best understood as lying on a continuum ranging from the most clearly inflectional patterns to the most clearly derivational patterns.

4.1 Inflectional categories

Morphologists usually talk in quite different terms about inflection and derivation. For instance, the different inflectional formations are referred to as **inflectional categories**, so that we say, for instance, that English verbs have the inflectional categories 'present tense' (e.g. *(he/she) walks*) and 'past tense' (e.g. *(he/she) walked*). But for derived lexemes like *walker* we would not normally say that it represents a 'derivational category' ('agent noun') – instead we simply talk about **derivational patterns, formations or meanings**. One reason for this distinction is that often inflectional categories do not have a clearly identifiable meaning, but only a syntactic function. Thus, *(he/she) walk-s* and *(they) walk* represent two different inflectional categories ('third person singular' and 'third person plural'), though they hardly differ in meaning.

Another instance of different terminology for inflection and derivation is the use of the term *allomorphy*. When an inflectional category is expressed by different markers (e.g. the German plural markers *-en, -er, -e*), linguists often say that these are different **allomorphs** of a single abstract plural morpheme. But, when a derivational meaning is expressed by different formal means (e.g. the English suffixes *-ation, -ment, -al* for action nouns, as in *reform-ation, entertain-ment, arriv-al*), linguists do not normally say that these are different allomorphs of a single abstract action-noun morpheme. In this case it is not so clear whether the difference in the terminology corresponds to a difference in the phenomena.

But a property that does seem to be specific to inflection is that inflectional categories are often naturally grouped together into super-categories that we will call **inflectional dimensions**.[1] Two categories belong to the same dimension if they share a semantic (or more generally, functional) property and are **mutually exclusive**. For instance, the English present and past tenses both have to do with the relation between event time and utterance time, and they cannot occur together with the same verb. Thus, they are categories of the dimension 'tense'.

The paradigm (i.e. the set of word-forms) of a lexeme is most conveniently represented in the form of a table (or **grid**) in which word-forms of the same category are shown in a column or row that is labelled with the name of the category. Each combination of inflectional categories from the relevant dimensions defines a **cell**. This is shown for two partial sample paradigms in Figure 4.1, where category labels are printed in small capitals and dimension names are enclosed in ellipses. The first paradigm is from English, where verbs primarily inflect for tense. The second paradigm is from Spanish, where verbs inflect for two categories of the dimension 'number' (singular and plural) and three categories of the dimension 'person' (first, second and third) (they also inflect for tense – see below).

When a lexeme inflects for three dimensions simultaneously, a two-dimensional representation is no longer sufficient, and we would need a three-dimensional table. Figure 4.2 is an attempt at drawing such a table.

For practical purposes, three-dimensional (and especially *n*-dimensional, for *n* > 3) paradigms are mostly shown in two spatial dimensions as well. Thus, Figure 4.2 is generally replaced by Figure 4.3.

---

[1] Morphologists' terminological usage is inconsistent and confusing here. Some morphologists use the term *inflectional category* (or *inflectional feature*) for our *inflectional dimension*, and *inflectional property* (or *inflectional (feature) value*) for our *inflectional category*.

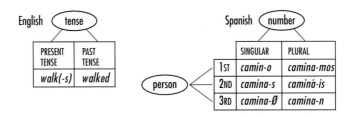

Figure 4.1 Inflectional dimensions and categories

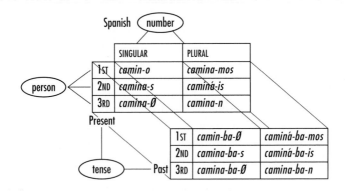

Figure 4.2 A three-dimensional representation of a three-dimensional paradigm

PRESENT TENSE

	SINGULAR	PLURAL
1ST	*camin-o*	*camina-mos*
2ND	*camina-s*	*caminá-is*
3RD	*camina-Ø*	*camina-n*

PAST TENSE

	SINGULAR	PLURAL
1ST	*camin-ba-Ø*	*caminá-ba-mos*
2ND	*camina-ba-s*	*caminá-ba-is*
3RD	*camina-ba-Ø*	*camina-ba-n*

Figure 4.3 A two-dimensional representation of a three-dimensional paradigm

The inflectional information contained in a word-form is often represented in a feature-value notation, as in the examples in (4.1).[2]

(4.1) a. Spanish
caminábamos
'we were walking'

$$\begin{bmatrix} \text{TENSE:} & \text{PAST} \\ \text{PERSON:} & \text{1ST} \\ \text{NUMBER} & \text{PLURAL} \end{bmatrix}$$

b. Sanskrit
dātṛṇoḥ
'of two givers'

$$\begin{bmatrix} \text{NUMBER:} & \text{DUAL} \\ \text{GENDER:} & \text{NEUTER} \\ \text{CASE:} & \text{GENITIVE} \end{bmatrix}$$

For practical purposes, the inflectional categories may also be written as subscripts of word-forms, e.g. *caminábamos*$_{\text{1PL.PAST}}$, *dātṛṇoḥ*$_{\text{GEN.DU.N}}$.

Different languages may vary quite dramatically in the amount of inflectional complexity that their words exhibit. Some languages, such as Vietnamese and Igbo, have no (or virtually no) inflectional categories, and others have inflection for more than a dozen categories (though it is uncommon for a single word-form to be inflected for more than half a dozen categories).

However, despite all this diversity, the types of inflectional categories that we find across languages are surprisingly uniform. Perhaps more than two-thirds of all inflectional categories fall into one of the classes of Table 4.1.

On nouns	On verbs	On nouns, verbs, adjectives and adpositions:
number (SINGULAR, PLURAL, …),	**tense** (PRESENT, FUTURE, PAST, …),	agreement in **number**, **case**, **person** and **gender**
case (NOMINATIVE, ACCUSATIVE, GENITIVE, …)	**aspect** (PERFECTIVE, IMPERFECTIVE, HABITUAL, …),	
	mood (INDICATIVE, SUBJUNCTIVE, IMPERATIVE, …)	

Table 4.1 Common inflectional dimensions and categories

We have already seen **number and case inflection** of nouns in Latin in (2.1). Latin is a fairly typical language in this respect: most languages have

---

[2] To be consistent with the terminology used in this book, we would have to say 'dimension-category notation' instead of the more widely used term *feature-value notation*.

nominal number marking, and only a few also distinguish a dual number in addition to the singular and the plural (we saw an example from Ancient Greek in (3.21)). Five different cases, as in Latin, are probably richer than average, because many languages have no case distinctions at all, and only a few have more than ten different cases.

Tense, aspect and mood inflection exists to some extent in virtually all languages that have any inflection at all. The three dimension names 'tense', 'aspect' and 'mood' suggest that categories from these different dimensions can be combined in the same way that case and number can be combined. Indeed, this is sometimes possible, for instance in Latin, which has three tense categories (present, past, future), two aspect categories (infectum and perfectum; the latter is similar to the English perfect) and two mood categories (indicative and subjunctive). See Figure 4.4.

However, the Latin system is not quite symmetrical: there are no future subjunctive forms. Moreover, this system is quite atypical. In most languages, different inflectional forms for tense, aspect and mood are difficult to combine. A language that contrasts with Latin in this respect and that is perhaps more typical is Swahili, where tense, aspect and mood are expressed by inflectional prefixes. In Figure 4.5, forms with the prefix *n(i)-* (first person singular) are given.

INDICATIVE			SUBJUNCTIVE		
	INFECTUM	PERFECTUM		INFECTUM	PERFECTUM
PRESENT	*canta-t*	*canta-v-it*	PRESENT	*cant-e-t*	*canta-v-eri-t*
PAST	*canta-ba-t*	*canta-v-era-t*	PAST	*canta-re-t*	*canta-v-isse-t*
FUTURE	*canta-bi-t*	*canta-v-eri-t*	FUTURE	—	—

Figure 4.4 Latin tense, aspect and mood forms (third person singular)

INDICATIVE			
	PRESENT	PAST	FUTURE
NORMAL	*n-a-fanya*	*ni-li-fanya*	*ni-ta-fanya*
PROGRESSIVE	*ni-na-fanya*	—	—
PERFECT	*ni-me-fanya*	—	—

HYPOTHETICAL			
	PRESENT	PAST	FUTURE
NORMAL	*ni-nge-fanya*	*ni-ngali-fanya*	—
PROGRESSIVE	—	—	—
PERFECT	—	—	—

Figure 4.5 Swahili tense, aspect and mood forms (first person singular, *-fanya* 'do')

In these grids, most of the cells are empty, and there are no obvious formal reasons for setting up such a paradigm with two mood categories, three tense categories and three aspect categories. The way the categories are arranged in Figure 4.5 is motivated exclusively by the meaning of the verb forms. From a formal point of view, positing just a single dimension ('tense/aspect/mood') with seven categories is simpler and does not seem to miss crucial generalizations. Thus, many linguists nowadays work with a single dimension 'tense/aspect/mood'. By contrast, nobody would collapse case and number into a single dimension, even though many Indo-European languages express case and number cumulatively (see the paradigms in (2.2) and (2.29)).

The explanation for the different behaviour of the combinations 'case + number' and 'tense + aspect + mood' lies in their semantic relations. While all combinations of different cases and numbers are roughly equally plausible, certain combinations of aspect, tense and mood are unusual or downright exotic. For instance, perfective aspect (which implies that an event is viewed in its totality) does not go together well with present tense (which implies that the speaker is still in the middle of the event). Even more obviously, the imperative mood (which expresses a command) does not combine with the past tense. It is not surprising that most languages lack straightforward inflectional means for these combinations (though that makes their inflectional patterns more difficult to describe in an elegant way).

The third important group of inflectional categories consists of **agreement markers**. Agreement is a kind of syntactic relation in which the inflectional behaviour of a word or phrase (the target) is determined by the properties of a nominal constituent (the controller) to which it is closely related. For instance, in *[the boy]*$_{NP}$ *[walk-s]*$_V$ and the *[girl-s]*$_{NP}$ *[walk]*$_V$, the target verb *walk(s)* agrees with the subject NP in number. And in *this girl* and *these boys*, the target demonstrative *this/these* agrees with its head noun (*girl/boys*) in number.

In agreement relations, the controller is almost always a noun or noun phrase, and the attested agreement dimensions are quite restricted: Agreement may be in person, number, gender and case. Two different types of agreement may be distinguished: **NP agreement** and **noun agreement**. The attested targets, controllers and agreement dimensions for these two types of agreement are shown in Table 4.2.

A few examples of different kinds of agreement are shown in (4.2)–(4.5). Note that, in NP agreement, person and number almost always go together, so that one might almost suggest that there is a single dimension person/number. Moreover, in most languages the controller NP may be omitted in NP agreement, i.e. the agreement markers may function as pronouns (see 4.3).

Agreement type	Possible targets	Possible controllers	Possible agreement dimensions
NP agreement	verb, noun, adposition	subject NP, object NP, possessor NP, complement NP	person, number, gender
noun agreement	adjective, determiner, genitive NP	modified head noun	case, number, gender

Table 4.2 Types of agreement relations and dimensions

(4.2) NP agreement: agreement of verb with subject and object in person, number and gender (Yimas)

Krayŋ   narmaŋ   k-n-tay.
frog.SG(G6)   woman.SG(G2) 3SG.G6.PAT-3SG.G2.AG-see
'The woman saw the frog.'

(Foley 1991: 194)

(4.3) NP agreement: agreement of noun with possessor NP in person, number and gender (Standard Arabic)

kitaab-ii   kitaabu-ka   kitaabu-humaa
book-1SG   book-2SG.M   book-3DU.M
'my book'   'your book'   'their book (i.e. book of the two of them)'

(4.4) NP agreement: agreement of postposition with complement NP in person and number (Classical Nahuatl)

i-pan   noyac
3SG-on   my.nose
'on my nose'

(Sullivan 1988:108)

(4.5) Noun agreement: agreement of demonstrative and adjective in number and gender

   a. Swahili
      wa-le   wa-tu   wa-refu
      PL.G2-that   PL-person(G2)   PL.G2-tall
      'those two tall people'

   b. Italian
      quest-a   nuov-a   casa
      this-SG.F   new-SG.F   house(F).SG
      'this new house'

It is important to note that only the agreement dimensions as marked on the target are dimensions of inflectional categories. The corresponding dimensions on the controller need not be inflectional categories. For instance, gender in Italian and Spanish is an inflectional dimension of determiners, adjectives and verbs, but not of nouns. Nouns are all lexically associated with one of the two genders (masculine/feminine), but they are not morphologically marked for gender: cf. Italian (*il* = masculine article, *la* = feminine article) *il poeta* 'the poet', *la mano* 'the hand', *la casa* 'the house', *il cuoco* 'the cook', *la chiave* 'the key', *il fiume* 'the river' (*-a* does not in general mean 'feminine', *-o* does not mean 'masculine').

Besides the three kinds of inflectional categories that we have seen up to now, there are quite a few others that are less easy to generalize about, but that are also less widespread. In English, adjectives have inflectional markers of **comparative** and **superlative degree** (*big, bigger, biggest*), but this kind of inflection is not common in the world's languages – it seems to be largely confined to the languages of Europe and south-western Asia.

In verbs, some languages have **passive voice** inflection, which indicates an unusual association of semantic roles and syntactic functions (e.g. Swedish *kasta* 'throw', *kasta-s* 'be thrown'). (For more on passives, see Section 11.1.2.) And many languages have inflectional expression of **polarity** (i.e. affirmative versus negative, e.g. Japanese *kir-u* [cut-PRES] 'cuts', *kir-ana-i* [cut-NEG-PRES] 'doesn't cut').

But the most important kind of inflection that we have not seen earlier is the group of **dependent verb forms**. Many languages have special verb forms that are confined to dependent clauses. Although the terminology is not uniform, a rough generalization says that verb forms marking relative clauses are called **participles**, verb forms marking adverbial clauses are called **converbs** and verb forms marking complement clauses are called **infinitives** or **masdars** (**action nouns**). Examples of a participle, a converb and an infinitive are given in (4.6)–(4.8).

(4.6) Korean participle
Hankwuk-ul   pangmwunha-nun   salam-i   nul-ko   iss-ta.
Korea-ACC   visit-PTCP   person-NOM   increase-ing   be-DECL
'Those who visit Korea are increasing.'

(S.-J. Chang 1996: 148)

(4.7) Hindi/Urdu converb
Banie   ke   beṭe   ne   ciṭṭhii   likh-kor   ḍaak   mẽ   ḍaal-ii.
grocer POSS son   ERG   letter(F).SG   write-CONV   box   in   put.PAST-F.SG
'The grocer's son wrote and posted a letter.'
(lit. 'having written a letter, posted (it).')

(4.8) Mparntwe Arrernte infinitive
    Re   lhe-tyeke   ahentyene-ke.
    she   go-INF   want-PAST
    'She wanted to go.'

                                                    (Wilkins 1989: 451)

4.2 Derivational meanings

Derivational meanings are much more diverse than inflectional categories. Besides cross-linguistically widespread meanings such as agent noun (e.g. *drink*$_V$ → *drink-er*$_N$), quality noun (e.g. *kind*$_A$ → *kind-ness*$_N$) and facilitative adjective (e.g. *read*$_V$ → *read-able*$_A$), we also find highly specific meanings that are confined to a few languages. For instance, Big Nambas has a suffix *-et* that derives reverential terms from ordinary nouns (e.g. *dui* 'man' → *dui-et* 'sacred man', *navanel* 'road' → *navanel-et* 'sacred road' (Fox 1979)). And French has a suffix *-ier* that derives words for fruit trees from the corresponding fruit nouns (e.g. *pomme* 'apple' → *pomm-ier* 'apple tree', *poire* 'pear' → *poir-ier* 'pear tree', *prune* 'plum' → *prun-ier* 'plum tree').

Derivational patterns commonly change the word-class of the base lexeme – i.e. nouns can be derived from verbs, adjectives from nouns, and so on. For such cases, the terms **denominal** ('derived from a noun'), **deverbal** ('derived from a verb') and **deadjectival** ('derived from an adjective') are in general use.

4.2.1 Derived nouns

Since creating new words for new concepts is one of the chief functions of derivational morphology, and since we have a greater need for naming diverse nominal concepts, languages generally have more means for deriving nouns than for deriving verbs and adjectives (Bauer, 2002). Some common meanings with examples from various languages are listed in Table 4.3.

Besides these widespread derivational meanings, many more specific derivational meanings are found in languages, but usually these are restricted to a few languages each. Thus, Russian has a suffix for nouns denoting kinds of meat (e.g. *lošad'* 'horse' → *lošad-ina* 'horse meat'). Tagalog has a pattern for nouns meaning vendors (e.g. *kandila* 'candle', *magkakandila* 'candle vendor' (Schachter and Otanes 1972: 103)). Various sciences have developed terminological conventions for creating new technical terms by suffixation (e.g. *-itis* as a suffix for inflammatory diseases, *-ite* as a suffix for minerals, *-ide* and *-ate* as suffixes for certain kinds of chemicals, and so on).

I.	**Deverbal nouns** (V → N)				
	agent noun	English	*drink*$_V$	→	*drink-er*$_N$
		Arabic	*ħamala*$_V$ 'carry'	→	*ħammaal*$_N$ 'carrier'
	patient noun	English	*invite*$_V$	→	*invit-ee*$_N$
	instrument noun	Spanish	*picar*$_V$ 'mince'	→	*pica-dora*$_N$ 'meat grinder'
	action noun	Russian	*otkry-t'*$_V$ 'discover'	→	*otkry-tie*$_N$ 'discovery'
II.	**Deadjectival nouns** (A → N)				
	quality noun	Japanese	*atarasi-i*$_A$ 'new'	→	*atarasi-sa*$_N$ 'newness'
	person noun	Russian	*umn-yj*$_A$ 'smart'	→	*umn-ik*$_N$ 'smart guy'
III.	**Denominal nouns** (N → N)				
	diminutive noun	Spanish	*gat-o* 'cat'	→	*gat-it-o* 'little cat'
	augmentative noun	Russian	*borod-a* 'beard'	→	*borod-išča* 'huge beard'
	status noun	English	*child*	→	*child-hood*
	inhabitant noun	Arabic	*Miṣr* 'Egypt'	→	*miṣr-iyyu* 'Egyptian'
	female noun	German	*König* 'king'	→	*König-in* 'queen'

Table 4.3 Common derivational meanings of nouns

4.2.2 Derived verbs

Languages generally have far fewer verbs than nouns, and verb-deriving patterns are less numerous and diverse. Most commonly, verbs are derived from other verbs. Denominal and deadjectival verbs are much less widespread than deverbal verbs (Bauer, 2002). Again, some typical examples are given in Table 4.4.

4.2.3 Derived adjectives

Derived adjectives are even less common than derived verbs, because adjectives are used more rarely than verbs, let alone nouns. Moreover, the semantic class of adjectives that is the most developed in a number of European languages, denominal relational adjectives (of the type *government* → *governmental*), seems to be quite rare in other areas of the world. Typical examples of derived adjectives are shown in Table 4.5.

I.   **Deverbal verbs** (V → V)

causative verb (see Section 11.1.4)	Korean	*cwuk-* 'die'	→	*cwuk-i-* 'kill'
applicative verb (see Section 11.1.5)	German	*laden* 'load'	→	*be-laden* 'load onto'
anticausative verb (see Section 11.1.2)	Swedish	*öppna* 'open (tr.)'	→	*öppna-s* 'open (intr.)'
desiderative verb	Greenlandic Eskimo	*sini-* 'sleep'	→	*sini-kkuma-* 'want to sleep'
repetitive verb	English	*write*	→	*re-write*
reversive verb	Swahili	*chom-a* 'stick in'	→	*chom-o-a* 'pull out'

II.   **Denominal verbs** (N → V)

'act like N'	Spanish	*pirat-a* 'pirate'	→	*pirat-ear* 'pirate'
'put into N'	English	*bottle$_N$*	→	*bottle$_V$*
'cover with N'	Russian	*sol'* 'salt'	→	*sol-it'* 'salt'

III.   **Deadjectival verbs** (A → V)

factitive	Russian	*čern-yj* 'black'	→	*čern-it'* 'make black'
inchoative	Spanish	*verde* 'green'	→	*verde-ar* 'become green'

Table 4.4 Common derivational meanings of verbs

4.3 Properties of inflection and derivation

Let us now look at the properties of inflectional and derivational morphology that can be used to distinguish between the two. Table 4.6 gives an overview of these properties. Some of these are all-or-nothing properties, and others are relative properties, i.e. a complex word may have the property to a greater or lesser extent. These relative properties are naturally unsuitable if one wants to arrive at a dichotomous classification of complex words into two non-overlapping classes. Proponents of the dichotomy approach have therefore primarily focused on the first three properties. Perhaps the most popular criterion is (i).

(i)   Inflection is **relevant to the syntax**; derivation is **not relevant to the syntax**.

That inflectional categories play a prominent role in the syntax is the most obvious for the agreement categories, because the syntactic relation of

I. Deverbal adjectives (V →A)

facilitative	Basque	*jan*	→	*jan-garri*
		'eat'		'edible'
agentive	Spanish	*habla-r*	→	*habla-dor*
		'talk'		'talkative'

II. Denominal adjectives (N →A)

relational	Russian	*korol'*	→	*korol-evskij*
(='related to N')		'king'		'royal'
proprietive	Ponapean	*pihl*	→	*pil-en*
(= 'having N')		'water'		'watery'
privative	Russian	*vod-a*	→	*bez-vod-nyj*
(= 'lacking N')		'water'		'waterless'
material	German	*Kupfer*	→	*kupfer-n*
		'copper'		'made of copper'

III. Deadjectival adjectives (A →A)

attenuative	Tzutujil	*kaq*	→	*kaq-koj*
		'red'		'reddish'
intensive	Turkish	*yeni*	→	*yep-yeni*
		'new'		'brandnew'
negative	German	*schön*	→	*un-schön*
		'beautiful'		'ugly'

Table 4.5 Common derivational meanings of adjectives

	Inflection	Derivation
(i)	relevant to the syntax	not relevant to the syntax
(ii)	obligatory	optional
(iii)	not replaceable by simple word	replaceable by simple word
(iv)	same concept as base	new concept
(v)	relatively abstract meaning	relatively concrete meaning
(vi)	semantically regular	possibly semantically irregular
(vii)	less relevant to base meaning	very relevant to base meaning
(viii)	unlimited applicability	limited applicability
(ix)	expression at word periphery	expression close to the base
(x)	less base allomorphy	more base allomorphy
(xi)	cumulative expression possible	no cumulative expression
(xii)	not iterable	iterable

Table 4.6 A list of properties of inflection and derivation

agreement is their sole *raison d'être*. Some other inflectional categories are also syntactically determined. For instance, case-markers are most commonly prescribed by the syntactic context (a direct object must be in the accusative case, an NP modifying a noun must be in the genitive, and so on), and speakers do not have much choice either with the various dependent verb forms (thus, the English verb *stop* requires a gerund complement, whereas *cease* needs an infinitive complement). But the categories of tense/aspect/mood and nominal number are not obviously relevant to the syntax. One might say that number categories are relevant in that they may serve as controller categories in agreement relations, but tense or at least aspect hardly ever occur in an agreement-like relationship. And, conversely, saying that derivational morphology is not relevant to the syntax is too vague. For instance, the two lexemes CONSTRUCT and CONSTRUCTION have a very similar meaning, but they differ considerably in their syntactic behaviour (cf. *The Arabs constructed the bridge* with *the construction of the bridge by the Arabs*) (see also Section 11.3.2).

Another commonly invoked criterion is (ii).

(ii)   Inflection is **obligatory**; derivation is **optional**.

This can be illustrated by the Latin nominal paradigm in (2.2) above: These 10 forms are the only forms in which the lexeme INSULA 'island' can occur – it must have some inflected category from each dimension, and the base *insul* is not a possible word-form. Derived lexemes, by contrast, generally coexist with a non-derived base lexeme (e.g. KIND and KINDNESS). Unfortunately, the application of this criterion is made difficult by the fact that many inflectional paradigms are unlike the INSULA paradigm in that one of the word-forms bears no affix (or bears a zero affix) and is identical with the stem, e.g. the paradigm of Spanish CAMINA- 'walk' in Figure 4.3. But here, proponents of criterion (ii) would argue, the absence of an affix is meaningful in itself: *camina* specifically expresses the grammatical function 'third person singular', so it is not an uninflected form, but an inflected form with zero expression. By contrast, in the lexeme KIND (as opposed to KINDNESS), the absence of the suffix -*ness* does not have meaning (KIND does not mean 'non-quality', as opposed to KINDNESS 'quality of being kind'). However, there are numerous cases where the semantic intuitions are not so clear. For instance, when a language has an inflectional negative form (e.g. Japanese *kir-ana-i* 'doesn't cut'), does the corresponding non-negative form (*kir-u* 'cuts') include the meaning 'non-negative'? This case at least does not seem to be all that different from derivational negation (e.g. English *happy/unhappy*).

Criterion (iii) looks very different from (i) but virtually amounts to the same.

(iii)   Inflected word-forms **cannot be replaced by simple words**; derived lexemes **can be replaced** by simple words.

In a specialized syntactic construction, inflected words cannot be replaced by simple words when an inflectional category is tailored precisely to that construction (e.g. *Brazil is bigger* (not: *big*) *than Argentina; Snoopy walks* (not: *walk*) *home*). But nominal plurals can be replaced by singulars (when nothing agrees with them), and verbal tense and aspect categories can be replaced as well (e.g. *The dogs* (or: *dog*) *walked home; Charlie lost* (or: *loses*) *the game*). Still, this criterion is somewhat better than (i) in that it generally makes correct claims about derived lexemes. That they can be replaced by simple words is because they do not normally have peculiar syntactic properties that no non-derived lexeme has. For instance, a derived action noun such as *construction* is not very different from a simple noun such as *book* (e.g. *the construction of the bridge by the Arabs; the book of songs by Tagore* – both with an *of*-phrase and a *by*-phrase).

Thus, dividing up complex words in a dichotomous fashion is not straightforward, because each of the three criteria that have been invoked for delimiting inflection from derivation has some problems. As an alternative to the dichotomy approach, it has been suggested that inflection and derivation form a continuum, with clearly inflectional formations at one extreme, clearly derivational formations at the other extreme, and intermediate formations in between. Proponents of the continuum approach typically mention a whole range of properties, the most important of which were listed in Table 4.6.

Properties (iv) and (v) have the disadvantage of being quite vague:

(iv) Inflected word-forms express the **same concept** as the base; derived lexemes express a **new concept**.

(v)   Inflectional categories express a relatively **abstract** meaning; derivational meanings are relatively **concrete**.

While everyone would probably agree that the same concept is expressed in *go* and *goes*, or in Latin *insula* ('island, nominative') and *insulae* ('island, genitive'), this is less clear with singular–plural pairs, for instance. On the other hand, although 'baker' is clearly a different concept from 'bake', in what sense is 'kindness' a different concept from 'kind'?

The abstractness criterion works quite well for inflectional meanings, because all of them are highly abstract (in some intuitive sense). And many derivational meanings are quite concrete (e.g. French *-ier*, which denotes a kind of tree). But there are also derivational meanings that are just as abstract as inflectional meanings (e.g. the meaning 'status' of *-hood* in *childhood*).

There are two other semantic criteria that are somewhat less vague and more important than (iv) and (v):

(vi) Inflected word-forms are **semantically regular**; derived lexemes can be **semantically irregular**.

(vii) The meanings of inflectional categories are **less relevant** to the meaning of the base; derivational meanings are **very relevant** to the meaning of the base.

While inflectional categories always make a predictable semantic contribution to their base, derived lexemes are often semantically idiosyncratic, i.e. **idiomatic**. We can distinguish two kinds of idiomaticity. In **weak idiomaticity**, the semantic contribution of the derivation is present, but the meaning of the derived lexeme is not exhaustively described by the base meaning and the derivational meaning. For instance, the Russian derivational suffix *-nik* means 'thing associated with (base concept)', and this meaning is clearly present in *dnev-nik* 'diary' (*dn-ev-* 'day'), *noč-nik* 'night lamp; night worker' (*noč* 'night'). However, the meaning of *dnevnik* is not exhausted by that of *dnev-* and *-nik*: a diary is indeed a kind of thing associated with days (or daily activities), but the additional meaning components 'notebook' and 'used for writing' cannot be predicted on the basis of the meaning of the two constituent morphemes and must be associated with the lexeme as a whole.

In **strong idiomaticity**, the regular derivational meaning is not present at all, and the meaning of the derived lexemes cannot even be guessed from the meanings of the components. For instance, the meanings of *ignorance* and *reparation* are probably only historically related to *ignore* and *repair*.

Besides exhibiting idiomaticity, derivational meanings may simply be heterogeneous. For example, the English action noun suffix *-ation* usually denotes the action of 'V-ing' (e.g. *The duplication of the manuscript took them many months*), but it may also denote a state (e.g. *Civilization is a recent stage in history*), a place (*fortification*), an object (*She sent us several of her publications*) or a group of people (*population*).

Of course, not all derivational formations exhibit semantic irregularity. For instance, German female nouns in *-in* (*König-in* 'queen', *Professor-in* 'female professor') are very regular.

The tendency for semantic irregularity is related to the higher degree of semantic relevance to the base meaning that we find in derivation (Bybee 1985: ch. 4). A grammatical (inflectional or derivational) meaning is relevant to the base meaning to the extent that it directly affects the base meaning. Agreement and case categories are not at all relevant to the base meaning – they just express the relation of the word to other words in its syntactic context. Likewise, tense is hardly relevant to the meaning of a verb, because the nature of an action does not depend in any way on its temporal relation to the speech event. The inflectional category of aspect is different: it expresses the internal temporal constituency of an event, and this interacts directly with the meaning of the base verb. Thus, in many languages aspect is expressed by derivational markers. Even more relevant to the base meaning is a derivational meaning such as 'cause' in causatives. Because of the higher relevance of derivational meanings, derivatives are more likely to develop idiomatic meanings. The notion of relevance is somewhat vague, but it does seem to capture a real semantic difference between inflection and derivation.

One of the most important criteria for telling inflection from derivation is (viii).

> (viii) Inflectional categories can be applied to their base **without arbitrary limitations**; derivational formations may be **limited** in an arbitrary way.

All lexemes of a language must have the relevant agreement and case-marked forms, otherwise they would not be able to function in every syntactic context. And in general all verbs of a language have all the tense–aspect–mood forms, and all adjectives have comparative forms. When exceptions occur, they can usually be explained easily by the incompatibility of the inflectional meaning and the base meaning. Thus, stative verbs may not have certain aspectual forms (e.g. English *She is knowing me*), and non-gradable adjectives do not have comparative forms (e.g. *Mammoths are deader than Neanderthals*). In derivation, by contrast, conceivable lexemes may be lacking without any obvious semantic explanation. For instance, English has female nouns in -*ess* such as *authoress, heiress, priestess*, but it is not possible to say *professoress* 'female professor', *presidentess* 'female president', and so on, although these make perfect sense semantically. The Spanish inchoative formation in -*ear* (see Table 4.4) occurs with colour adjectives (*verde* → *verdear* 'become green', *negro* → *negrear* 'become black', etc.), but it cannot be used freely with other adjectives where a 'become' sense would be just as appropriate and useful (e.g. *caro* → *carear* 'become expensive' – this word does not exist). It must be admitted, however, that this criterion is weakened by the fact that occasionally arbitrary gaps occur in inflection as well (see Section 7.7).

The next two properties concern the formal shapes of complex words:

> (ix) Inflection is expressed at the **periphery** of words; derivation is expressed **close to the root**.
> (x) Inflection induces **less base allomorphy**; derivation induces **more base allomorphy**.

These two properties can be used as distinguishing criteria only in special circumstances because they are relative and not absolute properties. The first is best illustrated by words that have one derivational affix and one inflectional affix on the same side of the root. In such cases, the derivational affix almost always occurs between the root and the inflectional affix:

(4.9) a. English *king-dom-s* root – status (D) – plural (I)
      b. English *real-ize-d* root – factitive (D) – past tense (I)
      c. English *luck-i-er* root – proprietive (D) – comparative (I)

d. Turkish   *iç-ir-iyor*   root – causative (D) – imperf. aspect (I)
            [drink-CAUS-IMPF.3SG]
            'makes (somebody) drink'
e. Arabic   *na-ta-labbasa* 1st plural subject (I) – reflexive (D) – root
            [1PL-REFL-clothe.PERF]
            'we clothed ourselves'

When there are more than two affixes, normally all the derivational affixes occur closer to the root than the inflectional affixes (e.g. German *nation-al-isier-te-n* '(they) nationalized': root – relational adjective (D) – factitive verb (D) – past tense (I) – third person plural subject agreement (I)).

The more frequent occurrence of base allomorphy with derivation is best illustrated with roots that show base allomorphy in derived lexemes, but not in comparable contexts in inflected word-forms:

(4.10)

		ROOT	INFLECTED FORM	DERIVED LEXEME
	a. English	*destroy*	*destroy-ed*	*destruc-tion*
	b. English	*broad*	*broad-er*	*bread-th*
	c. German	*Erde*	*Erde-n*	*ird-isch*
		'earth'	'earths (PL)'	'earthly'
	d. Latin	*honor*	*honor-is*	*hones-tus*
		'honour'	'honour-GEN'	'honest'
	e. Italian	*dialogo* [-g-]	*dialogh-i* [-g-]	*dialogico* [-dʒ-]
		'dialogue'	'dialogue-s'	'dialogical'
	f. Arabic	*kataba*	*katab-tu*	*kitaab*
		'he wrote'	'I wrote'	'book'

Finally we will mention two highly specific criteria that apply only to a small subset of cases, but are nevertheless interesting:

(xi)   Inflectional categories may be **expressed cumulatively**; derivational formations are **not expressed cumulatively**.

(xii) Inflectional categories **cannot be iterated**; derivational formations **can be iterated**.

We saw above (Section 2.6) that several inflectional categories may be expressed by a single affix, as in Latin *insularum* 'of the islands', where the suffix *-arum* expresses both 'genitive' and 'plural'. Such cases of cumulation seem to be very rare in derivational formations (a possible example is Dutch *-ster* 'agent' and 'female').

On the other hand, inflection is more restricted in that inflectional affixes cannot be iterated. Thus, although it would make sense logically to have an iterated plural (e.g. **cat-s-es* 'sets of cats'), such double plurals are virtually unattested. Or one could imagine a past-tense affix to be repeated to give a sense of remote past (e.g. **didded* 'had done'). With derivational formations, iteration is not common either, but it is possible, for instance, with diminutives in Afrikaans (*kind-jie-tjie* 'a little little child'), and with various prefixes in English (*post-post-modern*) and German (*Ur-ur-ur-großvater* 'great-great-great-grandfather'). Another instance is the double causative, as we find it in Huallaga Quechua: *wañu-* 'die', *wañu-chi-* 'kill', *wañu-chi-chi-* 'cause to kill' (Weber 1989: 164).

A further criterion that is frequently mentioned when the inflection/derivation distinction is discussed is the ability to change the word-class of the base. It is claimed that derivational formations always change the word-class of the base, while inflectional categories never do that. This is not correct, as is shown by inflectional deverbal nouns such as English *-ing* forms (e.g. *my raising (of) this issue*). Such word-class-changing inflection is discussed further in Section 11.4.

4.4 Conceptualizations in morphological theory

Let us now look at the major ways in which the phenomena surveyed in this chapter have been interpreted by theoretical morphologists. Despite intensive discussion since the 1980s, no consensus has been reached, and the two major views are quite incompatible: the dichotomy approach (which regards inflection and derivation as two disjoint classes) and the continuum approach (which sees the different patterns on a scale between minimally and maximally inflectional/derivational). Finally, there is a less well-known intermediate position, which assumes a tripartition of the domain. We now look at these three approaches in turn.

4.4.1 The dichotomy approach

As we saw earlier, morphologists who adopt the dichotomy approach usually choose one of the first three properties of Table 4.6 as the crucial criterion for distinguishing inflection and derivation. The other properties have to be ignored, because, if one takes a number of logically independent criteria into account, the danger always exists that they yield conflicting results and thus lead to a contradiction.

A popular version of the dichotomy approach builds the strict separation of inflection and derivation into the formal architecture of the grammar (this is also referred to as **split morphology**). It is assumed that rules of derivation (and compounding, i.e. all of word-formation) operate in a component of the grammar (called **lexicon**) that feeds into the syntax, and that inflectional rules apply only after the syntactic rules have applied. In other words, word-formation is **pre-syntactic**, inflection is **post-syntactic**. This architecture of the grammar is shown schematically in Figure 4.6.

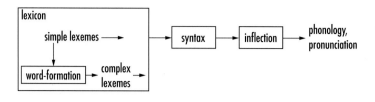

Figure 4.6 Word-formation and inflection in one possible grammatical architecture

Let us look at a concrete example of how this works. Our example sentence is (4.11) from Latin.

(4.11) *Imperator   saluta-v-it   popul-um.*
        emperor(NOM)   greet-PERF-3SG   people-ACC
        'The emperor greeted the people.'

The Latin lexicon contains simple lexemes such as IMPERARE 'command', SALUS 'health' and POPULUS 'people'. The word-formation rules create complex derived lexemes such as IMPERATOR 'commander, emperor' and SALUTARE 'greet'. Word-formation is said to operate 'in the lexicon' (i.e. in this approach, the lexicon contains both a list and rules), so both simple lexemes and derived lexemes are the output of the lexicon that can be inserted into abstract syntactic representations. The syntax contains phrase structure rules (e.g. S → NP VP, VP → V NP), case-assignment rules, which among other things ensure that the direct object gets accusative case ([$_{VP}$ V NP$_{ACC}$]), and agreement rules, which copy relevant features from the controller onto the target (here from the subject NP onto the head verb: NP$_{NOM/SG/3RD}$ ··· V → NP$_{NOM/SG/3RD}$ ··· V$_{SG/3RD}$). The syntactic rules might thus generate an abstract representation, as in (4.12). All of this is of course greatly simplified, but this much should be sufficient for our present purposes.

(4.12)

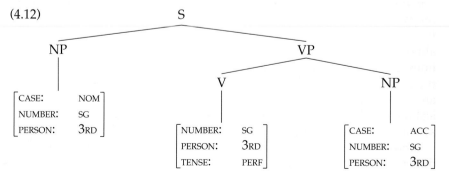

Now the lexemes (simple or complex) from the lexicon can be inserted, yielding a lexically specified syntactic representation as shown in (4.13) (the representation with labelled brackets and subscripts is equivalent to the tree representation in (4.12) and saves space).

(4.13) $[_S [_{NP} \text{IMPERATOR}_{\text{NOM}/\text{SG}/\text{3RD}}] [_{VP} [_V \text{SALUTARE}_{\text{SG}/\text{3RD}/\text{PERF}}]$
       $[_{NP} \text{POPULUS}_{\text{ACC}/\text{SG}/\text{3RD}}]]]$

Now the rules of inflection operate and create the correct word-forms from the lexemes with their feature specification: IMPERATOR$_{\text{NOM}/\text{SG}/\text{3RD}}$ becomes *imperator*, SALUTARE$_{\text{SG}/\text{3RD}/\text{PERF}}$ becomes *salutavit*, and POPULUS$_{\text{ACC}/\text{SG}/\text{3RD}}$ becomes *populum*. This gives us the output in (4.14a), which is then subjected to phonological rules, so that we finally get the pronunciation in (4.14b).

(4.14) a. *Imperator salutavit populum.*
       b. [ɪmpɛˈraːtɔrsaluːˈtaːwɪtˈpɔpʊlõ]

In addition to its intuitive plausibility, this architecture of the formal grammar also explains an important difference between inflection and derivation: the fact that derivation is generally 'inside' inflection, i.e. it occurs closer to the root (see (ix) in Section 4.3). If affixes are always attached peripherally by morphological operations, then the affix order of *king-dom-s* automatically follows from the order of application of the rules in Fig. 4.6. The lexicon creates KINGDOM from the simple lexeme KING, and the inflection *-s* is added after the syntactic component. There is no way a form like *king-s-dom* could ever arise, because inflected forms like *king-s* cannot be the input to word-formation rules.

Likewise, the model predicts that inflected forms should not occur inside compounds, because compounding is also a lexeme-forming rule in the lexicon. Thus, the impossibility of *trees plantation* or *trousers leg* in English follows from this as well (the correct forms are *tree plantation* and *trouser leg*, where the first part is uninflected, despite the plural meaning).

4.4.2. The continuum approach

The reason why some morphologists prefer the continuum aproach is that they want to avoid making an arbitrary choice from the criteria in Table 4.6. If all these criteria are taken seriously, then the continuum approach is almost inevitable, because different criteria may point in different directions. But what is particularly interesting is that the mismatches between the criteria are not random, but present a surprisingly orderly picture. As an example, let us look at Table 4.7. It gives a sample list of six morphological formations, which are evaluated by five of the twelve criteria that we saw in Section 4.3.

Table 4.7 is a simplification in various respects (e.g. in that it ignores the difficulties in applying some of the criteria), but it suffices to illustrate the

Language	Formation	Example	cum	obl	new	unl	sreg
English	3rd singular	*walk/walks*	+	+	+	+	+
English	noun plural	*song/songs*	−	+	+	+	+
Spanish	diminutive	*gato/gatito*	−	−	+	+	+
English	repetitive	*write/rewrite*	−	−	−	+	+
English	female noun	*poet/poetess*	−	−	−	−	+
English	action noun	*resent/resentment*	−	−	−	−	−

Note: cum= cumulative expression; obl = obligatory; new = new concept;

unl = unlimited applicability; sreg = semantically regular.

Table 4.7 A continuum from inflection to derivation

continuum approach. The English third person singular suffix -*s* cumulatively expresses person/number and present tense; the other formations show no cumulation. Both verbal agreement and nominal number are arguably present in any verb and noun form, so these two are obligatory, whereas this is not the case for the other formations. Diminutives are like classical inflected forms in that they do not (necessarily) denote a new concept – Spanish *gatito* often refers to the same kind of cat as *gato*, but occurs only under special pragmatic circumstances. Only the English female suffix -*ess* and the action-noun suffix -*ment* are limited in applicability, and only -*ment* is semantically irregular (as we can see in *govern/government*, which shows a different semantic relation from *resent/resentment*). On such a continuum view, agreement morphology such as -*s* (in *walks*) is **prototypical inflection** and English action nouns in -*ment* are **prototypical derivation**, but they are merely extremes of a continuum on which many intermediate items are found as well.

The continuum approach cannot use the architecture of the formal grammar to explain why derivational affixes occur closer to the root and inflectional affixes occur more peripherally. But this is not necessarily a drawback. For one thing, exceptions to this generalization are occasionally observed: inflection may exceptionally be closer to the root than derivation. For example, German has deadjectival factitive verbs that are based on the inflectional comparative form (e.g. *schön* 'beautiful' → *schön-er* 'more beautiful' → *ver-schön-er-n* 'make more beautiful'). And English allows plurals inside many compounds (e.g. *publications list, New York Jets fan*). Such exceptions cannot be accommodated if the regular cases are explained by the architecture of the grammar. And, second, the ordering of inflectional affixes with respect to derivational affixes is not the only generalization that can be made. Also within inflectional affixes and within derivational affixes, some orders are strongly preferred, and others are strongly dispreferred. For instance, the diminutive suffix in Spanish is always outside other derivational suffixes (e.g. the female noun suffix -es(a): baron-es-ita 'little baroness', not *baronitesa). And case suffixes almost always follow number suffixes, rather than vice versa (e.g. Turkish ev-ler-in [house-PL-GEN] 'of the houses', not *ev-in-ler). These additional tendencies cannot be explained by the architecture of the grammar, but whatever explains them can probably also explain the generalization about the larger classes of inflection and derivation.

It seems that the more derivational an affix is on the continuum of Table 4.7, the more likely it is to occur close to the root, and the more inflectional it is, the more likely it is to occur peripherally. Thus, the facts of affix ordering could even serve as an argument in favour of the continuum approach.

4.4.3 A tripartition: contextual inflection, inherent inflection and derivation

In order to respond to the challenge of the continuum approach, dichotomy theorists could weaken their claim and propose a tripartition instead of a dichotomy. The view that the domain of inflection is divided into two parts, **contextual inflection** and **inherent inflection**, has become increasingly influential recently. The resulting tripartition is shown in Table 4.8.

Contextual inflection	Inherent inflection	Derivation
N,V,A: agreement categories N: structural cases	N: number categories N: inherent cases A: comparative and superlative degrees V: tense, aspect, mood V: infinitive, participle	(as in other approaches)

Table 4.8 Contextual inflection, inherent inflection and derivation

Contextual inflection comprises categories of a purely syntactic nature which a word-form must possess because of the syntactic context in which it occurs. These are all the agreement categories, as well as **structural cases** on nouns (or noun phrases) – i.e. cases like nominative, accusative, and genitive, which are typically required by the syntactic environment in which they occur and thus express largely redundant information.

Inherent inflection comprises categories that, like derivation, convey a certain amount of independent information and that are not forced on the speaker by the syntactic context. Thus, a speaker may freely choose the verb's tense and aspect categories, the nominal number categories and also nominal **inherent cases**. (The term *inherent case* refers to cases such as locative (e.g. Turkish *ev-de* [house-LOC] 'in the house'), ablative (e.g. Huallaga Quechua *mayu-pita* [river-ABL] 'from the river') and instrumental (e.g. Russian *nož-om* [knife-INSTR] 'with a knife'), which clearly make their own semantic contribution and are mostly not syntactically determined.)

Inherent inflection is like derivation in that it may not be universally applicable. Thus, many English nouns do not have a plural form (e.g. **silvers, *informations*), many German adjectives do not have a comparative form (e.g. **tot-er*, literally 'deader') and several Russian verbs do not have an imperfective aspect form. (However, tense categories are normally applicable to all verbs.) Although both contextual and inherent inflection are usually semantically regular, occasionally inherent inflection is similar to derivation in that an inflected form has an unpredictable, idiosyncratic meaning. Some examples from Dutch are given in (4.15).

(4.15)

category	inflected word	expected meaning	observed meaning
comparative	*ouder*	'older'	'parent'
plural	*vaders*	'fathers'	'forefathers'
past participle	*bezeten*	'possessed'	'mad'
present participle	*ontzettend*	'appalling'	'very'
infinitive	*eten*	'(to) eat'	'food'

(Booij 1993)

Inherent inflection is also like derivation in that it is more likely to induce base allomorphy than contextual inflection. A few examples are given in (4.16).

(4.16)

	contextual inflection	inherent inflection
English	*sing/sings* (agreement)	*sing/sang* (past tense)
German	*warm-er/warm-e* (agr.)	*warm/wärmer* (comparative)
	'warm-MASC/warm-FEM'	'warm/warmer'
Arabic	*kitaab-un/kitaab-in* (str. case)	*kitaab-/kutub* (plural)
	'book-NOM/book-GEN'	'book.SG/book.PL'

Finally, those exceptional cases in which an inflectional affix is closer to the root than a derivational affix, and those in which an inflectional affix occurs on a first compound member, generally involve inherent inflection (recall the examples *verschönern* and *publications list* of Section 4.4.2).

Thus, whatever approach we choose ultimately for describing the relation between inflection and derivation, the conceptual distinction between contextual and inherent inflection is very useful because there are a number of points on which the two kinds of inflection behave rather differently.

Summary of Chapter 4

Morphologists use different terminology for talking about inflection and derivation. Inflection is described in terms of categories grouped into dimensions, and paradigms are usually described as grids consisting of cells occupied by word-forms. Derivation is described in terms of individual morphemes (or morphological patterns) and their meanings. The range of inflectional meanings found in languages is severely restricted; most of them fall under the general headings of number, case, tense, aspect, mood and agreement. Derivational meanings are more varied, but many recurrent types can be identified as well.

Linguists adopting the dichotomy approach to inflection and derivation have usually emphasized criteria such as relevance to the syntax and obligatoriness, whereas linguists favouring the continuum approach have considered a whole range of criteria, including semantic regularity, applicability and closeness to the root. Within inflection, a distinction between (more derivation-like) inherent inflection and contextual inflection can be made.

Further reading

A useful survey of the kinds of meanings that are expressed by derivational morphology is found in Bauer (2002).

The dichotomy approach to inflection and derivation is represented by works such as Scalise (1988), Perlmutter (1988) and Anderson (1992), and it is implicit in much further work. The continuum approach is defended by Stephany (1982), Bybee (1985), Dressler (1989) and Plank (1994) (and see Wurzel (1996)). The tripartition between contextual inflection, inherent inflection and derivation was proposed in Booij (1993, 1996).

Exercises

1. Give the inflectional information of the following word-forms in feature-value notation (see (4.1)):

Spanish	*caminabas*	(3 dimensions)
Latin	*insulam*	(2 dimensions)
Latin	*cantabit*	(4 dimensions, see Figure 4.4)

Spanish	*cantaré*	(3 dimensions, see (3.23))
English	*books*	(1 dimension)
Serbian/Croatian	*ovci*	(2 dimensions, see (2.29))
Classical Nahuatl	*incal*	(2 dimensions, see (2.8))
English	*bigger*	(1 dimension)

2. Lezgian verbs have suffixes for aspect (-*zawa* imperfective, -*nawa* perfect, -*da* habitual), followed by suffixes for polarity (-$\varnothing$ affirmative, -*č* negative), followed by suffixes for tense (-$\varnothing$ present, -*j*/-*ir* past; -*ir* is chosen after -*č*). For instance *katzawaj*$_{\text{IMPF.AFF.PAST}}$ 'was running', *katdačir*$_{\text{HAB.NEG.PAST}}$ 'would not run'. Give the whole three-dimensional paradigm in a two-dimensional representation (as in Figure 4.3), using the verb *kat*- 'run' (i.e. a grid with $3 \times 2 \times 2 = 12$ cells) (Haspelmath 1993).

3. Consider the meanings of the following denominal and deadjectival verbs of English and classify them using the categories of Table 4.4. For some of them, you need to set up new categories not represented in that table.

   butter, flatten, categorize, peel, legalize, phone, blacken, ground, cannibalize, unionize, skate, modernize, terrorize, husk, ski

4. At the beginning of this chapter, we asked whether the English deadjectival adverb-forming pattern (*nice* → *nicely*) is inflectional or derivational. Apply the criteria of Section 4.3 and try to form an opinion on this question.

5. Not only derived lexemes, but also compounds can be semantically irregular. Consider the meaning of the following English derivatives and compounds and say whether they are semantically regular, weakly idiomatic, or strongly idiomatic.

   darkroom, high-flown, hobbyhorse, lioness, neckband, observable, plasticity, snowboard, chalky, church school, doorbell, fishy, opportunity, permeable

Morphological trees

5

In this chapter, we will see that various kinds of morphologically complex words can be thought of as having hierarchical structure, commonly represented by tree diagrams. In this respect, morphological structure resembles syntactic structure, and the ways in which morphological and syntactic structure differ will be an important issue. Hierarchical structure is quite evident in compound words, and less so in derivationally derived words. Thus, we will start by examining compounds in some detail.

5.1 Compounding

A **compound** is a complex lexeme that can be thought of as consisting of two or more base lexemes. In the simplest case, a compound consists of two lexemes that are joined together (called *compound members*). Some examples from English are given in (5.1). English allows several types of combinations of different word-classes (N: noun, A: adjective, V: verb), but not all such combinations are possible.

(5.1) English compounds: some examples[1]

N + N	*lipstick*	$(lip_N + stick_N)$
A + N	*hardware*	$(hard_A + ware_N)$
V + N	*drawbridge*	$(draw_V + bridge_N)$
N + V	*babysit*	$(baby_N + sit_V)$
N + A	*leadfree*	$(lead_N + free_A)$
A + A	*bitter-sweet*	$(bitter_A + sweet_A)$

---

[1] Note that the spelling of English compounds is inconsistent: often they are written as a single word, but in many other cases (especially with N + N compounds), the constituents of the compound are separated by a space, like syntactic phrases (e.g. *sugar plantation, morpheme lexicon*). These spelling differences are irrelevant in the present context and should be ignored.

Like derivational rules, compounding rules may differ in productivity. In English, the N + N rule/pattern is extremely productive, so that novel compounds are created all the time and are hardly noticed. By contrast, the V + N rule/pattern is unproductive and limited to a few lexically listed items, and the N + V pattern is not really productive either (for instance, one cannot say *to hair-wash* 'wash one's hair'; but see Section 9.2).

However, there are many languages (especially morphologically rich, polysynthetic languages) that do allow compounds in which the notional object and the verb form a compound. Such compounding processes are called **incorporation** (metaphorically we say that the object is incorporated into the verb). An example from Alutor is given in (5.2). (For more on incorporation, see Section 11.2.1)

(5.2) *gəmmə   tə-məng-ilgətav-ək*
       I   1sg-hand-wash-1sg
       'I washed (my) hands.' (Lit.: 'I hand-washed.')
                   (Koptjevskaja-Tamm and Muravyova 1993: 298)

In a compound that consists of two lexemes, it is really the lexeme stems that are combined – in this respect compounding is no different from derivational affixes, which attach to stems, i.e. lexemes without their inflection. Thus, we get English compounds such as *lipstick* (not **lipsstick*), although it is used for both lips, and *child support* (not **children support*), even if several children are supported, and *drawbridge* (not **drewbridge*), even if the bridge was 'drawn' only in the past. That the first compound member is a stem, not an inflected word-form, can be seen even more clearly in languages with richer inflection, such as Sanskrit. In Sanskrit, the first compound member in N + N/A compounds shows a vowel-final (or -ṛ-final) form that does not occur as a member of the inflectional paradigm – this can thus be regarded as the pure stem.

(5.3) *deva-senā-*   'army of gods'   (*devaḥ* 'god')
       pitṛ-bandhu-   'paternal relation'   (*pitā* 'father')
       pati-juṣṭa-   'dear to the spouse'   (*patiḥ* 'spouse')

In German, many compounds even have a special semantically empty suffix (sometimes called **interfix**) on the first compound member, which forms the stem that is appropriate for compounding. Some examples are shown in (5.4).

(5.4) German compounds with interfixes
       Volk-s-wagen   lit. 'people's car' (*Volk* 'people' + *Wagen* 'car')
       Liebe-s-brief   'love letter'   (*Liebe* 'love' + *Brief* 'letter')
       Schwan-en-gesang 'swansong'   (*Schwan* 'swan' + *Gesang* 'song')

That the first member of a compound is a stem rather than a particular word-form is also clearly seen in German V + N compounds, as in (5.5).

(5.5)   German V + N compounds
   Wasch-maschine   'washing machine'
                        (*wasch-en* 'wash' +   *Maschine* 'machine')
   Schreib-tisch   '(writing) desk'
                        (*schreib-en* 'write' +   *Tisch* 'desk, table')
   Saug-pumpe   'suction pump'
                        (*saug-en* 'suck' +   *Pumpe* 'pump')

The elements *wasch-*, *schreib-* and *saug-* must be pure stems, because almost all word-forms of verbs have special suffixes (the suffix *-en* in (5.5) is the infinitive (and citation-form) suffix). The only suffixless word-form is the imperative, but it would not make sense semantically to claim that *wasch* in *Waschmaschine* is the imperative form of the lexeme WASCHEN.

From the point of view of semantics, not much needs to be said about the compounds that we have seen so far. The first compound member generally serves to modify and narrow the denotation of the second compound member, or, in other words, the compound is a **hyponym** of its second member. Thus, a lipstick is a special kind of stick (not a special kind of lip), a drawbridge is a special kind of bridge and a love letter is a special kind of letter. Since semantically the second member is in this sense more important, it is referred to as the **head** of the compound, and the modifying element is called the **dependent**. In English, the compound head is always the second member, but in other languages such as Spanish, the head is the first member.

(5.6)   *hombre-rana*   'frogman'   (*hombre* 'man' + *rana* 'frog')
   año luz   'light year'   (*año* 'year' + *luz* 'light')
   pez espada   'swordfish'   (*pez* 'fish' + *espada* 'sword')

The semantic relations that obtain between the head and the dependent in compounds are quite diverse: purpose (*writing desk, lipstick*), appearance (*hardware, sword fish*), location (*garden chair, sea bird*), event participant (e.g. agent: *swansong*, patient: *flower-seller*), and so on. However, such a classification is not particularly useful, because there seem to be almost no restrictions on the kinds of semantic relations that may hold between the dependent and the head in compounds (at least in the languages in which compound meanings have been studied extensively). It is our knowledge of the world that tells us that a *flower-seller* is someone who sells flowers, and that a *street-seller* is someone who sells something on the street. But it is easy to imagine a world (say, a fable about commercially active bees) in which selling goes on on flowers, and even easier to imagine a world in which people specialize in selling entire streets. English morphology does not seem to say more than that the dependent must be in some kind of pragmatically sensible relation to the head.

However, not all compounds are of the **head-dependent** or **endocentric** type that we have seen so far (the term *endocentric* means that the semantic head (or *centre*) of the compound is 'inside' (*endo-*) the compound). Compounds may also be **exocentric** (i.e. their semantic head is 'outside' (*exo-*) the compound). Exocentric compounds can be illustrated with examples from Ancient Greek.

(5.7) *kakó-bios*   'having a bad life'
                               (*kakós* 'bad' + *bíos* 'life')
       polu-phármakos   'having many medicinal herbs'
                               (*polús* 'much' + *phármakon* 'herb')
       hēdúoinos   'having sweet wine'
                               (*hēdús* 'sweet' + *oînos* 'wine')
       megaló-psukhos   'having a large mind, i.e. magnanimous'
                               (*mégas* 'large' + *psukhē* 'mind')

A compound such as *hēdúoinos* refers to someone who has sweet (*hēdú-*) wine (*oino-*), so its denotation is neither a hyponym of 'sweet' nor of 'wine'. The semantic head is 'outside' the compound: the reference to 'someone' must be inferred from the structure as a whole – there is no morpheme that refers to a person or to ownership. English has a few exocentric A + N compounds of this semantic type (*redhead* 'someone who has red hair', *highbrow, lazybones*), but this pattern is hardly productive in English.

Another type of exocentric compound is illustrated by the Italian examples in (5.8).

(5.8) *portabagagli*   'trunk'   (*portare* 'carry' + *bagagli* 'luggage')
       lavapiatti   'dishwasher'   (*lavare* 'wash' + *piatti* 'dishes')
       asciugacapelli 'hair dryer'   (*asciugare* 'dry' + *capelli* 'hairs')

Here the 'external' semantic head is an instrument for carrying out an action on an object. Again, English has a few exocentric V + N compounds as well (referring to people rather than instruments: *pickpocket, cutthroat, killjoy*), but this pattern is totally unproductive in English.

Exocentric compounds like those we have just seen provide another argument against a morpheme-based model of morphology, because complex words like *hēdúoinos* and *lavapiatti* have a meaning that cannot be derived exclusively from the meaning of their constituent parts. There is no morpheme in Italian *lavapiatti* that can be assigned the meaning 'instrument'. However, using our word-based notation of Section 3.2, the rules that yield these exocentric compounds can easily be represented formally.

(5.9) Rule for Italian exocentric compounds of (5.8)

$$\begin{bmatrix} /\text{Xre}/_{\text{V.INF}} \\ \text{'do}_x\text{'} \end{bmatrix} \quad \& \quad \begin{bmatrix} /\text{Y}/_{\text{N.PL}} \\ \text{'ys'} \end{bmatrix} \quad \leftrightarrow \quad \begin{bmatrix} /\text{XY}/_{\text{N.SG}} \\ \text{'instrument for doing}_x \text{ ys'} \end{bmatrix}$$

Here the compound word-schema on the right contains the additional meaning element 'instrument for', which is not associated with a particular element of phonological form, but with the pattern as a whole (cf. the rule in (3.12b–c), which is similar in this respect).

Another type of compound that cannot be easily accommodated by a morpheme-based model of morphology is what is called **affix compound** here. Affix compounds are patterns that consist of more than one stem plus an affix, as in the English examples in (5.10).

(5.10) *green-eyed*   'having green eyes'
       dark-haired   'having dark hair'
       red-roofed   'having a red roof'

These are similar to the Greek exocentric compounds of (5.7) in that they contain the meaning element 'having'. In contrast to the Greek compounds, these English compounds have the suffix *-ed*, which could in principle be described as expressing that meaning element. But, in addition, the semantic relation between 'green' and 'eye' is part of this pattern as well, and this cannot be attributed solely to the suffix *-ed*. Thus, the description in (5.11) seems preferable to any kind of morpheme-based description.

(5.11) $\begin{bmatrix} /X/_A \\ 'x' \end{bmatrix}$ & $\begin{bmatrix} /Y/_N \\ 'y' \end{bmatrix}$ $\leftrightarrow$ $\begin{bmatrix} /XYd/_A \\ \text{'having (a) } y\text{(s) with} \\ \text{the property } x' \end{bmatrix}$

Besides endocentric and exocentric compounds, there are also compounds that have more than one semantic head. In these compounds, both members are on an equal footing, and they can be paraphrased with 'and', so they are called **coordinative compounds**. Some examples from Korean are in (5.12).

(5.12) *elun-ai*   'adult and child'   (*elun* 'adult' + *ai* 'child')
       ma-so   'horses and cattle'   (*ma* 'horse' + *so* 'cow')
       non-path   'farm'   (*non* 'rice field' + *path* 'dry field')
       o-nwui   'brother and sister'   (*o* 'brother' + *nwui* 'sister')
       son-pal   'hand and foot'   (*son* 'hand' + *pal* 'foot')
                                                     (Sohn 1994: 416–7)

This type of additive compound is widespread in the world's languages, but it happens to be rare in European languages, including English. A more familiar type of non-headed compound is represented by examples such as (5.13) from Spanish, where both compound members have the same reference. Such compounds are also called **appositional compounds**.

(5.13) *poeta-pintor*   'poet who is also a painter'
       actor-bailarín   'actor who is also a dancer'
       compositor-director   'composer who is also a director'

English also has some compounds of this kind (*maidservant, Marxism-Leninism*), and adjective compounds such as *bitter-sweet* and *deaf-mute* can be subsumed under this type as well.

The last type of compound to be mentioned here is again exocentric (i.e. it has no semantic head), but it shares with coordinative compounds the feature of semantic equality of both compound members. A few examples from Classical Tibetan are given in (5.14).

(5.14) *rgan-gžon*   'age'   (*rgan* 'old' + *gžon* 'young')
        yag-ñes   'quality'   (*yag* 'good' + *ñes* 'bad')
        mtho-dman   'height'   (*mtho* 'high' + *dman* 'low')
        srab-mthug   'density'   (*srab* 'thin' + *mthug* 'thick')

(Beyer 1992: 105)

The semantic head of these compounds is something like 'property', so *rgan-gžon* is literally 'property (in the dimension) of old and young', i.e. 'age'.

5.2 Hierarchical structure and head-dependent relations in compounds

As we saw in the preceding section, the concept 'semantic head' is useful for talking about the kinds of semantic relations that may obtain between the members of an endocentric compound. In this section, we will see that not only a semantic notion of 'head', but also a formal notion of 'head' can play a role in morphology.

There are close parallels between compounds and syntactic phrases in many cases. Some minimal pairs are given in (5.15).

(5.15) COMPOUND   SYNTACTIC PHRASE
        childcare   *care for children, children's care*
        longhouse   *long house*
        leadfree   *free of lead*
        waterproof   *proof against water*

In syntactic phrases, the semantic criterion may serve to identify the head as in compounds: a long house is a kind of house, just as a longhouse, and something that is leadfree is 'free' in some specific sense. But, in syntax, there are also a number of purely formal properties that heads share:

(5.16) Syntactic head properties
        a. The head is the **morphosyntactic locus**, i.e. it bears inflectional markers that belong to the whole phrase.
        b. The head may **govern** the form of its dependents.
        c. The head may **agree** in person/number with its dependents.

These properties can be illustrated with the sentence in (5.17) (a Russian example is chosen because the inflectional properties are less salient in English). In Fig. 5.1, a tree diagram for this sentence is given.[2]

---

[2] The notation here differs somewhat from the notation in (4.12). In order to save space, the features are written as subscripts of syntactic nodes, and the dimension names are omitted.

(5.17) *Student-y*   *pomaga-l-i*   *zavedujušč-ej*   *kafedr-oj.*
       student-PL   help-PAST-PL   chairwoman-DAT   department-INSTR
       'The students helped the chairwoman of the department.'

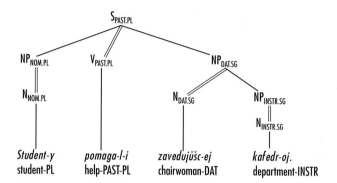

Figure 5.1 A tree diagram for (5.17)

In the tree in Figure 5.1, the head of each phrase is symbolized by a double line between the phrasal node and head node. We see that the verb *pomagali* is the morphosyntactic locus of the sentence in that is bears the tense marking that characterizes the whole clause. Likewise, nouns are the morphosyntactic locus of their NP in that they bear the case and number markers that must ultimately belong to the NP. In (5.17), all syntactic features of the head node are shared by the phrasal node (this sharing of head and phrase features is sometimes called **feature percolation**). We also see two examples of government in (5.17): The verb *pomagali* governs the dative case of its dependent object NP, and the noun *zavedujuščej* governs the instrumental case of its dependent complement NP. Finally, *pomagali* agrees with its dependent subject NP in number.

In compounds, two of the three syntactic head properties cannot be observed because the dependent in compounds does not in general bear inflectional features. As we saw in Section 5.1, the dependent member in compounds is an uninflected stem whose inflectional form cannot be governed and which cannot control agreement. However, the third syntactic head property, the morphosyntactic locus, applies to compounds as it does to syntactic phrases. Let us look at a number of examples of compounds and their tree diagrams, shown in Figure 5.2. Again, the head is shown by a double line. In *lipsticks*, the morphosyntactic property that is shared by the head and the compound word is plurality. One might object to the bracketing of *lipsticks* as *[[lip][stick-s]]* and propose the alternative *[[lip][stick]]s*, where the plural suffix attaches to the complete compound word rather than to the head. This alternative works for this particular example, but it does not work for a case like Spanish *años luz* 'light years' (singular: *año luz*

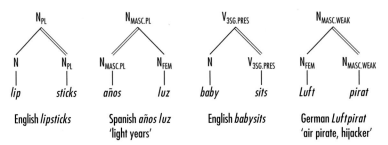

Figure 5.2 Compound trees

'light year'). As we saw in (5.6), Spanish has left-headed N + N compounds, and, if plurality is a property shared by the head and the compound, we expect the plural form *años luz* (not **año luz-es*), and indeed this is the correct Spanish form. Another head feature of compounds is the word-class, as shown by the English word *babysits*, which is a verb (third person singular present tense), just like its head *sits*. Spanish *años luz* and German *Luftpirat* 'air pirate, hijacker' illustrate the fact that gender is a head feature. While the nonheads *luz* 'light' and *Luft* 'air' are feminine, the compound nouns are masculine, just like their head. And in German *Luftpirat* we also see that the inflection class of the head is shared by the compound: both *Pirat* and *Luftpirat* are 'weak' nouns – i.e. their genitive singular suffix is *-en* rather than the more common *-s*. This can also be illustrated from English: the plural of *church mouse* is *church mice*, not **church mouses* – i.e. the head determines the way the plural of the compound is formed.

As we would expect, compounds that are not semantically endocentric do not behave formally like endocentric compounds either. Thus, in coordinative compounds we often find double plural marking (e.g. Spanish *actores-bailarines, compositores-directores,* etc.), and the English exocentric compound *sabertooth* ('a tiger whose teeth are like sabers', not 'a tooth that is like a saber') forms the plural *sabertooths* (not *saberteeth*).

Tree representations of compounds are useful also when a compound consists of members that are compounds themselves, because in that case several different hierarchical structures are possible. Two possibilities for three-term compounds are shown in Figure 5.3, and Figure 5.4 shows two possibilities for compounds with four terms.

Sometimes a compound with more than two nouns may allow two hierarchical structures simultaneously. For example, a compound like *nuclear power station* can be bracketed as [[*nuclear power*][*station*]] or as [[*nuclear*][*power station*]] with equal justification, because both make sense semantically, and both the compounds *nuclear power* and *power station* exist in English.

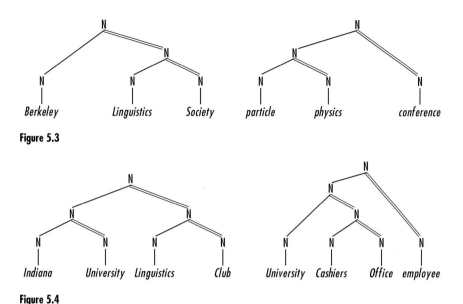

Figure 5.3

Figure 5.4

5.3 Hierarchical structure and head-dependent relations in derived lexemes

Complex lexemes formed by derivational affixes are not unlike compounds in several respects, and many morphologists use tree representations to show the relations between the base and affixes. Hierarchical tree structures are capable of showing semantic relations in a salient way. For example, the two trees in Figure 5.5 distinguish the two different meanings of *undoable* very clearly. *Undoable₁* ('which cannot be done') is derived from *doable* with the negative prefix *un-*, and *undoable₂* ('which can be undone') is derived

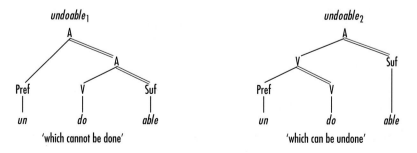

Figure 5.5 Two meanings and two structures of *undoable*

from *undo* with the suffix *-able*. The tree structures in Fig. 5.5 show these derivational origins quite directly.

Sometimes different orderings of affixes yield significantly different meanings, and then a hierarchical representation is appropriate as well. Consider (5.18) from Capanahua.

(5.18) a. *pi-catsih-ma-hue*
        eat-DESID-CAUS-IMPV
        'Make him hungry.' (Lit.: 'Make him want to eat.')
    b. *pi-ma-catsihqu-i*
        eat-CAUS-DESID-PRES
        'He wants to feed it.' (Lit.: 'He wants to make it eat.')
                 (Payne 1990: 228; data from Eugene Loos)

Here the different orderings of the causative ('make someone do something') and desiderative ('want to do something') suffixes are associated with different semantic scope, so that two very different readings arise. This is just like syntax, and a tree-like representation as in syntax captures the properties of these affixes quite well.

In addition to showing semantic relations, tree representations have also been used in morphology for expressing certain formal properties of derived lexemes. Some examples of such representations are given in Fig. 5.6.

The English suffix *-able* is mostly attached to verbs (and occasionally to nouns, as in *fashionable*), turning them into adjectives. As we saw in Chapter 4, it is quite typical of derivational affixes that they change the word-class of their base lexeme. This can be expressed by saying that the derivational affixes belong to a word-class (noun, verb, adjective) just like full lexemes and stems, and that they may be the heads of the corresponding derived lexemes. Since word-class is a head feature (as we saw for compounds in the preceding section), the word-class of the resulting lexeme is that of the derivational affix. Thus, *read-able* is an adjective (because of *-able*$_A$), Russian *carstvo* 'czardom' is a noun (because of *-stvo*$_N$) and Polish *awans-ować*

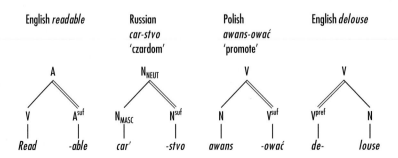

Figure 5.6 Tree representations of derived lexemes

'promote' is a verb (because of *-ować*_V). The fourth example in Fig. 5.6 shows that derivational prefixes may determine the lexeme's word-class as well. In addition to the word-class, derivational affixes also typically determine the gender of nouns (as is illustrated by Russian *-stvo*, which derives neuter nouns) and the inflection class of the derived lexeme (as is illustrated by Russian *-stvo*, which derives nouns of the *o*-declension, and Polish *-ować*, which derives verbs of the *-owa/-uj* conjugation).

However, not all derivational affixes are heads. Many derivational affixes do not determine the word-class and other properties of their derived lexemes. In the European languages, this is true in particular of prefixes and diminutive suffixes. Three such non-head affixes from three languages are listed in (5.19).

(5.19)

	English *co-*	Spanish *pre-*	Italian *-ino*
N	*co-author*	*pre-istoria* 'prehistory'	*tavol-ino* 'little table'
A	*co-extensive*	*pre-bélico* 'pre-war'	*giall-ino* 'yellowish'
V	*co-exist*	*pre-ver* 'foresee'	(Adv) *ben-ino* 'rather well'

Thus, derivational affixes often behave like heads of compounds, and this may be regarded as a sufficient reason for treating them as heads as in Figure 5.6. However, of the four head properties of syntactic heads (semantic hyponym, morphosyntactic locus, governor, person–number agreement target), only one is left in derivational affixes, because the semantic criterion does not apply here, for obvious reasons: *reality* is not a kind of *-ity*, something that is *yellowish* is not kind of *-ish*, and so on.

So the similarity to the syntactic notion of head is tenuous, and many morphologists have expressed scepticism about the usefulness of carrying over this notion to affixes. It must also be kept in mind that not all derivational patterns involve affixes. It may be possible to describe English *carri-er* as a headed structure, but Arabic *ħammaal* 'carrier' (from *ħamala* 'carry') cannot be so described.

Summary of Chapter 5

There are two main types of nominal compounds: endocentric compounds with a head-dependent structure, and various kinds of exocentric compounds (e.g. coordinative compounds and appositional compounds). Like syntactic phrases, (endocentric) compounds are often conveniently described as having hierarchical structure (using tree diagrams). Such hierarchical structures are often also applied to derived lexemes, and derivational suffixes are often described as the heads of their words, although they share only few properties with the heads of syntactic phrases.

Further reading

For a cross-linguistic survey of compounding, see Bauer (2001a). For noun incorporation, see Mithun (1984). For coordinative compounds, see Olsen (2001).

The word-syntactic approach that uses hierarchical structures is most prominently represented by works such as Selkirk (1982), Di Sciullo and Williams (1987) and Lieber (1992). On heads in morphology, see in particular Williams (1981a), Scalise (1988b) and Haspelmath (1992), and, for some sceptical voices, see Reis (1983) and Bauer (1990). A recent defence is found in Štekauer (2000).

Exercises

1. Formulate the word-based rule (analogous to (5.9) and (5.11) for German V + N compounds as given in (5.5).

2. Draw tree diagrams (analogous to those in Figs. 5.3–5.4) for the following English compounds:

   family planning adviser, undersea cable repair team, fixed-line phone system, mad cow disease hysteria, World Trade Center rescue worker, credit card agreement form, major league baseball game

   (For some of these, two different solutions may be correct.)

3. Consider the following Sanskrit compounds and, judging by their meaning, determine the type of compound in each case.

aśvakovida-	'knowledgeable about horses'
bahuvrīhi-	'having a lot of rice'
divyarūpa-	'having divine shape'
gṛhapati-	'houseowner'
mahārājā-	'great king'
mahātman-	'having a big soul, i.e. magnanimous'
priyasakhī-	'dear friend'
rājarṣi-	'king who is a wise man/wise man who is a king'
śuklakṛṣṇa-	'bright and dark'
sukhaduḥkha-	'joy and pain'

   A list of relevant Sanskrit nouns and adjectives:

ātman-	'soul'	*gṛha-*	'house'
aśva-	'horse'	*kovida-*	'knowledgeable'
bahu-	'much'	*kṛṣṇa-*	'dark'
divya-	'divine'	*mahā-*	'big'
duḥkha-	'pain'	*pati-*	'lord'

priya-	'dear'	*śukla-*	'bright'
ṛṣi-	'wise'	*sakhī-*	'friend'
rājā-	'king'	*sukha-*	'joy'
rūpa-	'shape'	*vrīhi-*	'rice'

4. In Spanish, there are two homophonous adjectives *inmovilizable*: *inmovilizable₁* 'unmobilizable' and *inmovilizable₂* 'immobilizable'. The morphological structure of these words corresponds closely to the structure of the corresponding English words (prefix *in-* 'un-', suffix *-able* '-able', suffix *-iz* '-ize', *móvil* 'mobile'). Draw the constituent structure trees of these two words.

5. Russian has a productive class of exocentric A + N compounds comparable to the Ancient Greek compounds in (5.7):

dlinno-ruk-ij	'long-armed'	*dlinnyj*	'long'	*ruka*	'arm'
krasno-borod-yj	'red-bearded'	*krasnyj*	'red'	*boroda*	'beard'
černo-kož-ij	'black-skinned'	*černyj*	'black'	*koža*	'skin'
tolsto-nog-ij	'thick-legged'	*tolstyj*	'thick'	*noga*	'leg'

Formulate the word-based rule, analogous to (5.11), for these compounds.

Productivity

6

6.1 Possible, actual and occasional words

As we saw in Section 3.1, a morphological rule or pattern is said to be productive if (and to the extent that) it can be applied to new bases and new words can be formed with it. The notion of productivity is in principle applicable both to word-formation and to inflection, but in this chapter we will focus on productivity in word-formation (see Section 7.5 for productivity in inflection)

Now one might ask why productivity should be such a big issue in morphology. After all, syntactic rules are productive as well, but few syntacticians worry much about how to define and determine their productivity (and no syntax textbook devotes an entire chapter to productivity). In syntax, linguists study **possible sentences**, and they do not care much whether these are actual sentences in some sense or not. Indeed, some morphologists have proposed that this procedure should be carried over to morphology: linguists who are interested in the morphological systems of languages should study **possible words**, regardless of whether these words happen to be in common use or not. In other words, linguists should focus on morphological **competence** (which comprises the possibilities of the system) and can afford to ignore morphological **performance** (which consists of the use of the system for communication and other tasks). If this position is adopted, productivity is uninteresting: whether or not a possible word is likely to become an actual word is not an issue.

Such a strict competence/performance division has the advantage of avoiding all the difficulties surrounding productivity, but it also has serious drawbacks. Most importantly, it is often very difficult to distinguish between possible and impossible words. Grammaticality judgements are not unproblematic in syntax either, but in morphology they are far more difficult to interpret than in syntax. To be sure, there are many cases in which speakers' judgements are just as unambiguous as in syntax: hypothetical words like *helpnessful* (with the wrong order of the suffixes *-ful* and *-ness*) or *frownity* (where the suffix *-ity* attaches to a verb) are clearly ungrammatical, as every speaker will agree. But in many other cases, it is less clear what speakers' judgements mean. Consider the set of words *bearded, winged, pimpled, eyed*. The last word in this set, *eyed*, seems odd, and many speakers would probably judge it unacceptable. But does that mean that it is truly ungrammatical, – i.e. not allowed by the morphological system? A straightforward explanation of the difference in the acceptability of *bearded, winged* and *pimpled*, on the one hand, and *eyed*, on the other, is that not all creatures have beards, wings and pimples, but virtually all have eyes, so one would rarely describe a person or an animal as *eyed*. But consider a context in which cave-dwelling bugs, worms and other lowly creatures are discussed, and the focus is on whether they have eyes or not. In such a context, the use of *eyed* suddenly becomes much more plausible, and, confronted with this context, speakers would perhaps reverse their acceptability judgements. Thus, linguists' descriptions need not account for the oddness of *eyed* – this turns out to be due to a non-linguistic factor that has no relevance to morphology.

A general problem is that speakers tend to be far more reluctant to accept new words than to accept new sentences, maybe because they do not encounter new words very often in ordinary life. Some morphologists have drawn from this the conclusion that speakers' negative judgements do not mean much. Words like *effectivity, refusive* or *illuxurious* have been regarded as possible English words (because they fit a pattern), although nobody would use them and they sound decidedly odd. But without the constraints of speakers' acceptability judgements, nothing prevents us from claiming that *coldth* (cf. *warmth*), *harrassion* (cf. *discussion*), *helpfulity* (cf. *tranquillity*), and even *oxes* (cf. *foxes*) or *horsen* (cf. *oxen*) are possible words of English. So, clearly, we cannot dispense with speakers' judgements entirely, but, as we saw in the preceding paragraph, just what these judgements mean is not always obvious.

For this reason, most morphologists are interested in **actual words** (in addition to speakers' acceptability judgements of hypothetical words), and many people study neologisms observed in the contemporary language. But what exactly is an actual word? The simplest definition would say that an actual word is one that has been used at least once, but, if it is never used again, that is hardly a sufficient reason to say that it has become part of the language. Words that have been observed at least on one occasion but have not really caught on in the speech community are called **occasionalisms** (or **nonce formations**). Most occasionalisms are probably never recorded, and, even among those that are recorded, many disappear soon afterwards. For instance, in 1943 the new word *deglamorize* was observed and recorded by a linguist, perhaps because it was used repeatedly around that time (Algeo 1991). But it seems that the word has not caught on and has not really become part of the English lexicon (even though the *OED* records it). Around the same time, the word *decolonize* arose. This word was more successful, and most English speakers nowadays know it. It has thus become a truly **usual word** of English.

So, from the point of view of lexicographers, only usual words (or actual) are significant, but, if we are interested in productivity, we should not ignore occasionalisms. Highly productive morphological patterns are quite prone to give rise to occasionalisms, whereas unproductive or little productive patterns rarely do so. Of course, all neologisms that have become established in the language once started their lives as occasionalisms, so the new usual words also contribute to our picture of productivity. But whether a word becomes usual or not depends on all kinds of circumstances, most of which have nothing to do with productivity. And under exceptional circumstances, a word may become usual, even if it is not formed according to a productive pattern at all (e.g. English *comeuppance*, which seems to consist of *come, up* and *-ance*, a quite impossible combination).

6.2 Productivity, creativity and analogy

When a rule is very productive, neologisms formed by that rule are hardly noticed – by speakers, hearers and lexicographers. For instance, English adjectives with the suffix *-less* can be formed quite freely (*childless, joyless, shoeless*, and so on), and if a speaker or writer creates a new word with *-less* (e.g. *commaless*: *the poet writes in long, commaless sentences*), this does not strike hearers or readers as particularly innovative. The author may not have noticed herself that she was using a new word. Dictionaries of neologisms are not likely to record new words with the suffix *-less* either.

Some linguists have proposed that the unconscious nature of the formation of new words is not merely a typical property of highly productive rules, but should be a necessary criterion for regarding a rule as productive. According to this view, there is a sharp distinction between **productivity** and **creativity**. A productive rule allows speakers to form new words unconsciously and unintentionally, whereas creative neologisms are always intentional formations that follow an unproductive pattern. An example of a creative neologism would be the word *mentalese* ('the mental language of our thoughts'), because new words with the suffix *-ese* (such as *motherese, computerese, translationese*) are probably always coined intentionally, and they immediately strike hearers and readers as new and unusual. (The word *mentalese* must have been coined by a philosopher in the middle of the twentieth century.)

However, in this book we will not adopt this terminological distinction between productivity and creativity. Instead, we will say that morphological rules can be more or less productive, and, the less productive a rule is, the more will a neologism be noticed and the fewer unconscious neologisms will be formed. The suffix *-ese* is less productive than the suffix *-less*, so we expect *-ese* neologisms to be more striking than *-less* neologisms. The proposed distinction between productivity and creativity has a methodological and an empirical problem. The methodological problem is that it defines productive rule application as unconscious or unintentional, but we have no way of knowing what speakers' intentions and state of consciousness are when they form a new word. Moreover, we can distinguish consciousness and intentionality at several levels. When the philosopher coined the word *mentalese*, he or she probably intended to create a catchy single-word expression for a highly abstract concept that would make that concept more popular. At this level the coinage was no doubt conscious. But why did he or she not choose *thoughtese* or *mindese*, two words that would have made perfect sense to describe the language of our thoughts in the mind? It so happens that English words with the suffix *-ese* have a strong preference for a stress pattern strong–weak–strong (e.g. *compùterése, mòtherése, translàtionése*, and also *Jàpanése*, not **Japànése, Vìetnamése*, not **Vietnàmése*), and the words *thòughtése* and *mìndése* would not conform to this pattern (Raffelsiefen 1996). It seems unlikely that the philosopher was aware of this phonological regularity, and in this sense the choice of *mèntalése* instead of *thoughtese* or *mindese* was probably unintentional.

The empirical problem with the distinction between productivity and creativity is that there are many rules that yield neologisms that are neither totally unremarkable nor immediately noticed. The English verb-deriving suffix *-ize*, for example, often forms new words, so it would be very odd to say that it is unproductive, but it may well be that quite a few of these new words are conscious creations (e.g. technical scientific terms such as *pronominalize, transistorize, multimerize*). It seems that it is more realistic to arrange rules on a continuous scale of productivity (as we did in Section 3.1) than to divide them into two disjoint classes.

Perhaps the term *creativity* is most appropriate when it is applied to violations of ordinary language norms by poets (this is called **poetic licence**). In the present context, we are interested in poetic licence that is manifested as the creation of novel words by unproductive rules. We saw in Section 5.1 that English V + N compounds of the type *killjoy* are unproductive, yet J. Thurber used *kissgranny*, and G. M. Hopkins coined *daredeath*. In Russian, the denominal suffix *-ač* (e.g. *trubač* 'trumpeter', from *truba* 'trumpet') is unproductive, but V. Mayakovsky created *stixač* 'verse-maker' (from *stix* 'verse'), and V. Khlebnikov used *smexač* 'laugher' (from *smex* 'laughter') (Dressler 1981). These cases should not be completely dismissed as abnormal use of language by a few exceptional individuals, because their poetry is intended for a (reasonably) wide audience, and readers must be expected at least to understand the neologisms. Thus, they provide interesting evidence that speakers are able to recognize the structure of unproductively formed words, and that the rules, even if unproductive by ordinary standards, at least exist.

More interesting than the productivity/creativity distinction is the distinction between creation by **rule** and creation by **analogy**. Sometimes a new word is created that is clearly formed on the basis of a single other word rather than on the basis of a general rule. For example, in French and Russian special words have been coined for 'land on the moon', which are clearly modelled on the words for 'land (on the earth)'.

(6.1) French   *terre*   'earth'   *atterrir*   'land (on the earth)'
                  lune   'moon'   *allunir*   'land on the moon'
     Russian   *zemlja* 'earth'   *prizemlit'sja* 'land (on the earth)'
                  luna   'moon'   *prilunit'sja* 'land on the moon'

The neologisms *allunir* and *prilunit'sja* cannot have been created by rule, because there is no productive rule in French and Russian that could have yielded these words. However, the structure of the words *atterrir* and *prizemlit'sja* is perfectly transparent, so speakers were able to create new words following the proportional equation in (6.2).

(6.2) *terre : atterrir*   = *lune* : X
                             X = *allunir*
     zemlja : prizemlit'sja = *luna* : X
                             X = *prilunit'sja*

The proportional formula of analogy seems to be a general feature of human cognition that is applied in all kinds of non-linguistic situations (e.g. in problem-solving, when people find analogous solutions to analogous problems, based on judgements of similarity). When the analogical proportion is applied in this way, with a single word as the analogical model, it is sometimes called **local analogy**. A few more examples are given in (6.3).

(6.3) neologism   model
     English *trialogue*   'conversation of   *dialogue* 'conversation of
                         three'   two'
     German *Hausmann* 'male homemaker' *Hausfrau* 'housewife'
     German *untertreiben* 'understate'   *übertreiben* 'exaggerate'
     Spanish *gaseoducto* 'gas pipeline'   *oleoducto*   'oil pipeline'

No general rule can be invoked to explain the creation of these neologisms. English *trialogue* must be based on *dialogue* because the element *-alogue* is a unique morpheme occurring only in *dialogue* (originally, in the Greek source of this word, the morpheme segmentation was *dia-logue*, but this is not transparent to English speakers). German *Hausmann* must be based on *Hausfrau*, because it has the highly specific meaning 'male homemaker', which one would not expect if it were simply a compound of *Haus* 'house' and *Mann* 'man'). The case of *untertreiben* is similar: The verb *übertreiben* is not semantically transparent (*über* 'over', *treiben* 'drive'), and *untertreiben* can get its meaning only from *übertreiben* and *unter*, not from *treiben* and *unter*. Spanish *gaseoducto* must be a local analogy, because it copies the part *-eo-* from *oleoducto*, which is originally part of *óleo* 'oil'.

In local analogy, there is just a single model on which a neologism is based. Now consider what happens if there are two or three possible models. For example, in Russian one might want to coin a word for 'land on Mars', which would be *primarsit'sja* (I do not know if this word has ever been used, but Russian speakers agree that it sounds not impossible). But now it is no longer clear what the model for this word was. Perhaps *prizemlit'sja*, perhaps *prilunit'sja*, but more likely both of these words. The analogical formula would thus look as in (6.4).

(6.4) *zemlja : prizemlit'sja*
      luna : prilunit'sja   =   *mars* : X
                                   X = *primarsit'sja*

But as soon as we admit more than a single model in analogical formations, the question arises as to what the difference is between analogical formations and word-based rule-governed formations of the kind we saw in Section 3.2.2. Thus, it is possible and not totally implausible to formulate a rule like (6.5) to account for *primarsit'sja*.

(6.5) $\begin{bmatrix} /\text{X}/_{\text{N}} \\ \text{'}x \text{ (= a celestial} \\ \text{body)'} \end{bmatrix} \leftrightarrow \begin{bmatrix} /\text{priXit'sja}/_{\text{V}} \\ \text{'land on } x\text{'} \end{bmatrix}$

And conversely, it would not be absurd to say that productive formations like *commaless* are formed by analogy with a large number of model words, as shown in (6.6).

(6.6) $\left.\begin{matrix} hat : hatless \\ child : childless \\ joy : joyless \\ \ldots : \ldots \end{matrix}\right\}$ = *comma* : X
                                  X = *commaless*

In a sense, then, the proportional analogical formula differs from the word-schema rules of Section 3.2.2 only in the number of models that are taken into account. Some morphologists have concluded from this that morphological analogy and morphological rules are really one and the same thing (see also the discussion in Section 3.3.3). The main difference between local analogy (as in 6.1–6.3) and more traditional rules is that the former is quite unproductive and cannot in general give rise to many neologisms.

6.3 Restrictions on word-formation rules

In many cases, we can give specific reasons why a word-formation rule does not give rise to words that it might be expected to permit. For example, the German female-noun suffix -*in* (as in *König-in* 'queen', *Löw-in* 'lioness') systematically fails to combine with the names of lower animals (*Käfer-in 'female beetle', *Wurm-in 'female worm'); and the English suffix -*ity* systematically fails to combine with adjectives ending in -*ish*, -*y* and -*ful* (*hopefulity). The set of bases to which a word-formation rule could apply in principle is called its **domain**. Whenever the domain is less than the entire word-class, we say that there are systematic **restrictions** on the rule. The kinds of restrictions that can be observed will be discussed in this section.

6.3.1 Phonological restrictions

Phonological restrictions on the domain of a word-formation rule are particularly common with derivational suffixes, much less so with prefixes and compounding. In most cases, there is a straightforward reason for the restriction: certain complex words are impossible because they would create difficulties for phonetic processing (i.e. pronunciation or perception). A common restriction rules out the **repetition of identical features**, e.g. the repetition of the phoneme /λ/ (spelled *ll*) in Spanish (which reduces the domain of the diminutive suffix -*illo*, (see (6.7)), or the repetition of the vowel /i(:)/ in English (which reduces the domain of the suffix -*ee* (see (6.8))).

(6.7) Spanish diminutive suffix -*illo*

mesa	*mesilla*	'(little) table'
grupo	*grupillo*	'(little) group'
gallo	*gallillo	'(little) rooster'
camello	*camellillo	'(little) camel'

(Rainer 1993: 18)

(6.8) English patient-noun suffix -*ee*

draw	*drawee*
pay	*payee*
free	*freeee
accompany	*accompanyee

(Raffelsiefen 1999a: 246)

Somewhat similar is the requirement that the derived word must have an alternating rhythm (strong–weak–strong). As a result, the English suffix -*ize* freely attaches to bases with a strong–weak rhythm, but does not attach to bases that end in a strong (i.e. stressed) syllable. (The suffix -*ese* behaves similarly, as we saw in Section 6.1.)

(6.9) English verbalizing suffix -*ize*

prívate	*prívatìze*
glóbal	*glóbalíze*
corrúpt	*corrúptìze
secúre	*secúrìze

(Raffelsiefen 1996; Plag 1999: ch. 6)

6.3.2 Semantic restrictions

In many cases, the meaning of an affix automatically restricts the domain of a word-formation rule, because some base–affix combinations simply make no sense. For example, it would be nonsensical to add the German female-noun suffix *-in* to a noun like *Baum* 'tree' (**Bäum-in*), because we do not conceive of trees as having gender distinctions. Similarly, the English reversive prefix *de-* (as in *de-escalate, decolonize*) can be combined only with verbal bases that denote a potentially reversible process. Combinations such as *deassassinate* or *deincinerate* are hard to interpret, except perhaps in a science-fiction context.

However, word-formation rules may also have semantic restrictions that seem quite arbitrary. For example, the Russian quality-noun suffix *-stvo* combines with adjectives that denote properties of human beings, not with adjectives denoting physical properties of objects.

(6.10) Russian quality-noun suffix *-stvo*

bogatyj	'rich'	*bogat-stvo*	'richness'
znakomyj	'acquainted'	*znakomstvo*	'acquaintance'
udaloj	'bold'	*udal'-stvo*	'boldness'
lukavyj	'wily'	*lukav-stvo*	'cunning'
krasivyj	'beautiful'	**krasiv-stvo*	
vjalyj	'withered'	**vjal'stvo*	
priemlemyj	'acceptable'	**priemlem-stvo*	

(Švedova 1980: 179)

Here there is no intrinsic reason why the suffix *-stvo* should not combine with other adjectives.

6.3.3 Pragmatic restrictions

In addition to being phonologically and semantically well-formed, a neologism must also be useful – this is what is meant by pragmatic restrictions. We noted at the beginning of this section that German does not have female nouns in *-in* denoting lower animals (**Käferin* 'female beetle', **Wurmin* 'female worm'). It seems clear that these gaps in the German lexicon are due to a pragmatic restriction: for animals like beetles and worms, it is simply not particularly useful to distinguish between males and females. Perhaps one should regard these derivations as potential German words, because it is not all that difficult to imagine a situation in which they might become useful (e.g. entomologists' specialized publications, or fairy tales). But ordinary speakers react to *Käferin* in much the same way as they would to *Bäumin*, and it is not easy to argue that the former is a possible word, while the latter is impossible.

6.3.4 Morphological restrictions

Some morphological patterns require special morphological properties of
the base. For example, Hebrew has a pattern for action nouns (*CiC(C)uC*)
that is applied only to verbs of one particular inflection class (*CiC(C)eC*).
Verbs of other inflection classes (*CaCaC, hiCCiC*, etc.) cannot form their
action nouns in this way.

(6.11) Hebrew action-noun pattern *CiC(C)uC*

diber	'speak'	*dibur*	'talk'
kibec	'gather'	*kibuc*	'gathering; kibbutz'
liked	'unite'	*likud*	'union; Likud'
tixnet	'program'	*tixnut*	'programming'
katav	'write'	**kituv*	
hamad	'desire'	**himud*	
hiškiv	'put to bed'	**hiškuv*	

In Russian, the female-noun suffix *-ja* combines only with bases that are
themselves derived by the suffix *-un* (see (6.12)). All other nouns must use
some other female-noun suffix (*-ka, -ša, -inja, -isa*).

(6.12) Russian female-noun suffix *-ja*

govor-it'	'talk'	*govor-un*	'talker'	*govor-un'-ja*	
beg-at'	'run'	*beg-un*	'runner'	*beg-un'-ja*	
pljas-at'	'dance'	*pljas-un*	'dancer'	*pljas-un'-ja*	
lg-at'	'lie'	*lg-un*	'lier'	*lg-un'-ja*	

(Švedova 1980: 203)

It appears that, with such nouns, the suffix *-ja* is 100 per cent productive.
Since the suffix *-un* is not particularly common and not particularly productive, nouns in *-ja* are very rare, yet it would be odd to say that *-ja* is not
productive.

6.3.5 Syntactic restrictions

Sometimes syntactic properties of words play a role in their options for
word-formation. This concerns particularly derivational meanings such as
the causative that have to do with transitivity. In many languages,
causatives can be formed only from intransitive verbs. A case in point is
Kiribatese, which has a *ka-* prefix that forms causatives:

(6.13) | | | | |
|---|---|---|---|
| *nako* | 'go' | *kanakoa* | 'make go, send away' |
| *kiba* | 'fly' | *kakibaa* | 'make fly, launch' |
| *am'arake* | 'eat (intr.)' | *kaam'arakea* | 'feed' |

(Groves *et al.* 1985: 88–9)

Ka-formations from transitive verbs are impossible.

6.3.6 Borrowed vocabulary strata

In some languages, a large part of the lexicon consists of loanwords from
another language that is (or has traditionally been) well known to many
speakers, at least educated or upper-class speakers. These loanwords
usually include many morphologically complex words. If an isolated
complex word is borrowed into another language, its morphological
structure inevitably gets lost (thus, the English word *orangutan* is
monomorphemic, although this is a compound noun in the source
language, Malay: *orang* 'man', *utan* 'forest'). But when a language borrows
many morphologically complex words from the same language, their
morphological structure may be preserved, and their patterns may remain
(or become) productive in the target language. For example, Japanese
borrowed many verb–noun compounds from Chinese – e.g. those in (6.14).

(6.14) Japanese V + N compounds (borrowed from Chinese)
doku-syo	'reading a book'
kyuu-sui	'supplying water'
satu-zin	'killing a man'
noo-zei	'paying tax'
tuu-gaku	'going to school'
tai-kyoo	'staying in Tokyo'
hoo-bei	'visiting the United States'

(Kageyama 1982: 221–31)

In some cases, the Chinese simple words were borrowed as well, but, in
many others, these noun and verb stems exist only in compounds (e.g. *bei-*
'US' occurs only in compounds such as *bei-koku* [US-country] 'United States').
The pattern of Chinese compounds is quite different from that of the
corresponding native Japanese compounds, which take the form N + V (e.g.
hito-dasuke [person-help] 'helping people', *yama-nobori* [mountain-climb]
'mountain climbing'). Thus, if Japanese had just borrowed a few compounds
of the type in (6.14), they would have lost their morphological structure, but
since they were borrowed in large quantities, these compounds are
analysable by Japanese speakers, and in effect Japanese borrowed the V + N
pattern along with the compounds from Chinese. The pattern is productive
in modern Japanese, and new compounds can be formed with it.

However, and this is crucial in the present context, only stems borrowed
from Chinese can be used in this compounding pattern. For example, the
noun *amerika* (used with the same meaning as *bei-koku*) cannot be a second
compound member (**hoo-amerika* 'visiting America'). Thus, the Chinese–
Japanese morphological pattern is still restricted to the vocabulary stratum
of Chinese–Japanese words.

A similar situation can be found elsewhere. Many languages of India have
borrowed heavily from the classical language Sanskrit and thus have many
derived lexemes of Sanskrit origin. In Kannada (a Dravidian language that

is not genealogically related to Sanskrit), many Sanskrit affixes are used extensively, but mostly with bases that are themselves Sanskrit loanwords. For instance, the quality-noun suffix *-te* can be used freely as in (6.15), but it does not combine with non-Sanskrit bases such as *kuḷḷa* 'short'.

(6.15)	*khacita*	'certain'	*khacitate*	'certainty'
	bhadra	'safe'	*bhadrate*	'safety'
	ghana	'weighty'	*ghanate*	'dignity'
	kuḷḷa	'short'	**kuḷḷate*	

(Sridhar 1990: 270, 278)

In many European languages, we find an analogous situation with loanwords from Latin. English has borrowed particularly extensively from Latin, and suffixes like *-ive, -ity, -ous* and adjectival *-al* (as in *parental, dialectal*) are mostly restricted to bases of Latin origin (these are often called **Latinate** bases).

(6.16)	*act*	*active*	*fight*	**fightive*
	brutal	*brutality*	*brittle*	**brittality*
	monster	*monstrous*	*spinster*	**spinstrous*
	parent	*parental*	*mother*	**motheral* (cf. *maternal*)

Now the question arises how speakers could learn whether a stem belongs to the native or to the borrowed stratum – after all, speakers do not acquire the historical information of etymological dictionaries during their normal process of language acquisition. In many cases, the phonological peculiarities of the borrowed stratum are probably of some help. Thus, in Kannada only Sanskrit loans have aspirated consonants (*kh, bh, gh*), and, in Japanese, Chinese loan morphemes never have more than two syllables. But otherwise the only way to infer that a word belongs to the borrowed stratum is by observing that it combines (or fails to combine) with certain affixes. However, that helps only if it is already known that those affixes belong to the borrowed stratum, so this procedure is somewhat circular.

Because of this learning problem, the restriction of a word-formation pattern to a borrowed stratum is often unstable. Thus, English *-ous* has also been applied to non-Latinate bases (e.g. *murderous, thunderous*), and the Kannada Sanskrit-derived suffix *-maya* (e.g. *haasya* 'humour', *haasya-maya* 'humorous') has also been applied to non-Sanskrit words (e.g. *lanca* 'bribe', *lanca-maya* 'corrupt'; *influuyens* 'influence', *influuyens-maya* 'influential' (Sridhar 1990: 282)). The English suffixes *-able, -ize, -ify, -ism* seem to have lost their restriction to Latinate bases almost entirely.

6.3.7 Synonymy blocking

Very often an otherwise productive derivational rule does not apply because it is pre-empted by an existing word that has the meaning of the potential neologism. For example, there is no agent noun in *-er* for the verb *steal* (**stealer*), because the word *thief* exists, which means the same as *stealer* would if it existed. Morphologists say that the rule is **blocked** under such circumstances. Apparently languages prefer not to have several words that mean exactly the same, so this is another kind of semantic restriction on productivity. Some other English examples are given in (6.17).

(6.17)	base	blocked word	blocking word	related pair
	broom	**to broom*	*to sweep*	*hammer/to hammer*
	to type	**typer*	*typist*	*to write/writer*
	linguistics	**linguistician*	*linguist*	*statistics/statistician*
	good	**goodly*	*well*	*bad/badly*

As the examples show, it is immaterial whether the blocking word is morphologically related to the blocked word or not.

A puzzling fact about blocking is that it has many exceptions. For instance, English has synonymous pairs like *piety/piousness, curiosity/ curiousness, accuracy/accurateness*, etc. (Plank 1981: 175–80), in which one would expect the second member to be blocked by the first one. This issue will be discussed further in Section 12.4.

(Blocking is also often invoked in inflectional morphology. For instance, morphologists often say that the past-tense form **goed* is blocked by *went*, and that the comparative form **badder* is blocked by *worse*.)

6.4 Measuring productivity

We have seen that productivity is best regarded as a gradeable property of morphological rules. Thus, for each rule we may want to ask how productive it is – i.e. we want to measure the degree of productivity of word-formation rules. Various measures have been proposed, but it turns out that they measure rather different things.

(i) The **number of actual words** formed according to a certain pattern (also called **degree of generalization, profitability** of a pattern or **type frequency**). This is an interesting concept, and it is fairly easy to measure by examining a comprehensive dictionary (though, of course, this works only to the extent that the dictionary faithfully records all the actual words of the language). However, type frequency is not the same as productivity: according to this measure, the English suffix *-ment* has a high type frequency (English has hundreds of words like *investment, harassment, fulfilment*), but it is not productive – only four neologisms with *-ment* are attested in the *OED* for the twentieth century. Conversely, there are not many usual words with the suffix *-ese* (as in *journalese*), but this can be used freely to coin new words denoting a special language or jargon.

(ii) The **number of possible words** that can be formed according to a certain pattern. This concept is much more difficult to measure, because it requires that we correctly identify all the restrictions on the pattern. But even then it is unlikely that the set of possible words equals the likelihood that a new word can be coined. There are simply too many cases of (more or less) unproductive rules that do not seem to be restricted in any general way. For instance, en-/em- prefixation in English should be possible with any noun that denotes a container-like object (e.g. *entomb, ensnare, embody*), but the rule is simply not productive (cf. *embox* 'put into a box', *encar* 'put in a car').

(iii) The **ratio of actual words to possible words** (also called the **degree of exhaustion**) (Aronoff 1976). Again, this requires that we be able to count the number of possible words, so it is not very practical. Moreover, when the possible bases include complex words that are themselves formed productively, the set of possible words becomes open-ended, and computing the ratio of actual to possible words is not really meaningful. For example, English or German N + N compounds can be formed freely without restrictions, and the compound members may be compounds themselves (see Section 5.1). Thus, the set of possible N + N compounds is staggeringly large (in principle, infinite), so the degree of exhaustion for N + N compounds is necessarily quite low (even though there are plenty of actual N + N compounds, and the pattern is highly productive).

(iv) The **number of neologisms** attested over a certain period of time (also called **diachronic productivity**). This measure can be determined if a good historical dictionary is available (such as the *OED*), but again only to the extent that the dictionary is reliable. And we saw earlier that, if a pattern is very productive, lexicographers are likely to overlook new words with this pattern. Another technique that is increasingly becoming available is the use of large text corpora. By looking at a newspaper corpus of the last three decades of the twentieth century, it should be possible, for instance, to observe how the English semi-suffix -*gate* (as in *Watergate, Irangate*, etc.) gained (and perhaps lost) productivity over the years. Probably diachronic productivity in this sense correlates with synchronic productivity, but again it is not quite the same, because the diachronic productivity can be determined only for periods of time, not for particular moments.

6.5 Speakers' knowledge of productivity

A widespread view among linguists holds that linguistic competence (speakers' knowledge of the words and the rules of the language) and linguistic performance (the actual use of that knowledge for speaking and understanding) are conceptually quite distinct and should therefore be studied separately. The different degrees of productivity that we observe in word-formation are a problem for this view, because rule productivity is not clearly a property of either competence or performance. To address this problem, some linguists have attempted to define away the whole issue of productivity.

One view says that productivity is exclusively a **diachronic** phenomenon. When a neologism is coined (and especially when it is accepted by the other speakers and becomes a usual word), this means that a new word enters the language and the language thereby changes. Thus, when a strictly synchronic point of view is adopted, the issue of productivity does not arise. However, speakers are perfectly capable of judging the likelihood of a new formation. When they are confronted in an experimental situation with two types of neologisms, formed by productive and by unproductive rules respectively, their acceptability judgements strongly correlate with the productivity of the rules as determined by linguists (Aronoff 1980). Since such acceptability judgements are otherwise routinely used to study linguistic competence, this suggests that the productivity of a rule should also be considered as a part of the speakers' (synchronic) knowledge of their language.

Another way in which the relevance of productivity to the study of linguistic competence has been denied is by equating the (un-)productivity of a rule with the (lack of) **restrictions** on the domain of that rule. On this view, all morphological rules are equally productive, but they are not equally restricted. Some are quite unrestricted (like English *-ness*, which attaches to almost any kind of adjective), whereas others are heavily restricted (like English deadjectival *-en* in *blacken, redden*, etc., which attaches only to monosyllabic adjectives ending in an obstruent). However, it is quite unlikely that this view is correct. There are simply too many rules that are not obviously restricted heavily and yet their productivity is limited. For example, the English diminutive suffix *-let* (e.g. *streamlet, piglet, booklet*) could in principle combine with any monosyllabic concrete noun, but in fact it is very rarely used for new words. It is, of course, possible that such unproductive rules are subject to restrictions that have not been discovered yet, but, until proponents of this view have identified these restrictions, we must regard it as more plausible that there is no such direct relation between the degree of productivity and unrestrictedness of a morphological rule.

Thus, we have to accept that speakers' knowledge of a language includes knowledge of the productivity of word-formation rules, in addition to knowledge of words and rules. But how do speakers come to have such knowledge? Is it something about the rule that determines its productivity?

One proposal is that the productivity of a rule depends on the semantic and phonological **regularity** of the actual words that were created by that rule. For example, it is not surprising that the rule of *-th* suffixation in English is unproductive, because many of the existing *-th* words are irregular phonologically (*depth, breadth, length, youth*) or semantically (*wealth* is not just 'being well', *dearth* is not just 'being dear'). This feature of a rule certainly correlates with productivity: semantic and phonological regularity is a prerequisite for neologisms because they cannot be formed and understood unless it is clear how they are pronounced and what they mean. But some completely regular rules are unproductive (e.g. the female-noun suffix *-ess* in English: *poetess, authoress, princess*), and some highly productive patterns have a fairly large number of irregular existing words (e.g. German *-chen* diminutives, as seen in idiomatized words like *Brötchen* 'bread roll', not 'little bread', *Teilchen* 'particle', not 'little part', *Weibchen* 'animal female', not 'little woman', *Zäpfchen* 'uvula', not 'little cone'). So regularity correlates with productivity, but it does not determine it.

Another proposal is that the productivity of a rule depends on the number of actual words that were created by that rule (i.e. the type frequency of the pattern). Again, there is probably a correlation (see also Section 7.5 for the analogous case in inflection), but this is not perfect (see the discussion in Section 6.4(i)).

The upshot of this discussion is that speakers can learn the degree of productivity of a rule only by observing the extent to which other speakers create neologisms using that rule (Rainer 1993: 34). Thus, if a linguist wants to predict a speaker's productivity judgement at a given moment, the best approach is probably to measure the diachronic productivity of the rule during the period immediately before that moment. Observing and recording neologisms in other speakers' speech is not the kind of activity that one would normally associate with the process of language acquisition, but there seems to be no way around the conclusion that this is what people do. And our linguistic knowledge comprises not only what one can and what one cannot say, but also what one is likely to say, at least in the (admittedly not very central) area of neologisms.

Summary of Chapter 6

Since the productivity of word-formation rules is often limited in ways that are difficult to understand, and speakers' judgements of morphological well-formedness are often hard to interpret, it is not advisable to limit one's attention to possible words – actual words and productivity itself must be objects of morphological study. Morphological patterns can be arranged on a scale from totally unproductive to highly productive. A rigid dichotomy between creativity and productivity, or between analogy and productivity, does not seem to be very useful, because there are always intermediate cases.

The productivity of a word-formation pattern may be limited in various ways: phonologically, semantically, pragmatically, morphologically and syntactically. Sometimes a pattern is productive only within a borrowed vocabulary stratum. Various quantitative measures of productivity have been proposed.

Productivity is often regarded as a phenomenon that exclusively concerns language use (performance) or language change, but, in the view defended here, productivity is one part of speakers' knowledge of language (competence) that has to be acquired.

Further reading

Excellent recent discussions of issues surrounding productivity are found in Plag (1999) and Bauer (2001b) (see also Kastovsky (1986) and Dressler and Ladányi (2000). The view that competence and performance should be strictly separated is expressed in Di Sciullo and Williams (1987). The distinction between productivity and creativity is proposed in the classical paper Schultink (1961) (see also van Marle 1985).

The non-distinctness of analogy and morphological rules is pointed out in Becker (1990). On productivity as a scalar notion, see Bauer (1992).

A sophisticated approach to measuring productivity is developed by Baayen and Lieber (1991) and Baayen (1992).

Exercises

1. The productivity of the suffix -ity in English is heavily restricted (see the examples below). What might be the nature of the restriction, and into which of the categories of Section 6.3 does it fall?

static	*staticity
important	*importantity
probable	probability
readable	readability
proactive	*proactivity
bagelizable	bagelizability
murderous	*murderosity
radical	*radicality
apposite	*appositity

2. Recall Exercise 2 of Chapter 3. Of the words listed there, you have probably characterized *reknow* and *happytarian* as impossible words in English, although the affixes *re-* and *-(t)arian* are widely attested and productive in English. What is it about the nature of these affixes that makes them unsuitable for these bases? (In other words, in what way is their productivity restricted?)

3. Modern Greek has two action-noun suffixes, *-simo* and *-ma*, which are both productive, but in different, complementary domains. Try to extract a generalization from the following examples that predicts when *-simo* occurs and when *-ma* is used. (Note that the phonological stem alternations are irrelevant.)

VERB	MEANING	ACTION NOUN	MEANING
ðjavázo	'I read'	ðjávasma	'reading'
kóvo	'I cut'	kópsimo	'cutting'
lúzo	'I bathe'	lúsimo	'bathing'
mangóno	'I squeeze'	mángoma	'squeezing'
pjáno	'I seize'	pjásimo	'seizing'
skondáfto	'I stumble'	skóndama	'stumbling'
tinázo	'I shake'	tínaɣma	'shaking'
tréxo	'I run'	tréksimo	'running'

4. Which of the following words are impossible because of synonymy blocking?

*musting   (e.g. *I hate musting get up every morning.*)
*foots   (e.g. *Bobby played outside and has dirty foots now.*)
*cooker   (e.g. *This meal is superb. The cooker is a real artist.*)
*bishopdom   (e.g. *The bishop often travels through his bishopdom.*)
*teacheress   (e.g. *Our teacheress is a very competent lady.*)
*ignorement   (e.g. *The government's ignorement of the protests was foolish.*)

5. What is the reason for the impossibility of the following English words?

*writation   (e.g. *The writation of this article took me three weeks.*)
*certainness   (e.g. *Nowadays there is less certainness about church teachings.*)
*sisterlily   (e.g. *She embraced her sisterlily.*)
*two-carred   (e.g. *Two-carred people need two garages.*)

6. How did the suffixes (or perhaps bound roots) -erati and -scape come into being? Consider the following examples:

literati, glitterati, liberati, chatterati, digiterati, soccerati (Kemmer, 2002)
landscape, seascape, cloudscape, skyscape, waterscape, winterscape (Aldrich 1966).

Inflectional paradigms

7.1 Types of inflection classes

Perhaps the most important challenge for an insightful description of inflection is the widespread existence of allomorphy in many languages. Phonological and morphophonological allomorphy will be the topic of Chapter 10, and in this section we will focus on **suppletive allomorphy**. We saw some examples of suppletive allomorphy in inflection in Section 2.5, and two more are given in (7.1)–(7.2).

(7.1) Irish nominative/genitive singular

NOMINATIVE	GENITIVE	
focal	*focail*	'word'
muc	*muic-e*	'pig'
corón	*corón-ach*	'crown'

(7.2) Old English infinitive, 3rd singular present, 3rd singular past

INFINITIVE		3RD SG PRESENT		3RD SG PAST	
dēm-an	'to deem'	*dēm-ð*	'deemeth'	*dēm-de*	'deemed'
luf-ian	'to love'	*luf-að*	'loveth'	*luf-ode*	'loved'

When different lexemes show different suppletive allomorphs, morphologists say that they belong to different **inflection classes**. Typically, a given pattern is valid for a number of lexemes, and languages are described as having between two and two dozen such classes. In (7.1), three different nominal inflection classes (or **declensions**) are illustrated, and, in (7.2), two verbal inflection classes (or **conjugations**) are shown. The existence of different inflection classes is a hallmark of Indo-European languages, so many examples in this chapter will come from Indo-European. Of course, the phenomenon is not restricted to Indo-European, but there are many languages with fairly complex morphological systems in which suppletive allomorphy of this kind is not found or is at least much less prominent (for instance, Turkish, Korean, Quechua and Tamil).

The term **inflection class** is not generally used for phonological allomorphy of inflectional affixes. For example, Basque nouns have somewhat different case suffixes depending on whether they end in a consonant (like *lagun* 'friend') or in a vowel (like *ume* 'child'):

(7.3) Basque definite nominal case paradigm (partial), phonological allomorphs

ABSOLUTIVE	*lagun-a* 'the friend'	*ume-a* 'the child'
LOCATIVE	*lagun-ean*	*ume-an*
ALLATIVE	*lagun-era*	*ume-ra*
LOCATIVE GENITIVE	*lagun-eko*	*ume-ko*

(Saltarelli 1988: 300)

Here the difference between the postconsonantal suffixes *-ean/-era/-eko* and the postvocalic suffixes *-an/-ra/-ko* has a straightforward phonological explanation and is of no great interest to the morphologist. Affix variants that help avoid consonant clusters (as in the example just seen) or vowel sequences (as in the Korean example (2.23a)) are extremely common in the world's languages. However, intermediate phenomena also exist. In Turkish, the third person singular possessive suffix is *-i* after consonants (e.g. *ev-i* 'her house'), but *-si* after vowels (e.g. *içki-si* 'her drink'). Although the distribution of these allomorphs makes good sense from a phonological point of view, they probably have to be described as suppletive allomorphs because there is no general phonological rule that inserts or deletes an *s*.

Inflection classes may be very large and may contain hundreds or thousands of lexemes, or they may be small and contain only a handful of lexemes. The limiting case would be an inflection class with just a single lexeme; for most purposes, this would amount to saying that the inflection of that lexeme is **irregular**. In English, we do not normally recognize an inflection class for nouns with the plural suffix *-en*, which has the lone member *ox*, but we say that *ox-en* is an irregular plural form. But note that, in pedagogical descriptions, the term 'irregular' is sometimes used where a morphologist would recognize a small inflection class. Thus, English present–past pairs such as *keep/kept, sleep/slept, sweep/swept, bereave/bereft, cleave/cleft, deal/dealt, dream/dreamt* form a distinct class of their own, a fact that is obscured when they are simply added to a list of 'irregular' verbs.

Remembering which lexeme belongs to which inflection class is difficult not only for a second-language learner, but also for first-language learners, so most inflection classes are not arbitrary but are linked to some non-morphological property of the lexeme that has to be learned anyway. This non-morphological property may be a **phonological** one (i.e. the allomorphy may be phonologically conditioned). We saw an example of this from Martuthunira in (2.27a); more examples are given in (7.4).

(7.4) a. Lezgian aorist participle: *-j(i)* after low vowel *(a, e)*, *-r* after high
vowel *(u, ü, i)*

AORIST FINITE	*awu-na*	*t'ü-na*	*fe-na*	*ata-na*
AORIST PARTICIPLE	*awu-r*	*t'ü-r*	*fe-ji*	*ata-j*
	'did/done'	'ate/eaten'	'went/gone'	'came/come'

(Haspelmath 1993: 131)

b. Eastern Armenian plural: *-er* with monosyllabic bases, *-ner* with
polysyllabic bases

SG	*jeřk'*	*yuɣ*	*erexa*	*tari*
PL	*jeřk'-er*	*yuɣ-er*	*erexa-ner*	*tari-ner*
	'hand(s)'	'oil(s)'	'child(ren)'	'oil(s)'

c. Standard Arabic plural: *CVCCVC* → *CaCaaCiC*,
CVCVVC → *CaCaaCiiC*

SG	*qayṣar*	*daftar*	*dirham*	*dustuur*	*quftaan*
PL	*qayaaṣir*	*dafaatir*	*daraahim*	*dasaatiir*	*qafaatiin*
	'emperor'	'notebook'	'drachma'	'statute'	'caftan'

Very often inflection classes are linked to **semantic** properties of the
lexeme. Particularly widespread are **animacy** distinctions. In German,
only animate nouns belong to the masculine *n*-declension ending in *-e* in
the nominative singular (*Hase* 'hare', *Affe* 'ape', *Junge* 'boy'). In Tamil, the
locative suffix is *-il* with non-human nouns (e.g. *nāṭṭ-il* 'in the country'),
but *-itam* with human nouns (e.g. *manitan-itam* 'in the man') (Annamalai
and Steever 1998: 105). Welsh has a special plural suffix for nouns denoting animals, *-od* (e.g. *cath/cathod* 'cats', *draenog/draenog-od* 'hedgehog(s)',
eliffant/eliffantod 'elephant(s)') (King 1993: 59). Lezgian has a special
oblique-stem marker that is used with all consonant-final proper names, *-a*
(e.g. *Farid-a* 'Farid', *Talibov-a* 'Talibov'). Lezgian also illustrates the potential relevance of the **mass-count distinction**: mass nouns tend to have the
oblique-stem suffix *-adi/-edi* (e.g. *naq'w-adi* 'soil', *kf-adi* 'foam', *hüm-edi*
'haze') (Haspelmath 1993: 75–6). In verbs, **transitivity** often plays a role.
For example, in Ossetic intransitive and transitive verbs show different
agreement inflection in the past tense. The singular forms of the intransitive verb *xuyssy-* 'sleep' and of the transitive verb *dzur-/dzyr-* 'say' are
given in (7.5).

(7.5)

	intransitive pattern	transitive pattern
1SG	*xuyssy-d-æn* 'I slept'	*dzyr-d-on* 'I said'
2SG	*xuyssy-d-æ*	*dzyr-d-aj*
3SG	*xuyssy-d*	*dzyr-d-a*

(Isaev 1966: 247)

In languages with gender distinctions, inflection classes are often linked
to **gender** in some way. This link is evident when the agreement markers
that reflect the gender on other words are formally similar to the inflectional
affixes on nouns themselves, as for instance in the Bantu languages. For

example, Zulu has the four inflection classes illustrated in (7.6), among others.

(7.6)

SG PREFIX	PL PREFIX	EXAMPLE	MEANING	AGR PREFIXES
um-	aba-	umfazi/abafazi	'woman/-men'	u-/ba-
um-	imi-	umfula/imifula	'river(s)'	u-/i-
i-	ama-	itafula/amatafula	'table(s)'	li-/a-
isi-	izi-	isicathulo/izicathulo	'shoe(s)'	si/zi-

The agreement prefixes for the genders corresponding to the four inflection classes are given in the last column in (7.6). Two examples of their use as subject prefixes on verbs are given in (7.7).

(7.7) a. *Aba-fazi*   *ba-biza*   *aba-fana*
       PL.G2-woman   3PL.G2.SUBJ-call   PL.G2-boy
       'The women call the boys.'
    b. *Isi-hambi*   *si-buza*   *um-gwaqo.*
       PL.G8-traveller   3PL.G8-ask   SG.G3-road
       'The traveller asks the road.'

(Ziervogel *et al.* 1981: 34, 46)

There is thus a close correspondence between gender classes and inflection classes, so that Bantuists generally treat them as one and the same thing ('noun classes'). However, the two kinds of classes need to be kept apart conceptually, as becomes clear from the Italian examples (7.8)–(7.9). (In Italian, verbs do not generally show agreement in gender, so (7.9) shows adjectival agreement.)

(7.8) Two Italian inflection classes

SG SUFFIX	PL SUFFIX	EXAMPLE	MEANING	AGR SUFFIXES	
-o	-i	giardino/giardini	'garden(s)'	-o/-i	(masc.)
-a	-e	casa/case	'house'	-a/-e	(fem.)

(7.9) Italian gender agreement
       a. *il mi-o giardin-o nuov-o*   'my new garden'
       b. *la mi-a cas-a nuov-a*   'my new house'

In Italian we clearly need to distinguish between inflection classes and genders, because there are nouns that have the singular suffix -o but are feminine (e.g. *mano* 'hand') and nouns that have the singular suffix -a but are masculine (e.g. *poeta* 'poet'). Such nouns are much rarer than the nouns where gender and inflection class match perfectly, but they exist. Thus, the correspondence between gender and inflection class is not more than a strong tendency. But it is a tendency that is noticed not only by linguists, but also by Italian speakers, as becomes clear when we look more closely at masculine nouns of the *a*-class (*poeta* 'poet', *linguista* 'linguist', and many others). In Latin, these had a nominative plural form ending in -ae, just like the feminines in -a (*poeta/poetae* 'poet(s)', just like *insula/insulae* 'island(s)'). If no morphological change had occurred, Italian would have the paradigm *poeta/poete* 'poet(s)', but in fact the plural of *poeta* is *poeti*, with the suffix -*i* from the *o*-declension. So, although there is no perfect match between gender and inflection class, the plural suffix -*i* seems to have been perceived as a marker of masculine plural and was used also for masculine nouns in -*a*.

Similarly, Sanskrit originally had a single inflection class of nouns with a stem-final -*i*, which included both masculine and feminine nouns. However, since nouns in the *a*-class are generally masculine and nouns in the *ā*-class are generally feminine, their markers came to be associated with masculine and feminine gender, and the *i*-class split up into two subclasses, a masculine *i*-class and a feminine *i*-class.

(7.10) Some partial Sanskrit nominal paradigms

		masculine *i*-class	feminine *i*-class	*a*-class (masc.)	*ā*-class (fem.)
SG	NOM	*agniḥ* 'fire'	*matiḥ* 'mind'	*devaḥ* 'god'	*senā* 'army'
	ACC	*agnim*	*matim*	*devam*	*senām*
	GEN	*agneḥ*	*mateḥ/matyāḥ*	*devasya*	*senāyāḥ*
	DAT	*agnaye*	*mataye/matyai*	*devāya*	*senāyai*
	INSTR	*agninā*	*matyā*	*devena*	*senayā*
PL	NOM	*agnayaḥ*	*matayaḥ*	*devāḥ*	*senāḥ*
	ACC	*agnīn*	*matīḥ*	*devān*	*senāḥ*

The differences in the instrumental singular and accusative plural, as well as the innovated forms *matyai* and *matyāḥ* in the feminine *i*-class are clearly due to the influence from the *a*-class and the *ā*-class. Thus, speakers seem to have a propensity to link inflection classes to gender, even though that makes the system still more complicated.

Besides phonological and semantic properties and gender, **morphological** properties of the lexeme may be decisive for the assignment to one or another inflection class. Most typically, the **derivational** pattern of a derived lexeme determines its inflectional behaviour. For example, Welsh has about a dozen different plural patterns, which are often unpredictably associated with individual nouns. However, when a noun has a derivational suffix, it is mostly predictable which plural affix the noun takes:

(7.11) -*og*/-*ogion*	*swydd*	'job'	*swyddog(-ion)*	'official(s)'
	march	'horse'	*marchog(-ion)*	'horseman/men'
-*es*/-*esau*	*tywysog*	'prince'	*tywysoges(-au)*	'princess(es)'
	Sais	'Englishman'	*Saesnes(-au)*	'Englishwoman/-men'
-*adur*/-*aduriaid*	*pechu*	'sin'	*pechadur(-iaid)*	'sinner(s)'
	cachu	'shit'	*cachadur(-iaid)*	'coward(s)'

(King 1993: 53–61)

As we saw in Section 5.3, this is one of the reasons why some morphologists regard derivational affixes as heads of their lexemes.

Another example of derivational patterns determining inflectional behaviour comes from Tagalog. In this language most verbs have a derivational affix (prefix, suffix or infix) that indicates in some way the transitivity or voice of the verb (e.g. actor voice -*um*-, *ma*-, patient voice -*in*, -*an*). The perfective form of the verb can be formed in four different ways: (i) zero (when the voice affix is -*um*-), (ii) *m*- becomes *n*- (e.g. when the voice affix is *ma*-), (iii) infix -*in*- (e.g. when the voice affix is -*an*) and (iv) infix -*in*- and subtraction of -*in* (when the voice affix is -*in*):

(7.12) root	basic form with voice affix		perfective form
takbo	*tumakbo*	'run'	*tumakbo*
tulog	*matulog*	'sleep'	*natulog*
hugas	*hugasan*	'wash'	*hinugasan*
basah	*basahin*	'read'	*binasah*

Again, this illustrates the dependence of inflection-class membership on a morphological property of the lexeme (its derivational pattern). But the derivational pattern need not be characterized by an affix. In Arabic, nouns derived by the pattern $C_1aaC_2iC_3$ tend to have the plural $C_1uC_2C_2aaC_3$ (e.g. *kaafir* 'infidel', plural *kuffaar*; *kaatib* 'writer', plural *kuttaab*; *zaahid* 'ascetic', plural *zuhhaad*). Here it is not possible to identify a head of the derived lexeme that would determine its inflection class.

The inflectional behaviour of a lexeme may depend not only on its derivational properties, but also on its other inflectional properties. For example, we can say that a Latin noun in -*us* (like *hortus* 'garden', *gradus* 'step') has a genitive plural in -*orum* if its genitive singular is -*ī*, and a genitive plural in -*uum* if its genitive singular is -*ūs*. To make this clearer, we can look at the complete paradigms of the two words:

(7.13)			*o*-declension	*u*-declension
SG	NOM		*hort-us*	*grad-us*
	ACC		*hort-um*	*grad-um*
	GEN		*hort-ī*	*grad-ūs*
	DAT		*hort-ō*	*grad-uī*
	ABL		*hort-ō*	*grad-ū*
PL	NOM		*hort-ī*	*grad-ūs*
	ACC		*hort-ōs*	*grad-ūs*
	GEN		*hort-ōrum*	*grad-uum*
	DAT		*hort-īs*	*grad-ibus*
	ABL		*hort-īs*	*grad-ibus*

Both these nouns are non-derived, so their inflectional behaviour cannot be determined by a derivational pattern. Phonological, semantic and gender properties do not help either. However, the distribution of the various suppletive allomorphs is by no means arbitrary. If it were, we might expect that some nouns in Latin have the genitive singular -*ī*, the ablative singular -*ū*, the accusative plural -*ōs*, and the dative plural -*ibus*, for instance. But, in fact, a noun can only choose a complete package of suffixes, either the package of *hortus* (generally called the *o*-declension) or the package of *gradus* (generally called the *u*-declension). Thus, we can say that the genitive plural depends on the genitive singular, as we did above, but with equal justification we can say that it depends on the dative singular or on the nominative plural. In fact, all word-forms depend on every other word-form (except for the nominative and accusative singular, which are identical in both classes and therefore have no predictive value). Of course, in practice some dependencies are more useful than others. For example, learners of Latin probably heard the genitive singular of a new word more often than its genitive plural, so the ability to predict the genitive plural from the genitive singular is more relevant than the ability to make the reverse prediction.

When an inflectional paradigm exhibits extensive dependencies among its word-forms in the choice of suppletive allomorphs, we may speak of **global inflection classes**. These are particularly characteristic of Indo-European nominal inflection, but they occur elsewhere, too. For example, Martuthunira has three conjugation classes, which are illustrated in (7.14) (only some exemplary inflected forms are given).

(7.14)	Ø-conjugation	L-conjugation	R-conjugation
PRESENT	*nyina-nguru*	*thani-rnuru*	*kanyja-rnuru*
PAST	*nyina-lha*	*thani-lalha*	*kanyja-rralha*
PASSIVE PERFECTIVE	*nyina-yangu*	*thani-rnu*	*kanyja-rnu*
FUTURE	*nyina-layi*	*thani-rninyji*	*kanyja-rninyji*
IMPERATIVE	*nyina-Ø*	*thani-lyu*	*kanyja-rryu*
LEST	*nyina-wirri*	*thani-lwirri*	*kanyja-rrwirri*
PRESENT RELATIVE	*nyina-nyila*	*thani-rnura*	*kanyja-rnura*
PURPOSE SAME-SUBJECT	*nyina-lu*	*thani-ru*	*kanyja-ru*
	'sit'	'hit'	'keep'

(Dench 1995: 139–40)

But global inflection classes, and more generally interdependence of inflected forms, do not seem to be particularly widespread. In many languages there is no dependence between case allomorphy and number allomorphy, or between the allomorphs of different tense–aspect forms. Although global inflection classes can be thought of as typical of Indo-European languages, even in Ancient Greek aspect inflection, there is no obvious dependence among the various allomorphs of the present, aorist and perfect stem markers. Some Ancient Greek verbs are given in (7.15), where person/number suffixes, prereduplication (in the perfect) and the past-tense prefix *e*- (in the aorist) are parenthesized in order to focus attention on the pure stems.

(7.15)   PRESENT STEM   AORIST STEM   PERFECT STEM
 allomorphs: (i) *-nCan(-ō)*   (i) Ø   (i) *-ēk(-a)*
             (ii) *-n(-ō)*   (ii) *-ēs(-a)*   (ii) Ø
             (iii) stem vowel *-e-* (iii) *-s(-a)*   (iii) vowel change
                                           (iv) stop aspiration
                                           (v) *-k(a)*

'bite'   *dák-n(-ō)* (ii)   *(é-)dak(-on)* (i)   *(dé-)dēkh(-a)* (iii+iv)
'flee'   *pheúg(-ō)* (iii)   *(é-)phug(-on)* (i)   *(pé-)pheug(-a)* (ii)
'learn'   *ma-n-th-án(-ō)* (i) *(é-)math(-on)* (i)   *(me-)máth-ēk(-a)* (i)
'strive' *mél(-ō)* (iii)   *(e-)mél-ēs(a-)* (ii) *(me-)mél-ēk(-a)* (i)
'happen' *téukh(-ō)* (iii)   *(é-)teuk-s(-a)* (iii) *(té-)teukh(-a)* (ii)
'arrive' *phthá-n(-ō)* (ii)   *(é-)phtha-s(-a)* (iii) *(é-)phtha-k(-a)* (v)

The allomorphy in the three stem classes is complicated, but it is by no means random. However, knowing one stem rarely helps one remembering another one, and, consequently, grammarians of Ancient Greek have not attempted to group verbs into conjugation classes globally.

7.2 Describing global inflection classes

The insightful description of inflection classes, particularly global inflection classes, has long been an important issue in morphology. First we observe that the morpheme-combination approach fares particularly badly here. If we wanted to describe the two Latin declensions in (7.13) in this framework, for instance, we would have to say that the lexeme stem *hort-* is marked in the lexicon for combining with the *-ī* allomorph of the genitive singular morpheme, the *-ō* allomorph of the dative singular morpheme, and so on. But, clearly, our description must contain more than just a list of morphemes and allomorphs with their combinatory potentials, because otherwise we would miss the generalization that not any choice of allomorphs in (7.13) is possible in Latin.

Now let us see what a word-based description along the lines of Section 3.2.2 would look like. The relation between the inflected forms of a global inflection class can be seen as parallel to the relation between two derivationally related lexemes. Thus, the relation between *hortī* 'garden, NOM.PL' and *hortōrum* 'garden, GEN.PL' can be characterized by the rule in (7.16). The full form of the rule is given in (7.16a), and (7.16b) shows an equivalent abbreviated notation.

(7.16) a.
$$\begin{bmatrix} /X\bar{\imath}/_N \\ 'x' \\ \text{CASE:} \quad \text{NOMINATIVE} \\ \text{NUMBER: PLURAL} \end{bmatrix} \leftrightarrow \begin{bmatrix} /X\bar{o}rum/_N \\ 'x' \\ \text{CASE:} \quad \text{GENITIVE} \\ \text{NUMBER: PLURAL} \end{bmatrix}$$

    b. $[/X\bar{\imath}/_{\text{NOM.PL}}] \leftrightarrow [/X\bar{o}rum/_{\text{GEN.PL}}]$

The fact that there is no Latin noun with a nominative plural in -*ī* and a genitive plural in -*uum* is thus expressed by the non-existence of a rule that would link these two suffixes.

(7.16) is certainly part of what speakers know, but they know more: a correct genitive plural form can be created on the basis of every other word-form in the paradigm, and in fact every form can be created on the basis of every other form. Since there are ten forms in the paradigm, we can posit 45 pairwise rules like (7.16). Now recall from Section 3.2.2 that, even in derivational morphology, there is sometimes reason for positing rules that involve more than two word-schemas. If we adopt the formalism proposed in (3.20), we can formulate the rule in (7.17), which contains 10 corresponding word-schemas.

(7.17) {[/Xus/$_{\text{NOM.SG}}$], [/Xī/$_{\text{GEN.SG}}$], [/Xō/$_{\text{DAT.SG}}$], [/Xum/$_{\text{ACC.SG}}$], [/Xō/$_{\text{ABL.SG}}$], [/Xī/$_{\text{NOM.PL}}$], [/Xōrum/$_{\text{GEN.PL}}$], [/Xīs/$_{\text{DAT.PL}}$], [/Xōs/$_{\text{ACC.PL}}$], [/Xīs/$_{\text{ABL.PL}}$]}

Clearly, this word-based rule is just a notational variant of the paradigms that we find in Latin school grammars and in (7.13) above. Latin school grammars do not usually have a variable, instead giving a concrete lexeme like *hortus* to make the description more concrete. But everyone understands that *hortus* is just an example and really stands for /Xus/. Thus, the word-based description is just a somewhat more explicit variant of what school grammars have long been doing. In what follows, we will call rules like (7.17) **paradigm rules**.

Such word-based rules capture the generalization that the allomorphs within the paradigm all depend on each other, but we still need to ask what information is contained in the lexical entry of *hortus* or *gradus* that tells speakers which of the competing paradigms should be followed. In these two cases at least, the nominative singular, which is used as citation form, is of no help. One traditional approach consists in giving arbitrary diacritic names to the paradigm rules that describe the inflection classes, and marking each lexeme with a **diacritic feature** in its lexical entry. In Latin, there is a tradition of numbering the declension classes that goes back to the grammarian Priscian. In this tradition, *hortus* would be said to belong to the second declension, and *gradus* to the fourth declension. For example, the lexical entry of *hortus* would contain, in addition to its phonological, syntactic and semantic features, a purely morphological diacritic feature '[second declension]'. Thus this approach requires a special look-up procedure that creates the correct inflected forms on the basis of the paradigm rules that are stored in the grammar. This is a very economical solution in some sense, because numerical diacritics are easy to handle, and many dictionaries of languages with global inflection classes have adopted it. However, it is questionable whether the human cognitive apparatus allows the device of diacritic features for inflection classes. Diacritic features are very efficient in computer programs, but there does not seem to be any other evidence that human memory ever makes use of such arbitrary diacritics.

Thus, linguists who are interested in cognitively realistic descriptions of inflection have looked for alternatives. A possibility that has often been adopted by dictionaries as well is to list several **reference forms** of the lexeme that together permit a unique assignment to one of the inflection classes. For example, descriptions of Latin often give the genitive singular form of a noun in addition to the nominative (*hortus, hortī; gradus, gradūs*). Since there are no two declension classes that have the same suffixes in the nominative and genitive singular, this method provides the same information as the declension class diacritic. And, unlike the diacritic, it can plausibly be applied to models of the mental lexicon. Speakers can be assumed to remember the nominative and genitive singular forms of each lexeme, and, by matching these two forms against the word-schemas in their paradigm rules, they can determine all the other forms of the paradigm. Remembering two inflected forms instead of a stem and a diacritic feature is less economical, but probably more realistic.

This approach in terms of stored reference forms also has the advantage that it can explain **class shifts** – i.e. diachronic changes by which a lexeme changes its inflection class. For example, in later Latin quite a few nouns of the *u*-declension shifted to the *o*-declension – e.g. *senātus* 'senate' (older genitive form *senātūs*, newer genitive *senātī*), *exercitus* 'army', *frūctus* 'fruit'. To explain this shift, we need assume only that the innovating speakers did not remember the genitive form of these nouns for some reason (perhaps because it had become less frequent as a result of semantic change). Now if they remember only the nominative form, the word matches both paradigm rules – i.e. it could belong either to the *o*-declension or to the *u*-declension. In such situations of choice, speakers naturally opt for those rules that generalize over more items. Latin always had many more *o*-declension nouns than *u*-declension nouns, so that the *o*-declension rule was stronger. This explains why shifts from the *u*-declension to the *o*-declension are common in Latin, but shifts in the opposite direction do not occur (see Wurzel 1987: 79). Similarly, verbs belonging to the R-conjugation in Martuthunira (see (7.14)) have been shifting to the L-conjugation. If a speaker only remembers the (probably more frequent) present-tense form of a verb of the R-conjugation, then there is no indication that it could not belong to the L-conjugation. Since there are many more L-conjugation verbs than R-conjugation verbs, the L-conjugation rule is stronger and we expect shifts to occur only in one direction, from R-conjugation to L-conjugation. This is indeed what we observe; the closely related language Panyjima has carried the change even further and has lost the R-conjugation completely.

The solution to the class-assignment problem in terms of stored reference forms leads to the question of which forms of the paradigm are the reference forms. In a pedagogical description or a dictionary, a consistent answer to this question has to be found for practical reasons. However, a cognitively oriented morphological description need not necessarily make a commitment here. Recall from Section 3.1 that it is quite plausible to assume that many inflected forms are stored even though they could in principle be derived by rules. Thus, all we have to assume is that a speaker who knows the inflectional behaviour of a word remembers enough forms of the word to determine its behaviour. Thus, a speaker of Latin might know the genitive singular of some words, the accusative singular of others and the nominative plural of yet others. And different speakers of Latin might store different reference forms for different words. Purely linguistic methods do not permit us to determine what exactly speakers have in their mental lexicons.

7.3 Inheritance hierarchies

From what we have said so far, one might get the impression that inflection classes may differ arbitrarily in the kinds of markers that they exhibit. But in fact different inflection classes often show great similarities, to the point where it is unclear whether a separate inflection class needs to be set up. Let us consider the seven most important inflection classes of Modern Greek nouns, shown in the traditional way in (7.18). (To simplify the presentation, stress is ignored here.)

		os-declension	*as*-declension	*us*-declension	
SG	NOM	*nomos*	*pateras*	*papus*	
	ACC	*nomo*	*patera*	*papu*	
	GEN	*nomu*	*patera*	*papu*	
PL	NOM	*nomi*	*pateres*	*papuðes*	
	ACC	*nomus*	*pateres*	*papuðes*	
	GEN	*nomon*	*pateron*	*papuðon*	
		'law (masc.)'	'father (masc.)'	'grandfather (masc.)'	

		a-declension	*i1*-declension	*i2*-declension	*u*-declension
SG	NOM	*imera*	*texni*	*poli*	*maimu*
	ACC	*imera*	*texni*	*poli*	*maimu*
	GEN	*imeras*	*texnis*	*poleos*	*maimus*
PL	NOM	*imeres*	*texnes*	*poles*	*maimuðes*
	ACC	*imeres*	*texnes*	*poles*	*maimuðes*
	GEN	*imeron*	*texnon*	*poleon*	*maimuðon*
		'day (fem.)'	'art, skill (fem.)'	'town (fem.)'	'monkey (fem.)'

(7.18)

In the more abstract notation of our paradigm rules, these could be written as (7.19).

(7.19) a. Paradigm rule for the *os*-declension
   $\{ [/\mathrm{Xos}/_{\mathrm{NOM.SG}}], [/\mathrm{Xo}/_{\mathrm{ACC.SG}}], [/\mathrm{Xu}/_{\mathrm{GEN.SG}}],$
   $[/\mathrm{Xi}/_{\mathrm{NOM.PL}}], [/\mathrm{Xus}/_{\mathrm{ACC.PL}}], [/\mathrm{Xon}/_{\mathrm{GEN.PL}}] \}$
   b. Paradigm rule for the *as*-declension
   $\{ [/\mathrm{Xas}/_{\mathrm{NOM.SG}}], [/\mathrm{Xa}/_{\mathrm{ACC.SG}}], [/\mathrm{Xa}/_{\mathrm{GEN.SG}}],$
   $[/\mathrm{Xes}/_{\mathrm{NOM.PL}}], [/\mathrm{Xes}/_{\mathrm{ACC.PL}}], [/\mathrm{Xon}/_{\mathrm{GEN.PL}}] \}$
   and so on.[1]

None of the seven classes in (7.18) is completely identical to any other class, but the similarities among them are evident. Theoretically, given seven different declensions and six cells in the paradigm, we could have ($6 \times 7 =$) 42 totally different suffixes. In reality we have almost the opposite: the declensions seem to differ only slightly from each other. One might even propose that some of them could be lumped together, especially the *a*-declension and the *i1*-declension.

In order to express these generalizations, we will introduce one additional descriptive device: the **rule-schema**, which generalizes over rules in much the same way as word-schemas generalize over words. Thus, given the paradigm rules for the *a*-declension and the *i1*-declension in (7.20), we can formulate the rule-schema in (7.21), which subsumes both rules. In addition to the stem variable X, this also contains the variable V for the vowel, which may be instantiated by *a* or *i*.

(7.20) a. Paradigm rule for the *a*-declension
   $\{ [/\mathrm{Xa}/_{\mathrm{NOM.SG}}], [/\mathrm{Xa}/_{\mathrm{ACC.SG}}], [/\mathrm{Xas}/_{\mathrm{GEN.SG}}],$
   $[/\mathrm{Xes}/_{\mathrm{NOM.PL}}], [/\mathrm{Xes}/_{\mathrm{ACC.PL}}], [/\mathrm{Xon}/_{\mathrm{GEN.PL}}] \}$
   b. Paradigm rule for the *i1*-declension
   $\{ [/\mathrm{Xi}/_{\mathrm{NOM.SG}}], [/\mathrm{Xi}/_{\mathrm{ACC.SG}}], [/\mathrm{Xis}/_{\mathrm{GEN.SG}}],$
   $[/\mathrm{Xes}/_{\mathrm{NOM.PL}}], [/\mathrm{Xes}/_{\mathrm{ACC.PL}}], [/\mathrm{Xon}/_{\mathrm{GEN.PL}}] \}$

(7.21) Rule schema for (7.19a–b)
   $\{ [/\mathrm{XV}/_{\mathrm{NOM.SG}}], [/\mathrm{XV}/_{\mathrm{ACC.SG}}], [/\mathrm{XVs}/_{\mathrm{GEN.SG}}],$
   $[/\mathrm{Xes}/_{\mathrm{NOM.PL}}], [/\mathrm{Xes}/_{\mathrm{ACC.PL}}], [/\mathrm{Xon}/_{\mathrm{GEN.PL}}] \}$

To make the notation more reader-friendly, let us introduce the formalism in Figure 7.1, where the slashes for the phonological representation and the inflectional categories are omitted for the sake of simplicity. In this figure, the two declensions and the rule schema are shown in a tree format, the standard format for representing taxonomic hierarchies. In effect, the *a*-declension and the *i1*-declension are subtypes of the declension described by the rule-schema of (7.21), in much the same way as, say, a violin and a cello are subtypes of stringed instruments, and these are again a subtype of musical instrument (see Figure 7.2). The taxonomic hierarchy of declension classes is completely parallel to hierarchies of this familiar kind.

---

[1] There is no point in rewriting all the paradigms of (7.18) in this format, because the tabular format is more perspicuous than the format with brackets and subscripts.

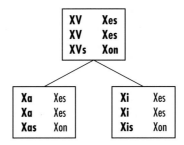

Figure 7.1 A hierarchy of declension classes

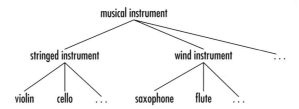

Figure 7.2 A hierarchy of musical instruments

By setting up the hierarchy in Figure 7.1, we claim that the similarity between the two declensions is captured in the speakers' internalized grammar. Now, if the speakers do indeed abstract such a rule-schema from the individual paradigm rules, this means that they do not have to store all the details of the individual rules. Those pieces of information that are identical in the rule-schema and in the individual rule need not be specified twice. They can be specified once in the rule-schema, and the individual paradigm rule can **inherit** the information from the superordinate node in the hierarchy. This is symbolized by the use of boldface and normal print in Figure 7.1: boldface information is necessary, and normal-print information is redundant and could in principle be inherited from the superordinate node. (If we wanted a completely redundancy-free representation of grammatical information, normal-print material could simply be omitted. However, as we saw earlier in the discussion of word storage (Section 3.1), lack of redundancy does not seem to be a priority for human memory.)

The taxonomic hierarchy in Figure 7.1 is thus called an **inheritance hierarchy**. Let us now extend this hierarchy to subsume the other Modern Greek inflection classes that we saw earlier. Figure 7.3 shows an attempt to draw a single inheritance hierarchy for the seven classes of (7.18) that has four different levels of abstractness.

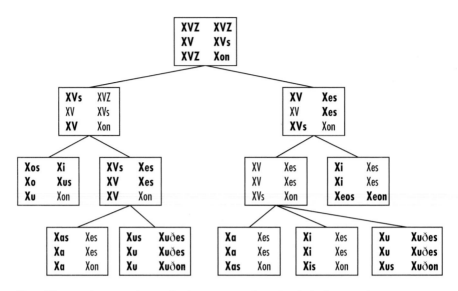

Figure 7.3 An inheritance hierarchy for seven Modern Greek declension classes

The top-level rule-schema is so abstract that it consists almost exclusively of variables (X for the stem, V for a vowel following the stem and Z for anything else, including zero, that follows that vowel). The only concrete elements that all classes share are the genitive plural suffix -*on* and the last consonant of the accusative plural suffix (-*s*). The major split is between the masculine classes (-*os*, -*as*, -*us*), on the one hand, and the feminine classes (-*a*, -*i1*, -*i2*, -*u*), on the other: all masculines are characterized by an -*s* in the nominative singular, and all feminines are characterized by an -*s* in the genitive singular (Modern Greek is thus like Sanskrit and Italian in that gender plays an important role in inflection classes (see Section 7.1)).

The inheritance network allows us a flexible and sophisticated answer to the question of how many different inflection classes should be set up for the Modern Greek data in (7.18). At the lowest level, there are seven classes, and we may call these **microclasses** (the *os*-class and the *i2*-class are microclasses as well, although they are shown only at the intermediate level in Figure 7.3). At an intermediate level, we might say that there are four classes (some of them with subclasses), and at a higher level, we could say that it has just two **macroclasses**, the masculine and feminine declension types.

The hierarchy in Figure 7.1 is just a single tree with no cross-classification, but in reality such cross-classifications are possible, and examples are easy to find. This is again parallel to other domains of knowledge. To return to the example of Figure 7.2, one could cross-classify musical instruments into classical instruments (violin, cello, flute) and modern instruments (saxophone, electric guitar). One obvious generalization that is missed by Figure 7.3 but

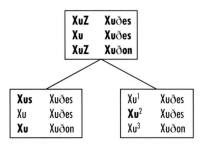

Figure 7.4 A rule-schema/inheritance hierarchy for two inflection classes

that is certainly not lost on speakers of Greek is the similarity between the
us-class and the *u*-class. This may be expressed by the hierarchy in Figure 7.4.
The topmost rule-schema in Figure 7.4 and the links to the two paradigm
rules should be added to the hierarchy in Figure 7.3. This would no longer
be a single hierarchy, and the resulting structure is more complicated, but this
kind of multiple inheritance must clearly be allowed in morphology.

We should now ask what evidence we have for positing ever more
abstract rule-schemas, as in Figure 7.3. Could it not be that speakers simply
memorize the seven concrete paradigm rules and do not relate them to one
another? Of course, linguists easily recognize further generalizations and
are eager to express them, but can we be sure that speakers recognize them
as well? This is an important question if we want our descriptions to be not
just elegant, but also cognitively realistic. As we saw in Section 3.1, only if a
linguistic pattern is productive can we be sure that the pattern exists in the
speakers' minds and not just in the eye of the linguistic beholder.
Determining productivity or lack thereof is relatively straightforward for a
morphological rule (see Chapter 6) and for an inflection class (see Section
7.5), but can a rule-schema for inflection classes be said to exhibit productivity? Normally morphologists do not talk about rule-schemas being
productive, but there is an analogue of productivity for inflectional rule-
schemas: diachronic change by which an inflection class is attracted to a
rule-schema and changes to conform to it. For example, the Modern Greek
i2-declension used to have the ending *-is* in the nominative singular
($\{[/\text{Xis}/_{\text{NOM.SG}}], [/\text{Xi}/_{\text{ACC.SG}}], [/\text{Xeos}/_{\text{GEN.SG}}], \ldots\}$), e.g. *polis/poli/poleos* 'town'. The
change from /Xis/ to /Xi/ in the nominative singular was clearly a mor-
phological, not a phonological change. The paradigm rule of the
i2-declension clashed with the general schema for the other feminine microclasses in an important respect (the nominative singular in *-is*), and, by
changing this, that schema was able to subsume the rule for the *i2*-declen-
sion as well. If the speakers had had only the rules for the individual
declensions, this change would be mysterious. Thus, diachronic change in
inflection classes may provide a crucial check for the reality of linguistic
generalizations.

Before leaving the topic of inheritance hierarchies, we should mention the possibility of mismatches within such a hierarchy. In the hierarchy of Figure 7.3, there is never a conflict between a lower and a higher node; higher nodes are merely less specific. Now it has been suggested that such conflicts should be allowed, and that specifications in a lower node should be able to **override** specifications in a higher node. For example, the Greek *os*-declension and the *a*-declension could be subsumed under the same rule schema as shown in Figure 7.5.

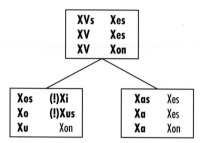

Figure 7.5 An inheritance hierarchy with a mismatch

Here there is a **mismatch** between the nominative and accusative plural forms /Xi/ and /Xus/ and the corresponding forms specified in the higher node (/Xes/). The exclamation mark in the notation shows that a higher specification is overridden. The forms /Xes/ in the higher rule schema are no longer fully schematic, but they are a **default** that applies unless it is over-ridden. By using the device of **default specifications** and overrides, the inheritance hierarchy can be simplified. Thus, in Figure 7.3 one of the rule schemas could be dispensed with if the description of Figure 7.5 were adopted.

7.4 The role of stems in inflection

In many languages, it is useful in the description of inflection to set up **abstract stems**, formal entities without any coherent meaning to which further elements are added to yield the inflected forms. Consider the Persian verb forms in (7.22).

(7.22) INFINITIVE		PAST TENSE	PRESENT TENSE
mundæn	1SG	*mundæm*	*mimunæm*
'to stay'	2SG	*mundi*	*mimuni*
	3SG	*mund*	*mimune*
	1PL	*mundim*	*mimunim*
	2PL	*mundid*	*mimunid*
	3PL	*mundænd*	*mimunænd*

(Mahootian 1997: 28, 236)

All past-tense forms share the stem *mund-*, and all present-tense forms share the stem *mun-*. All Persian verbs behave like *mundæn* in this respect. But the formal relation between the two stems is not always the same, as the seven verbs in (7.23) show.

(7.23)

INFINITIVE	1ST SG PAST TENSE	1ST SG PRESENT TENSE	
mundæn	mundæm	mimunæm	'stay'
xæridæn	xæridæm	mixæræm	'buy'
mordæn	mordæm	mimiræm	'die'
šekaftæn	šekaftæm	mišekafæm	'split'
šetaftæn	šetaftæn	mišetabæm	'hurry'
nešæstæn	nešæstæm	minešinim	'sit'
didæn	didæm	mibinæm	'see'

(Mahootian 1997: 231–7)

In these and all other Persian verbs, the infinitive and the past-tense forms share a common element: *xærid-, mund-, mord-*, etc., called the **past stem** in Persian grammar, which is opposed to the **present stem** (*xær-, mun, mir-*, etc.). Once we know these two stems of a verb, all its inflected forms can be easily created on the model of the paradigm (7.22). The past stem is often formed from the present stem by adding a suffix (*-id/-d/-t*), and one might want to say that this suffix expresses the past tense in Persian, just as the suffix *-ba* expresses the past tense in Spanish (see the paradigm in Figures 4.2–4.3). That does not work in Persian, however, because the infinitive (which semantically has nothing to do with the past tense) also takes this suffix and then adds the further element *-æn*. This could in principle be a case of an accidental inflectional homonymy, but when we examine the data in (7.23) more closely, we see that this is impossible: the relation between the past stem and the present stem is quite unpredictable for many verbs, occasionally even suppletive. So many parallels between the formation of the past tense and the infinitive cannot be accidental. Thus, morphologists find it convenient to recognize an abstract stem here that has no meaning attached to it but is justified because it allows an economical description of the forms.

Such abstract stems in morphology are quite common in Indo-European languages, but they are also found elsewhere. Consider the data from Lezgian in (7.24).

(7.24)

MASDAR	OPTATIVE	IMPERFECTIVE	PROHIBITIVE	
raxun	raxuraj	raxazwa	raxamir	'talk'
kiẑin	kiẑiraj	kiẑizwa	kiẑimir	'write'
qʰürün	qʰürüraj	qʰürezwa	qʰüremir	'laugh'
at'un	at'uraj	at'uzwa	at'umir	'cut'
q'in	q'iraj	req'izwa	req'imir	'die, kill'
atun	aturaj	qwezwa	qwemir	'come'
t'ün	t'üraj	nezwa	neda	'eat'

(Haspelmath 1993: 122–30)

Again, for an economical description we need one stem from which the masdar (action noun) and the optative are derived, and one stem from which the imperfective and the prohibitive are derived. And, again, no clear meaning can be assigned to these stems. (See also (2.33) for an abstract stem in Lezgian noun inflection.)

An alternative to the description in terms of abstract stems would be a description in terms of **Priscianic formation** (so called because it was used by the Latin grammarian Priscian, in the sixth century CE), whereby a member of an inflectional paradigm is formed from another member of the paradigm to which it need not be closely related semantically. A well-known case in Latin is the past passive participle and the future active participle, which are based on the same stem. Some representative forms are given in (7.25).

(7.25)

INFINITIVE	PAST PASS. PART.	FUTURE ACT. PART.	
laudāre	laudātus	laudātūrus	'praise'
monēre	monitus	monitūrus	'warn'
dūcere	ductus	ductūrus	'lead'
vehere	vectus	vectūrus	'carry'
mittere	missus	missūrus	'send'
haerēre	haesus	haesūrus	'stick'
premere	pressus	pressūrus	'press'
ferre	lātus	lātūrus	'bear'

(Aronoff 1994: ch. 2)

A Priscianic description would say that the form of the future active participle is obtained by replacing the case-number ending (-us in the citation form) by the ending -ūr(us). The meaning is quite independent of this: obviously the *future active* participle cannot be based semantically on the *past passive* participle.

A description in terms of Priscianic formation is equivalent to a description in terms of stems for most purposes, but twentieth-century linguists have generally adopted analyses in terms of abstract stems. Pedagogical grammars, however, have continued the tradition of Priscianic formation. But even for a linguist, a stem-based analysis is perhaps less attractive in cases like the following from Tümpisa Shoshone. This language has two non-nominative case forms, an objective case and a possessive case. The formation of these cases is illustrated in (7.26).

(7.26)

NOMINATIVE	OBJECTIVE	POSSESSIVE	
mupin	mupitta	mupittan	'nose'
tümpi	tümpitta	tümpittan	'rock'
nümü	nümi	nümin	'person'
piammütsi	piammütsia	piammütsian	'baby'
kahni	kahni	kahnin	'house'

(Dayley 1989: 185–6)

The objective case is formed from the nominative in various ways (one of them being identity to the nominative), but the possessive is systematically formed from the objective by adding a further suffix -*n*. If we wanted to describe this pattern in terms of abstract stems, we would have to set up a non-nominative stem that yields the possessive form by addition of -*n* and the objective form by addition of nothing. Of course, such a description is perfectly possible, but nothing seems to be gained when compared to the Priscianic solution.

As we noted, affixes that form an abstract stem cannot be assigned any clear meaning, and they are often treated as **empty morphemes** by morphologists, where 'empty' means that they are meaningless, though of course not functionless (see Section 2.6). In morphological practice, they are often called *stem affixes, stem extensions, thematic affixes*[1] or simply *thematic vowels* when they are vowels (as in the Lezgian case in (7.24)). They behave like ordinary morphemes in several other respects: for example, they may exhibit allomorphy (as in all the cases we saw in this section), their allomorphy constitutes inflection classes, they may be productive and unproductive, and so on.

7.5 Productivity of inflection classes

Like word-formation patterns, inflection classes may be more or less productive, but the productivity criterion of applicability to new bases must be used in a somewhat different way than in word-formation. In word-formation, a new base can be an existing word that has simply never been used before with a certain pattern, but in inflection this does not work, because all lexemes are expected to have inflected forms for all categories. For instance, we cannot test whether the Welsh inflection class constituted by the plural suffix -*edd* (e.g. *bys/bysedd* 'finger(s)') is productive by trying to apply it to bases that have not been used with -*edd* before, because all nouns have a plural form. Thus, the fact that -*edd* cannot be used with *llestr* 'dish' (**llestredd*) does not tell us much, because the conventionally fixed plural of *llestr* is *llestri* 'dishes' (using the plural allomorph -*i*).

Thus, applicability to new bases must mean one of two things in inflection: either (i) it means the ability of an inflection class to attract new members by **inflection class shift** in diachronic change, or (ii) it means the ability to apply to novel lexemes that come into the language, either as **loanwords** or as **neologisms** formed by productive word-formation rules. We can distinguish at least three degrees of inflection-class productivity on the basis of these criteria (Dressler 1997), as summarized in Table 7.1.

---

[1] Note that *theme* is an older term for 'stem'.

Criteria and examples	Highly productive classes	Classes with intermediate productivity	Unproductive classes
Criteria			
Apply to loanwords	YES	NO	NO
Attract class-shifting lexemes	YES	NO	NO
Apply to productively formed neologisms	YES	YES	NO
Examples			
Welsh plurals	*-au, -iaid*	*-oedd*	*-edd*
Italian verbs	*-are*	*-ire*	*-ere*
Italian nouns	*-o/i*	*-a/i, -e/i*	—
Russian nouns	*-C* (M), *-a*(F)	*-o* (N)	*-ja* (N)
English past tense	*-ed*	—	vowel change
English plural	*-s*	—	vowel change

Table 7.1 Three degrees of inflection-class productivity

Only highly productive classes are able to accommodate loanwords and to attract class-shifting lexemes from other, unstable classes. Productively formed neologisms, by contrast, often go into classes with intermediate productivity. Completely unproductive classes do not get new members at all, and, since they inevitably lose some members (e.g. when a word becomes obsolete), they are ultimately doomed to disintegration.

For exemplification, let us go back to Welsh plurals (King 1993: 52–64). Welsh has several highly productive plural classes that can accommodate loanwords from English – for instance, the suffix *-au*, which is the most common Welsh plural suffix (e.g. *siop/siopau* 'shop(s)', *trên/trenau* 'train(s)'), or *-iaid*, which is often used with nouns denoting persons (e.g. *doctor/doctoriaid* 'doctor(s)', *biwrocrat/biwrocratiaid* 'bureaucrat(s)'). Both these classes also apply to regularly formed neologisms. Thus, *-au* is always used with quality nouns in *-deb* (e.g. *ffurfioldeb* 'formality', *ffurfioldebau* 'formalities'), and *-iaid* is always used with agent nouns in *-dur* (e.g. *pechadur* 'sinner', *pechaduriaid* 'sinners'). The class in *-au* also shows its productivity in attracting members of other classes – for instance, from the class of plurals in *-oedd*. For example, *amser* 'time' has an older plural *amseroedd* and a newer plural *amserau*, and *cylch* 'circle' has an older plural *cylchoedd* and a newer plural *cylchau*. The plural class in *-oedd* is thus losing members, but it has at least intermediate productivity in that productively formed place-nouns in *-fa* have *-oedd* plurals (e.g. *meithrinfa* 'nursery', *meithrinfaoedd* 'nurseries'). Completely unproductive is, for instance, the plural suffix *-edd* of *bys/bysedd* 'finger(s)', as well as the various classes of vowel-changing plurals (e.g. *ffordffyrd* 'road(s)', *asgell/esgyll* 'wing(s)').

In Italian, the verbal inflection class in *-are* is highly productive: It accommodates loanwords (e.g. *dribblare* 'dribble') and occurs in homegrown neologisms (e.g. in *-izzare* '-ize' or *-ificare* '-ify'). The inflection class in *-ire* is not used with loanwords, but it can be used with newly formed lexemes such as *imbruttire* 'make ugly' (from *brutto* 'ugly'). The inflection class in *-ere* (e.g. *vedere* 'see', *cadere* 'fall') is not productive at all. In Italian nouns, the classes *-o/-i* (masculine) and *-a/-e* (feminine) are highly productive: they are used with loanwords (e.g. *il chimono*, plural *i chimoni* 'kimono(s)', *la giungla*, plural *le giungle* 'jungle(s)'), and occasionally they attract members from other inflection classes in non-standard varieties of Italian (e.g. *il pane* 'bread' becomes *il pano* 'bread', *la moglie* becomes *la moglia* 'wife'). The class in *-a/-i* (masculine) cannot be used with loanwords: the noun *lama* 'Tibetan monk' does not get the plural *-i* (**i lami* 'lamas') but remains unchanged in the plural (i.e. it joins the class of indeclinables, like all consonant-final loanwords). However, the *-a/-i* class is not totally unproductive, as it is used with the productive suffix *-ista* (e.g. *leghista* 'follower of the Lega', plural *leghisti*). There is no real unproductive class in Italian, unless one regards the few irregular nouns (*uomo/uomini* 'man/men', *bue/buoi* 'ox(en)', etc.) as classes of their own.

In Russian, consonant-final masculines and the *a*-class are the two highly productive classes that have been absorbing many lexemes from other inflection classes over the past millennium. They can be used with loanwords, e.g. *komp'juter* becomes a consonant-final masculine, and *disketta* joins the *a*-class. The *o*-class (consisting almost entirely of neuters) is not highly productive – even loanwords ending in *-o* (such as *pal'to* 'coat' from French *paletot*) do not follow this class but are indeclinable. However, the class still gets new members through productive suffixes like *-stvo* (e.g. *professor-stvo* 'professorship'). There is a small class of neuters in *-ja* (e.g. *vremja* 'time') that is totally unproductive.

Inflection classes and their productivity have been hotly debated among psycholinguists since the 1980s. In this book, psycholinguistic issues of language processing and acquisition had to be left aside, but the controversy over inflection classes should be briefly mentioned. One school of thought has defended the idea that there are two quite different modes of processing inflected words (hence, this is called the **dual-processing model**): productive, regular forms are processed by **rules**, whereas irregular, unproductive forms are **stored** in the mental lexicon as an associative network. The opposing view is that there is just a single mechanism of processing involving a network of connections (hence, this is called the **connectionist** or **single-mechanism model**). Most of the psycholinguistic evidence that has been cited in this debate comes from English, where both nouns and verbs show an impoverished pattern. In both cases there is a single large productive class (past tense *-ed*, plural *-s*), and a rather unsystematic set of unproductive miniclasses or individual words (mostly involving vowel

changes). English completely lacks inflection classes with intermediate productivity, and it also lacks an unproductive but still sizeable (and hence
regular) class such as Welsh *-edd* plurals or German *-er* plurals. Thus,
(ir)regularity and **(un)productivity** largely coincide in English, and such
data may easily lead one to the view that language possesses two completely different kinds of processing modes. It seems that the debate over
dual versus single processing can be resolved only if data from inflectionally richer languages are taken into account so that the various factors can
be separated more clearly.

Finally, we need briefly to address the question of how speakers know
whether an inflection class is productive or unproductive. This is not a problem for intermediate productivity, because speakers just have to observe
which inflection class a productive word-formation pattern chooses. But
how do they know whether a pattern is highly productive? In the case of
loanword integration, there may exist learned conventions (especially when
a language routinely borrows from another one), but this seems implausible for productivity as evinced in class shift. We saw in Section 7.2 that, in
class shifts, classes with a higher type frequency (i.e. with a larger number
of members) usually attract members from smaller classes, whereas the
reverse case (shift from a larger to a smaller class) is quite unusual. Type frequency makes the right prediction in all cases that we saw in this section,
and in general in inflection it seems to work better as a predictor of productivity than in word-formation (see the discussion in Sections 6.4–6.5).
However, there are again cases where type frequency and productivity do
not go together, e.g. German plural formation: German has three productive
plural suffixes, *-en*, *-e* and *-s*. The former two suffixes have a much higher
type frequency than the latter suffix, but still *-s* is very productive in loanwords as well as in words where *-en* and *-e* are not appropriate for phonological reasons (however, it does not seem to attract class-shifting members).

7.6 Syncretism

Not uncommonly, two word-forms in an inflectional paradigm are phonologically identical, or, in other words, **homonymous**. For example, in the
present-tense paradigm of German verbs, the third person singular and the
second person plural, and the first and third person plural have the same
endings:

(7.27)	1SG	(ich)	spiele	'I play'
	2SG	(du)	spielst	'you(SG) play'
	3SG	(er/sie)	spielt	'he/she plays'
	1PL	(wir)	spielen	'we play'
	2PL	(ihr)	spielt	'you(PL) play'
	3PL	(sie)	spielen	'they play'

When the inflectional homonymy is systematic, we speak of **syncretism**, and homonymous forms of a paradigm are called **syncretic**.

7.6.1 Systematic versus accidental inflectional homonymy

How can we distinguish between systematic and accidental homonymy (see Zwicky 1991)? We will discuss three criteria, a quantitative criterion, a qualitative syntactic criterion and a diachronic criterion.

The quantitative criterion of systematicity is the extent to which the homonymy is found in different inflection classes. The two pairs of homonymous forms in (7.27) behave differently by this criterion. German has a small class of vowel-changing verbs that have a different stem vowel in the second and third person singular, e.g. *gebe/gibst/gibt* 'give', *falle/fällst/fällt* 'fall'. In these verbs, the third person singular and the second person plural are not identical, because the vowel alternation is restricted to the third person singular (3sg *gibt* versus 2pl *gebt*, 3sg *fällt* versus 2pl *fallt*), but the first person and third person plural are still identical. In fact, the first person and the third person plural are identical in all German verb paradigms, including the suppletive paradigm of *sein* 'be' (singular: *bin/bist/ist*, plural: *sind/seid/sind*). So in this respect, the 1pl/3pl homonymy (*spielen*) is more systematic than the 3sg/2pl homonymy (*spielt*).

The qualitative criterion concerns an interesting syntactic property of syncretic forms: they can be used in situations where two conflicting syntactic requirements must be fulfilled simultaneously. One such construction is shown in (7.28a), where the verb *spielt* has to agree simultaneously with both coordinands of the disjunction. Now there are situations where the two requirements are in conflict, as in (7.28b), where the verb is supposed to agree both with *ich* (first person singular) and with *du* (second person singular). Since there is no verb form that can do this, the sentence is ungrammatical.

(7.28) a. *Entweder Bierhoff oder Matthäus spielt gegen Bulgarien.*
'Either Bierhoff or Matthäus will play in the Bulgaria match.'
b. **Entweder ich oder du spiele/spielst gegen Bulgarien.*
'Either I or you(sg) will play in the Bulgaria match.'
c. *Entweder wir oder sie spielen gegen Bulgarien.*
'Either we or you will play in the Bulgaria match.'
d. **Entweder Bierhoff oder ihr spielt gegen Bulgarien.*
'Either Bierhoff or you(pl) will play in the Bulgaria match.'

However, when the two requirements are first or third person plural, as in (7.28c), there is a way to resolve the feature conflict: the syncretic form *spielen* can serve simultaneously as a first person plural and as a third person plural form. In this, it contrasts with the two homonymous forms *spielt* '3rd sg' and *spielt* '2nd pl': as we see in (7.28d), the form *spielt* cannot resolve the feature conflict, and hence we say that, in the case of *spielen*, we have systematic homonymy (i.e. syncretism), whereas, in the case of *spielt*, we are dealing with accidental homonymy. The syntactic criterion is much stronger than the quantitative criterion because it shows that speakers treat the two syncretic forms as related. In the case of German verbs, the quantitative criterion and the syntactic criterion give the same results: The identity of *spielt* (3SG) and *spielt* (2PL) is accidental, but the identity of *spielen* (1PL) and *spielen* (3PL) is systematic – i.e in the latter case we are dealing with syncretism.

The ability to resolve a feature conflict can be taken as a sufficient criterion for systematic homonymy, but it cannot be a necessary criterion because sometimes there are no relevant syntactic constructions that would impose conflicting requirements. For instance, if we want to know whether the frequent homonymy of the English past tense and the past participle (as in forms like *played, fed, thought*) is systematic, we cannot apply the syntactic criterion, because there are no constructions in which a verb should simultaneously be a past tense and a past participle. It is true that, for the vast majority of verbs, these forms are homonymous, but in Old English they were distinct for all verbs, and the present-day homonymy could be explained in almost all cases by regular phonological changes. Thus, the homonymy might still be accidental for English speakers. However, here the diachronic criterion can be invoked: there are a few verbs whose past-participle form became identical with the past-tense form through morphological, not phonological change: *stand/stood/stood* (cf. Old English *standan/stōd/gestanden*), *sit/sat/sat* (cf. Old English *sittan/sæt/geseten*). The morphological change is a strong indication that, at the time of the change, the homonymy of the two forms was perceived as systematic by the speakers.

7.6.2 Polyfunctionality versus vagueness

Once we have established that a case of identity is systematic and not accidental, the question arises whether we are really dealing with two different (though formally identical) forms that fill two cells in the paradigm, or whether there is perhaps just a single form that simply does not distinguish the relevant categories (i.e. that is vague with respect to the categories). Consider another example, Standard Arabic case inflection:

(7.29)

	SINGULAR	PLURAL
NOM	*ḥaywaan-un*	*ḥaywaan-aat-un*
GEN	*ḥaywaan-in*	*ḥaywaan-aat-in*
ACC	*ḥaywaan-an*	*ḥaywaan-aat-in*
	'animal'	'animals'

In the plural, both the genitive and the accusative end in *-in*, and the usual analysis is that we are dealing with syncretism here (this genitive–accusative homonymy is found in all non-singular forms, so it is unlikely to be accidental homonymy). But should we perhaps say instead that Arabic has a different case system in the plural, that it distinguishes only a direct and an oblique case? In other words, instead of (7.29), the standard analysis, one might propose (7.30) as an alternative, where the oblique case is vague with respect to the genitive/accusative distinction.

(7.30)

	SINGULAR
NOM	*ḥaywaan-un*
GEN	*ḥaywaan-in*
ACC	*ḥaywaan-an*

	PLURAL
NOM	*ḥaywaan-aat-un*
OBL	*ḥaywaan-aat-in*

Most linguists would not adopt this description, because it would make the rules of syntax more complicated. Instead of saying that a direct object is in the accusative case, we would have to say that it is in the accusative case in the singular and in the oblique case in the plural.

On the other hand, sometimes linguists do not find such a complication of the syntactic rules too inconvenient. For instance, many people would say that, in English, the direct object is marked by a special accusative case only when it is a personal pronoun (*The dog saw her*$_{ACC}$ versus *She*$_{NOM}$ *saw the dog*). This is a little awkward, but the alternative, that all other nouns exhibit nominative–accusative syncretism, does not seem very attractive either. In the next subsection we will see how we can reach a satisfactory description of these English facts from both a syntactic and a morphological point of view.

7.6.3 Natural syncretism

Sometimes the cells of a paradigm that exhibit syncretism form a natural class – i.e. they can be defined by a single set of inflectional categories. Consider the Lithuanian verb paradigm in (7.31) (present tense, indicative mood of *sup-* 'shake, swing').

(7.31)

	SINGULAR	PLURAL
1ST	*supu*	*supame*
2ND	*supi*	*supate*
3RD	*supa*	*supa*

Here the two syncretic cells are the third person singular and the third person plural, which form a natural class, because these are all and only the third person forms of the paradigm. Such syncretisms may be called **natural syncretisms**, and they are quite easy to describe. We can simply say that the Lithuanian third person form of the verb is *supa* – i.e. we do not have to mention the number dimension at all. We can visualize this description by a representation in which the syncretic form occupies an enlarged cell, as in (7.32).

(7.32)

	SINGULAR	PLURAL
1ST	*supu*	*supame*
2ND	*supi*	*supate*
3RD	*supa*	

In the more formal representation format of (7.17), we would say that the paradigm of *sup-* is described by the paradigm rule in (7.33), in which nothing is said about the number dimension for the form *supa*.

(7.33)   {[/Xu/$_{1.SG}$], [/Xi/$_{2.SG}$], [/Xa/$_3$], [/Xame/$_{1.PL}$], [/Xate/$_{2PL}$]}

Such a mode of description is called **underspecification**: we simply do not specify the value of certain dimensions in the paradigm rule. For the syntactic rule of agreement that interacts with these inflectional categories, this means that it should not require **feature identity**, but only **feature compatibility**. Both a singular and a plural subject NP are compatible with a form like *supa*, so the agreement relation works, even though *supa* is not specified for number.

A very similar account solves the problem of the English case syncretism in a word like *dog*, because the nominative and accusative form a natural class of categories. We can thus describe the inflectional paradigm of *dog* in the familiar way as in (7.34a). Unlike the personal pronoun *he* (see (7.34b)), *dog* is always underspecified for case.

(7.34) a. {[/dog/$_{SG}$], [/dogs/$_{PL}$]}
         b. {[/he/$_{NOM.SG}$], [/him/$_{ACC.SG}$], [/they/$_{NOM.PL}$], [/them/$_{ACC.PL}$]}

If we require just feature compatibility rather than feature identity, we can have a single syntactic rule for all types of nouns in English: 'A direct object is in the accusative case.' Since [/dog/$_{SG}$] is compatible with 'accusative', it is permitted as a direct object.

Thus, in the case of natural syncretisms, the underspecification analysis implies that we are dealing with vagueness rather than polyfunctionality.

But, of course, there are many instances of syncretism that cannot be described by underspecification. For these, we need a special type of rule: rules of referral, as discussed in the next subsection.

7.6.4 Rules of referral

Consider the three Old Chuch Slavonic nominal inflection classes in (7.35). Only the case endings are given here in order to save space.

(7.35)

	ŭ-class			a-class			ĭ-class		
	SG	DU	PL	SG	DU	PL	SG	DU	PL
NOM	-ŭ	-a	-i	-a	-ě	-y	-ĭ	-i	-i
ACC	-ŭ	-a	-y	-o	-ě	-y	-ĭ	-i	-i
GEN	-a	-u	-ŭ	-y	-u	-ŭ	-i	-ĭju	-ĭjĭ
LOC	-ě	-u	-ěxŭ	-ě	-u	-axŭ	-i	-ĭju	-ĭxŭ
DAT	-u	-oma	-omŭ	-ě	-ama	-amŭ	-i	-ĭma	-ĭmŭ
INSTR	-omĭ	-oma	-y	-ojǫ	-ama	-ami	-ĭ	-ĭma	-ĭmĭ

Especially in the dual, we have a lot of syncretism: The nominative and accusative, the genitive and locative, and the dative and instrumental are systematically homonymous (this is true also of the other inflection classes not shown here). These syncretisms are clearly not natural syncretisms, because these three pairs of cases do not have any exclusive properties. Another case of an unnatural syncretism was seen in (7.27): the first and third person plural do not constitute a natural class, yet they are identical in all inflection classes and all tenses and moods in German.

For unnatural syncretisms, we need a special type of rule that says that several forms in the paradigm are identical. Such rules are called **rules of referral**. We can formulate the rule for the nominative–accusative dual as in (7.36).

$$(7.36) \quad \begin{bmatrix} /X/_N \\ \text{'NOM.DU'} \end{bmatrix} \leftrightarrow \begin{bmatrix} /X/_N \\ \text{'ACC.DU'} \end{bmatrix}$$

This rule generalizes over all the paradigms of Old Church Slavonic. It can be thought of as a kind of paradigm rule schema that relates two cells in the paradigm to each other.

That such rules of referral are real rules for speakers and not just thought up by linguists becomes clear when they trigger morphological changes. An example comes from Old High German (Wurzel 1987: 70–1). The paradigm of neuter nouns of the a-declension that must have existed in pre-Old High German is shown in (7.37).

(7.37)

		SINGULAR	PLURAL	SINGULAR	PLURAL
	NOM	wort	wort	faz	fazzu
	ACC	wort	wort	faz	fazzu
	GEN	wortes	worto	fazzes	fazzo
	DAT	worte	wortum	fazze	fazzum
		'word'		'barrel'	

The original suffix of the nominative/accusative was -u, as is clear from comparative evidence. This suffix was lost by regular sound change in heavy-syllable words like *wort*, but it was preserved in light-syllable words like *faz*. Now apparently speakers formulated a rule of referral '[/X/_{N.NEUT} 'NOM/ACC.SG'] ↔ [/X/_{N.NEUT} 'NOM/ACC.PL']' – i.e. the singular and the plural forms of the nominative and accusative are identical. This rule was originally based only on nouns of the *wort* class, but since the *faz* class had a much lower type frequency, it was also affected by this rule, and by the time of Old High German the paradigm of (7.37) has changed: the forms *fazzu* have been replaced by *faz*, in accordance with the rule of referral.

7.7 Missing cells: defectiveness, deponency and periphrasis

Nobody is perfect, not even inflectional paradigms. In the previous section we encountered one way in which cells in an inflectional paradigm may be imperfect. They may be identical to other cells in the paradigm. In this section, we look at other ways in which cells fail to correspond to the ideal of Chapter 4.

First of all, they may simply lack word-forms. Lexemes with missing word-forms are called **defective lexemes**. An example is the Italian verb *incombere* 'be incumbent', which lacks a past participle and therefore cannot be used in the compound past tense. In French, the verbs *frire* 'fry', *déchoir* 'fall' and *clore* 'close' lack an imperfective past tense. In English, the verb *abide* sounds strange in the past tense (*??They abided/abode by the referee's decision*). In Russian, a number of verbs do not have a first person singular in the present/future tense (e.g. *pobedit'* 'win, defeat'), and the noun *mečta* 'dream' lacks a genitive plural form.

Defectiveness is surprising not only because it disturbs the functionality of the language. Sometimes one wants to say 'I'll win' in Russian, but the system does not allow it. Of course, speakers are not condemned to silence in such cases – there is always a way around the defective form. For instance, a Russian speaker can resort to the expression *oderžu pobedu* 'I'll be victorious', and an English speaker can avoid *abided* by choosing a semantically similar verb such as *respect* or *accept*. What is primarily surprising about defectiveness is that speakers can learn the negative fact that a lexeme lacks certain forms. Normally there is at least one productive pattern for each inflectional category, a **default** pattern that is used when no other pattern is remembered. Since this option is unavailable in the defective verbs that we just mentioned, one must assume that speakers learn all the existing forms of these (and perhaps many other words). Otherwise it would be difficult to see how they could learn that certain forms do not exist. In contrast to other irregular lexemes, which usually show a high frequency of use (see Section 12.3), defective lexemes seem to be rather rare in general, and often they represent remnants of older paradigms that have become unproductive but have been neither regularized nor eliminated.

The term defectiveness is usually applied only to lexemes, not to entire categories. One could, for instance, say that the Latin subjunctive is defective because it lacks future-tense forms (see Figure 4.4), but this is not normally done.

Another phenomenon of paradigm imperfectness that is related to defectiveness is **deponency**, where a formal marker of an inflectional category is used in the 'wrong' function, to express a different category. Consider the Modern Greek active and reflexive forms of *pléno* 'wash' in (7.38a). The verb *érxome* 'come' exhibits the same inflection pattern as the reflexive, although it is not a reflexive verb semantically.

(7.38)   a.

	ACTIVE	REFLEXIVE	b. (ACTIVE)
1SG	*pléno*	*plénome*	*érxome*
2SG	*plénis*	*plénese*	*érxese*
3SG	*pléni*	*plénete*	*érxete*
1PL	*plénume*	*plenómaste*	*erxómaste*
2PL	*plénete*	*plenósaste*	*erxósaste*
3PL	*plénun*	*plénonde*	*érxonde*

Verbs like *érxome*, which have a paradigm from a different category but not the meaning of that category, are called **deponents**. Reflexive and passive deponents are the best-known cases of deponency, but there are also tense deponents – e.g. Latin *ōdī* 'I hate', which has a present-tense meaning despite its perfect-tense form.

Not uncommonly, missing cells are not completely empty, but may be filled by syntactic processes that express the needed concepts in a roundabout way. For example, many English adjectives lack ordinary comparative forms in *-er*. We have *warm-er*, *nic-er*, *pretti-er*, but for phonological reasons we do not have **beautifuller*, **interestinger*, **activer*. However, morphologists do not say that the lexemes *beautiful*, *interesting* and *active* are defective in lacking a comparative form, because there is a well-established conventional way of expressing the category by a syntactic phrase: *more beautiful*, *more interesting*, *more active*. Such comparatives are called **periphrastic**, and the phenomenon is called **periphrasis**. Another example comes from Romanian, where nouns inflect for an oblique case (e.g. *prietenul* 'the friend (NOM)', *prietenului* 'the friend (OBL)', *Ana* 'Ana (NOM)', *Anei* 'Ana (OBL)'). However, masculine personal names such as *Petre* lack an ordinary oblique case. In order to use them in a syntactic slot that requires the oblique case, a periphrasis involving the pronoun *lui* 'him' is used (*lui Petre* 'Petre (OBL)').

So far we have seen only cases of **lexical periphrasis**, where certain (groups of) lexemes lack word-forms for certain categories. But we also find **paradigmatic periphrasis** – i.e. cases in which entire word-classes lack certain combinations of inflectional categories. A well-known example of this is the Latin passive, which lacks ordinary inflected forms in the perfect, pluperfect and future perfect tenses. In (7.39) we see the third person singular forms of some tense–aspect–voice combinations of the verb *scribere* 'write'. The perfect and pluperfect passive forms are expressed by the past passive participle plus the verb *esse* 'be'.

(7.39)

	PRESENT	IMPERFECT	PERFECT	PLUPERFECT
ACTIVE	*scribit*	*scribebat*	*scripsit*	*scripserat*
PASSIVE	*scribitur*	*scribebatur*	*scriptum est*	*scriptum erat*

Thus, inflectional paradigms may sometimes contain syntactic phrases – or at least grammarians have often found it useful to pretend that they do.

We should be careful to distinguish this **gap-filling periphrasis** from another kind of periphrasis that we may call **categorial periphrasis**: For example, French is sometimes said to have a periphrastic future involving the auxiliary verb *aller* 'go', e.g. *je vais faire* 'I'm going to do', *tu vas faire* 'you're going to do', *il va faire* 'he's going to do', and so on. In contrast to gap-filling periphrasis, such cases of categorial periphrasis have nothing to do with morphology. The French periphrastic future is similar to inflectional future formations in that it has a future tense meaning, but this meaning is expressed purely syntactically – the morphologist can ignore such periphrases.

In gap-filling periphrasis, the normal situation is the existence of ordinary single-word forms in the cells of a paradigm, and the gap is the special situation that calls for special measures. But we also find the reverse quantitative distribution: sometimes multi-word expressions are the normal situation, and a single-word expression is the special case. Consider negation in Lezgian. The normal way to express negation in certain categories is by means of the negative verb *tawun* 'not doing' – e.g. *čüxün* 'washing', *čüxün tawun* 'not washing'. However, there are about a dozen verbs that allow non-syntactic single-word expression of negation by means of the prefix *ta-* (e.g. *xun* 'becoming', *taxun* 'not becoming', *gun* 'giving', *tagun* 'not giving') (Haspelmath 1993: 133). This is actually not unlike colloquial English, which generally requires the negative verb *don't*, but has a few verbs in which negation may be expressed morphologically by single-word forms (e.g. *can/can't, must/mustn't, ought/oughtn't*).

In such cases, it is conceptually awkward to say that the single-word forms constitute the inflectional paradigm, which has gaps that are filled by the multi-word forms to express the same notions periphrastically. Instead, we must change the perspective and recognize that the multi-word forms are basic and constitute a kind of 'syntactic paradigm', some of whose cells are filled by single-word forms that express the same notions in a more compact way. We may call this phenomenon **symphrasis**. Another example of symphrastic expression comes from Spanish, where the comparative of adjectives is usually formed syntactically, by means of the adverb *más* 'more' (e.g. *oscuro* 'dark', *más oscuro* 'darker'). However, there are four adjectives that have a symphrastic (i.e. single-word) comparative that is at the same time suppletive: *bueno* 'good'/*mejor* 'better', *malo* 'bad'/*peor* 'worse', *grande* 'great'/*mayor* 'greater', *pequeño* 'small'/*menor* 'smaller'.

Both periphrasis and symphrasis thus challenge the widely held belief

that morphology and syntax are separate domains that interact only minimally with each other.

Summary of Chapter 7

Three major issues in inflectional morphology are allomorphy,
productivity and syncretism. Suppletive allomorphy constitutes
inflection classes, which are typically linked to non-morphological
properties such as the phonological shape of the base, the lexeme's
meaning (animacy, transitivity) and the lexeme's gender, or to
morphological properties such as the derivational pattern. Global
inflection classes can be described by word-based paradigm rules and
rule-schemas that form inheritance hierarchies (possibly interpreted
as defaults that can be overridden). Sometimes abstract stems formed
by semantically empty morphemes must be assumed. The productivity of inflection classes can be seen in their ability to apply to novel
lexemes (loanwords or productively formed neologisms) and in their
ability to attract class-shifting lexemes. Inflectional homonymy may
be accidental or systematic, in which latter case we speak of syncretism. Syncretism may be natural or unnatural; the former is best
described by underspecification, the latter by rules of referral. There
are three ways in which cells in a paradigm may be missing: defectiveness (simple lack of a form), deponency (a form has an unexpected
function) and periphrasis (a cell is filled by a syntactic phrase).

Further reading

Book-length studies on inflection are Carstairs (1987), Wurzel (1989) and
Stump (2001a). A typologically oriented overview article is Bickel and
Nichols (forthcoming).

For inflection classes and stems, see Aronoff (1994), and for inheritance
hierarchies, see Corbett and Fraser (1993) and Stump (2001b). For
productivity, see Dressler (1997). For syncretism, see several of the papers in
Plank (1991). Periphrasis is discussed in Haspelmath (2000) (note that the
term *symphrasis* is first introduced in this book). The distinction between
systematic and accidental homonymy is discussed in Zwicky (1991).

The most important representatives of the debate on processing of inflection classes are Pinker and Prince (1994) for the dual-processing model (see
also Pinker (1999) for a book-length treatment written in an entertaining
and highly accessible style) and Bybee (1988, 1995) for the single-mechanism model (see also Sánchez Miret *et al.* 1997 for a third view).

Exercises

1. Using the rules given in connection with (7.12), form the perfective form of the following Tagalog verbs:

root	basic form with voice affix	
langoy	*lumangoy*	'swim'
wagayway	*wumagayway*	'wave'
takot	*matakot*	'be afraid'
uhaw	*mauhaw*	'be thirsty'
buhat	*buhatin*	'raise'
punit	*punitin*	'rip'
punas	*punasan*	'wipe'

2. At the end of Section 7.3, we said that 'in Figure 7.3, one of the rule schemas could be dispensed with if the description of Figure 7.5 were adopted'. Which rule schema could be dispensed with? What would the modified version of Figure 7.3 look like?

3. Take a complete list of English 'irregular verbs' and try to group them into small inflection classes. Which classes can be established? Which verbs must be said to be truly irregular – i.e. cannot be put into a class with some other verb(s)?

4. Consider the following three inflection classes of Ancient Greek (only singular forms are given). Class (i) consists of feminines (like the Latin class of *insula* 'island'), class (ii) consists of masculines denoting men (like the Latin class of *poeta* 'poet') and class (iii) mostly consists of masculines. The nouns of class (ii) originally inflected just like class (i). What may have motivated the change?

	(i)	(ii)	(iii)
NOM	*hēmérā*	*neaníās*	*phílos*
ACC	*hēmérān*	*neanían*	*phílon*
GEN	*hēmérās*	*neaníou*	*phílou*
DAT	*hēmérāi*	*neaníāi*	*phíloɔi*
	'day'	'young man'	'friend'

5. Consider the following four inflection classes of Russian nouns, and try to set up an inheritance hierarchy corresponding to Figure 7.3. (see Corbett and Fraser 1993). (Note that <y> and <i>, and <t'> and <tj> stand for the same phoneme.)

	(i)	(ii)	(iii)	(iv)
NOM.SG	zakon	komnata	kost'	boloto
ACC.SG	zakon	komnatu	kost'	boloto
GEN.SG	zakona	komnaty	kosti	bolota
DAT.SG	zakonu	komnate	kosti	bolotu
INST.SG	zakonom	komnatoj	kost'ju	bolotom
LOC.SG	zakone	komnate	kosti	bolote
NOM.PL	zakony	komnaty	kosti	bolota
ACC.PL	zakony	komnaty	kosti	bolota
GEN.PL	zakonov	komnat	kostej	bolot
DAT.PL	zakonam	komnatam	kostjam	bolotam
INST.PL	zakonami	komnatami	kostjami	bolotami
LOC.PL	zakonax	komnatax	kostjax	bolotax

6. English has few cases in which syncretism could be observed. However, consider the present-tense and past-tense paradigms of *be*:

I	am	was
you	are	were
he/she	is	was
we	are	were
they	are	were

Apply the criteria of Section 7.6.1 to see whether the homonymy of *are*, *was* and *were* is systematic.

Words and phrases

8.1 Dividing text into words

So far in this book we have pretended that the segmentation of a sentence into tokens of word-forms is a straightforward matter. But this is an illusion that is reinforced by our writing system in which blank spaces provide a very clear indication of the boundaries between word-forms. But not all writing systems have this feature. In Chinese, for instance, there are never blank spaces between characters. Not surprisingly, there is much less agreement about word division among linguists of Chinese than among linguists of modern European languages. But even in languages that use the modern European writing system, the conventional spelling is occasionally ambiguous. Sometimes the spelling vacillates, as in English compounds (e.g. *flower pot, flower-pot, flowerpot*). Sometimes boundary symbols other than a blank space are used – for example, the apostrophe (as with the English genitive *s*, e.g. *Joan's book*) or the hyphen (as with object pronouns in the French imperative, e.g. *donne-le-moi* 'give it to me'). These symbols seem to indicate that the elements linked by them belong together, but not as closely as ordinary affixes and bases.

Sometimes the same element is spelled differently under different circumstances. In Spanish, weak object pronouns are spelled separately when they precede the verb (e.g. *lo hacemos* 'we do it'), but together with the verb when they follow it (*hacerlo* 'to do it'). In German, the infinitive marker is spelled separately in most cases (e.g. *zu bringen* 'to bring'), but together with the verb when it is preceded by a prefix such as *ein-* 'in' (e.g. *einzubringen* 'to bring in'). In Turkish, the interrogative marker *mu* is spelled separately from the verb (e.g. *okuyor* 'he or she is reading', *okuyor mu?* 'is he or she reading?'), suggesting that it is a separate word. However, when the verb is followed by a non-zero person-number suffix (e.g. *okuyorsun* 'you are reading'), the interrogative marker precedes the person-number suffix and is spelled together with it, but still separately from the verb stem (e.g. *okuyor musun?*

'are you reading?'). In all these cases, the hints from the spelling are clearly contradictory. The rules for orthographic word division are to some extent simply traditional in languages with a long written history. And when a language is first written down, the language-users often disagree on where to put blank spaces between words, and when a conventional spelling is agreed on, the decisions are sometimes clearly arbitrary.

However, although there are often disagreements, there is equally often agreement among speakers, and it does seem to be the case that dividing sentences into words (i.e. word-forms) is possible in roughly the same sense of *word* (or *word-form*) in all languages. Indeed, it seems that most languages have a word for 'word', the smallest unit of language that people with no training in linguistics or writing have an awareness of (non-educated speakers of course have no awareness of syllables, morphemes or phonological segments). In this chapter we will review the criteria that are most often used to distinguish complex words from phrases, and words from parts of words.

There are two types of situations in which we may have doubts whether a complex expression is a word-form or a syntactic phrase. On the one hand, the boundaries between compounds and phrases with two content words may be unclear (for instance, are the expressions *back-bench, back door, back seat* compounds or phrases?). On the other hand, the boundaries between affixed words and phrases with a content word and a function word may be unclear (for instance, is French *donne-le-moi* 'give it to me' a single word-form or a phrase consisting of three word-forms?). It may be that in the end it will turn out that sharp boundaries cannot be drawn and that there is instead a continuum from compound to phrase and from function word-form to affix, but it will still be useful to try as hard as possible to come up with criteria for distinguishing different cases.

One way in which the word/affix distinction has been refined is by identifying a third, intermediate category of **clitics** that is neither a real affix nor a prototypical independent word-form. A term for the category of elements that comprises both affixes and clitics is **bound form**, as opposed to **free form** for independent word-forms. The relations among the terms *affix, clitic, bound, free* and *word-form* are summarized in Figure 8.1.

bound forms		free forms
affixes	word-forms	
	clitics (= bound word-forms)	free word-forms

Figure 8.1 Terms for distinctions on the affix–word continuum

In Section 8.2 we will first discuss criteria for telling bound forms from free forms, and in Section 8.3 we will go on to distinguish affixes from clitics. Then in Section 8.4 we will discuss compounds and phrases, and finally in Section 8.5 we will briefly look at a general principle distinguishing between morphological and syntactic structures, the Lexical Integrity Principle.

8.2 Free forms versus bound forms

First and foremost, a free form contrasts with a bound form in that it is **prosodically independent**, while bound forms are **prosodically dependent**. This means, first, that an utterance may be interrupted at a boundary between two free forms, but not at the boundary between two bound forms (e.g. *Paul ... uh ... started to play*, or *Paul started ... uh ... to play*, but not **Paul start ... uh ... ed to play*). When a speaker is asked to repeat an utterance slowly for dictation (e.g. an utterance heard on a tape in a typical fieldwork situation), he or she will repeat the utterance free form by free form, not morpheme by morpheme. In languages that use stress to express contrast, free forms can be **stressed contrastively**, whereas bound forms generally cannot. Thus, in English we can have PAUL *started to play*, or *Paul started to* PLAY, but not **Paul start*ED *to play*, or **Paul started* TO *play*, because past-tense *-ed* and infinitival *to* are not free forms. In languages like French, where contrast is expressed by **clefting** rather than by stress, free forms can be clefted, but bound forms cannot. The sentence in (8.1a) can have the clefted variant (8.1b), but (8.2a) cannot have the clefted variant in (8.2b), because the weak subject pronoun *il* 'he' is not a free form.

(8.1) a. *Paul   commenç-ait   à   jou-er.*
          Paul   begin-3SG.IMPF   to   play-INF
          'Paul started to play.'
      b. *C'   est   Paul   qui   commenç-ait   à   jou-er.*
          it   is   Paul   who   begin-3SG.IMPF   to   play-INF
          'It's Paul who started to play.'

(8.2) a. *Il commençait à jouer.*
          'He started to play.'
      b. **C'est il qui commençait à jouer.*
          'It's he who started to play.'

In the clefted variant of (8.2a), French has to use its independent pronoun *lui* 'he' (*C'est lui qui commençait à jouer*).

Two other syntactic constructions that, like clefting, are limited to free forms are **topicalization** and **coordination**. Since French weak subject pronouns (as in *je joue* 'I play', *tu joues* 'you play', *il joue* 'he plays') are not free forms, in topicalization, the independent pronouns must be used (*moi,* *je joue* 'as for me, I play', not **je, je joue*), and likewise in coordination (*moi et toi jouons* 'you and I play', not *je et tu jouons).

Prosodic independence also means that free forms constitute a separate **domain for word stress**, whereas bound forms do not constitute such a separate domain. Bound forms are often unstressed, and, when they are stressed, they bear the stress of the larger unit consisting of free form and bound form, not their own stress. For example, in the French imperative *joue-le!* 'play it!', the weak object pronoun *le* bears stress (*joue-lé*), but this is the stress of the whole expression (which happens to be on the final syllable), not *le*'s own stress.

Free-form boundaries are often the boundaries for **(morpho-)phonological rules** that apply to combinations of free and bound forms, but do not apply across several free forms. Thus, the rule of vowel harmony in Finnish applies to combinations of free forms with clitics and affixes: bound elements like the suffix *-nsa/-nsä* 'his' and the clitic *=ko/=kö* (question marker) agree in backness with the vowel of the stem or host (*koira-nsa* 'his dog', *ystävä-nsä* 'his friend'; *koira=ko* 'dog?', *ystävä=kö* 'friend?'). Phonological rules may also apply across free-form boundaries, but this is much less common than with bound-form boundaries.

The criteria for distinguishing between free forms and bound forms are summarized in Table 8.1.

Free forms	Bound forms (= affixes and clitics)
prosodically independent	prosodically dependent
utterance interruptible at free-form boundary	utterance not interruptible at bound-form boundary
contrastively stressable	not contrastively stressable
cleftable	not cleftable
topicalizable	not topicalizable
coordinatable	not coordinatable
separate domain for word stress	not a separate domain for word stress
fewer phonological rules across free-form boundaries	more phonological rules across bound-form boundaries

Table 8.1 Free forms versus bound forms

8.3 Clitics versus affixes

The criteria seen so far distinguish between free forms and bound forms, but this is not yet the distinction that interests us primarily: that between word-forms and affixes. The notion 'bound form' comprises not just affixes, but also the class of **clitics**, elements that are in many ways intermediate between affixes and free forms. Clitics are generally regarded as a type of word-forms, but they are different from free word-forms in that they are prosodically dependent and have all the other features of bound forms that we have seen. Thus, the rules by which clitics are combined with their **hosts** (the elements to which they attach and which they rely on for 'prosodic support') are considered to be not in the domain of morphology, but in the domain of syntax (and/or perhaps phonology). Moreover, clitics may be morphologically complex themselves and consist of a root with affixes (though such clitics are not particularly common). The expression formed by a clitic and its host is called a **clitic group**.

Perhaps the most salient property of clitics that distinguishes them from affixes is that they often have **freedom of movement** – i.e. they can occur in different positions in the sentence. For example, the Polish clitic pronoun *go* 'him' (which contrasts with the independent, stressable pronoun *jego*) can be in several different positions in the sentence in (8.3). (In this and other examples of clitics, we follow the convention of linking them to their hosts by an equal sign, even though Polish spelling has a space here.)

(8.3)   a. *Tak bardzo =*   **go**   *chcia-tby-m*   *spotkać*   *w*   *Krakowie.*
           so much   him   want-HYP-1SG   meet   in   Cracow
        b. *Tak bardzo*   *chcia-tby-m =*   **go**   *spotkać*   *w*   *Krakowie.*
           so much   want-HYP-1SG   him   meet   in   Cracow
        c. *Tak bardzo*   *chcia-tby-m*   *spotkać =* **go**   *w*   *Krakowie.*
           so much   want-HYP-1SG   meet   him   in   Cracow
        'I would so much like to meet him in Cracow.'

Of course, this property of clitics can be illustrated only with languages that allow freedom of movement in comparable non-clitic positions. Thus, in English we would not expect clitics such as *='ve* to show freedom of movement, because the corresponding full form *have* does not show such freedom either (e.g. *They='ve done it/*They done='ve it; They have done it/*They done have it*). And the clitics' freedom of movement may not be as complete as that of free forms. For instance, the Polish clitic pronoun *=go* is always **enclitic** (it follows its host) and thus cannot be in sentence-initial position, unlike the independent pronoun *jego*.

Sometimes the restrictions on the movement of clitics are so great that they no longer have any freedom, as happens with **second-position clitics**, a fairly common class of clitics that must occur directly after the first element of the sentence. For instance, in Serbian/Croatian the auxiliary verb *je* is such a second-position enclitic, as is illustrated by the sentence in (8.4), again with a number of variant word orders.

(8.4)   a. *Čovek=je*   *voleo*   *Mariju.*   (**Čovek voleo=je Mariju*)
           man=has   loved   Marija
        b. *Voleo=je*   *čovek*   *Mariju.*   (**Voleo čovek Mariju=je.*)
           loved=has   man   Marija

c. *Mariju=je   čovek   voleo.*
   Marija=has   man   loved
   'The man has loved Marija.'

But, although Serbian/Croatian *=je* has no freedom of movement, it still has **freedom of host selection** – i.e. it can occur with hosts of various syntactic categories, and its host need not be syntactically related to it. The clitic *=je* is syntactically related to *voleo*, the main verb, but it may also follow other constituents of the clause. Affixes do not have such freedom of host selection – they combine with a stem to which they are syntactically related.

Another widespread property of clitics is that they are less **prosodically integrated** with their host than affixes – i.e. fewer prosodic rules take the clitic group as their domain. For instance, Spanish stress is usually on the last or penultimate syllable of the word, and rarely on the antepenultimate (e.g. *caminár* 'walk.INF', *camína* 'walk.PRES.3SG', *caminábamos* 'walk.PAST.1PL'), but never on the fourth syllable from the end. But this is possible with clitic groups, e.g. *díga=me=lo* 'say it to me!'.

Moreover, there are many **(morpho-)phonological rules** that operate within the **domain of the word-form**, but not across a word boundary. For example, in Dutch a word-final obstruent is devoiced, but no such devoicing occurs when a vowel-initial suffix follows it (see (8.5a)). However, when a vowel-initial clitic follows such a word, devoicing still occurs, as can be seen in (8.5b).

(8.5) a. *verband*   [vər'bɑnt]   *verband-ig*   [vər'bɑndɪx]
          'bandage'   'bandage-like'
       b. *ik brand*   [ɪg'brɑnt]   *brand=ik*   ['brɑntɪk]
          'I burned'   'I burned'

Thus, the clitic is as it were invisible for the rule of final devoicing. Similarly, in Ponapean there is a rule of vowel lengthening at the end of the word that does not apply when a suffix follows. However, when a clitic such as demonstrative *=et* follows the noun, vowel lengthening still occurs (Ponapean spelling marks vowel length by the letter *h*):

(8.6) *sahpw*   'land'   *sapw-ei*   'my land'   *sahpw=et*   'this land'
       ngihl   'voice'   *ngil-ei*   'my voice'   *ngihl=et*   'this voice'
       pwuhs   'novel'   *pwus-ei*   'my novel'   *pwuhs=et*   'this novel'
                                               (Rehg 1981: 169–70, 186)

Affix-base combinations are often **idiosyncratic** in one way or another, whereas clitic-host combinations are usually very regular, as one would expect for combinations of syntactic units. For one thing, affixes may **trigger idiosyncratic morphophonological alternations**, whereas clitics do not. An example is the English plural suffix *-s*, which requires idiosyncratic voicing of the final fricative in a number of nouns (e.g. *knives, lives, calves, houses, mouths*). By contrast, the English genitive clitic *='s* never triggers such voicing (e.g. *knife'* = *s, life'* = *s, calf'* = *s*). Second, affixes may **undergo idiosyncratic morphophonological alternations**, whereas clitics do not. For example, the Russian reflexive suffix *-sja* (as in *ty moeš'-sja* 'you (SG) wash yourself') has the reduced phonological allomorph *-s'* when it follows a vowel-final word (e.g. *vy moete-s'* 'you (PL) wash yourselves'). The corresponding Polish element *się* is not an affix, but a clitic, and it undergoes no morphophonological alternation (e.g. *myjesz* = *się* 'you wash yourself', *myjecie* = *się* 'you wash yourselves').

Third, affixes may **trigger idiosyncratic suppletive alternations** in the base, whereas clitics do not. For example, in Finnish many nouns alternate between a stem-final sequence *-nen* and a sequence *-se*. The former occurs when the word is uninflected (i.e. in the nominative singular form), and the latter occurs when any kind of suffix follows, inflectional or derivational.

(8.7) *nainen*   'woman'   *naise-llinen*   'woman-like, feminine'
                                        naise-n   'woman's (GEN.SG)'
                                        naise-lla   'to the woman (ALL.SG)'
                                        naise-nsa   'his woman'
                                                         (Kanerva 1987: 506)

But when a clitic follows the noun 'woman', the stem *nainen* is used (e.g. *nainen=ko?* 'the woman?'), showing that clitics behave differently from affixes.

Fourth, affixes may **undergo idiosyncratic suppletive alternations**, whereas clitics do not. For instance, Polish has several different inflection classes of verbs, and the first person singular suffix is either *-m* or *-ę*, depending on the class (*kocha-m* 'I love', *umie-m* 'I'm able', *ucz-ę* 'I teach', *pij-ę* 'I drink'). Object pronouns, however, are clitics, and they have an invariable shape (*kocham go* 'I love him', *piję go* 'I drink it', *uczę go* 'I teach him', etc.).

Fifth, affix–base combinations may have an **idiosyncratic meaning**, whereas clitic–host combinations never do. Idiosyncratic meanings of affixes are mostly observed in derivational morphology, but occasionally they are found in inflection as well (e.g. plurals with a special meaning, as in (4.15)). And, finally, affix–base combinations may exhibit **arbitrary gaps**, whereas clitic–host combinations are always possible. Again, arbitrary gaps are more characteristic of derivation than of inflection, but we saw in Section 7.7 that defective paradigms occasionally occur.

The criteria for distinguishing between affixes and clitics are summarized in Table 8.2.

8.4 Compounds versus phrases

In many cases, compounds are easy to tell apart from phrases with two content words. Compounds consist of two (or rarely more) lexeme stems

Clitics	Affixes
freedom of movement	no freedom of movement
freedom of host selection	no freedom of stem selection
not prosodically integrated	prosodically integrated
may be outside the domain of a phonological rule	always within the domain of a phonological rule
may not trigger/undergo morpho-phonological or suppletive alternations	may trigger/undergo morpho-phonological or suppletive alternations
(clitic–host combinations:)	(affix–base combinations:)
• may not have idiosyncratic meanings	• may have idiosyncratic meanings
• may not have arbitrary gaps	• may have arbitrary gaps

Table 8.2 Clitics versus affixes

that are juxtaposed in a single word-form, and, when a language does not allow phrases consisting of two juxtaposed lexemes of the same word-classes, the combination must be a compound. For example, German *Holzhaus* [wood-house] must be a compound noun because two juxtaposed nouns cannot form a noun phrase in German. Two rough paraphrases of *Holzhaus* would be *Haus aus Holz* 'house from wood' and *hölzernes Haus* 'wooden house', but these are clearly distinct from the compound because of different word order, an additional preposition, or additional adjectival morphology. Similarly, Italian *segnalibri* [indicate-books] 'bookmark' must be a compound, because it is not similar to a phrase with a similar meaning. It is true that Italian has a phrase *segna libri* whose pronunciation is the same, but this is an imperative verb phrase and means 'indicate books!', so both syntactically and semantically it is clearly distinct from the compound *segnalibri*. Occasionally compounds even have a special segmental marker. Thus, in Coast Tsimshian an *-m-* interfix between the two members indicates a compound, e.g. *gyemg-m-dziws* [light-INTF-day] 'sun', *güünks-m-hoon* [dry-INTF-fish] 'dried fish' (Dunn 1979: 55). But such special markers are rare (see also (5.4)).

However, there are also a great many cases in which compounds are quite similar to phrases with a similar meaning, and then we have to take a closer look in order to distinguish the two patterns. For example, in Lango the inalienable possessive construction shows the order head–possessor and is expressed by simple juxtaposition (e.g. *wì rwòt* [head king] 'the king's head', *bàd dàktàl* [arm doctor] 'the doctor's arm'). Now Lango has expressions that look like compounds at first blush, e.g. *wàŋ ɔ̀t* [eye house] 'window', *dɔ́g bɔ́ŋɔ́* [mouth dress] 'hem' (Noonan 1992: 115, 157–8). However, their most striking property is that they are **idiomatic** – i.e. their meaning cannot be determined from the meaning of their constituents.

Idiomaticity is a typical property of compounds, but it is neither a necessary nor a sufficient criterion for compound status. On the one hand, all languages with productive compounding must have semantically regular (i.e. compositional) compounds (English examples are *piano-tuner, brake cable, spring festival*). On the other hand, not all idioms are compounds. Idioms like English *spill the beans*, French *roulette russe* 'Russian roulette' or German *goldenes Zeitalter* 'golden age' are formally just like ordinary syntactic phrases in the language, and the general assumption is therefore that they are idiomatic phrases. Thus, one might suspect that Lango expressions like *wàŋ ɔ̀t* 'window', *dɔ́g bɔ́ŋɔ́* 'hem' are simply phrases that happen to be semantically idiomatic.

(In actual fact, this seems unlikely, because Lango also has clear compounds of the type N–N, e.g. *ɔ̀t cɛ̀m* [house-eating] 'restaurant', *mɔ̀ɔ̀ ɲìm* [oil sesame] 'seame oil'. These cannot be phrases, because *ɔ̀t* and *mɔ̀ɔ̀* are not inalienable nouns, and the juxtapositional possessive construction is possible only with inalienable nouns such as kinship terms and body part terms. Thus, *wàŋ ɔ̀t* and *dɔ́g bɔ́ŋɔ́* are probably compounds, although existing descriptions of Lango are insufficient to be completely sure.)

A semantic property of almost all compounds is that a dependent noun does not denote a particular referent but the entire class; in other words, a dependent noun in a compound is not **referential** but **generic**. For example, in the compound *piano-tuner*, the element *piano* cannot refer to a particular piano, but must refer to pianos in general. In syntactic phrases, by contrast, a noun is typically referential. Generic meaning is also a general feature of dependent nouns in verb-headed N–V compounds (i.e. **noun incorporation**), as the examples in (8.8)–(8.9) show. The (a) examples show a non-incorporated, phrasal version, and the (b) examples show an incorporated version of the sentence (note the absence of the determiner in both cases).

(8.8) Lakhota
    a. *Wičháša   ki   čhą́   ki   kaksá-he.*
       man   the   wood   the   chop-CONT
      'The man is chopping the wood.'
    b. *Wičháša   ki   čhą-káksa-he.*
       man   the   wood-chop-CONT
      'The man is chopping wood.' (Lit.: 'The man is wood-chopping.')
                       (Van Valin and LaPolla 1997: 123)

(8.9) Ponapean
    a. *I   pahn   kang   wini-o.*
      1SG   FUT   eat   medicine-DEM
      'I will take that medicine.'
    b. *I   pahn   keng-wini.*
      1SG   FUT   eat-medicine
      'I will take medicine.' (Lit.: 'I will do medicine-taking.')
                       (Rehg 1981: 209–14)

However, a dependent noun in a noun phrase need not necessarily be referential. In the German phrase *Haus aus Holz* 'house from wood' that we saw above, *Holz* 'wood' is just as generic as in *Holzhaus*. This means that, just because a dependent noun is generic, we cannot conclude that the expression is a compound. But, conversely, if a dependent noun is referential (as in Lango *wì rwòt* 'the king's head', which refers to the head of a particular king), we can be fairly certain that the expression is a phrase and not a compound.

Since the typical semantic properties of compounds are not unique to compounds, we have to rely on additional phonological, morphological and syntactic properties to identify compounds when compound and phrase patterns are otherwise formally similar. Quite generally, compounds exhibit greater phonological, morphological and syntactic **cohesion** than phrases.

A well-known **phonological** criterion is a characteristic compound stress. In English, main stress on the first element of a compound-like expression is a sufficient criterion for compound status. Thus, the words in (8.10a) are compounds, whereas those in (8.10b) are generally taken to be phrases. (As these examples show, word division in the spelling correlates only imperfectly with the criterion of stress.)

(8.10) a. *góldfish*
            báckdròp
            Whíte Hòuse
        b. *gòld médal*
            bàckbénch
            whìte kníght

Stress is also one of the criteria that show that Lakhota incorporation (see 8.8b)) is a compounding pattern, and Ponapean shows a segmental phonological change in the verb (see (8.9b)). (However, other nouns show even more drastic changes when they occur as an incorporated dependent member, so that we have to posit a special incorporation stem in Ponapean; this is thus really a morphological criterion for compound status.)

In Chukchi, compounding creates a single **domain** for vowel harmony. Within such a domain, only vowels of one of the two sets [i], [e], [u] and [e], [a], [o] may occur, and, if one morpheme of a word has vowels of the second set, all other morphemes must have such vowels. Thus, when *kupre-n* 'net' occurs in a compound, it may have to be changed to *kopra-* (e.g. *pəlvəntə-kopra-n* 'metal net'). However, Chukchi is actually atypical in this respect. In most better-known languages with vowel harmony, compound nouns do not count as a single domain for vowel harmony (cf. Turkish compound nouns like *bin-başı* [thousand-head] '(army) major' and *deniz-altı* [sea-below] 'submarine', which have both front vowels (*i, e*) and back vowels (*ı, a*)). Thus, although compounds exhibit greater phonological cohesion than phrases, there are also clear signs that their phonological cohesion is less than that of other complex words.

In some cases, **morphological cohesion** can give us decisive criteria for compound status. In the relevant examples, a morphological pattern clearly takes the whole compound in its domain rather than just the head. Consider the English word *sister-in-law*, which for many speakers has the (non-standard) plural form *sister-in-laws*. The older (standard) form *sisters-in-law*, which has the plural suffix on the head noun, could be a compound noun or a phrase, but *sister-in-laws* can only be a compound because the English plural suffix is attached to words, not to phrases. Similarly, in Ponapean the aspectual suffix *-(a)la* is suffixed to a word, as in (8.11).

(8.11) a. *I*   *kang-ala*   *wini-o.*
        1SG   eat-COMPL   medicine-DEM
        'I completed taking that medicine, i.e. I took all of that medicine.'
     b. *I*   *keng-winih-la.*
        1SG   eat-medicine-COMPL
        'I completed my medicine-taking.'

The fact that *-(a)la* follows *wini(h)* in (8.11b) is another piece of proof that *keng-wini(h)* is a compound rather than a phrase. (However, recall from Section 5.2 that in compounds the morphosyntactic locus is often the head. Such compounds do not provide this kind of evidence.)

   Where phonological and morphological criteria are not decisive, criteria of **syntactic cohesion** should be able to differentiate between compounds and phrases. Most obviously, syntactic phrases are often **separable**, whereas compounds are **inseparable**. For example, Hausa has N–N compounds that clearly resemble possessive constructions in that they show head-dependent order and a relation marker (*-n* (masculine)/*-r̃* (feminine)) on the head, e.g. *gida-n-sauroo* [house-REL.M-mosquito] 'mosquito net'. There are no phonological or morphological properties that would distinguish such compounds from possessive phrases like *gida-n Muusaa* 'Musa's house'. However, when an adjective modifies these expressions, it becomes clear that the compound is inseparable, whereas the phrase is separable.

(8.12) a. *gida-n-sauroo*   *bàbba*   (**gidaa bàbba na sauroo*)
            house-REL.M-mosquito   big
            'big mosquito net'
     b. *gidaa*   *bàbba*   *na*   *Muusaa*
        house   big   REL.M   Musa
        'Musa's big house'

(Newman 2000: 109)

   Another clear indication of phrasal status is the **expandability** of the dependent element, because dependents in compounds cannot be expanded by modifiers such as adjectives or adverbs (e.g. English *kingmaker* versus **illegitimate kingmaker* 'someone who makes an illegitimate king'; *crispbread* versus **very crispbread* 'bread that is very crisp'). Some languages seem to allow short phrases to be dependent compound members (e.g. English *open-air concert, African history teacher, small claims court*), but this is quite unusual cross-linguistically, and it works mainly with fixed phrases (cf. **thin-air concert, *recent history teacher, *large claims court*).

In compounds, the dependent noun cannot be replaced by an **anaphoric pronoun** (**the king and the him-makers*), but this is not a very useful syntactic criterion because it follows from the semantic condition that the dependent noun in a compound must be generic: anaphoric pronouns cannot be interpreted generically, so they cannot occur as dependent members of compounds. However, in compounds not even the head noun can be replaced by an anaphoric pronoun. For instance, English allows (8.13a), but not (8.13b).

(8.13) a. *My aunt has one gold watch and three silver ones*
             (i.e. three silver watches).
        b. **My aunt knows one goldsmith and three silver ones*
             (i.e. three silversmiths).

This contrast can be taken to show that *gold watch* is an adjective–noun phrase, whereas *goldsmith* is a compound word.

In Japanese, complex verbal expressions like *benkyoo suru* [study do] 'study' and *rakka suru* [fall do] 'fall' are sometimes regarded as N–V compound verbs. However, the noun in these combinations can be omitted with an anaphoric interpretation (see 8.14)), suggesting that these expressions are phrases after all.

(8.14) *Sore   wa   rakka   si-masi-ta   ka? – Hai,   si-masi-ta.*
        it   TOP   fall   do-POLITE-PAST   INT   yes   do-POLITE-PAST
        'Did it fall? – Yes, it did.'

(Matsumoto 1996: 41)

Another criterion for distinguishing between compounds and phrases is the possibility of **extraction** (or **fronting**) – i.e. the movement of an element out of the compound/phrase to the clause-initial position. The following examples show that, in English, extraction is generally possible with phrases, but impossible with compound members (see also (1.9)).

(8.15) a. *History, which I've been teaching __ for years, still fascinates me.*
        b. **History, which I've been a __ teacher for years, still fascinates me.*
             (cf. history teacher)

A problem with this criterion is that this kind of extraction is possible only with referential phrases, so (8.15b) is impossible for semantic reasons as well and thus cannot serve as a syntactic argument. But when (exceptionally) the first compound member is referential, extraction is still not possible:

(8.16) a. *Nixon, who she has baited ___ for years, still angers her.*
   b. **Nixon, who she has been a ___baiter for years, still angers her.*
   (cf. Nixon-baiter)

A type of extraction is **topicalization**. Again, this is possible with dependent phrases in NPs, but not with dependents in compounds. In (8.17)–(8.18), we see examples from Italian, which has head-dependent compounds such as *nave ospedale* 'hospital boat' and *capo-stazione* 'station master'.

(8.17) a. *Dei   passeggeri,   è   efficiente   il   trasporto ___.*
           of.the   passengers   is   efficient   the   transport
           'Of the passengers, the transportartion is efficient.'
           (cf. *il trasporto dei passeggeri* 'the transportation of the passengers')
     b. **Ospedale,   hanno   costruito   una   nave ___.*
           hospital   they.have   built   a   boat
           'Hospital, they have built a ___ boat.'

(8.18) a. *Della   carta,   è   stata   sospesa   la   produzione ___.*
           of.the   paper   has been   stopped   the   production
           'Of the paper, the production has been stopped.'
           (cf. *la produzione della carta* 'the production of the paper')
     b. **Stazione,   hanno   licenziato   il   capo-___.*
           station   they.have   fired   the   master
           'Station, they have fired the ___ master.'
           (Bisetto and Scalise 1999: 38–9)

Finally, **coordination ellipsis** is often said to be restricted to phrases. For instance, in Italian (8.19a) is possible, but (8.19b) is not.

(8.19) a. *il   transporto   dei   passeggeri   e   ___   delle   merci*
           the   transport   of.the passengers   and   of.the   goods
           'the transportation of the passengers and of the goods'
     b. **il   capo-stazione   e   ___ -reparto*
           the   master-station   and   department
           'the station master and department ___'
           (Bisetto and Scalise 1999: 37)

However, this criterion is weakened by the fact that some well-known languages do allow coordination ellipsis within semantically regular compounds (e.g. German *Landes- und Bundesstraßen* 'state and federal roads', English *lion and elephant hunters*).

Thus, compounds are in principle distinguishable from phrases, though not all criteria are applicable to all languages and all compounds. A particular difficulty is distinguishing idiomatic phrases with a generic dependent element from compounds. For example, the English expression *house of cards* is generally taken as a somewhat idiomatic phrase, not as a compound. However, because of its idiomatic meaning, expandability and anaphoric replacement cannot be tested, and separability cannot be tested because English has no modifiers that would follow the noun but precede the *of*-phrase. Thus, we will probably have to live with some indeterminacy.

The criteria for distinguishing between phrases and compounds are summarized in Table 8.3.

Phrases	Compounds
dependent noun may be referential	dependent noun always generic
less phonological cohesion	greater phonological cohesion (e.g. special compound stress)
no morphological cohesion	greater morphological cohesion
separable	inseparable
dependent noun is expandable	dependent noun not expandable
head may be replaced by an anaphoric expression	head may not be replaced by an anaphoric expression
extraction of dependent possible	extraction of dependent impossible
coordination ellipsis possible	coordination ellipsis impossible

Table 8.3 Phrases versus compounds

8.5 Lexical integrity

We saw in the preceding section that compounds are different from syntactic phrases in a number of crucial respects. It has often been suggested that this difference between compounds and phrases is due to a deeper principle of Universal Grammar that is called the *Lexical Integrity Principle*:

(8.20) **Lexical Integrity Principle** (first version)
Syntactic rules cannot apply to parts of words.

This principle in turn could be seen as following from the architecture of grammar if a model like the one sketched in Figure 1.1 is adopted: if morphology and syntax are two completely separate components of grammar – i.e. if the morphological component delivers complete words that are then the input to syntactic rules – it can be expected that syntactic rules do not 'look inside' the complete words received from the morphology. And this in turn would explain why compound members cannot be replaced by anaphoric pronouns, and why they cannot be extracted or undergo coordination ellipsis.

However, counterexamples to the Lexical Integrity Principle as stated in (8.20) have sometimes been observed. For example, in some languages verbs show agreement with incorporated nouns (i.e. with compound members), as is the case in Southern Tiwa:

(8.21) a. *ti-khwian-mu-ban*
1SG.SUBJ/SG.OBJ-dog-see-past
'I saw the dog.'
b. *bi-khwian-mu-ban*
1SG.SUBJ/PL.OBJ-dog-see-past
'I saw dogs.'

(Allen *et al.* 1990: 322)

Here the agreement prefixes register the number of the incorporated noun *-khwian-* 'dog(s)'. Agreement is a syntactic rule, so here the incorporated noun is visible to the rules of syntax. And in some languages, incorporated nouns may have non-incorporated modifiers, for instance in Greenlandic Eskimo: (8.22b) is the incorporated counterpart of (8.22a). These examples show that the incorporated noun is a true syntactic argument of the verb.

(8.22) a. *Ammassan-nik   marlun-nik   neri-vunga.*
sardine-INSTR.PL   two-INSTR.PL   eat-INDIC.1SG
'I ate two sardines.'
b. *Marlun-nik   ammassat-tor-punga.*
two-INSTR.PL   sardine-eat-INDIC.1SG
'I ate two sardines.'

Thus, it may be necessary to weaken the Lexical Integrity Principle somewhat and state it as in (8.23).

(8.23) **Lexical Integrity Principle** (second version)
Syntactic rules of word order and constituency cannot apply to parts of words.

Even in this form, the Lexical Integrity Principle is very controversial, because it is possible to analyse an incorporated structure like *ammassat-tor-punga* in (8.22b) as arising through a movement transformation from a structure corresponding to (8.22a). There are a large number of ways in which syntactic rules can be formulated, so it will inevitably be difficult to reach a consensus about the exact relation between syntax and morphology. Clearly, morphology and syntax are different, but the question of whether the difference is minor and gradual or major and sharp will probably be debated for a long time to come.

Summary of Chapter 8

There are two main difficulties that we encounter in dividing texts into word-forms: distinguishing affixed word-forms from phrases that contain a function word, and distinguishing compounds from phrases with two content words. Word-forms that are intermediate between fully independent word-forms and fully dependent affixes are called clitics, and clitics and affixes are grouped together as bound forms. Free forms differ from bound forms in that they are phonologically independent, cleftable, topicalizable and coordinatable. Clitics differ from affixes in that they have greater freedom of movement and host selection, are phonologically less dependent, do not trigger or undergo morphophonological alternations and show no idiosyncrasies of meaning or distribution. Phrases differ from compounds in that they allow referential dependent members and exhibit less phonological, morphological and syntactic cohesion. Often a 'Lexical Integrity Principle' is postulated that forbids syntactic rules to apply to parts of words.

Further reading

Much influential work on clitics and the affix/clitic distinction is due to Arnold Zwicky (e.g. Zwicky 1977, 1985 and Zwicky and Pullum 1983) (see also Kanerva 1987). For compounds versus phrases, see Bauer (1998) and Bisetto and Scalise (1999).

Lexical integrity is discussed and defended in Di Sciullo and Williams (1987) and Bresnan and Mchombo (1995) (and see Rosen (1989) and Mohanan (1995) for incorporation). Syntactic approaches to incorporation that do not assume the Lexical Integrity Principle are Baker (1988) and Sadock (1991).

Exercises

1. Provide arguments to show that English *-s*, the suffix of the third person singular of present-tense verbs, is an affix, not a clitic.

2. What is wrong with the following sentences?

   a. Polish
*Go	spotka-t-em	w	Krakowie.
him	meet-PAST-1SG	in	Cracow

   'I met him in Cracow.'

b. French

*A:	Qui	joue?	Robert?	– B:	Non,	TU	joues.
	who	plays	Robert		no	you	play

'A: Who is playing? Robert? – B: No, YOU are playing.'

c. Serbian/Croatian

*Klara	čovek	voleo = je.
Klara.ACC	man.NOM	loved has

'The man has loved Klara.'

d. Ponapean

*I	keng-wini-o-la.
1SG	eat-medicine-DEM-COMPL

'I completed my taking of that medicine.'

e. Russian

*Sergej	= sja	moet.
Sergej	self	washes

'Sergej is washing (himself).'

3. Sometimes the various criteria for distinguishing clitics from affixes contradict each other. For instance, in Spanish the bound pronominals undergo a morphophonological alternation when a third person dative pronominal cooccurs with an accusative pronominal: *-le* is replaced by *-se* because another *l* follows:

diga-me	'tell me'	
diga-le	'tell him'	
diga-me-lo	'tell me it'	
diga-se-lo	'tell him it'	(**diga-le-lo*)

Given what we said in this chapter about Spanish bound pronominals, where is the contradiction?

4. Another case of a contradiction comes from Lithuanian, which forms reflexive verbs by means of an element *s(i)*. (The letter *ė* stands for a long [eː].)

	'rock'	'rock oneself'	'not rock oneself'
1SG	*supu*	*supuosi*	*nesisupu*
2SG	*supi*	*supiesi*	*nesisupi*
3	*supa*	*supasi*	*nesisupa*
1PL	*supame*	*supamės*	*nesisupame*
2PL	*supate*	*supatės*	*nesisupate*

In what ways is this element like an affix, and in what way is it like a clitic?

5. Look at the example of noun incorporation in Guaraní (ex. (11.26)). Which criteria can be applied to show that (11.26b) contains a compound, not a phrase like (11.26a)?

Word-based rules

9

9.1 Syntagmatic and paradigmatic relations in morphology

The relations between linguistic units are of two broad kinds: **syntagmatic** relations are between units that (potentially) follow each other in speech, and **paradigmatic** relations are between units that could (potentially) occur in the same slot. In other words, syntagmatic relations have to do with concatenation, while paradigmatic relations have to do with substitution. Syntagmatically related units co-occur in speech, while paradigmatically related units coexist in the lexicon. These two dimensions are illustrated in (9.1), where (in line with common notational practice) the horizontal dimension shows syntagmatically related units, and the vertical dimension shows paradigmatically related units.

(9.1) *In* $\left\{ \begin{array}{l} the \\ {}^*\varnothing \end{array} \right\}$ *beginning* $\left\{ \begin{array}{l} God \\ Allah \\ he \\ {}^*why \end{array} \right\}\left\{ \begin{array}{l} created \\ made \\ {}^*create \\ {}^*rested \end{array} \right\}$ *the* $\left\{ \begin{array}{l} heaven \\ heavens \end{array} \right\}$ *(and the earth) (*not).*

Parentheses and curly brackets show optionally occurring linguistic units, and asterisks show impossible units.

In a concrete linguistic utterance, we always have a chain of units, so the syntagmatic relations are in a sense more salient. However, paradigmatic relations are no less important for the structure of language. Morphology can be looked at from both a syntagmatic and a paradigmatic point of view. In a syntagmatic approach to morphology, morphological analysis consists in the **segmentation** of words into **morphemes** and the description of the conditions under which different morphemes can occur (see Definition 2 of Section 1.1). In syntagmatic morphology, tree representations are often used to show constituency relations within words, as we saw in Chapter 5.

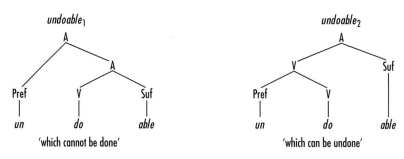

Figure 9.1 Two meanings and two structures of undoable

In a paradigmatic approach to morphology, paradigmatic relations are emphasized more than syntagmatic relations. In Section 3.2.2, we saw that word-based descriptions have various advantages over syntagmatic morpheme-based descriptions. Word-based descriptions of the sort outlined in Section 3.2.2 represent a paradigmatic point of view, because morphological structure is seen as consisiting not in the combination of morphemes, but in the **parallel formal and semantic resemblances** among words in the lexicon (see Definition 1 of Section 1.1). Such resemblances lead speakers to set up word-schemas, and correspondences between word-schemas are morphological rules.

In Section 5.3 we saw that in the syntagmatic approach we have an elegant way of describing the difference between the two senses of the word *undoable*. Figure 9.1 essentially repeats Figure 5.5. In the paradigmatic approach, words are not segmented into constituent morphemes and no tree representations are used, but the two senses of *undoable* can be described equally well. *Undoable₁* is paradigmatically related to words such as *unhappy, uninteresting, unequal*, as well as to *doable*, and it matches the second word-schema in (9.2) (this corresponds to the segmentation *un + doable*).

(9.2) $\begin{bmatrix} /X/_A \\ \text{'having quality}_X\text{'} \end{bmatrix} \leftrightarrow \begin{bmatrix} /unX/_A \\ \text{'not having quality'}_X \end{bmatrix}$

Undoable₂, by contrast, is paradigmatically related to words such as *readable, washable, approachable*, as well as to *undo*, and it matches the second word-schema in (9.3) (this corresponds to the segmentation *undo + able*). In the same way, *doable* (the close relative of *undoable₁*) is related to *do* (this corresponds to the segmentation (*do + able*).

(9.3) $\begin{bmatrix} /X/_V \\ \text{'do}_X\text{'} \end{bmatrix} \leftrightarrow \begin{bmatrix} /Xable/_A \\ \text{'capable of being done}_X\text{'} \end{bmatrix}$

Finally, the relationship between *undo* and *do* is shown in (9.4). The second word-schema also subsumes words such as *uncover, unfold, untie*.

(9.4) $\begin{bmatrix} /X/_V \\ \text{'do}_X\text{'} \end{bmatrix} \leftrightarrow \begin{bmatrix} /unX/_V \\ \text{'reverse the effect of doing}_X\text{'} \end{bmatrix}$

Thus, with respect to this example, the syntagmatic and the paradigmatic descriptions work equally well, but this is not always the case.

Although the syntagmatic approach to morphology was perhaps more prominent in twentieth-century linguistics than the paradigmatic approach, in this textbook I tend to emphasize the paradigmatic approach. This reflects the growing recognition among morphologists that the syntagmatic approach has its limitations and that important insights can be gained by adopting a paradigmatic approach. In this chapter, some further evidence will be presented for the word-based model of morphology that was introduced in Section 3.2.2. However, in the final section of this chapter I will end by giving some reasons why we may also need the syntagmatic approach.

9.2 Subtraction and back-formation

In the syntagmatic model of morphology, the most expected situation is one in which a form /X/ meaning 'x' is combined with a form /Y/ meaning 'y', so that an addition of form corresponds to an addition of meaning. This is indeed the most common situation in morphology, but it is not the only possibility.

On the one hand, it is possible for morphological rules to involve subtraction of form. We have already seen an example of this in Section 2.4 (ex. 2.21). Another famous example comes from Tohono O'odham:

(9.5)

INCOMPLETED	COMPLETED	
hi:nk	*hi:n*	'bark(ed)'
ñeid	*ñei*	'see/saw'
ñeok	*ñeo*	'speak/spoke'
golon	*golo*	'rake'
si:sp	*si:ṣ*	'nail'

(Zepeda 1983: 59–60)

Like the Murle case of Section 2.4, this must be analyzed as formally subtractive, because in an additive analysis it would be impossible to predict which shape the additional elements have.

The reverse case of this, the **subtraction of meaning**, is also possible. For example, Russian has a productive anticausative suffix -*sja* whose semantic effect is to subtract the meaning component 'cause' from the base's meaning (Mel'čuk 1991). For instance, *otkryt'* means 'open (tr.), cause to become open', and the anticausative derivative *otkryt'sja* means 'open (intr.), become open'. The word-based rule for this pattern is shown in (9.6).

(9.6) $\begin{bmatrix} /X/_V \\ \text{'A causes B to happen'} \end{bmatrix} \leftrightarrow \begin{bmatrix} /Xsja/_V \\ \text{'B happens'} \end{bmatrix}$

Both subtraction of form and subtraction of meaning are difficult to represent in a morpheme-based model, but the representation is straightforward in a word-based model.

Another kind of morphological formation that might be considered as subtractive in nature is back-formation (see Section 3.2 for earlier discussion). In such well-known examples as *to burgle* (back-formed from *burglar*), *to peddle* (back-formed from *pedlar*) and *to sculpt* (back-formed from *sculptor*), one could say that the new lexeme was formed by simultaneous subtraction of form (the suffix /-ər/) and meaning ('agent noun'). However, an even simpler analysis of back-formation would say that there is no special rule here at all: back-formation involves only the creative use of the ordinary rule of agent–noun formation (see (3.16) in Section 3.2.2) in the reverse direction, a possibility that is entirely expected if morphological rules are not inherently directed.

One important question that now arises (and that we left open at the end of Section 3.2.2) is why back-formation is relatively rare, compared to 'forth-formation', or in other words why derivational rules are typically productive only in one direction. We saw in Chapter 6 that it is not in general possible to predict the degree of productivity of a rule on the basis of its structural properties, but at least one inhibiting factor can be easily identified: when one of the word-schemas in a morphological rule contains some highly specific constant elements, there will be very few words matching that schema, apart from those that were coined by using it in the first place. Thus, in such a case the domain of the rule is automatically quite limited and the rule will have a hard time producing many neologisms. For example, a rule such as '[/X/$_A$ 'having quality$_X$'] $\leftrightarrow$ [/Xness/$_N$ 'the state of having quality$_X$']', which is often used to create neologisms with the suffix -*ness* (e.g. *floweriness*), will rarely be used for neologism-creating back-formations, simply because there are extremely few (if any) non-derived words ending in -*ness* that denote the state of having a certain quality. In the last sentence I added the qualification 'neologism-creating' because it is much more likely that individual speakers use the rule to back-form an adjective from a complex form that they may have heard. Recall, for example, the noun *defectiveness* from the heading of Section 7.7. Some readers of this book probably never encountered this word before (at least in its specialized morphological sense), but quite possibly they back-formed the adjective *defective* from it even before they read it in the text of Section 7.7. This would be creative use of the -*ness* rule in the reverse direction, but it is not neologism-creating back-formation, because the adjective *defective* (in its linguistic sense) is not a neologism for the speech community as a whole.

It is for this reason that the main area of productivity of back-formations is in compounds of the type *to air condition* and *to babysit*. The bases of these compounds, *air conditioning* and *babysitter*, have the right semantic and formal properties, but they were not created by invoking the rule of action–noun formation in *-ing* or agent-noun formation in *-er* (at least not directly). Thus, such compounds with action–noun and agent–noun heads are a fertile ground for back-formations. And, indeed, this type is highly productive in English, with well over 100 attested neologisms for the first half of the twentieth century alone (Algeo 1991: 144–5). This can be taken as evidence that there is nothing peculiar about back-formation: if the conditions are right, it functions exactly like 'forth-formation'. The word-based model, in which correspondences are not inherently directed, leads us to expect just this.

Another argument against the traditional definition of back-formation in terms of double subtraction is the possibility of back-formation in non-concatenative correspondences such as conversions. Consider the English rule in (9.7), which describes pairs of words such as $call_V/call_N$, $kick_V/kick_N$, $shove_V/shove_N$.

$$(9.7) \quad \begin{bmatrix} /X/_V \\ \text{'do}_X\text{'} \end{bmatrix} \leftrightarrow \begin{bmatrix} /X/_N \\ \text{'act of doing}_X\text{'} \end{bmatrix}$$

The direction of diachronic derivation seems clear: The nouns were created on the basis of the verbs. For example, the verb *call* is first attested in English around 1000, but the noun *call* is attested only around 1300. However, this rule may occasionally also be used in the opposite direction – e.g. $crusade_N \rightarrow crusade_V$, $pirouette_N \rightarrow pirouette_V$.

But if we do not define back-formation in terms of 'double subtraction', and if morphological correspondences (=rules) are not inherently directed, how can we distinguish between back-formation and forth-formation? It seems that the best way to define back-formation is as an application of a morphological rule in the less productive direction (Becker 1993a). This accounts both for the standard *babysit* case and for $crusade_V$. It also expresses the fact that back-formation refers only to the **creative** aspect of a morphological rule. Once a back-formed word has become a usual word, it is synchronically indistinguishable from a non-derived word (thus, only historical linguists, but not speakers of English, know that *edit* was back-formed from *editor*). For the **descriptive** aspect of morphology, we do not need the distinction between back-formation and forth-formation.

9.3 Cross-formation

A cross-formation is a morphological rule in which both word-schemas in the correspondence exhibit a constant phonological element (Becker 1993a). A set of words that are related by cross-formation is shown in (9.8a), and the rule is formulated in (9.8b).

(9.8) a. *socialist*   *socialism*
      hedonist   *hedonism*
      fascist   *fascism*
      pessimist   *pessimism*

$$\text{b.}\begin{bmatrix} /Xist/_N \\ \text{'ideology}_X \text{ or attitude}_X\text{'} \end{bmatrix} \leftrightarrow \begin{bmatrix} /Xism/_N \\ \text{'follower of ideology}_X/\text{attitude}_X\text{'} \end{bmatrix}$$

Cross-formations are in no way unusual or uncommon. We saw examples earlier, in Chapter 3 ((3.18c) and (3.30b)), and especially in Chapter 7, when we discussed inflection. Cross-formations can be described easily in a word-based model, but they are often problematic in a morpheme-based model. The easiest case is perhaps the pair *socialist/socialism*, which could be described as two separate derivations: *social + ist* and *social + ism*. Less straightforward for a morpheme-based description are pairs like *hedonist/hedonism*, for which we would need to postulate an abstract stem *hedon-* that does not occur elsewhere. But, of course, abstract stems are often posited, and for good reasons (as we saw in Section 7.4), so let us leave this issue aside. The main problem with the syntagmatic morpheme-based account of *socialist/socialism* and *hedonist/hedonism* is the fact that the two words are always closely related semantically. If the *-ist* word and the *-ism* word were not related to each other directly, but were related directly only to their base, then one would expect that some *-ist/-ism* words could differ in meaning.

But the really difficult cases of cross-formation are those in which the needed simple base exists but does not have the right meaning. Consider the German verb pairs in (9.9).

(9.9) a. *einklammern* 'put in   *ausklammern* 'remove from
                      parentheses'   parentheses'
      eintragen   'make a note'   *austragen*   'remove a note'
      einfassen   'mount (jewelry)' *ausfassen*   'dismount (jewelry)'
    b. *zudecken*   'cover'   *aufdecken*   'uncover'
      zusperren   'lock'   *aufsperren* 'unlock'
      zuschließen 'lock'   *aufschließen* 'unlock'
                              (Becker 1993a: 11; 1993b: 186)

We see that the German prefixed particle *aus-* can be used to form a reversive derivation from bases that contain the prefixed particle *ein-*. This can be captured by the rule in (9.10), with an analogous rule for *zu/auf*.

$$(9.10)\begin{bmatrix} /ein\,X/_V \\ \\ \text{'do}_X\text{'} \end{bmatrix} \leftrightarrow \begin{bmatrix} /aus\,X/_V \\ \\ \text{'reverse the action of doing}_X\text{'} \end{bmatrix}$$

The logical alternative approach in the morpheme-based model would be to derive both *ein-/zu-* verbs and *aus-/auf* verbs separately from simple verbs. However, this does not yield the right meanings. The verbs *klammern, tragen, fassen, decken, sperren, schließen* exist as simple verbs, but they are semantically only distantly related to the left-hand verbs in (9.9). For instance, *klammern* means 'clip, cling', *tragen* means 'carry', *fassen* means 'grasp', *decken* means 'set (the table)', and so on. The morpheme-based model would thus have to set up artificial stems that are formally identical to, but semantically quite different from, the existing simple verbs.

Cross-formation also exists in compounding. Consider the pairs of words in (9.11).

(9.11)		
	seasick	*airsick*
	sealane	*airlane*
	seafare	*airfare*
	seaborne	*airborne*
	seamanship	*airmanship*
	seaworthy	*airworthy*
	seaman	*airman*

(Becker 1993a: 13–14)

For the first few words one can still imagine that the *sea* and *air* compounds were created idependently of each other – i.e. *airsick* from *air* + *sick*, without direct relation to the older word *seasick*, or *airlane* from *air* + *lane*, without direct relation to *sealane*. But for some of the others this seems very unlikely because the meaning is noncompositional. A *seaman* is a low-ranking navy member, not any man with some relation to the sea, and similarly an *airman* is a low-ranking air force member. Thus, we are probably dealing with a rule as in (9.12).

(9.12)
$$\begin{bmatrix} /seaX/ \\ \text{'an } x \text{ having to do} \\ \text{with sea travel'} \end{bmatrix} \leftrightarrow \begin{bmatrix} /airX/ \\ \text{'an } x \text{ having to do} \\ \text{with air travel'} \end{bmatrix}$$

9.4 Output constraints in morphology

In a substantial number of cases, morphologically complex words have properties that can be described only as properties of the complex pattern, or in other words properties that cannot be ascribed to any of the constituents. Such properties are called **output constraints**. This is very common in the phonological part of a morphological pattern and apparently less common in the semantic part.

9.4.1 Phonological output constraints

Let us consider two examples, the first from Dutch. Dutch inhabitant nouns have the suffix *-er* or *-aar*, depending on the phonological shape of the base.[1]

(9.13) a. *Ámsterdàm*   *Ámsterdàmmer*   'inhabitant of Amsterdam'
            Blóemendàal   *Blóemendàler*   'inhabitant of Bloemendaal'
       b. *Díemen*   *Diemenàar*   'inhabitant of Diemen'
            Úddel   *Úddelàar*   'inhabitant of Uddel'

(Booij 1998)

This is a case of phonologically conditioned weak suppletion, for which we need two different rules (9.14a–b). In the phological part of the schema, v́ stands for any stressed vowel bearing secondary or primary stress, and L stands for a coronal sonorant (i.e. *n*, *l* or *r*). Parentheses indicate prosodic constituency – i.e. parsing into feet.

(9.14) a. $\left[\begin{array}{c} /(X)_F(Cv́C)_F/_N \\ \text{'town}_X\text{'} \end{array} \right]$ $\leftrightarrow$ $\left[\begin{array}{c} /(X)_F(Cv́Cər)_F/_N \\ \text{'inhabitant of town}_X\text{'} \end{array} \right]$

       b. $\left[\begin{array}{c} /(CVCəL)_F/_N \\ \text{'town}_X\text{'} \end{array} \right]$ $\leftrightarrow$ $\left[\begin{array}{c} /(CVCə)_F\,(Là:r)_F/_N \\ \text{'inhabitant of town}_X\text{'} \end{array} \right]$

It would theoretically be possible to describe the affix suppletion exclusively on the basis of the input: town names that end in a stress-bearing syllable get the suffix [-ər], town names that end in a schwa syllable get the suffix [-a:r]. However, only when we see the complex forms, the outputs, does this distribution begin to make sense. $(Cv́Cər)_F$ and $(La:r)_F$ are possible feet in Dutch. If we had the reverse distribution of suffixes, we would get [Cv́Cà:r] and $(CVCəLər)_F$, two patterns that are not prosodically well formed (in the first, we would have a stress clash, and in the second, a three-syllable foot).

In a word-based model, outputs have a clear status: they are word-schemas just like inputs – i.e. they have a direct representation in the grammar. Special well-formedness constraints on outputs are therefore entirely expected.

9.4.2 Semantic output constraints (or constructional meanings)

Semantic output constraints are semantic properties of the derived words that cannot be attributed to any of the constituent morphemes. We have

---

[1] The stress marks indicate main stress (v́) and secondary stress (v̀). (The spelling differences between *Amsterdam* and *Amsterdamm-(er)* and between *Bloemendaal* and *Bloemendal-(er)* are due to peculiarities of Dutch spelling that are irrelevant here. There is no alternation in the pronunciation.)

already seen two examples of this phenomenon: noun-to-verb conversion, e.g. *hammer*$_N$ → *hammer*$_V$ (cf. 3.12)), and certain types of compounds, such as Italian *lavapiatti* 'dishwasher' (cf. (5.8)). Here the meaning components 'use' and 'agent' are present in the derivative, but there is no morpheme that corresponds to them. Some linguists have postulated a zero morpheme in these cases that bears the relevant meaning, but the main purpose of this device seems to be to save the morpheme-based model.

9.5 Triangular relationships

In derivational morphology, most morphological relationships can be described as simple base-derivative relationships, i.e. as rules involving just two word-schemas. All the rules that we have seen so far in this chapter have been of this simple type, but we saw earlier that sometimes more than two word-schemas may be in correspondence. In Section 3.2.2, a rule was formulated for putting triples of the type *attract/attraction/attractive* in correspondence, repeated here as (9.15).

$$(9.15) \quad \begin{bmatrix} /X/_V \\ \text{'do}_X\text{'} \end{bmatrix} \quad \longleftrightarrow \quad \begin{bmatrix} /Xion/_N \\ \text{'action of doing}_X\text{'} \end{bmatrix}$$
$$\begin{bmatrix} /Xive/_A \\ \text{'prone to doing}_X\text{'} \end{bmatrix}$$

The argument for positing such a triangular relationship in this case was the existence of pairs like *aggression/aggressive*, where no verb **aggress* exists. But there is an additional motivation, which was not mentioned earlier. Consider the additional triples in (9.16).

(9.16)
describe	*description*	*descriptive*
repeat	*repetition*	*repetitive*
multiply	*multiplication*	*multiplicative*
destroy	*destruction*	*destructive*
permit	*permission*	*permissive*
acquire	*acquisition*	*acquisitive*

In these and other lexeme triples, the noun and adjective are formally similar and differ only (if we confine ourselves to the spelling for expository simplicity) in the endings *-ion* and *-ive*. The formal relation between the noun–adjective root and the verb root, however, is unpredictable and must be learned individually for each of these verbs. Thus, a more precise version of (9.15) should be as in (9.17), where the verb root appears as /X/ and the noun–adjective root appears as /Y/.

(9.17) $\begin{bmatrix} /X/_V \\ \text{'do}_X\text{'} \end{bmatrix} \leftrightarrow \begin{bmatrix} /Yion/_N \\ \text{'action of doing}_X\text{'} \end{bmatrix}$

$\begin{bmatrix} /Yive/_A \\ \text{'prone to doing}_X\text{'} \end{bmatrix}$

In this triangle, the relationships between the verb and the noun and between the verb and the adjective are semantically regular and formally irregular, whereas the relationship between the noun and the adjective is regular both formally and semantically, but indirect (a cross-formation, both formally and semantically).

A very similar triangle must be posited for German country names, inhabitant nouns and country adjectives. Consider the triples in (9.18).

(9.18)

country	inhabitant	adjective	
Libanon	*Libanese*	*libanesisch*	(Lebanon)
Finnland	*Finne*	*finnisch*	(Finland)
Türkei	*Türke*	*türkisch*	(Turkey)
Zypern	*Zypriote*	*zypriotisch*	(Cyprus)
Böhmen	*Böhme*	*böhmisch*	(Bohemia)
Korsika	*Korse*	*korsisch*	(Corsica)
Guatemala	*Guatemalteke*	*guatemaltekisch*	(Guatemala)

(Becker 1990: 43–4)

The formal relationship between the country name and the other two words is quite unpredictable, whereas the relationship is completely regular between inhabitant noun and country adjective. Semantically, however, both the noun and the adjective refer to the country name. The adjective *türkisch*, for instance, means 'relating to Turkey', as is clear from phrases like *türkischer Kurde* 'Turkish Kurd (= Kurd living in Turkey)' or *türkische Landschaft* 'Turkish landscape (= landscape of Turkey)'. The triangular correspondence is shown in (9.19).

(9.19) $\begin{bmatrix} /X/_N \\ \text{'country}_X\text{'} \end{bmatrix} \leftrightarrow \begin{bmatrix} /Ye/_N \\ \text{'inhabitant of country}_X\text{'} \end{bmatrix}$

$\begin{bmatrix} /Yisch/_A \\ \text{'relating to country}_X\text{'} \end{bmatrix}$

Such triangular relationships are also the formal mechanism by which **Priscianic formation** can be described in the word-based model. Recall from Section 7.4 that in inflection we sometimes need abstract stems that do not correspond to a semantic category. Basically we have the same phenomenon here in the domain of derivation.

9.6 Bracketing paradoxes

In a morpheme-based model, morphemes are often arranged in a hierarchical structure, as we saw in Chapter 5. Now there are a number of cases in which establishing such a hierarchical structure is problematic because of a mismatch between meaning and form. Consider person-denoting expressions of the type in (9.20a), which seem to be derived from the corresponding bases in (9.20b).

(9.20) a. *nuclear physicist, functional grammarian, atomic scientist*
   b. *nuclear physics, functional grammar, atomic science*

From a semantic point of view, the bracketing of *nuclear physicist* has to be *[[nuclear physic][-ist]]*, because the noun denotes a specialist in nuclear physics, not a physicist who is nuclear in some sense. But, from a formal point of view, the bracketing should be *[[nuclear] [physic-ist]]*, because a suffix like *-ist* cannot attach to a phrase consisting of noun + adjective (morphological rules cannot apply to syntactic phrases, just like syntactic rules cannot apply to morphological elements (see Section 8.5)). Moreover, the choice of the suffix is clearly lexically determined: *physics* takes *-ist*, not *-ian*, and *grammar* takes *-ian*, not *-ist*. In *science/scientist*, we further have an idiosyncratic alternation in the shape of the base. This contradiction between semantic and formal constituent structure is often called **bracketing paradox**. The tree representations corresponding to the two bracketings are shown in Figure 9.2.

Morphologists have proposed various solutions to deal with this apparent contradiction. One obvious possibility that linguists often resort to when faced with contradictions is to assume different levels of representation. At an underlying representation, the bracketing would be

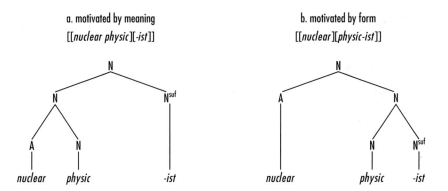

Figure 9.2 A bracketing paradox: two hierarchial structures of *nuclear physicist*

[[nuclear][physic-ist]], and this would be changed into the semantically appropriate *[[nuclear physic][-ist]]* by some kind of transformational rule.

In a word-based model, such cases could be described by a triangular relationship of the sort we saw in the preceding section, or rather a quadrangular relationship, because four terms are involved: the field of activity (e.g. *physics*), the practitioner of that field (e.g. *physicist*), the additionally qualified field (e.g. *nuclear physics*) and the practitioner of the qualified field (e.g. *nuclear physicist*). The rule could be formulated as in (9.23).

$$(9.23) \quad \begin{bmatrix} /X/_N \\ \text{'field of activity}_X' \end{bmatrix} \qquad \longleftrightarrow \qquad \begin{bmatrix} /Y/_N \\ \text{'practitioner of field}_X' \end{bmatrix}$$

$$\updownarrow \qquad\qquad\qquad\qquad\qquad\qquad \updownarrow$$

$$\begin{bmatrix} /ZX/_N \\ \text{'field}_X \text{ with qualification}_Z' \end{bmatrix} \qquad \longleftrightarrow \qquad \begin{bmatrix} /ZY/_N \\ \text{'practitioner of field}_{XZ}' \end{bmatrix}$$

The formal relations between the field and the practitioner noun are unpredictable, so the rule simply contains a different variable $/Y/$, as in the cases of *destroy/destruction* and *Türkei/Türke* in Section 9.5. The pair of word-schemas on the left-hand side is an instance of a more general rule of compounding, and the correspondence between the two word-schemas on the right-hand side is the unusual part of this quandrangular rule. The right-hand correspondence cannot be subsumed under any more general rule, but within the quadrangular relationship it makes sense and is thus productive in English.

The advantage of the rule in (9.23) is that it can subsume further similar pairs such as those in (9.24) (see Spencer 1988), which are also 'paradoxical' in that they cannot be derived by other, more ordinary rules, but which are not really bracketing paradoxes because they cannot be described by the two hierarchical structures in Figure 9.2.

(9.24) a. *moral philosopher*   *moral philosophy*
           urban sociologist   *urban sociology*
      b. *baroque flautist*   *baroque flute*
           modern hispanist   *modern Spain/Spanish*
      c. *electrical engineer*   *electrical engineering*
           theoretical linguist   *theoretical linguistics*

In (9.24a) both the practitioner and the field noun bear an affix and, in (9.24b), the relation between the practitioner noun and the field noun is that of weak suppletion. In (9.24c) the practitioner noun has no affix and the field noun has an affix. Thus, the formal relations are quite diverse, but the semantic relations are constant, as is expressed by the rule in (9.23).

9.7 Are morphemes unnecessary?

We could conclude this chapter by noting that there is overwhelming evidence in favour of word-based rules, and that the paradigmatic, word-based model of Section 3.2.2 and this chapter is therefore superior to the syntagmatic, morpheme-based model of Section 3.2.1, so that we do not need morphemes at all in morphology. A number of morphologists have drawn this conclusion, but at this stage a few words of caution seem in order.

First, at the practical level, it is simply very convenient to talk about morphemes as if they were real entities, and not just an aspect of abstract paradigmatic relations between words. Morphologists routinely talk about prefixes, suffixes, roots, allomorphs, etc., and it would be very difficult to do without them. These notions can all be defined in terms of the morpheme concept, but, if we wanted to abandon that concept in favour of purely paradigmatic rules, we would have to develop a completely new set of terms for practical purposes. Note also that descriptive linguists routinely segment complex words and provide morpheme-by-morpheme glosses – e.g. Japanese *waraw-ase-rare-ta* [laugh-CAUS-PASS-PAST] 'was made to laugh'. This has proved extremely useful, and there is no obvious alternative to this procedure.

Second, there is some evidence that words are seen as consisting of morphemes by speakers as well. Some linguists have claimed that morphological rules never make reference to word-internal structure, so that there is no need to assume that words 'have structure' once they have been formed according to the rules. But this does not seem quite right. For one thing, we saw in Section 5.3 that there often is evidence for **head operations** – i.e. morphological rules that affect the head constituent of a complex word. And, second, allomorphy is often conditioned by the morphological structure of the base (see Section 2.5). For example, Dutch past participles are marked by the prefix *ge-* (e.g. *spreken* 'speak', *ge-sproken* 'spoken') unless the verb bears a derivational prefix such as *be-* (e.g. *be-spreken* 'discuss', *be-sproken* 'discussed', not **ge-be-sproken*). The Sanskrit converb is formed by the suffix *-tvā* if the verb has no prefix (e.g. *ga-tvā* 'having gone', *nī-tvā* 'having led'), but by the suffix *-ya* if the verb has a prefix (e.g. *ā-gam-ya* 'having come', not **ā-ga-tvā; pari-ṇī-tvā*) (Carstairs-McCarthy 1993).

Third, morphemes also seem to have relevance for phonology. For example, many languages have phonological **morpheme structure conditions** – i.e. restrictions on the co-occurrence of sounds within a morpheme. For example, English allows combinations such as [tθ] and [dθ] in complex words like *eighth* and *width*, but not within a single morpheme. German allows syllable-final consonant clusters such as [rpsts] as in *Herbst-s* (genitive of *Herbst* 'autumn'), but within a single morpheme four consonants (e.g. [rpst]) are the maximum. In addition, phonological alternations may be sensitive to morpheme boundaries. Standard Northern Italian has an alternation in the pronunciation of *s* between [s] and [z], whereby the latter pronunciation is chosen if the s occurs between vowels (e.g. *santo* [s-] 'saint', *casa* [-z-] 'house'). However, if the *s* is morpheme-initial, it is pronounced [s] even if it occurs between vowels (e.g. *asimmetrico* [-s-] 'asymmetric', *rosocializzare* 'resocialize') (Baroni 2001). These phenomena, too, seem to require that we recognize morphemes as real entities.

And, fourth, while the word-based model as presented here clearly allows us to describe some phenomena that would be difficult to describe in a pure morpheme-based model, one may ask why there are so few cases that are difficult for the morpheme-based model. Most morphology looks morpheme-based in most languages, so should we change our entire approach just to accommodate a few uncommon phenomena? If all of morphology is word-based, why do we not have more non-concatenative processes? Why are so few languages like Arabic and Hebrew, with massive use of non-concatenative morphology?

Now it turns out that there is a good answer to these latter questions: new morphology mostly arises from syntactic constructions when lexical items are grammaticalized to become affixes (see Section 3.3.2). As a result, all languages are constantly being enriched by new concatenative morphological processes that can easily be described by the morpheme-based model (Bybee and Newman 1995). So the predominance of concatenative operations would have a diachronic explanation and need not be attributed to the architecture of the grammar.

And the evidence for morphemes as real entities need not be incompatible with the word-based model. It is perhaps possible to define a morpheme as a special case of a formal relationship in a morphological correspondence: a constant element in the phonological part of a corresponding word-schema or lexical entry could be called a morpheme – e.g. /un/ in (9.2) or /able/ in (9.3). This definition would not be too different from the usual definition of a morpheme, and it would make it possible to continue to make use of morphemes, roots and affixes for practical purposes. It might also help us with the other problems for a morpheme-free morphology that were mentioned in this section. Under this view, the difference between the word-based model and the morpheme-based model would be the status of the morpheme as secondary or primary, not its very existence.

Summary of Chapter 9

Morphological structure can be considered from a syntagmatic and a paradigmatic perspective. In contrast to Chapter 5, where the syntagmatic, morpheme-based perspective was highlighted, this chapter emphasizes those phenomena that are better understood from a paradigmatic, word-based perspective. Subtraction and back-formation are necessarily rare phenomena, but they cannot be accommodated naturally by the syntagmatic approach. Cross-formation is more common, and certain types of cross-formation can be described only paradigmatically. The paradigmatic, word-based approach is further motivated by output constraints and triangular relationships, and 'bracketing paradoxes' cease to be paradoxical in this light. It is thus possible that the morpheme concept can be entirely dispensed with, although there are also some arguments in favour of keeping this concept.

Further reading

Word-based rules of the kind proposed and defended in this chapter have been proposed especially in works such as Becker (1990, 1993a,b), Bochner (1993) and Ford and Singh (1991). See also Spencer (1988) and Booij (1997).

Phonological output conditions are discussed in Booij (1998), and bracketing paradoxes are discussed by Spencer (1988), Stump (1991) and Beard (1991).

The view that morphemes are unnecessary is defended most forcefully in Anderson (1992) and in Dasgupta *et al* (2000).

Exercises

1. The following pairs of English lexemes are related by cross-formation. Formulate the rule for them, analogous to (9.8b).

astronomy	*astronomer*
philosophy	*philosopher*
ethnography	*ethnographer*

2. For French adjectives, linguists have often advocated an analysis in terms of subtraction: the masculine form is formed from the femine form by subtracting the final consonant (Bloomfield 1933: 217):

plat/platte	'flat'	[pla/plat]
laid/laide	'ugly'	[lɛ/lɛd]
long/longue	'long'	[lõ/lõg]
soul/soule	'drunk'	[su/sul]
gris/grise	'gray'	[gri/griz]

Why is this an attractive analysis?

3. Assuming that the possessive case in Tümpisa Shoshone (see (7.27)), is best described by Priscianic formation, formulate the word-based rule, which will have the form of a triangular relationship, analogous to (9.19) and (9.21).

4. English compounds such as *pickpocket, cut-throat, kill-joy, spoil-sport* have a meaning element that does not have a corresponding formal constituent. How can this be captured by a word-based rule?

5. A kind of form-meaning mismatch is found in words such as the following (Spencer 1988):

southern Dane
East German
South Korean

A southern Dane is not a Dane who is southern, but someone who comes from southern Denmark. Formulate a quadrangular rule (analogous to the one in (9.23)) that shows both the formal and the semantic relations.

Morphophonology **10**

10.1 Two types of sound alternations

In Chapter 2, we saw that morphemes often have different phonological shapes depending on the environment (i.e. the other morphemes and sounds with which they co-occur in a word). For example, the stem of the English lexeme *leaf* is pronounced [li:f] in the singular, but [li:v] in the plural (*leaves*); the stem of *pat* is always pronounced [pæt] if it occurs without any suffix, but in many varieties the pronunciation is [pæɾ] if a vowel-initial suffix follows (*patting* [pæɾɪŋ]). Such alternations are called **sound alternations**, and they are relevant for a morphology textbook because they come in two kinds: **automatic alternations** (also called **phonetic alternations**) and **morphophonological alternations** (also called **lexical alternations**). While automatic alternations clearly belong in the realm of phonology, morphophonological alternations (as their name says) have both phonological and morphological properties and must be considered in some detail in this book.[1]

As is the case with morphological patterns, sound alternations (whether automatic or morphophonological) are often described in process terms. Thus, the well-known German alternation of voiced and voiceless obstruents in syllable-final position (e.g. *Tag* [ta:k] 'day' / *Tage* [ta:gə] 'days', (see (2.24a)) is referred to as **final devoicing**. Again, this terminology must be understood as metaphorical – the process is happening in the linguist's

---

[1] A note on terminology: many linguists use the term *phonological alternation* as a general term both for automatic alternations and for morphophonological alternations, implying that both belong in the same component of grammar. But since there are so many differences between the two alternation types, this is a controversial view, and other linguists would say that only automatic alternations are truly phonological, whereas morphophonological alternations are really morphological in nature. Thus, I avoid the term *phonological alternation* in this chapter and use the more neutral term *sound alternation*.

imagination, not in language or speech. But the process terminology is very convenient because it gives more information than purely static terminology. If we simply referred to the German alternation in [ta:k]/[ta:gə] as *voiceless/voiced alternation*, we would not know that there are many voiceless obstruents that are never affected by this alternation – e.g. [k] in *Volk* 'people'/*Völker* 'peoples'. If, on the other hand, we call the alternation *devoicing*, it is immediately clear that the existence of such non-alternating voiceless obstruents is completely expected. Note also that in the case of sound alternations, such 'synchronic processes' are usually the result of diachronic processes of sound change. In Old High German (c.800–1100 CE), voiced obstruents did occur in syllable-final position, but around 1100 a sound change occurred by which all syllable-final obstruents became voiceless. Now, of course, modern speakers of German do not know this, so diachronic processes and 'synchronic processes' must be kept strictly apart conceptually. But linguists can profit from this historical knowledge when they happen to have it because it throws light on the synchronic alternations that it gave rise to.

Before we examine the properties that distinguish between automatic and morphophonological alternations, let us look at a few representative cases of both types.

(10.1) Some automatic alternations[2]

a. German **Final Devoicing**
   Voiced obstruents are pronounced voiceless when they occur in a syllable-final position.

Tage [ta:gə]	'days'	*Tag* [ta:k]	'day'
Liese [li:zə]	'Liese (name)'	*Lieschen* [li:sçən]	'little Liese'
Monde [mo:ndə]	'moons'	*Mond* [mo:nt]	'moon'
beige [be:ʒə]	'beige (inflected)	*beige* [be:ʃ]	'beige (uninfl.)'

b. English **Flapping**
   Alveolar plosives ([d] and [t]) are pronounced as voiced flaps [ɾ] when they occur in front of an unstressed vowel, in many varieties of English.

pat [pæt]	*patting* [pæɾɪŋ]
fat [fæt]	*fatter* [fæɾər]
pad [pæd]	*padding* [pæɾɪŋ]

c. Russian **Akanie** (neutralization of unstressed *o* and *a*)
   The vowel [o] is pronounced [a] when it occurs in the syllable immediately before the stressed syllable, and both [o] and [a] are

---

[2] The names of sound alternations are capitalized here because they are often traditional names that reflect the actual phonological properties only partially. Not uncommonly, the terms used in the respective language is in general use among linguists (e.g. German *Umlaut*, Russian *Akanie*, Japanese *Rendaku*).

pronounced [ə] when they occur in an earlier syllable, or in a syllable after the stressed syllable.

vol [vol]	'ox (NOM.SG)'	*vol-ɨ* [va'lɨ]	'oxen (NOM.PL)'
nós-it ['nos'it]	'carries'	*nos-í* [na's'i]	'carry!' (IMPV)
bórod-ɨ ['borədɨ]	'beards'	*borod-á* [bəra'da]	'beard'
bandít [ban'd'it]	'gangster'	*bandit-ízm* [bənd'i't'izm]	'gangsterism'

    d. Japanese **Palatalization**
       Alveolar obstruents ([t] and [s]) are pronounced as palatals ([tɕ] and [ɕ], commonly written as *ch* and *sh*) when they occur before the high palatal vowel [i].

kas-e	'lend' (imperative)	*kash-i*	'lend' (continuative)
kat-e	'win' (imperative)	*kach-i*	'win' (continuative)
			(Vance 1987: 177)

(10.2) Some morphophonological alternations

    a. English **Trisyllabic Shortening**
       The vowels or diphthongs [ei], [i:], [ai] and [ou] alternate with the short vowels [æ], [e], [ɪ] and [ɒ] when followed by two syllables the first of which is unstressed.

[ei]	*nation*	[æ]	*national*
[i:]	*extreme*	[e]	*extremity*
[ai]	*divine*	[ɪ]	*divinity*
[ou]	*globe*	[ɒ]	*globular*

    b. German **Umlaut** (vowel fronting)
       The back vowels and diphthongs *a, o, u* and *au* alternate with front vowels *ä* [ɛ], *ö* [ø, œ], *ü* [y, ʏ] and *äu* [ɔʏ] in certain morphological environments (plural of nouns, past subjunctive of verbs, female-noun suffix -*in*)

Buch	'book'	*Bücher*	'books'
Vater	'father'	*Väter*	'fathers' (cf. (2.6))
bot	'offered'	*böte*	'would offer'
Jude	'Jewish person/man'	*Jüdin*	'Jewish woman'

    c. Russian *Jer* **deletion** (alternation of *o/e* and zero)[3]
       The vowels *o/e* in the last syllable of the stem sometimes alternate with zero when a vowel-initial suffix follows.

zámok	'castle (NOM)'	*zámk-i*	'castles (NOM)' (cf. 2.25b)
ókon	'windows (GEN)'	*okn-ó*	'window (NOM)'

---

[3] The term *jer* refers to two short vowels of Old Russian that were lost in some environments, but became *o/e* in others, thus giving rise to the contemporary alternation.

zemél'-nyj	'relating to land'	*zemlj-á*	'land'
umén	'clever (predicative)'	*umn-yj*	'clever (attributive)'

d. Hebrew **Spirantization** (fricativization)
The stops *p, b, k* alternate with the fricatives *f, v, x* when a vowel precedes.

yi-spor	'he will count'	*sofer*	'he counts'
kotev	'he writes'	*yi-xtov*	'he will write'
pilpel	'he peppered'	*me-falpel*	'he peppers'
bakaša	'request'	*be-vakaša*	'please'

e. Turkish *k/ğ* **alternation**
The consonant *k* alternates with *ğ* when a vowel follows. (In standard Turkish, the letter *ğ* is no longer pronounced, so *yatağ-ı* is [jataɨ], but some non-standard varieties preserve a velar fricative.)

inek	'cow'	*ineğ-i*	'his cow'
kuyruk	'tail'	*kuyruğ-u*	'its tail'
köpük	'foam'	*köpüğ-ü*	'its foam'
yatak	'bed'	*yatağ-ı*	'its bed'

f. Japanese **Rendaku** (Sequential Voicing)
Morpheme-initial obstruents alternate with voiced obstruents when a vowel precedes (mostly when they occur initially in a second compound member).

kami	'paper'	(*iro*	'color')	*iro-gami*	'colored paper'
tooroo	'lantern'	(*ishi*	'stone')	*ishi-dooroo*	'stone lantern'
shirushi	'mark'	(*hoshi*	'star')	*hoshi-jirushi*	'asterisk'
hone	'bone'	(*se*	'back')	*se-bone*	'backbone'
chi	'blood'	(*hana*	'nose')	*hana-ji*	'nosebleed'

(Vance 1987: ch. 10)

The main differences between automatic alternations (as in (10.1)) and morphophonological alternations (as in (10.2)) are summarized in Table 10.1.

(i) Help for phonetic processing. In most cases, sound change is motivated by phonetics in the sense that it occurs because phonetic processing is made easier by a change. For example, pronouncing an alveolar or velar consonant before [i] is relatively more difficult than pronouncing a palatal (or palatalized) consonant, and this explains why the diachronic change of palatalization before front vowels is so common in the world's languages (e.g. (10.1d)). Final devoicing helps pronunciation because maintaining the vibration of the vocal chords (which is made difficult by the oral obstruction of obstruents anyway) is particularly difficult in the final position when no voiced sound follows (e.g. (10.1a)). Neutralization of unstressed vowels occurs for perceptual reasons: when a vowel is not stressed, it is less

Automatic alternations	Morphophonological alternations
help phonetic processing	do not necessarily help phonetic processing
phonetically coherent	not necessarily phonetically coherent
alternants are phonetically close	alternants may be phonetically distant
only phonologically conditioned	at least in part morphologically or lexically conditioned
not contradicted by simple morphemes	may be restricted to derived environments
extend to loanwords	need not extend to loanwords
may be optional and sensitive to speech style	obligatory, not sensitive to speech style
can create new segments	do not lead to new segments
not necessarily restricted to the word level	generally restricted to the word level

Table 10.1 Two types of sound alternations

loud and thus differences between vowels are harder to perceive (e.g. (10.1c)). Since automatic alternations result from relatively recent sound changes, the phonetic motivation is still transparent.

Morphophonological alternations generally reflect older sound changes, and the phonetic motivation may have been lost completely. For instance, German Umlaut (vowel fronting (10.2b)) was originally motivated by assimilation to a high front vowel in the following syllable (e.g. *Jude/Jüdin*). But in most contemporary words, this original front vowel has been lost completely or reduced to schwa, as shown in the examples in (10.3).

(10.3) Old High German   Modern German
    apful/epfili   *Apfel/Äpfel* [ɛpfl]   'apple(s)'
                                      (complete loss of final [i])
    kalb/kelbir   *Kalb/Kälber* [kɛlbər]   'calf/calves'
                                        (reduction to schwa)

Similarly, English Trisyllabic Shortening (10.2a) is no longer phonetically useful for English speakers. However, in some other cases of (10.2) the original phonetic motivation is still present, so this criterion is not sufficient for classifying an alternation as automatic.

(ii) Phonetic coherence. Often a whole range of different sounds is affected in a similar way by a sound change, and the resulting alternation may then be phonetically coherent in the sense that both the affected sounds and their replacements are natural classes. For example, German Final Devoicing affects all voiced obstruents and turns them into the corresponding voiceless obstruents; and English Flapping affects all alveolar plosives.

In morphophonological alternations, the coherence of the set of affected sounds may have been lost by subsequent sound changes. Thus, the class of English vowels affected by Trisyllabic Shortening is not a natural class; the class of Hebrew consonants affected by Spirantization is not a natural class; and the vowels resulting from German Umlaut are not a natural class (in particular, *äu* [ɔʏ], the umlauted counterpart of *au* [aʊ], can be described as 'fronted' only with great difficulty).

(iii) Phonetic distance. In automatic alternations, the alternating sounds tend to differ in one feature only, but in morphophonological alternations they may differ quite drastically. For instance, English [i:]/[ɛ], [oʊ]/[ɒ], Turkish [k]/Ø and Japanese *h/b* show a phonetic distance that is only possible because the sound changes that originally created the alternations occurred a long time ago and subsequent changes have made the connections opaque. (For instance, Japanese Rendaku originally led to *p/b* alternations, comparable to *k/g* and *t/d* alternations, but later *p* became *h*.)

(iv) Phonological versus morphological/lexical conditioning. In automatic alternations, the conditions under which the alternations occur can always be described in purely phonological terms. In morphophonological alternations, by contrast, the conditions always have a morphological (and sometimes also lexical) component. For example, English Trisyllabic Shortening is restricted to certain suffixes (e.g. *globular* versus *globalize*) and to certain words (e.g. *national* versus *notional*; the latter is pronounced [noʊʃn̩l], not [nɒʃn̩l]). Hebrew has many words where *k* does not undergo Spirantization although the phonological condition, a preceding vowel, is met (e.g. *kocer* 'reaps', *yikcor* 'will reap'). In the extreme case, a morphophonological alternation occurs under purely morphological and lexical conditions. This can be illustrated by German Umlaut, which was originally conditioned by [i] in the following syllable. Nowadays this phonological condition is irrelevant. Umlaut occurs always with certain suffixes such as plural *-er* (e.g. *Buch/Bücher* 'book(s)'). With other suffixes, it occurs only subject to further lexical conditions. Thus, with the plural suffix *-e*, the application of Umlaut has to be learned individually for each lexeme (e.g. *Hund/Hunde* 'dog(s)' versus *Bund/Bünde* 'league(s)').

(v) Derived environments. Automatic alternations result from constraints on pronunciation that are valid for all environments, and an alternation is just a special case that arises when different morphological contexts provide different phonological conditions. For instance, syllable–final obstruents are always voiceless in German, Russian [o] can never occur in an unstressed syllable and Japanese never allows [t] and [s] in front of [i] (Vance 1987: 21). Morphophonological alternations, by contrast, may be restricted to derived environments. For instance, Turkish [k] is deleted between vowels in a derived environment (see (10.2d)), but inside a morpheme there is nothing wrong with intervocalic [k] (e.g. *sokak* 'street', *sitreptokok* 'streptococcus'). In Hebrew, [b] is spirantized to [v] after a vowel, but inside a morpheme there is no problem with [b] (e.g. *kibuc* 'gathering;

kibbutz'). English long vowels and diphthongs may get shortened when a two-syllable suffix follows (e.g. *divine – divinity*), but inside a morpheme there is nothing wrong with a diphthong in the antepenultimate syllable (e.g. *vitamin* ['vaɪtəmɪn]).

(vi) Loanwords. Automatic processes apply to loanwords and foreign names as they do to native words. Thus, the city *Madrid* is pronounced with a final [t] in German because of final devoicing; in Russian, not only *Moskvá* is pronounced with [a] where the spelling has *o*, but also *Mombása* and *Montána* (and in *Mogadíšo*, the pronunciation is [ə], because *o* is not immediately before the stressed syllable). In Japanese, loans from English have *chi* and *shi* for English [ti] and [si] (e.g. *shiisoo* from *seesaw*, *shiizun* from *season*). By contrast, the effects of morphophonological alternations need not be found in loanwords. Thus, Turkish loanwords sometimes preserve their final [k] (e.g. *sitreptokok* 'streptococcus', *sitreptokoku*), and Russian *jer* deletion is never applied in loanwords (e.g. *baron/barony* 'baron', not **barny*).

(vii) Speech style and obligatoriness. When a phonological process has entered the language quite recently, it may still be optional and sensitive to the speech style. In formal, slow speech the process is less likely to occur than in informal, fast speech. For instance, English flapping may be suppressed in formal speech. Morphophonological alternations are always obligatory and are never sensitive to the speech style. It should be noted, however, that most automatic alternations that are described in grammars are obligatory as well.

(viii) New segments. Automatic alternations sometimes create segments that are not found under other conditions. For instance, English [ɾ] only occurs under the conditions of Flapping, and Russian [ə] occurs only under the conditions of Akanie. By contrast, morphophonological alternations only lead to segments that occur independently in the language. Thus, German has front vowels like *ö* and *ü* in basic words that have nothing to do with Umlaut (e.g. *öde* 'bleak', *Mühle* 'mill'), and Hebrew has the fricatives *f*, *v* and *x* in basic words that have nothing to do with Spirantization (e.g. *finjan* 'coffee cup', *ʕaxšav* 'now'). (This property of morphophonological alternations is also called **structure preservation**.)

(ix) Word level. Automatic alternations may apply across word boundaries. Thus, flapping occurs in English also within phrases, as in *a lot of stuff* [ə lɒɾ əv stʌf]. This is not generally possible with morphophonological alternations.

It should be noted that the distinction between automatic and morphophonological alternations that is described in this section is not the same as that between **allophonic** (i.e. involving non-distinctive sound differences) and **phonemic** alternations. It is true that there are some similarities: allophonic alternations are always automatic, and morphophonological alternations are always phonemic (i.e. they always involve sounds that can distinguish different words in the language). However, automatic alternations can be allophonic or phonemic, and it is the phonemic alternations that could be mistaken for (or could at a later stage turn into) morphophonological alternations. The four cases in (10.1) are all phonemic, as can be seen in the resulting neutralization of distinctions (cf. English [pærɪŋ], which could be from *pat* or from *pad*, and Russian [valá], which could be from *vol* or from *val*).

10.2 Process descriptions of sound alternations

We saw earlier in this chapter that it may be convenient to describe sound alternations in process terms rather than purely static terms, although no actual process in language or speech is implied. Now many linguists have argued that such process descriptions are not merely a descriptive convenience, but are a good model of the speakers' knowledge of their grammatical system. This approach is called **derivational phonology**, because it describes sound alternations by (morpho-)phonological rules that **derive**[4] the **surface form** (i.e. the form that is actually pronounced and perceived) from an abstract **underlying representation**. Let us illustrate this again with the example of German Final Devoicing. Somewhat more formally, this can be represented as in (10.4). (In the usual formalism for derivational phonological rules, the symbol '→' means 'changes into', and after the slash comes the statement of the conditions under which the change occurs, primarily the phonological environment.)

(10.4) a. Rule: German Final Devoicing[5]
voiced obstruent → voiceless / in syllable-final position
b. Sample derivation

underlying representation	[taːg]
Final Devoicing (g → k)	[taːk]
surface form	[taːk]

The advantage of this derivational approach for morphology is that the statement of phonological allomorphy becomes simpler because the morphology proper can work with underlying representations. In a description that works only with surface forms, the German lexicon would have to contain two different allomorphs of hundreds of words that display this alternation. In a description that allows abstract underlying representations, the German lexicon becomes much simpler, because words like *Tag*

---

[4] Note that this sense of *derive* is different from the sense that we saw earlier (Section 2.4).
[5] In the statement of phonological rules, linguists often use a special set of phonological features and special abbreviatory conventions. Thus, the rule of Final Devoicing would be stated as:

$$[- \text{sonorant}] \quad \rightarrow \quad [- \text{voice}] \ / \ \underline{\quad}]_\sigma$$

Since this is not a book on phonology, we will use more informal equivalent notations.

now need only a single allomorph in the lexicon, and the surface variation is dealt with by the phonological rule.

Moreover, the phonological rule is not restricted to a particular morphological context, so we can, for example, express the generalization that Final Devoicing in German nouns (as in *Ta*[k]/*Tage* 'day(s)', *Mon*[t]/*Monde* 'moon(s)') is the same phenomenon as in verbs (e.g. *fegen*/*fe*[k] 'sweep (infinitive/imperative)', *heben*/*he*[p] 'lift (infinitive/ imperative)'. If we just listed the alternants for each morpheme, this generalization would be lost.

Underlying representations are particularly useful when there are more than two phonological allomorphs. Consider the case of Russian *borodá* 'beard', which has four different alternants:

(10.5) [bərad]   in   *borodá*   [bəra'da]   NOM.SG
        ['borəd]   in   *bórody*   ['borədi]   NOM.PL
        [ba'rot]   in   *boród*   [ba'rot]   GEN.PL
        [ba'rod]   in   *dlinnoboródyj* [dlinnəba'rodij] 'long-bearded'

If we assume an underlying representation [borod], these forms are easily derived by the three rules in (10.6).

(10.6) a. Russian Final Devoicing
            voiced obstruent → voiceless / in word-final position
        b. Pre-stress Akanie
            o → a / in the syllable immediately before the stressed syllable
        c. Akanie Elsewhere
            o → ə / in any other unstressed syllable

The sample derivations in (10.7) show how the surface forms are derived.

(10.7) a. underlying representation   [boro'd + a]
            Pre-stress Akanie (o → a)   [bora'da]
            Akanie Elsewhere (o → ə)   [bəra'da]   (= surface form)
        b. underlying representation   ['borod + i]
            Akanie Elsewhere (o → ə)   ['borədi]   (= surface form)
        c. underlying representation   [bo'rod]
            Pre-stress Akanie (o → a)   [ba'rod]
            Final Devoicing (d → t)   [ba'rot]   (= surface form)
        d. underlying representation   [(dlinnə-)bo'rod + ij]
            Pre-stress Akanie (o → a)   [(dlinnə-)ba'rodij] (= surface form)

In such cases, inferring the underlying representation from the surface forms is a more difficult task for speakers and linguists, because there is no surface alternant that is identical to the underlying representation. But if they manage to infer it, they are rewarded with much simpler grammars.

An even stronger argument for the derivational approach in (morpho-) phonology comes from alternations that can be described by **ordered rule application**. In (10.6), we saw that a single morpheme may undergo more than one rule, but here the order of the application was immaterial. In the following example from Zulu, the order is crucial. Zulu has a locative case that is formed by suffixing *-ini (-eni/-ni)* and replacing the initial vowel by *e*, as illustrated in (10.8).

(10.8) *umuthi*   'tree'   *e-muthi-ni*   'at the tree'
         indlebe   'ear'   *e-ndlebe-ni*   'in the ear'
         intaba   'mountain'   *e-ntabe-ni*   'at the mountain'
         into   'thing'   *e-ntw-eni*   'by the thing'
         inkukhu   'fowl'   *e-nkukhw-ini*   'at the fowl'
                                       (Ziervogel *et al.* 1981: 64)

It seems best to assume that the underlying forms of the stems are identical to the non-case-marked forms, and that the underlying form of the locative suffix is *-ini*. Zulu nouns always end in a vowel, and, since vowel sequences are phonetically difficult, the sequences of vowel + *ini* do not show up as such on the surface. We are not concerned here with the sequences *-i + ini* ($\rightarrow$ *-ini*), *-e + ini* ($\rightarrow$ *-eni*), and *-a + ini* ($\rightarrow$ *-eni*), which can be taken care of by straightforward rules of vowel deletion and coalescence. More interesting are the combinations *-o + ini* and *-u + ini*. For these, we need the two rules in (10.9).

(10.9) a. Vowel Height Assimilation
            high *i* $\rightarrow$ mid *e* / after mid *o* in the preceding syllable
     b. Glide Formation
            o, u $\rightarrow$ *w* / before a vowel

These rules need to be ordered as in (10.9) – i.e. Vowel Height Assimilation must precede Glide Formation for the derivation to work. In (10.10), the derivation of *enkukhwini* and *entweni* is shown.

(10.10) underlying representation   *ento + ini*   *enkukhu + ini*
         Vowel Height Assimilation (*i* $\rightarrow$ *e*)   *ento-eni*   (no change)
         Glide Formation (*o/u* $\rightarrow$ *w*)   *entw-eni*   *enkukhw-ini*

If Glide Formation were applied before Vowel Height Assimilation, the result would be the incorrect form **entwini*.

Now some Zulu nouns show still another alternation, as illustrated in (10.11). (Note that orthographic *j* = [dʒ], *sh* = [ʃ], *ny* = [ɲ]; otherwise the spelling reflects the pronunciation directly.)

(10.11) *isigubhu*   'calabash'   *esigujini*   'in the calabash'
         impuphu   'meal'   *empushini*   'in the meal'
         umlomo   'mouth'   *emlonyeni*   'in the mouth'
         umthombo   'fountain'   *emthonjeni*   'in the fountain'
         iphompo   'gossip'   *ephontsheni*   'by the gossip'
                                         (Ziervogel *et al.* 1981: 64)

These forms can be derived by the additional rule of Labial Palatalization in (10.12), as illustrated in the sample derivation in (10.13).

(10.12) Labial Palatalization

$$\left\{\begin{array}{c} bh \\ ph \\ m \\ mb \\ mp \end{array}\right\} \;+\; w \;\rightarrow\; \left\{\begin{array}{c} j \\ sh \\ ny \\ nj \\ ntsh \end{array}\right\}$$

(In this rule, no specification of an environment is needed, because it applies everywhere. The *w* cannot be treated as an environmental specification because it is deleted and must be part of the input to the rule.)

(10.13)	underlying representation	*esigubhu + ini*	*emthombo + ini*
	Vowel Height Assimilation	(no change)	*emthombo-eni*
	Glide Formation	*esigubhw-ini*	*emthombw-eni*
	Labial Palatalization	*esiguj-ini*	*emthonj-eni*

Again, these alternations are difficult to describe without the device of an underlying representation and an ordered sequence of (morpho-)phonological rules that effect various changes.

A final example comes from English, where we find a rule of palatalization that is somewhat similar to the Zulu rule in (10.12). Compare the English examples in (10.14).

(10.14)	a. *commune*	[-n]	*communion*	[kəmju:njən]
	rebel	[-l]	*rebellion*	[rêbɛljən]
	discuss	[-s]	*discussion*	[dɪskʌʃən]
	digest	[-t]	*digestion*	[daɪdʒɛstʃən]
	fuse	[-z]	*fusion*	[fju:ʒən]
	b. *professor*	[-r]	*professorial*	[prəfɛsɔrjəl]
	face	[-s]	*facial*	[feɪʃəl]
	essence	[-s]	*essential*	[ɪsɛnʃəl]

On the basis of stems that end in *-n, -l* and *-r*, we can postulate that both suffixes start with yod underlyingly: [-jən] and [-jəl]. In order to derive words like *discussion*, we need the rule of Yod Fusion (10.15).

(10.15) Yod Fusion

$$\{s, z, t, d\} + j \;\rightarrow\; \{ʃ, ʒ, tʃ, dʒ\}$$

But this rule does not make the right prediction for the pairs in (10.16).

(10.16)	*insert*	[-t]	*insertion*	[-ʃən]
	extend	[-d]	*extension*	[-ʃən]
	expand	[-d]	*expansion*	[-ʃən]
	permit	[-t]	*permission*	[-ʃən]
	create	[-t]	*creation*	[-ʃən]

For this alternation, we need an additional morphophonological rule that changes [t] and [d] into [s]. We call the rule Latinate Assibilation here because it is restricted to loanwords from Latin.

(10.17) Latinate Assibilation

{t, d} → s / before the suffix [-jən], if no [s] precedes

A sample derivation is shown in (10.18).

(10.18) underlying representation   [ɪkstɛnd + jən]   [daɪdʒɛst + jən]
Latinate Assibilation   [ɪkstɛnsjən]   (no change)
Yod Fusion   [ɪkstɛnʃən]   [daɪdʒɛstʃən]

Again, the order of the rules is crucial. If Yod Fusion preceded Latinate Assibilation, we would get the incorrect form *[ɪkstɛndʒən].

We noted earlier (in Section 10.1) that synchronic sound alternations originate in sound changes whose realization depends on the phonological environment. This insight helps us understand why the order of phonological rules is sometimes crucial for a synchronic description. When a sound change occurred significantly earlier than another sound change that interacted with it, this means that the contemporary words that show the effects of both sound changes can be described only by ordered phonological rules. We have no good historical records for Zulu that would demonstrate this for the first example of this section. But for the English rules of Latinate Assibilation and Yod Fusion, it is clear that the former occurred earlier, in fact much earlier. The alternation of *t*/*d* and *s* already existed in Latin and goes back to a sound change that may have occurred as early as 3000 years ago. By contrast, Yod Fusion is a fairly recent event in English phonology. Thus, the intermediate stage in the derivation in (10.18), [ɪkstɛnsjən], was also an intermediate stage in the historical development of English; probably Shakespeare's pronunciation was still close to it. Similarly, we may hypothesize that *entoeni* was an earlier pronunciation of modern Zulu *entweni* (see (10.10)).

The historical origin of synchronic sound alternations thus explains why languages are often elegantly described by a sequence of ordered rules. Whether such descriptions are not merely elegant but also cognitively realistic – i.e. whether the speakers' internal rules also make use of ordered rule application – is a separate question that is more difficult to answer than the question of descriptive elegance. We will come back to this question in Section 10.4.

10.3 Three types of morphophonological alternations

In Section 10.1, we focused on the differences between automatic and morphophonological sound alternations. When we look at morphophonological alternations in greater detail, we see that these show quite a bit of internal diversity. In terms of the relevance of the alternations to the grammar, we can distinguish three different classes (although they are probably just three points on a continuum): relic alternations, common alternations and productive alternations. Their properties are summarized in Table 10.2.

Relic alternations	Common alternations	Productive alternations
apply to very few items	apply to many items	apply to many items
do not apply to novel words	do not apply to novel words	apply to novel words
probably not recognized by speakers	probably recognized by speakers	clearly recognized by speakers

Table 10.2 Three types of morphophonological alternations

(i) **Relic alternations** are found only in a few words, and it is therefore doubtful whether a rule should be formulated for them. An example is the *s/r* alternation in German. This was quite regular in Old High German: in vowel-changing verbs, the past-tense plural forms and the past participle showed *r*, whereas the other forms showed *s*:

(10.19)

PRESENT TENSE	PAST TENSE SINGULAR	PAST TENSE PLURAL	PAST PARTICIPLE	
lesan	*las*	*lārum*	*gileran*	'read'
ginesan	*ginas*	*ginārum*	*gineran*	'be saved'
kiusan	*kōs*	*kurum*	*gikoran*	'choose'
friusan	*frōs*	*frurum*	*gifroran*	'freeze'

In Modern German, most of these alternations have been levelled: the modern forms are *lesen/las/lasen/gelesen*, *genesen/genas/genasen/genesen* and *frieren/fror/froren/gefroren*. However, in the high-frequency verb 'be', the alternation was preserved (*war/gewesen*). And, when we take derived lexemes into account, we also see it in *Frost/frieren* 'frost/freeze'. In these cases it really takes a historical linguist to discover anything systematic about these alternations. For contemporary speakers, the relation between *war* 'was' and *gewesen* 'been' is probably as suppletive and non-systematic as the relation between *bin* 'am' and *war* 'was'.

(ii) **Common alternations** are found in many words in a language, and often in different morphological contexts. An example is the Diphthongization alternation in Spanish, whereby *ue* and *ie* occur in stressed syllables, and *o* and *e* occur in unstressed syllables:

(10.20)

ciérro	'I close'	*cerrár*	'to close'
cuénto	'I tell'	*contár*	'to tell'
buéno	'good'	*bondád*	'goodness'
cuérpo	'body'	*corpóreo*	'bodily'

Spanish has dozens of verbs such as *cerrar* and *contar* that show this alternation, and there are many derivational relationships such as *bueno/bondad*
where it shows up as well. So at least as linguists we want to formulate a
rule rather than just say that all these cases show (weak) suppletion. It
would seem reasonable to assume that speakers, too, have some kind of
rule and do not have to memorize the different stems for each individual
verb. However, this is difficult to show, because the Diphthongization alternation is not productive. When a stem with a diphthong becomes the stem
of a novel verb (e.g. a verb formed by the denominal pattern *des-N-ar*
'remove N'), the diphthong appears throughout the paradigm (as in
deshuesár 'remove bones' from *huéso* 'bone', not **deshosár*). When a stem
with a monophthong appears in a novel verb, it shows no alternation (e.g.
filosofár 'philosophize', which has stem-stressed forms such as *filosófo* 'I
philosophize'). Similarly, when a diminutive in *-ito* is formed from a noun
with a diphthong, the diphthong is preserved (e.g. *cuerpíto* 'little body',
from *cuérpo* 'body').

(iii) **Productive alternations** are not merely found in many words, but are
also extended to new words such as neologisms and borrowings. The
German Umlaut is a famous example of such an alternation. In older
German, it was productively extended to new plurals such as
Mutter/Mütter 'mother(s)', *Garten/Gärten* 'garden(s)', which did not have
Umlaut in the plural originally because their old plural suffix (now lost) did
not contain an [i]. However, in modern German the Umlaut is no longer
productive in plurals, and neither is it in female-noun formations of the
type *Jude/Jüdin* (a newly formed female noun from *Luchs* 'lynx' would have
to be *Luchsin*, not **Lüchsin*). But there is one pattern in which the Umlaut is
required: diminutives in *-chen* and *-lein*. For instance, one could form a
diminutive *Fäxchen* from the new word *Fax* 'fax', and parents might refer to
a medicine called *Vitamnol* as *Vitamnölchen* when talking to a small child.
The German Umlaut thus demonstrates clearly that a morphophonological
alternation may be productive in some morphological contexts but unproductive in others.

Some other productive morphophonological alternations are:

- Turkish *k/ ğ*. This is extended to loanwords, e.g. *kartotek/kartoteği* 'card
  catalog', *frikik/frikiği* 'free kick', *barok/baroğu* 'baroque'. (However, other
  loanwords preserve *k* (see the example *sitreptokok/sitreptokoku* in Section
  10.1)).
- Polish Second Palatalization. This process changes the velars *k, g* and *ch*
  [x] to *c* [ts], *dz* and *sz* [ʃ] in certain environments – e.g. in the locative
  singular of nouns of the *a*-declension (e.g. *mucha* 'fly', locative *musze*;
  stuga 'servant', locative *studze*; *matka* 'mother', locative *matce*). This alternation is completely regular, and it always applies to loanwords – e.g.
  Braga (city in Portugal), locative *Bradze*; *alpaka* 'alpaca', locative *alpace*,
  and so on.

- Indonesian Nasal Substitution. In this alternation, the initial voiceless stop of a verb root is deleted and replaced by a nasal stop at the same place of articulation when the active-voice prefix *meng-* is attached to the root. In addition to *t, k* and *p*, this alternation also affects *s*, where the replacing nasal is *ny* [ɲ]. (The letters *ng* stand for [ŋ].)

(10.21) *meng* + *urus*   *mengurus*   'take care'
         meng + *tulis*   *menulis*   'write'
         meng + *kirim*   *mengirim*   'send'
         meng + *pakai*   *memakai*   'use'
         meng + *sewa*   *menyewa*   'rent'

That this alternation is productive can again be seen in the behaviour of loanwords, which are also subject to Nasal Substitution:

(10.22) *meng* + *kritik*   *mengritik*   'criticize'
         meng + *sukses* + *kan*   *menyukseskan*   'make successful'
         meng + *protes*   *memrotes*   'protest'
                                                           (Sneddon 1996: 9–13)

However, in recent borrowings the initial consonant tends to be retained, and, besides the forms (10.22), the forms *mengkritik, mensukseskan* and *memprotes* are possible as well. This may indicate that the alternation is losing its productivity.

10.4 The diachrony of morphophonological alternations

We have seen that synchronic sound alternations have their origin in phonological changes, but we have not yet explained why these sound changes sometimes result in automatic alternations and sometimes in morphophonological alternations. On one level, the answer is straightforward: sound changes always yield automatic alternations initially, and automatic alternations then become morphophonological alternations in a further step of development:

(10.23)   sound change → automatic alternation → morphophonological alternation

The reverse change, from morphophonological alternation to automatic alternation, is quite impossible. This is because the rules of phonology in the strict sense (i.e. the rules of pronunciation) are motivated exclusively by factors of phonetic processing. Diachronic sound changes and synchronic automatic alternations are thus limited to phonological conditioning factors. Phonetics and phonology are to a large extent **autonomous** from morphology, or, to put it in even more metaphorical terms, they act blindly, without seeing the consequences of their actions for morphology. If sound changes could, so to speak, predict the outcome of their actions and cared about morphology, they might exercise some restraint. For example, Hebrew Spirantization (see (10.2d)), which turned intervocalic [p] into [f], could have been satisfied with changing non-alternating words like *safa* 'lip' (from earlier *sapa*), and it could have spared verbs like *soper/yispor*, which became alternating (*sofer/yispor*) as a result of the sound change. Modern Hebrew speakers are still struggling with the consequences of these ancient changes, as attempts at analogical levelling show. Thus, phonetics and phonology mostly mind their own business and do not respond to the needs of morphology. This explains why morphophonological alternations (which are to a large extent morphological in nature) cannot revert to become automatic alternations.

But this does not explain yet why automatic alternations change into morphophonological alternations rather than simply disappearing when the phonological rules change. For instance, in early Old High German, the Umlaut must have been an automatic alternation, so that, for instance, *Jüdin* 'Jewish woman' (derived from *Jude* 'Jew') could not have been pronounced otherwise because a back vowel had to be assimilated to a front vowel in the next syllable. But subsequently the phonological restriction that made *u-i* sequences unpronounceable was lost, and already in Middle High German words like *Luchsin* 'female lynx' were no problem. But why was the alternation retained? Why did *Jüdin* not revert to its earlier pronunciation *Judin*? The reason is apparently that speakers do not store words in terms of their underlying representations, as the approach of derivational phonology (see Section 10.2) would seem to suggest. If Old High German speakers had stored *Jüdin* as [ju:din] underlyingly, producing the surface form by applying the rule of *u*-fronting before [i] in the next syllable, then we might expect that the underlying form would have become the surface form again that speakers actually pronounce. But this did not happen, and such things do not normally happen in general. If, however, speakers store words as surface forms which they hear, we expect that the effects of automatic alternations do not disappear together with the rules of alternation. This would thus be an argument for the view that derivational process descriptions of sound alternations are a descriptive convenience rather than a realistic reflection of speakers' knowledge of their language.

When a phonological constraint has disappeared and a sound alternation has thus lost its phonological motivation, speakers are faced with the problem of learning and remembering the alternants. One possibility is that they simply store individually all the alternants that they can remember, so that the alternation is exclusively lexically governed and there is no morphophonological rule at all. This was apparently what happened to the Old High German *r/s* alternation of (10.19). Such alternations become vulnerable to analogical levelling, and they are preserved only in the most frequent words. After some time, the alternation thus becomes a relic alternation and is doomed to disappear from the language.

But another possibility is that the speakers find some other way of remembering the alternation, for example by reinterpreting it as signalling (or co-signalling) a particular morphological pattern. This has happened, for example, with Zulu Labial Palatalization (see (10.12) above) in passive verb forms. In Zulu, the passive voice is marked by a suffix -*w(a)*, as illustrated in (10.24a). In (10.24b), we see the effects of Labial Palatalization (note that the *w* has been preserved in these cases, in contrast to (10.11), where it was lost; this is probably because the *w* is the main carrier of the passive meaning).

(10.24) a. *bon-a*   'see'   *bon-w-a*   'be seen'
           shay-a   'beat'   *shay-w-a*   'be beaten'
         b. *gubh-a*   'hollow'   *guj-w-a*   'be hollowed'
           khiph-a   'take out'   *khish-w-a*   'be taken out'
           lum-a   'bite'   *luny-w-a*   'be bitten'
           bamb-a   'catch'   *banj-w-a*   'be caught'
         c. *khumul-a*   'loosen'   *khunyul-w-a*   'be loosened'
           khumbul-a   'remember'   *khunjul-w-a*   'be remembered'
           bophel-a   'harness'   *boshel-w-a*   'be harnessed'
           gijimis-a   'make run'   *gijinyis-w-a*   'be made to run'
           bophis-a   'make fasten'   *boshis-w-a*   'be caused to fasten'
                                 (Ziervogel *et al*. 1981: 106–7, 160, 163)

When Labial Palatalization ceased to be a phonetically motivated automatic alternation, Zulu speakers evidently reinterpreted it as co-signalling the passive meaning and introduced it into words that could never have developed palatals by phonological processes. Such words are shown in (10.24c). In all these verbs, the root-final labial consonant is followed by some segments that would have protected it from undergoing Labial Palatalization as a sound change. The fact that it was extended to these cases shows that the alternation is now part of the morphological pattern.

The history of the German Umlaut was very similar. When it lost its phonological motivation, it became associated with particular morphological environments, as we saw earlier. For some time it was productive with plurals (*Vater/Väter* 'father(s)') and female nouns (*Gott/Göttin* 'god/goddess'), and now it is productive mainly with diminutives (*Fax/Fäxchen* 'fax/little fax').

Thus, when a sound alternation has become closely associated with a morphological pattern, it has become part of the morphology, and we expect it to behave like other ingredients of morphological patterns. For example, it is possible for the alternation to become the sole formal marker of a pattern – e.g. when the original marker disappears for phonological reasons. This has happened in Modern Irish, where the past tense of verbs is marked by Lenition of the initial consonant. Lenition involves fricativization and some other changes and originally it occurred only in intervocalic position (like Hebrew Spirantization (10.2d)).

(10.25) Modern Irish Lenition
{k, g, t, d, p, b, s, f} → {x, ɣ, h, ɣ, f, w, h, Ø}
(spelling: *c, g, t, d, p, b, s, f → ch, gh, th, dh, ph, bh, sh, fh*)

(10.26) PRESENT TENSE	PAST TENSE	
molaim	*mhol mé*	'I praise(d)'
brisim	*bhris mé*	'I break/broke'
sábhálaim	*shábháil mé*	'I save(d)'
díbrím	*dhíbir mé*	'I banish(ed)'

The past tense was originally formed with a prefix *do-*, but this was lost, and nowadays only the Lenition is a unique signal of the past tense (but there are also different person-number markers, *-(a)im* and *mé* for first person singular). We saw similar cases earlier: the German plurals signalled solely by the Umlaut (see (2.6)) and the Albanian plurals signalled solely by Palatalization (see (2.12)). In Section 2.4, we referred to these cases as 'base alternation', signalled by 'a phonological change of some kind'. Now it becomes clear that the 'phonological change' must be a morphophonological alternation, and, since such alternations need not be phonetically coherent (see Section 10.1), the alternations that we find in cases like the Irish past tense need not be phonetically coherent either. As a result, there is strictly speaking no single aspect of form that all Irish past-tense forms share (most, but not all, have an initial fricative), and we need abstract (and perhaps artificial) concepts such as the Lenition rule in (10.25) to describe the generalization.

Since morphophonological alternations are ingredients of morphological rules, it is not surprising that we also find back-formation with them, as with segmental morphological patterns. An example of this comes from Polish. A widespread (and productive) alternation in Polish is the First Palatalization, whose effects are shown in (10.27). (Note that this is somewhat different from the Second Palatalization, which we saw in Section 10.3, and which occurs in different environments.)

(10.27) $\begin{bmatrix} [k] \\ [g] \\ [x] \end{bmatrix} \rightarrow \begin{Bmatrix} [t\int] \\ [3] \\ [\int] \end{Bmatrix}$ (spelling: $\begin{Bmatrix} k \\ g \\ ch \end{Bmatrix} \rightarrow \begin{Bmatrix} cz \\ ż \\ sz \end{Bmatrix}$)

The First Palatalization occurs, for instance, with the verb-deriving suffix *-yć*, with the adjective-deriving suffix *-ny* and with the diminutive suffixes *-ek* and *-ka*:

(10.28) | *kaleka* | 'cripple' | *kaleczyć* | 'mutilate' |
|---|---|---|---|
| *dynamika* | 'dynamics' | *dynamiczny* | 'dynamic' |
| *pończocha* | 'stocking' | *pończoszka* | 'little stocking' |
| *krąg* | 'circle' | *krążek* | 'little circle' |

Polish has a productive pattern of back-forming words from non-diminutive words ending in *-ek* or *-ka*. These derivatives get an augmentative interpretation, as in (10.29).

(10.29) *ogórek*   'cucumber'   *ogór*   'big cucumber'
       szpilka   'pin'   *szpila*   'big pin'

Now when this rule of 'subtractive' augmentative-formation is applied to words ending in *-szka* or *-czka*, the result is a new word ending in *-cha* or *-ka*:

(10.30) *broszka*   'brooch'   *brocha*   'big brooch'
       flaszka   'bottle'   *flacha*   'big bottle'
       gruszka   'pear'   *grucha*   'big pear'
       Agnieszka   (name)   *Agniecha* 'big Agnieszka'
       beczka   'barrel'   *beka*   'big barrel'
       taczka   'wheelbarrow'   *taka*   'big wheelbarrow'

The words in the left-hand column in (10.30) all have [ʃ] (*sz*) and [tʃ] (*cz*) originally. For example, *broszka* was borrowed from French *broche* [bʀɔʃ], *flaszka* was borrowed from German *Flasche* and *gruszka* was derived from *grusza* 'pear tree'. The *ch/k* in the back-formed augmentatives is clearly new, and it shows that morphophonological rules can be used in the reverse direction under certain circumstances. In this respect, they are just like morphological rules and very different from phonological rules.

10.5 Integrated versus neutral affixes

In some languages, it is useful to distinguish between two types of affixes, depending on their behaviour with respect to phonological and morphophonological rules and alternations. We call these two types **integrated** and **neutral affixes** here. Their typical properties are summarized in Table 10.3. In the following we examine integrated and neutral affixes in three languages, Lezgian, Yidiny and English, before discussing a widely adopted proposal for describing this contrast in English (level ordering).

Integrated affixes	Neutral affixes
are in the domain of stress assignment	are not in the domain of stress assignment
trigger and undergo morphophonological alternations	do not trigger or undergo morphophonological alternations
words with integrated affixes show the phonotactics of monomorphemic words	words with neutral affixes may show phonotactic peculiarities
tend to occur closer to the root	tend to occur further away from the root

Table 10.3 Integrated and neutral affixes

10.5.1 Lezgian

In Lezgian, most inflectional suffixes are neutral, but some are integrated (all prefixes are integrated, but there are so few of them that they can be neglected here). To see the difference between the two types of suffixes, we need to consider the rule of stress assignment and two relevant morphophonological alternations (see (10.31)).

(10.31) a. Lezgian Stress Rule
Stress is on the second syllable in the stress domain if there are at least two syllables in it. Otherwise stress is on the single syllable of the stress domain.

b. Aspirate Ejectivization
A word-final voiceless aspirate consonant alternates with an ejective if the plural suffix follows:

meth	met'-ér	'knee(s)'
neth	net'-ér	'louse/lice'
wakh	wak'-ár	'pig(s)'
haqh	haq'-ár	'truth(s)'

c. Vowel Harmony
The stressed syllable and the prestress syllable agree in backness and in labialization – i.e. the only allowed sequences of unlike vowels are *a–u, u–a, i–e, e–i, ü–e, e–ü*. (Disallowed are *a–e, e–u, i–ü*, etc.; note that Lezgian has the five vowel phonemes *a, e, i, u, ü*.) The suffix vowels *a/e* and *i/u/ü* alternate:

q'al	q'al-ár	'stick(s)'	ǧal	ǧal-úni	'thread'
q'ul	q'ul-ár	'board(s)'	č'ul	č'ul-úni	'belt'
q'il	q'il-ér	'head(s)'	ric'	ric'-íni	'bowstring'
q'ül	q'ül-ér	'dance(s)'	q'ül	q'ül-üni	'dance'

(Haspelmath 1993: 56–8)

The suffixes -er/-ar (plural) and -uni/-ini/-üni (oblique stem) that are illustrated in (10.31) are examples of integrated suffixes. As the examples show, they are in the stress domain (i.e. they receive stress, because they attach to a monosyllabic base) and they trigger and undergo morphophonological alternations. Besides these, Lezgian also has neutral plural suffixes and neutral oblique-stem suffixes, as illustrated in (10.32).

(10.32) a. Lezgian oblique-stem suffix -di (neutral)

fil	fíl-di	'elephant'
tip	típ-di	'type'
nur	núr-di	'beam'
din	dín-di	'religion'

b. Lezgian plural suffix *-ar* (neutral)[6]

tip	*típ-ar*	'type(s)'
kür	*kü'r-ar*	'shed(s)'
kar	*kár-ar*	'enclosure(s)'
li	*lí-jar*	'hide(s)'

(Haspelmath 1993: 68–9)

These are not in the stress domain, so that the stress is on the first syllable in these words, and they neither undergo any alternations (in particular, they are not subject to vowel harmony) nor do they trigger them. Integrated suffixes always follow the root immediately, whereas neutral suffixes may also come after a derivational suffix. For instance, the noun *čečen-wi* 'Chechen person' (derived fron *Čečen* 'Chechnya') has the plural *čečen-wi-jar* and the oblique-stem suffix *-di* (*čečen-wi-di*).

Lezgian words with neutral suffixes are immediately recognizable as morphologically complex: consonant sequences like *pd* (in *tipdi*) are impossible morpheme-internally, and disyllabic words with initial stress must be morphologically complex. By contrast, all words in (10.31b–c) could be monomorphemic in principle.

10.5.2 Yidiny

Another language in which neutral and integrated affixes can be distin-guished is Yidiny (Dixon 1977:88-98). Three relevant morphophonological alternations of Yidiny are given in (10.33).

(10.33) a. Penultimate Lengthening
In every word with an odd number of syllables, the vowel of the penultimate syllable is lengthened, e.g.

absolutive case	*guda:ga*	*mudyam*	*yabu:lam*
purposive case	*gudaga-gu*	*mudya:m-gu*	*yabulam-gu*
	'dog'	'mother'	'loya-cane sp.'

b. Final Syllable Deletion
In odd-syllabled words, if the two final syllables are CVL(C)V, the final syllable (C)V is deleted (where V stands for any vowel, C for any consonant, and L for a sonorant consonant: l, r, m, n, ɲ, ŋ)

Penultimate Lengthening must be ordered before Final Syllable Deletion. Because of the condition of an odd number of syllables, odd-syllabled and even-syllabled verb roots behave quite differently. This is illustrated by (10.34), which shows the underlying representations of present-tense and past-tense forms of two verbs and sample derivations.

---

[6] The neutral plural suffix *-ar* is similar in shape to the integrated plural suffix *-er/-ar*, but it is a distinct suffix.

(10.34)

underlying rep.	*gali-ŋ*	*gali-ɲu*	*madyinda-ŋ*	*madyinda-ɲu*
Pen. Lengthening	—	*gali:ɲu*	*madyi:ndaŋ*	—
Fin. Syll. Deletion	—	*gali:ɲ*	—	—
surface form	*gali-ŋ*	*gali:-ɲ*	*madyi:nda-ŋ*	*madyinda-ɲu*
	go-PRES	go-PAST	walk.up-PRES	walk.up-PAST

The present-tense suffix *-ŋ* and the past-tense suffix *-ɲu* are integrated and thus are in the domain of the two rules of Penultimate Lengthening and Final Syllable Deletion. The same is true of the suffix *-ŋal*, which can be glossed as 'do together with someone' (e.g. *gali-ŋal-* means 'go with, accompany, take'). As (10.35) shows, verbs with this suffix behave just like monomorphemic verbs such as *wawal-* 'see' and undergo the two rules if they have an odd number of syllables.

(10.35)

	wawal-ɲu	*gali-ŋal-ɲu*	*gali-ŋal*	*madyinda-ŋal-ɲu*
underlying rep.				
Pen. Lengthening	*wawa:l-ɲu*	—	*gali:-ŋal*	*madyinda-ŋa:l-ɲu*
Fin. Syll. Deletion	*wawa:l*	—	—	*madyinda-ŋa:l*
surface form	*wawa:l*	*gali-ŋal-ɲu*	*gali:-ŋal*	*madyinda-ŋa:l*
	see(PAST)	go-with-PAST	walk.up-PRES	walk.up-with(PAST)

However, some verb suffixes are neutral and are not in the domain for the two rules, or, rather, they constitute a new domain for them. Examples of neutral suffixes are *-daga* 'become' (e.g. *milba-daga-* 'become clever', *gumari-daga-* 'become red') and *-ŋali* 'go and'. As the examples in (10.36) show, the number of syllables of the root is irrelevant for words derived by these suffixes. Penultimate lengthening applies to *guma:ridaga:ɲ* and *dyadya:maŋali:ɲ* as if no suffix were present.

(10.36)

underlying rep.	*milba-daga-ɲu*	*gumari-daga-ɲu*
Pen. Lengthening	*milba-daga:-ɲu*	*guma:ri-daga:-ɲu*
Fin. Syll. Deletion	*milba-daga:-ɲ*	*guma:ri-daga:-ɲ*
	'became clever'	'became red'

underlying rep.	*dyuŋga-ŋali-ɲu*	*dyadyama-ŋali-ɲu*
Pen. Lengthening	*dyuŋga-ŋali:-ɲu*	*dyadya:ma-ŋali:-ɲu*
Fin. Syll. Deletion	*dyuŋga-ŋali:-ɲ*	*dyadya:ma-ŋali:-ɲ*
	'went and ran'	'went and jumped'

Thus, Yidiny words with neutral suffixes can be immediately recognized as morphologically complex, because they may have two long vowels. In contrast to Lezgian neutral suffixes, Yidiny neutral suffixes do undergo morphophonological alternations, but they do not trigger them, i.e. the roots to which they attach behave as if no suffix were present. Yidiny is different from Lezgian also in that neutral affixes occur closer to the root than integrated affixes, contrary to the generalization of Table 10.3.

10.5.3 English

Let us now look at English, where the distinction between integrated and neutral affixes has occupied many morphologists and phonologists. Some examples of both types of affixes are given in (10.37).

(10.37) integrated affixes: *-ity, in-, -ical, -ion, -ian, -al, -y₁, -ous, -ive*
neutral affixes: *-ness, un-, -ly, re-, -ize, -able, -ful, -y₂, -ism*

Integrated suffixes often lead to a stress shift, whereas neutral suffixes never do:

(10.38)

BASE	WITH INTEGRATED SUFFIX	BASE	WITH NEUTRAL SUFFIX
réal	*reálity*	*nátural*	*náturalness*
cómedy	*comédian*	*accómpany*	*accómpaniable*
phótograph	*photógraphy (-y₁)*	*ríckets*	*ríckety (-y₂)*
pseúdonym	*pseudónymous*	*bóunty*	*bóuntiful*

Integrated suffixes may trigger Trisyllabic Shortening (cf. (10.2a)), whereas neutral suffixes never do. The integrated prefix *in-* shows Nasal Assimilation of the *n* to the first consonant of the base (*elegant/inelegant*, but *possible/impossible, literate/illiterate, regular/irregular*), whereas the *n* of the neutral prefix *un-* is always preserved (*unpretentious, unlimited, unrealistic*, etc.). The attachment of neutral affixes may lead to the violation of morpheme-internal phonotactic constraints – e.g. *cleanness* and *unnecessary* show two consecutive instances of [n], something that never occurs within a morpheme. Likewise, the suffix *-ful* brings about consonant sequences such as [pf] (e.g. *hopeful*) and [kf] (e.g. *thankful*) that do not occur morpheme-internally. The integrated affixes, by contrast, do not create structures that are impossible morpheme-internally.

And, finally, English shows a strong tendency for integrated suffixes to occur close to the root, whereas neutral suffixes occur further away from the root. Integrated affixes do not, as a rule, attach to words derived by a neutral affix (**[hope-ful]-ity, *in-[friend-ly], *[kind-ness]-ical*), whereas the opposite order is unproblematic (*[natur-al]-ness, un-[product-ive], [Rastafari-an]-ism*).

10.5.4 Level ordering

The contrast between integrated and neutral affixes in English has given rise to the idea that the innate architecture of the grammar provides the possibility of several **levels** of affixes that are linked to particular morphophonological or phonological rules. English would have two levels, commonly called level I and level II (see Table 10.4). The basic idea of this

Level	Affixes	(Morpho)phonological rules
level I: (≈ integrated affixes)	*-ity, in-, -ical, -ion, -ian,* *-al, -y₁, -ous, -ive*	morphophonological rules Trisyllabic Shortening, Stress Assignment, Nasal Assimilation
level II: (≈ neutral affixes)	*-ness, un-, -ly, re-, -ize,* *-able, -ful, -y₂, -ism*	phonological rules Flapping

Table 10.4 The two levels of English morpho(phono)logy

approach is that the rules introducing affixes are ordered in much the same way as the phonological rules have been said to be ordered (see Section 10.2), and that sets of affixes are paired with sets of rules that apply after the affix has been introduced. Thus, this architecture requires level I affixes to be attached before level II affixes, thereby explaining the ordering restriction that prohibits integrated affixes from attaching to words with neutral affixes. In addition, it explains why level II affixes are not affected by the morphophonological rules of level I.

This theory of **level ordering** became influential among generative morphologists, but its application to English encounters some serious problems. Some counterexamples to the ordering restriction are obvious: the level I suffix *-ity* can attach to the level II suffix *-able* as in *readability*, and *-ation* (a variant of *-ion*) can attach to *-ize* (e.g. *realization*). There are also problems with the pairing of affixes and rules. For example, the rule of Velar Softening (which changes underlying [k] into [s], and [g] into [dʒ] before certain suffixes – e.g. *electric/electricity*) is a clear example of an old morphophonological rule that should go with level I affixes. And, indeed, many level I affixes do trigger this rule (e.g. *analogous/analogy, demagogue/demagogic, music/musician, opaque/opacity*), but there are also two level I suffixes that trigger it, *-ize* and *-ism* (e.g. *public/publicize, fanatic/fanaticism*). Also with respect to stress, integrated and neutral affixes may behave alike: words prefixed with *in-* and *un-* both share the same stress pattern, with secondary stress on the prefix (*ùnnátural, ùnafráid, ìmmóral, ìmprecíse*). This stress pattern contrasts with that of monomorphemic words like *ínnocent, ínfamous, ímpudent, ínfidel*. Thus, in this respect *in-* behaves as we would expect from a level II prefix (Raffelsiefen 1999b).

Now a few counterexamples do not in general invalidate a generalization, but, if the generalization is supposed to be a direct consequence of the architecture of the grammar, they do become a big problem, because there is no way in which they could arise if the system of Table 10.4 is assumed.

Even more damaging to the level ordering hypothesis is the fact that there appears to be a ready alternative explanation for the observed ordering restriction. Most integrated affixes in English are quite unproductive anyway, so it seems unnecessary to invoke a level ordering architecture in order to explain why they do not attach to words derived with neutral affixes. Even the most common suffix, *-ity*, cannot in general be used with new bases (cf. **chivalrosity, *naturality, ?*effectivity*), only in the special case of adjectives derived by *-able* (*readability, bagelizability*, etc.). True, within strict limits it is sometimes possible to form new words with the integrated affixes (for instance, one could imagine words like *telescopy, grammophonic* or *credentious* in some technical context). But it seems that only speakers with some kind of philological education would form such words, and this historical knowledge probably prevents them from coining or accepting neologisms with Latinate (= integrated) suffixes that are attached to non-Latinate bases (see Section 6.3.6).

Thus, it seems that for English we can explain the different behaviour of integrated and neutral affixes with respect to their history: the integrated affixes were borrowed along with the complex words from French or Latin, and most of them never became truly productive in English. The rules of Velar Softening and Nasal Assimilation were borrowed along with the complex words and did not become really productive either. Those Latin/French affixes that did become productive (in particular, *-able, -ize, -ism, re-*) did not take their stress-changing properties along with them to the new words (thus, a productively formed *-able* adjective of *defer* would be *deferrable*, not **déferable*, despite the existence of *préferable*). The non-borrowed neutral suffixes mostly derive from second compound members (*-ly, -dom, -ful*) and it is for this reason that they are not fully integrated phonologically.

It remains to be seen how the properties of integrated versus neutral affixes are to be explained in other languages. If there is indeed a general tendency for integrated affixes to occur closer to the root, this would make sense, because affixes occurring closer to the root are more relevant semantically (in the sense of Section 4.3(vii)), and semantic relevance generally correlates with a greater amount of morphophonological alternations. But we also saw the example of Yidiny, where neutral affixes occur closer to the root than integrated affixes. In Yidiny, it is clear what determines the neutral versus integrated status of an affix: monosyllabic suffixes are integrated, disyllabic suffixes are neutral, presumably because an item that constitutes its own prosodic domain must have a minimal size.

Thus, languages exhibit considerable diversity in this area, and at present we do not know very well what the generalizations are, so it is perhaps premature to attempt ambitious explanations.

Summary of Chapter 10

Two types of sound alternations can be distinguished: automatic alternations and morphophonological alternations. Only the latter are relevant to morphology. They differ in a variety of ways: automatic alternations show clear signs of their phonetic motivation, may be optional and may apply across word boundaries, whereas morphophonological alternations have lost their connection to phonetics, are obligatory and apply within words. Sound alternations are often described in terms of rules that change an abstract underlying representation into a surface representation, thus simplifying the morphological rules, which make reference to the underlying representation. Morphophonological alternations can be divided into three types: relic alternations, common alternations and productive alternations. Diachronically, automatic alternations turn into morphophonological alternations, never the other way round. Some languages distinguish between neutral and integrated affixes, depending on the way in which sound alternations apply to the affixes.

Further reading

Sound alternations and derivational phonology are discussed in every phonology textbook (e.g. Gussenhoven and Jacobs 1998: ch. 6). The most influential work in derivational phonology was Chomsky and Halle (1968). The difference between automatic alternations (which are truly phonological) and morphophonological alternations (which really belong to the morphology) is highlighted in Hooper (1976) and Bochner (1993), among many others. An opposing view is defended in Kiparsky (1996). A variety of approaches to morphophonology are discussed in the papers in Singh (1996).

For diachronic change from phonological to morphophonological rules, see Wurzel (1980).

For the theory of level ordering (also called 'Lexical Phonology'), see Kiparsky (1982, 1985) and Kaisse and Shaw (1985).

The most comprehensive book on morphophonology is Dressler (1985). Important insights on morphophonology are found in Bybee (1985) and (2001).

Exercises

1. Is the voicing alternation of English fricatives in

   leaf/leaves
   knife/knives
   house/houses, etc.

   an automatic or a morphophonological alternation?

2. English has a morphophonological alternation of [ŋ] and [ŋg] – e.g. *young* [jʌŋ], *younger* [jʌŋgər]. Is this a relic alternation, a common alternation or a productive alternation?

3. Decide whether the following sound alternations are automatic or morphophonological, on the basis of the (necessarily incomplete) information given here.

   a. In Hausa, the alveolars *t, d, s, z* may palatalize to *c* [tʃ], *j* [dʒ], *sh* [ʃ], *j* [dʒ] when they occur before a front vowel (Newman 2000: 414–15):

kàazaa	'hen'	*kàajii*	'hens'
cìizaa	'bite'	*cìiji*	'bite' (imperative)
Hausa	'Hausa'	*Bàhaushèe*	'Hausa person'
gwadàa	'measure'	*gwajìi*	'experiment' (deverbal noun)

      Recent sound changes have created new cases of *ee* and *i*:

	original form		current form	
ai > ee	*tàibà*	>	*tèebà*	'cooked cassava flour'
	ƙoosai	>	*ƙoosee*	'fried beancake'
u > i	*tukaatukii*	>	*tikàatikii*	'calf, shin'

      Some English loanwords:

laasiisìi	'licence'
teebur	'table'
gàzêt	'gazette'

   b. In Spanish, the voiced stops *b, d, g* alternate with the fricatives [β, ð, ɣ] if a vowel or fricative precedes them:

el dedo [el deðo]	'the finger'
los dedos [loz ðeðos]	'the fingers'
Damiano viene [damjano βjene]	'Damiano is coming'
viene Damiano [bjene ðamjano]	'Damiano is coming'

c.   In Modern Greek, the velar phonemes [k], [g], [x], [ɣ] alternate with the palatal phonemes [c], [ɟ], [ç], [j] whenever they precede a front vowel ([e] or [i]), e.g.

1SG	steko	exo
2SG	stecis	eçis
3SG	steci	eçi
1PL	stekume	exume
2PL	stecete	eçete
3PL	stekun	exun
	'stand'	'have'

Some loanwords: [cinino] 'chinine', [ɟemi] 'reins' (from Turkish *gem*)

d.   In Polish, the vowel [o] alternates with [u] (spelled *ó*) in certain morphological forms when the morpheme-final consonant does not start a new syllable, e.g.

gtowa	'head.NOM.SG'	*gtów*	'head.GEN.PL'
gtodu	'hunger.GEN.SG'	*gtód*	'hunger.NOM.SG'
woda	'water'	*wódka*	'vodka'

However, there are numerous exceptions to this rule, not just loanwords:

spora	'spore.NOM.SG'	*spor*	'spore.GEN.PL'
kodu	'code.GEN.SG'	*kod*	'code.NOM.SG'
wódeczka	'little vodka'	*wódka*	'vodka'

4.   We saw that Zulu Labial Palatalization is a morphophonological alternation (and not an automatic alternation), because it is tied to particular morphological contexts. What other criteria can be invoked to support that conclusion?

5.   Consider the following nominal forms of Yidiny. The proprietive suffix -*yi* expresses 'having', and the privative suffix -*gimbal* expresses 'lacking' (Dixon 1977: 91–2).

ABS	*mugaru-yi*	*gala:-y*	*muga:ru-gimbal*	*gala-gimbal*
ERG	*mugaru-yi:-ŋ*	*gala-yi-ŋgu*	*muga:ru-gimba:l-du*	*gala-gimba:l-du*
	'having a fishnet'	'having a spear'	'lacking a fishnet'	'lacking a spear'

What are the underlying forms of these eight words? What might be the reason that the number of syllables is irrelevant when -*gimbal* is attached? (Note that due to a further morphological condition on the rule of Final Syllable Deletion, the ergative suffix -*du* does not delete; -*ŋgu* and -*du* are phonologically conditioned suppletive allomorphs.)

Morphology and valence

11

So far we have focused our attention primarily on formal aspects of morphology. But this chapter will be entirely devoted to one type of function of morphological patterns. We will examine various ways in which morphology can affect valence – i.e. the expression of arguments in verbs and deverbal formations. We will first look at valence-changing operations such as passives and causatives (Section 11.1), then move on to the way in which valence is affected by compounding (Section 11.2), and finally discuss what happens to verbal arguments in transpositional derivation (i.e. derivational patterns that change the base's word-class) (Section 11.3) and transpositional inflection (Section 11.4).

11.1 Valence-changing operations

11.1.1 Semantic valence and syntactic valence (argument structure and function structure)

Most verbs are associated with one, two or three arguments as part of their lexical entries (verbs with zero or more than three arguments are very rare, and many languages lack them completely). When we know a verb's meaning, we also know the **semantic roles** of the participants of the verbal event. For example, a verb that means 'eat' will have an **agent** and a **patient** participant in all languages, a verb meaning 'please' will have an **experiencer** and a **stimulus** participant, and a verb that means 'steal, rob' will have an **agent**, a **theme** (the thing that is taken away) and a **source** participant. But this knowledge is not sufficient if we want to use these verbs, because the **syntactic functions** (such as subject, object, oblique) by which these participants are expressed differ from language to language and from verb to verb. As a concrete example, the semantic-role structures and the syntactic-function structures of five English verbs are given in (11.1).

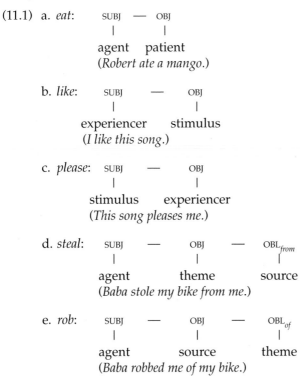

(11.1) a. *eat*:   SUBJ — OBJ
  | |
  agent patient
  (*Robert ate a mango.*)

  b. *like*:   SUBJ — OBJ
  | |
  experiencer stimulus
  (*I like this song.*)

  c. *please*: SUBJ — OBJ
  | |
  stimulus experiencer
  (*This song pleases me.*)

  d. *steal*: SUBJ — OBJ — OBL$_{from}$
  | | |
  agent theme source
  (*Baba stole my bike from me.*)

  e. *rob*: SUBJ — OBJ — OBL$_{of}$
  | | |
  agent source theme
  (*Baba robbed me of my bike.*)

The verbs *please* and *like*, and the verbs *steal* and *rob*, are roughly synonymous, so that there is no way to predict their different behaviour from their meanings. Hence speakers must store not only the meaning of every verb, but also the syntactic functions that are associated with the semantic roles. Thus, the lexical entry of the verbs *please* and *rob* would look as in (11.2).

(11.2) a. $\begin{bmatrix} \text{/pli:z/}_V \\ \text{SUBJ} \quad - \quad \text{OBJ} \\ \quad | \qquad\qquad | \\ \text{stimulus} \quad \text{experiencer} \\ \text{'please'} \end{bmatrix}$ b. $\begin{bmatrix} \text{/rɒb/}_V \\ \text{SUBJ} \; - \; \text{OBJ} \; - \; \text{OBL}_{of} \\ \quad | \qquad\quad | \qquad\quad | \\ \text{agent} \quad \text{source} \quad \text{theme} \\ \text{'rob'} \end{bmatrix}$

The information that these entries contain in addition to the pronunciation, the word-class and the meaning is called the **valence** of the verb. The valence has two parts: the syntactic-function structure ('syntactic valence', also called simply **function structure**),[1] and the

---

[1] The most important syntactic functions are subject (SUBJ), (direct) object (OBJ), and oblique (OBL – i.e. adpositional phrases and phrases in oblique cases). Two further functions that are needed less commonly are indirect object (IOBJ) and adverbial (ADV). A syntactic function that is needed for noun phrase structure is possessor (POSS).

semantic-role structure ('semantic valence', also called **argument structure**).[2]

The semantic-role structure can in principle be derived form the meaning (or **conceptual structure**, or **event structure**) of a verb. For example, a formal decomposition of the meaning of *steal* or *rob* looks as in (11.3) (see Jackendoff 1990).

$$(11.3) \left[\begin{array}{l} \text{CAUSE} ([A], [\text{GO}_{\text{POSS}} ([B], [\text{FROM} ([C])])]) \\ \{\text{BY-FORCE}\} \end{array} \right]$$

(11.3) can be paraphrased as '*A* causes *B* to go from *C*'s possession by force' – i.e. *A* robs *C* of *B*. The participant *A* must be an agent because it is the first role of the semantic element CAUSE; the participant *B* must be a theme because it is the first role of the semantic element GO; and *C* must be a source because it is the participant of FROM. Thus, it would in principle be possible to formulate the linking rules and lexical linking specifications as direct links between the conceptual structure and the function structure. The lexical entry of the verb *steal* would then be as in (11.4), where there is no separate argument structure.

$$(11.4) \left[\begin{array}{lll} /\text{sti:l}/_V & & \\ \text{SUBJ} & \text{OBJ} & \text{OBL}_{from} \\ | & | & | \\ \text{'CAUSE} ([A], [\text{GO}_{\text{POSS}} ([B], [\text{FROM} ([C])])])' \\ \{\text{BY-FORCE}\} \end{array} \right]$$

Although it is actually quite likely that the format of (11.4) is closer to the truth than the format of (11.2), in the present context a practical problem is that there is much less agreement about the right form of the conceptual decomposition of verb meanings than about semantic roles. Thus, we will mostly continue to use the simplified format of (11.2), bearing in mind that this is just an abbreviation and that the complete picture requires a more elaborate specification of verb meaning along the lines of (11.3).

Now morphological operations may change the valence of a verb in two different ways. On the one hand, they may change the linking of semantic roles to syntactic functions. Such operations are called **function-changing operations** (or **voice**). On the other hand, they may change the conceptual structure (or event structure) of the verb in such a way that the argument structure is affected. We will refer to such operations as **event-changing operations**. Examples of both types of operations will be seen in the following subsections.

---

[2] The **linking** between argument-structure positions and function-structure positions (indicated here by lines) is governed by a set of rules that have been extensively discussed by syntacticians and that we cannot go into here. The crucial point is that these rules cannot cover all cases. At least for some verbs such as *like* and *please* the function structure must be part of the lexical entry.

11.1.2 Agent-backgrounding operations

The best-known valence-changing operation is the **passive**, where the agent is backgrounded in that it is no longer the subject: instead, the patient usually becomes the subject. Examples of an active and a passive sentence from Chichewa are given in (11.5).

(11.5) a. *Naphiri*   *a-na-lemba*   *kalata.*
         Naphiri   3SG-PAST-write   letter
         'Naphiri wrote a letter.'
      b. *Kalata*   *i-na-lemb-edwa*   *(ndi Naphiri).*
         letter   3SG-PAST-write-PASS   by   Naphiri
         'The letter was written (by Naphiri).'

(Dubinsky and Simango 1996: 751–2)

In Chichewa, the passive is marked by the suffix *-idw/-edw*, which is attached directly to the verb stem (the ending *-a* is a stem extension that need not concern us here). Its syntactic effect is that the patient is linked to the subject function and the agent is linked to the OBL_{ndi} function. As in English, the oblique agent is optional, as is indicated by the parentheses. Thus, we can formulate the rule for passivization as in (11.6).

$$
(11.6)
\begin{bmatrix}
/\text{Xa}/_v \\
\text{SUBJ} \quad\text{—}\quad \text{OBJ} \\
\;\mid\qquad\qquad\mid \\
\text{agent}\quad\text{patient} \\
\text{'do}_x\text{'}
\end{bmatrix}
\leftrightarrow
\begin{bmatrix}
/\text{Xidwa}/_v \\
(\text{OBL}_{ndi}) \quad\text{—}\quad \text{SUBJ} \\
\;\mid\qquad\qquad\mid \\
\text{agent}\quad\text{patient} \\
\text{'be done}_x\text{'}
\end{bmatrix}
$$

Here all that changes is the phonological form of the verb and the function structure of the verb (as well as the linking to the thematic roles). The verb meaning (and thus the argument structure) is unaffected. Even when the oblique agent is omitted, it is still present implicitly: the sentence *kalata inalembedwa* means that some unspecified agent wrote the letter (not just that some agentless letter writing took place), as is clear from a sentence like (11.7), where the adverb *mwadala* 'deliberately' presupposes such an agent.

(11.7) *Chitseko*   *chi-na-tsek-edwa*   *mwadala.*
        door   3SG-PAST-close-PASS   deliberately
        'The door was closed deliberately.'

(Dubinsky and Simango 1996: 751)

The passive in English and other European languages is very similar in its syntactic effects, but it is more complicated formally (involving both an auxiliary and a participle), so that the Chichewa passive serves our purposes better (the Chichewa type is far more common in the world's languages anyway).

The passive is thus a prototypical example of a function-changing operation, or voice. Another example is the **reflexive**, where the agent and the
patient are coreferential and can hence be thought of as occupying a single
syntactic function. Examples of an active and a reflexive verb in Eastern
Armenian are given in (11.8), and the rule is given in (11.9).

(11.8) a. *Mayr-ə*   *lvan-um*   *e*   *Seda-yi-n.*
           mother-ART   wash-PRES   AUX   Seda-DAT-ART
           'Mother is washing Seda.'
        b. *Seda-n*   *lva-cv-um*   *e.*
           Seda(NOM)-ART   wash-REFL-PRES   AUX
           'Seda is washing (herself).'

(Kozinceva 1981: 83)

$$(11.9) \begin{bmatrix} /Xnum/_v \\ \text{SUBJ} \quad — \quad \text{OBJ} \\ | \qquad | \\ \text{agent} \quad \text{patient} \\ \text{'A acts}_x \text{ on B'} \end{bmatrix} \leftrightarrow \begin{bmatrix} /Xcvum/_v \\ \text{SUBJ} \\ \overbrace{\text{agent}_i \quad \text{patient}_i} \\ \text{'A acts}_x \text{ on self'} \end{bmatrix}$$

In the reflexive voice, the meaning of the verb remains the same, but it is
specified that the agent and the patient are coreferential (indicated in the
right-hand word-schema in (11.9)). Thus, although the reflexive is not really
event-changing, its effect is not strictly limited to function changing either.
It is thus a borderline case between the two types.
    A clear example of an event-changing operation is the **anticausative**,
where the agent-backgrounding is much more radical than in the passive:
The agent is completely removed from the argument structure. An example
comes from Russian, where the anticausative is expressed by the suffix *-sja/*
-s' (we have already seen this example in Section 9.2 in a different context).

(11.10) a. *Vera*   *zakryla*   *dver'.*
            Vera.NOM   closed   door.ACC
            'Vera closed the door.'
        b. *Dver'*   *zakryla-s'.*
            door.NOM   closed-ANTIC
            'The door closed.'

$$(11.11) \begin{bmatrix} /X/_v \\ \text{SUBJ} — \text{OBJ} \\ | \qquad | \\ \text{agent patient} \\ \text{'CAUSE ([}A\text{], [BECOME ([STATE}_x \text{ ([}B\text{])])])'} \end{bmatrix} \leftrightarrow \begin{bmatrix} /Xsja/_v \\ \text{SUBJ} \\ | \\ \text{patient} \\ \text{'BECOME ([STATE}_x \text{ ([}B\text{])])'} \end{bmatrix}$$

In (11.11) we see that not only is the agent removed from the argument structure, but also the CAUSE element is eliminated from the conceptual event

structure (hence the term 'anticausative'). It is in this sense that the anti-causative is event changing and not merely function changing. The function change (patient becoming subject) is an almost trivial consequence of the main function of the anticausative. That the agent is not present in the argument structure and in the verb meaning can also be seen from the fact that it cannot appear as an oblique argument (*Dver' zakrylas' Veroj 'The door closed through Vera'), and no agent-oriented adverbials may occur in the sentence (*Dver' zakrylas' namerenno 'The door closed deliberately'; this sentence is possible only in an unlikely world in which doors have intentions).

An even more radical change in the event structure of the verb is effected by the **resultative** (or **stative**) operation, which removes not only the 'cause' part of the event structure together with the agent, but also the 'become' part. An example of a resultative (marked by the suffix *-ik/-ek*) from Chichewa, which contrasts with the passive in (11.7), is given in (11.12a). The active and resultative event structures are given in (11.12b).

(11.12) a. *Chitseko   chi-na-tsek-eka.*
         door   3SG-PAST-close-RESULT
         'The door was closed (= in a closed state).'

       b. 'CAUSE ([A], [BECOME ([CLOSED ([B])])])' ↔ 'CLOSED ([B])'

As in the Russian anticausative, neither an oblique agent nor an agent-oriented adverb is permitted (*Chitseko chinatsekeka ndi Naphiri 'The door was in a closed state through Naphiri'; *Chitseko chinatsekeka mwadala 'The door was in a closed state deliberately') (Dubinsky and Simango 1996: 751).

As we saw in Section 9.2, an interesting feature of the anticausative and resultative operations is that they are semantically **subtractive** – i.e. the derived form removes part of the conceptual structure of the base.

11.1.3 Patient-backgrounding operations

Antipassive is the term for a morphological operation whose effect is to background the patient in much the same way as the agent is backgrounded in the passive. An example of an active and an antipassive construction from Greenlandic Eskimo is shown in (11.13a–b). Note that the oblique patient is marked by the instrumental case in Greenlandic. The relevant part from the antipassive rule is given in (11.14).

(11.13) a. *Qimmi-p   inu-it   tuqup-pai.*
         dog-ERG.SG   person-ABS.PL   kill-3SG.SUBJ/3SG.OBJ.INDIC
         'The dog killed the people.'

       b. *Qimmiq   (inun-nik)   tuqut-si-vuq.*
          dog(ABS)   person-INSTR.PL   kill-ANTIP-3SG.INDIC
          'The dog killed (people).'

(Fortescue 1984: 86, 206)

(11.14) $$\begin{bmatrix} \text{SUBJ} & \text{---} & \text{OBJ} \\ | & & | \\ \text{agent} & & \text{patient} \end{bmatrix} \leftrightarrow \begin{bmatrix} \text{SUBJ} & \text{---} & (\text{OBL}_{instr}) \\ | & & | \\ \text{agent} & & \text{patient} \end{bmatrix}$$

Now we might ask whether there is also a patient-backgrounding operation that completely removes the patient from the argument structure. And, indeed, some languages have a valence-changing affix whose effect is that the patient cannot be expressed at all. We may call this operation **deobjective**. An example comes from Tzutujil.

(11.15) a. *x-Ø-uu-ch'ey*
         PAST-3SG.OBJ-3SG.SUBJ-hit
         'he hit him'
      b. *x-Ø-ch'ey-oon-i*
         PAST-3SG.SUBJ-hit-DEOBJ-PAST
         'he was hitting'

(Dayley 1985: 89, 116)

(11.15b) is an intransitive verb in all respects: it has the suffix *-i* in addition to the prefix *x-* in the past tense (cf. *x-eel-i* 'he went out', contrasting with *x-uu-ch'ey* in (11.15a) where there is no *-i*), it has only a single person–number prefix for the subject, and it does not allow a patient to be expressed. However, it is unlikely that (11.15b) has a different event structure from (11.15a), because it is difficult to conceive of a hitting event without a patient participant. In anticausatives, agents can be eliminated from the event structure because the 'cause' element is eliminated: we can think of opening, breaking and similar events as occurring either through an external agent or spontaneously, but we cannot easily think of such events as occurring without a patient. Thus, the most likely valence-changing effect of the deobjective is that shown in (11.16). The crossed linking line above 'patient' means that this semantic role cannot be linked to any syntactic function.

(11.16) $$\begin{bmatrix} \text{SUBJ} & \text{---} & \text{OBJ} \\ | & & | \\ \text{agent} & & \text{patient} \end{bmatrix} \leftrightarrow \begin{bmatrix} \text{SUBJ} & & \\ | & & \not\mid \\ \text{agent} & & \text{patient} \end{bmatrix}$$

Thus, patient-backgrounding operations seem to be exclusively function changing.

11.1.4 Agent-adding operations: causatives

When a new participant is added to a verb, the event structure must be enriched as well, so the causative is clearly an event-changing operation. Two examples of a non-causative and a corresponding causative from

Japanese are given in (11.17a–b)–(11.18a–b), and (11.17c)–(11.18c) shows the valence-changing rules.

(11.17) a. *Taroo   ga   ik-u.*
          Taro   NOM   go-PRES
          'Taro goes.'

    b. *Hanako   ga   Taroo   o   ik-ase-ta.*
        Hanako   NOM   Taro   ACC   go-CAUS-PAST
        'Hanako made Taro go.'

                               (Shibatani 1990: 308–10)

    c. $\begin{bmatrix} \text{SUBJ} \\ | \\ \text{agent} \end{bmatrix} \leftrightarrow \begin{bmatrix} \text{SUBJ} & \text{---} & \text{OBJ} \\ | & & | \\ \text{causer} & & \text{agent} \end{bmatrix}$

(11.18) a. *Taroo   ga   hon   o   yom-u.*
          Taro   NOM   book   ACC   read-PRES
          'Taro reads a book.'

    b. *Hanako   ga   Taroo   ni   hon   o   yom-ase-ta.*
        Hanako   NOM   Taro   DAT   book   ACC   read-CAUS-PAST
        'Hanako made Taro read a book.'

                               (Shibatani 1990: 310)

    c. $\begin{bmatrix} \text{SUBJ} & \text{---} & \text{OBJ} \\ | & & | \\ \text{agent} & & \text{patient} \end{bmatrix} \leftrightarrow \begin{bmatrix} \text{SUBJ} & \text{---} & \text{IOBJ} & \text{---} & \text{OBJ} \\ | & & | & & | \\ \text{causer} & & \text{agent} & & \text{patient} \end{bmatrix}$

The semantic change in the event structure is obvious: it consists in adding the element 'cause' and with it a causer role (e.g. for 'go': [GO ([A])] ↔ [CAUSE ([D], GO ([A]))]). The linking of semantic roles to syntactic functions in causatives is complicated because languages cannot simply create a new syntactic function for the new role. Instead, causative verbs are made to fit into the existing function structures. The agent of an intransitive verb becomes an object as in (11.17b–c), but the agent of a transitive verb often becomes an indirect object (as in 11.18b–c), especially in languages that do not allow two equal objects.

Causatives are probably the most common type of morphological valence-changing operation in the world's languages. Since they happen to be rare in Europe, linguists working on European languages have often paid more attention to the agent-backgrounding constructions that are so common and varied in Europe.

11.1.5 Object-creating operations: applicatives

The **applicative** operation creates a completely new object in the function structure of the verb or shifts a non-object to the object function. An example of the latter kind comes from German, where the productive verbal prefix *be-* can have the effect of turning an indirect object into a direct object. The original direct object can be omitted or expressed as an oblique phrase.

(11.19) a. *IKEA   liefert   dem   Nachbar-n   die   Möbel.*
IKEA   delivers   the   neighbour-DAT   the   furniture.ACC
'IKEA delivers furniture to the neighbour.'

   b. *IKEA   be-liefert   den   Nachbar-n   (mit   Möbeln).*
IKEA   APPL-delivers   the   neighbour-ACC   with   furniture
'IKEA delivers furniture to the neighbour.'

   c. $\begin{bmatrix} \text{SUBJ} & - & \text{OBJ} & - & \text{IOBJ} \\ | & & | & & | \\ \text{agent} & & \text{patient} & & \text{recipient} \end{bmatrix} \leftrightarrow \begin{bmatrix} \text{SUBJ} & (\text{OBL}_{mit}) & \text{OBJ} \\ | & | & | \\ \text{agent} & \text{patient} & \text{recipient} \end{bmatrix}$

This construction is called a **recipient applicative** because it is the recipient that becomes a direct object. Almost all roles apart from the agent can become direct objects when an applicative marker is added to the verb. An example of a **locative applicative** from Ainu is shown in (11.20).

(11.20) a. *A-kor   kotan   ta   sirepa-an.*
1SG-POSS   village   to   arrive-1SG.INTR
'I arrived at my village.'

   b. *A-kor   kotan   a-e-sirepa.*
1SG-POSS   village   1SG.TR-APPL-arrive
'I arrived at my village.'

(Shibatani 1990: 65)

   c. $\begin{bmatrix} \text{SUBJ} & - & \text{ADV} \\ | & & | \\ \text{agent} & & \text{location} \end{bmatrix} \leftrightarrow \begin{bmatrix} \text{SUBJ} & - & \text{OBJ} \\ | & & | \\ \text{agent} & & \text{location} \end{bmatrix}$

Ainu has no case marking, but the subject-agreement marker *a-*, which is restricted to transitive verbs, clearly shows that the applicative prefix *e-* creates a direct-object function in the derived verb's function structure.

However, an applicative may also add an object argument that was not in the function structure of the verb before. For example, Chamorro has a **benefactive applicative**, illustrated in (11.21).

(11.21) a. *Ha   hatsa   i   acho'.*
he.ERG   lift   ABS   stone
'He lifted the stone.'

   b. *Ha   hatsa-yi   si   Pedro   ni   acho'.*
he-ERG   lift-APPL   ABS   Pedro   OBL   stone
'He lifted the stone for Pedro.'

(Topping 1973: 253)

Thus, here the applicative adds a new participant (a beneficiary) to the argument structure, like the causative:

(11.21) c.
$$
\begin{bmatrix}
\text{SUBJ} & - & \text{OBJ} \\
| & & | \\
\text{agent} & & \text{patient}
\end{bmatrix}
\leftrightarrow
\begin{bmatrix}
\text{SUBJ} & - & \text{OBL} & - & \text{OBJ} \\
| & & | & & | \\
\text{agent} & & \text{patient} & & \text{beneficiary}
\end{bmatrix}
$$

This means that applicatives can be either function changing or event changing. One might propose that these two subtypes of applicatives should be given different names, but it is in fact not so easy to keep them apart. One might argue, for instance, that the 'location argument' of the Ainu verb *sirepa* is not in fact an argument but an adjunct, so that this would be event changing as well. Moreover, some languages use the same affix for benefactive and recipient applicative, suggesting that this is indeed the same kind of operation. Thus, the distinction between event-changing and function-changing operations is not always un-problematic.

11.1.6 General properties of valence-changing operations

As we have seen, valence-changing operations primarily affect agents/subjects and patients/objects. Other participants can be promoted to object (or occasionally to subject) status, but there are no operations that change an oblique to an indirect object, for example. Explaining such possible restrictions on valence changing is a matter for syntactic and semantic theories of verbal event structure and argument linking.

Here it still needs to be pointed out that the semantic/syntactic contrast between event-changing and function-changing operations shows a clear correlation with derivational and inflectional status of the valence-changing affixes. Passives and antipassives are primarily inflectional, whereas anti-causatives, resultatives and causatives are primarily derivational. Reflexives and applicatives tend to show mixed behaviour, again correlating with their intermediate status with respect to the event-changing/function-changing contrast.

An important consequence of this contrast is also the prediction that it should be possible to apply a function-changing operation to an event-changing operation, but not vice versa. For example, in Chichewa the passive suffix *-idw* can be attached to a benefactive applicative verb in *-ir*.

(11.22) a. *Chibwe*   *a-na-phik-ir-idwa*   *nyemba.*
        Chibwe   3SG-PAST-cook-APPL-PASS   beans
        'Chibwe was cooked beans for.'
                                    (Dubinsky and Simango 1996: 752)

b. active: benefactive applicative: passive:

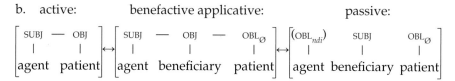

The reverse ordering is not possible in Chichewa, although it would make sense semantically (cf. 11.23a). However, the applicative suffix can follow the resultative suffix, as in (11.23b), because the applicative and the resultative are both event-changing operations.

(11.23) a. *Chitseko   chi-na-tsekul-idw-ira   Chibwe.
                door   3SG-PAST-open-PASS-APPL   Chibwe
                'The door was opened for Chibwe.'

         b. Chitseko   chi-na-tseku-k-ira   Chibwe.
                door   3SG-PAST-open-RESULT-APPL   Chibwe
                'The door was opened (= in an opened state) for Chibwe.'
                                    (Dubinsky and Simango 1996: 757)

   Valence-changing operations are in many ways syntactic phenomena, but since they are often signalled by specific morphological patterns, they also belong to morphology. However, most of the operations that we have seen in this section also occur with no specific formal coding. For instance, English has alternations such as (11.24)–(11.25).

(11.24) a. *I opened the door.*
         b. *The door opened.*

(11.25) a. *I baked a cake for her.*
         b. *I baked her a cake.*

The alternation in (11.24) clearly resembles the anticausative and the causative operation, and (11.25) is very much like a benefactive applicative. The English alternations are not usually discussed under the heading of morphology, but there is really no deep reason why they should not. Morphological operations need not be associated with a particular change in the pronunciation, as we saw earlier (3.12). When they are not, morphologists speak of conversion, and, while this term is mostly applied to uncoded word-class-changing operations, it could easily be transferred to uncoded valence-changing operations. Note also that such valence-changing operations may vary in productivity, from sporadic to extremely productive, much like other morphological processes.

11.2 Valence in compounding

When one of the members of a compound has a valence potential and takes arguments, this may be affected by the compound structure and the result may be a kind of valence change. We will look at three different compound types: noun incorporation, V–V compound verbs and synthetic compounds.

11.2.1 Noun incorporation

Noun incorporation is the traditional term for N–V compounds with a verbal head. Since verbs typically have a valence potential and require arguments, it is natural for incorporated nouns to occupy an argument position of the verb. Consider (11.26a–b) from Guaraní.

(11.26) a. *A-jogua-ta   petei   mba'e.*
        1ACT-buy-FUT   one   thing
        'I will buy something.'

     b. *A-mba'e-jogua-ta.*
        1ACT-thing-buy-FUT
        'I'll go shopping.'

(Velázquez-Castillo 1996: 107)

In the compound verb *-mba'e-jogua-* 'shop', the dependent noun *-mba'e-* clearly has the patient role of the verb *-jogua-* 'buy', but the question is whether this is necessarily part of the compounding rule. An alternative description would simply say that the semantic relation between the head verb and the dependent noun is vague, as in English N–N compounds. The patient interpretation ('buy things') would then be a natural implicature, but not strictly speaking part of the compound verb's meaning. If this is so, we would expect incorporated nouns to be able to fulfil other semantic roles as well, and this is indeed possible in quite a few languages with noun incorporation. Example (11.27) is from Huahtla Nahuatl.

(11.27) *Ya'   ki-koččillo-tete'ki   panci.*
        he   3SG.OBJ-knife-cut   bread
        'He cut the bread with the knife.'

(Merlan 1976)

Thus, it may be that the noun incorporation rule in these languages does not affect the syntax of the verb at all, and that the valence change is only apparent. However, in many languages there is clear morphosyntactic evidence for a valence-changing effect of noun incorporation. This is the case, for example, in Ainu, which has different subject-agreement affixes in transitive and intransitive sentences, as we saw earlier in (11.20) (e.g. *-an* for first person singular intransitive, *a-* for first person singular transitive).

(11.28) a. *Inaw   a-ke.*
           inaw   1SG.TR-make
           'I make an *inaw* (a wooden prayer symbol).'

b. *Inaw-ke-an.*
   inaw-make-1SG.INTR
   'I make an *inaw*.'

(Shibatani 1990: 11, 28)

In contrast to the transitive simple verb *ke* 'make', the compound verb *inaw-ke* 'make an *inaw*' is intransitive, as is clearly seen in the choice of the subject affix. Thus, it is not sufficient to say that the patient interpretation in (11.28b) arises as a pragmatic implicature – it must be part of the compounding rule, which can be formulated as in (11.29).

$$(11.29) \quad \begin{bmatrix} /X/_N \\ \\ \\ \\ 'x' \end{bmatrix} \& \begin{bmatrix} /Y/_V \\ \text{SUBJ} \quad\quad\quad \text{OBJ} \\ | \quad\quad\quad\quad\quad | \\ \text{agent}_i \quad\quad \text{patient}_j \\ \text{'A}_i \text{ acts on B}_j' \end{bmatrix} \leftrightarrow \begin{bmatrix} /XY/_V \\ \text{SUBJ} \\ | \\ \text{agent}_i \\ \text{'A}_i \text{ acts on } x' \end{bmatrix}$$

As this rule shows, the patient variable of the semantic structure of the simple verb is filled by the meaning of the incorporated noun, so that the semantic structure of the compound verb contains only a single variable and hence only a single argument. As in the case of the reflexive voice (Section 11.1.2), we have here a borderline case between event changing and function changing.

11.2.2 V–V compound verbs

A compound type that is not found in European languages but that is very interesting from the point of view of valence is V–V compounding. Two well-known languages in which such compounds are common are Chinese and Japanese.

The simplest and least problematic case involves two verbs with the same argument structure – e.g. Japanese *ukare-sawagu* [make.merry-be.noisy] 'go on a spree', Mandarin Chinese *tang-huai* [iron-break] 'ruin by ironing'. Example (11.30) shows how this Chinese verb is used.

(11.30) *Meimei   tang-huai   le   nei   jian   xin   yi.*
         sister   iron-break   PERF   that   CLF   new   clothes
         'Sister ruined those new clothes by ironing them.'

(C. H. Chang 1998: 82)

The rule for Chinese *tang-huai* could be formulated as in (11.31).

$$(11.31) \begin{bmatrix} /X/_v \\ \text{agent}_i \quad \text{patient}_j \\ \text{'A}_i \text{ acts}_x \text{ on B}_j' \end{bmatrix} \& \begin{bmatrix} /Y/_v \\ \text{agent}_i \quad \text{patient}_j \\ \text{'A}_i \text{ acts}_y \text{ on B}_j' \end{bmatrix} \leftrightarrow \begin{bmatrix} /XY/_v \\ \text{agent}_i \quad \text{patient}_j \\ \text{'A}_i \text{ acts}_x \text{ and acts}_y \\ \text{on B}_j' \end{bmatrix}$$

However, both Chinese and Japanese allow verbs with different argument structures to be compounded as well. In Japanese, where compounds are usually right-headed, it is mostly the second verb that determines the argument structure of the compound. For example, in *uchi-agaru* [hit-go.up] 'be hit high up in the air', the first verb is transitive and the second is intransitive (with an additional direction argument). An example is given in (11.32), and the correspondence is shown in (11.33).

(11.32) *Sono   booru   wa   sora   takaku   (*Jon   ni yotte)   uchi-agat-ta.*
　　　　 the　　 ball　 TOP　 sky　 high　　 John　 by　　　 hit-go.up-PAST
　　　　 'The ball was hit high up in the air (by John).'
　　　　　　　　　　　　　　　　　　　　　　　　　　　 (Matsumoto 1996: 204)

(11.33) $\begin{bmatrix} /\text{uchi}/_v \\ \text{agent}_i \quad \text{patient}_j \\ \text{'A}_i \text{ hits B}_j\text{'} \end{bmatrix}$ & $\begin{bmatrix} /\text{agaru}/_v \\ \text{theme}_j \quad \text{direction}_k \\ \text{'A}_j \text{ goes up to B}_k\text{'} \end{bmatrix}$ ↔ $\begin{bmatrix} /\text{uchiagaru}/_v \\ \text{theme}_j \quad \text{direction}_k \\ \text{'A}_j \text{ is hit upwards} \\ \text{to B}_k\text{'} \end{bmatrix}$

In this compound, the theme of the head verb is identified with the patient of the dependent verb. The agent of the dependent verb completely disappears from the argument structure, as is shown by the fact that it cannot be expressed as a kind of passive agent.

The association of intransitive theme and transitive patient is very natural (both of these semantic roles are affected by the processes in which they are involved), but an intransitive theme may also be identified with an intransitive agent:

(11.34) a. Japanese
　　　　　　 hataraki-tsukareru　 [work-get.tired]　 'get tired from working'
　　　　　　 tatakai-yabureru　　 [battle-lose]　　　 'lose as a result of fighting'
　　　　　　　　　　　　　　　　　　　　　　　　　　　 (Matsumoto 1996: 204)

　　　　 b. Chinese
　　　　　　 zou-lei　　　　　　 [walk-get.tired]　 'get tired from walking'
　　　　　　 xiao-jiang　　　　　 [laugh-stiff]　　　 'be stiff from laughing'
　　　　　　　　　　　　　　　　　　　　　　　　　　　 (C. H. Chang 1998: 83)

Perhaps the most interesting type of V–V compound is the **argument-mixing** type, in which the compound verb's argument structure has arguments from both constituent verbs. An example is Japanese *mochi-kaeru* [have-return] 'bring back' – see (11.35) and the correspondence in (11.36).

(11.35) *Jon   wa   kamera   o   ie   ni   mochi-kaet-ta.*
　　　　 John　 TOP　 camera　 ACC　 house　 to　 have-return-PAST
　　　　 'John brought the camera back home.'
　　　　　　　　　　　　　　　　　　　　　　　　　　　 (Matsumoto 1996: 208)

(11.36)

$$\begin{bmatrix} /\text{mochi}/\text{v} \\ \text{possessor}_i \quad \text{theme}_j \\ \text{'A}_i \text{ has B}_j' \end{bmatrix} \& \begin{bmatrix} /\text{kaeru}/\text{V} \\ \text{agent}_i \quad \text{direction}_k \\ \text{'A}_i \text{ returns to B}_k' \end{bmatrix} \leftrightarrow \begin{bmatrix} /\text{mochikaeru}/\text{V} \\ \text{agent}_i \quad \text{theme}_j \quad \text{direction}_k \\ \text{'A}_i \text{ brings B}_j \text{ back to C}_k' \end{bmatrix}$$

In this compound verb, all arguments of the constituent verbs end up as arguments of the compound verb. In this way, *mochikaeru* contrasts with *uchiagaru*. Clearly, Japanese V–V compounding consists of different sub-rules in which the argument linking is crucially different.

The final case to be mentioned here is the ambiguous type represented by Chinese *qi-lei* [ride-tired]. This can mean two different things:

(11.37) *Zhangsan*   *qi-lei*   *le*   *ma.*
       Zhangsan   ride-tired   PFV   horse
       a. 'Zhangsan was tired from riding horses.'
       b. 'The horse was tired from Zhangsan's riding/Zhangsan rode the
           horse tired.'

                                            (C. H. Chang 1998: 82)

Thus, here the theme argument of *lei* 'tired' can be identified either with the agent or with the patient of *qi* 'ride'.

11.2.3 Synthetic nominal compounds

A nominal compound whose dependent noun fills an argument position in the head's valence is often called a **synthetic compound**. According to this definition, incorporating compound verbs as discussed in Section 11.2.1 are of course also synthetic compounds, but the term *synthetic compound* is mostly used in discussions of European languages. In this context, it refers to N–N compounds like *truck-driver* and *whale hunting*, which have a deverbal noun head that is said to **inherit** (see Section 11.3) the verb's valence requirements. Thus, the noun *driver* can be analysed as taking a patient argument, like its base verb *drive*, and the noun *hunting* can be analysed as taking a patient argument like its base verb *hunt*.

There are at least three different ways in which such synthetic compounds could be described. The simplest approach is to deny that any special rule is needed at all. Compounds like *truck-driver* and *whale hunting* can be described as ordinary N_1–N_2 compounds that do not mean more than 'N_2 that has some relation to N_1' (see Section 5.1). In *truck-driver*, this meaning ('driver who has some relation to a truck') is then naturally interpreted as 'driver who drives a truck' by a pragmatic implicature. Similarly, *whale hunting* really means only 'hunting that has some relation to whales', but a natural pragmatic implicature gives rise to the interpretation 'hunting in which whales are hunted'. This analysis does not imply that individual compounds cannot be lexicalized and acquire the argument interpretation as a special meaning. But it does mean that there would be no general rule to account for argument interpretation in synthetic compounds.

An argument in favour of the simple approach is the fact that the dependent noun in compounds with a deverbal head need not have an argument interpretation. Consider the compounds in (11.38).

(11.38) a. *chain smoker*   b. *food poisoning*
        vacuum cleaner   *gang shooting*
        freedom fighter   *breast feeding*

                                (Oshita 1995: 183, 189)

A chain smoker does not smoke chains (cf. *pipe-smoker*), a freedom fighter does not fight freedom (cf. *fire-fighter*), and food poisoning does not involve poisoning food (cf. *rat poisoning*). The compounds in (11.38) are conventionalized, but novel compounds of this type can easily be created. It is even possible to imagine an unusual context in which *truck driver* means 'someone who drives around on trucks' (like *desert driver* or *moon driver*), or a context in which *whale hunting* means 'hunting with whales' (like *dog hunting* or *falcon hunting*).

Another approach to synthetic compounds derives their argument interpretation from a special word-syntactic structure that is different from that of ordinary N–N compounds. In this approach, the structure of *pipe-smoker* would be as in (11.39a), contrasting with that of *chain smoker* in (11.39b).

(11.39) a.   b.

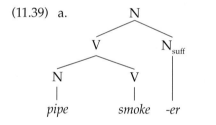 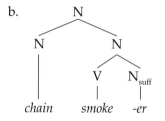

An argument in favour of having different structures for synthetic and non-synthetic compounds is the fact that, in more complex compounds, the dependent noun that is interpreted as an argument must be closest to the deverbal head:

(11.40) *chain pipe smoker*   *beach hat seller*
        *pipe chain smoker   **hat beach seller*

If we assume the structures in (11.39), the impossible compounds cannot be formed, so this approach accounts for the ungrammatical cases in (11.40).

Another argument is the existence of compounds like *caretaker* and *churchgoer*, which can hardly be said to be derived by compounding *care* and *taker*, and *church* and *goer*, because *taker* and *goer* cannot be used by themselves. Thus, the first approach does not work well with them. But, unfortunately, the second approach has a similar problem: The combinations **pipe-smoke*, **hat-sell* and **church-go* are not English verbs; if these were to come into existence, they would be created by back-formation from the corresponding compounds, not directly as N–V compounds.

The third approach to synthetic compounds involves a special rule of argument linking, analogous to the incorporation rule above in Section 11.2.1 (ex (11.29)). Let us assume that the noun *hunting* has the argument structure [agent patient], just like the verb *hunt*, and the function structure [POSSESSOR$_{of}$ — OBLIQUE$_{by}$] (e.g. *hunting of whales by traditional fishermen*). Then the compound *whale hunting* eliminates the patient/POSSESSOR$_{of}$ argument and the resulting compound is 'intransitive' – i.e. it takes only a single OBLIQUE$_{by}$ argument (e.g. *whale hunting by traditional fishermen*). The complete rule is shown in (11.41).

$$(11.41) \quad \begin{bmatrix} /X/_N \\ \\ \\ \\ 'x' \end{bmatrix} \quad \& \quad \begin{bmatrix} /Y/_N \\ \text{POSS} \text{ — } \text{OBL}_{by} \\ | \qquad | \\ \text{patient}_j \text{ agent}_i \\ \text{'event of A}_i \text{ acting}_y \\ \text{on B}_j' \end{bmatrix} \quad \leftrightarrow \quad \begin{bmatrix} /XY/_N \\ \text{OBL}_{by} \\ | \\ \text{agent}_i \\ \text{'event of A}_i \text{ acting}_y \\ \text{on } x' \end{bmatrix}$$

This approach is less radical than the second approach in that it does not assume a completely different compounding rule for synthetic compounds. (11.41) is an instantiation of the general English compounding rule (3.15), being merely more specific in that it specifies what happens to the arguments and the syntactic functions. This seems necessary, at least for action nouns like *hunting*, because the possibilities of associating semantic roles and syntactic functions are severely restricted (for instance, we cannot have **fisherman hunting of whales*, or **?whale hunting of fishermen*).

Thus, there are good arguments for all three approaches, and it is possible that different approaches are appropriate for different compounds or for different languages (this topic has been most intensively discussed for English). Other things being equal, it would of course be desirable to have just a single type of rule, but it remains to be seen whether other things are in fact equal.

11.3 Transpositional derivation

11.3.1 Transposition and argument inheritance

A derivational process is called **transpositional** when it changes the word-class of the base lexeme. Some typical examples of transpositional derivation are shown in (11.42).

(11.42) a. N → V English *computer* → *computerize*
        b. V → N Russian *napolnit'* 'fill' → *napolnenie* 'filling'

     c. A → V Basque   *luze* 'large' → *luza-tu* 'lengthen'
     d. V → A Italian   *mangiare* 'eat' → *mangiabile* 'edible'
     e. A → N Japanese *atarashii* 'new' → *atarashisa* 'newness'
     f. N → A Indonesian *tahun* 'year' → *tahunan* 'annual'

Valence may be affected by transposition when a verb or an adjective is transposed into another word-class (non-derived nouns normally cannot be said to have a valence potential, so transpositional derivations of nouns are hardly relevant here). When a verb such as *examine* is transposed into an action noun such as *examination*, its basic meaning (referring to an event with an agent and patient) is still intact, but the arguments cannot be expressed in the same way as with the base verb. We can say *The vet examined the pet*, but not *[The vet examination the pet]$_{NP}$ (took one hour)*. This is because deverbal nouns behave much like ordinary nouns in that they do not take subject and object arguments, but only possessor and oblique arguments. Thus, we have *The examination of the pet by the vet (took one hour)*. The patient argument becomes an *of*-possessor, and the agent argument becomes a *by*-oblique. The resulting noun phrase is similar to noun phrases with non-derived noun heads such as *the portrait of Charles V by Titian*. The relation between the valences of *examine* and *examination* can be described with our usual notation as in (11.43).

(11.43)
$$
\begin{bmatrix}
/\text{examine}/_V \\
\text{SUBJ} \quad\text{---}\quad \text{OBJ} \\
| \qquad\qquad | \\
\text{agent} \quad \text{patient}
\end{bmatrix}
\leftrightarrow
\begin{bmatrix}
/\text{examination}/_N \\
(\text{OBL}_{by}) \quad\text{---}\quad \text{POSS}_{of} \\
| \qquad\qquad | \\
\text{agent} \qquad \text{patient}
\end{bmatrix}
$$

In transpositional derivation, when a derived word has a valence that corresponds to the valence of the base in this way, we say that the derivative **inherits** the base's valence.

In the following subsections, we will take a closer look at various kinds of transpositional derivation.

11.3.2 Action nouns (V → N)

Perhaps the most interesting type of transpositional derivation is the **action noun** (or **event noun**), because action nouns show the greatest variety of argument structure phenomena both within a language and across languages. In English and other European languages, two different types of event noun can be distinguished, the **simple event noun** (e.g. (11.44a)) and the **complex event noun** (e.g. (11.44b)).

(11.44) a. *I have an examination tomorrow.*
       b. *The vet's careful examination of Fido's eyes took a long time.*

The basic difference between them is that complex event nouns preserve more verbal properties than simple event nouns. Sometimes a third type of event noun is distinguished, called **concrete noun**, and illustrated in (11.44c).

(11.44) c. *The examination is on your desk.*

However, this is not really an event noun, because it does not refer to an event. But it is necessary to mention this type in the present context because this is a widespread phenomenon: in many languages, the derivational patterns used for action nouns can also have concrete meanings. However, the kinds of concrete meanings are unpredictable: the product of an action (*building, painting, judgement, composition*), a group of people (*management, government*) or a manner (*conjugation*). Concrete nouns seem to arise by ill-understood and unsystematic (though frequent) processes of metonymic meaning shift, not by a word-formation rule, so we need not discuss them further.

Returning to simple and complex event nouns, we note that, when the verbal arguments are expressed with an event noun, it must be definite (see (11.45b)) and cannot be pluralized (see (11.45c)).

(11.45) a. *the examination of Fido's eyes by the vet*
         b. **an examination of Fido's eyes by the vet*
         c. **three examinations of Fido's eyes by the vet*

These two properties are characteristic of complex event nouns, while simple event nouns are more like ordinary nouns in that they can be indefinite or definite (*Tomorrow I have an/the examination*), and they can be pluralized (*Tomorrow I have three examinations*). Moreover, complex event nouns can be modified by duration adverbs like *frequent* and *constant*, whereas simple event nouns cannot (cf. *the frequent examination of Fido's eyes/*a frequent examination*). But, in the present context, the most important difference between complex event nouns and simple event nouns is that only the former inherit the verb's argument structure. Thus, for complex event nouns, the function-changing transposition rule in (11.43) is appropriate, whereas, in simple event nouns, the argument structure is not preserved. As a result, simple event nouns may occur on their own, with no arguments expressed, as in (11.46).

(11.46) a. *The examinations took a long time.*
         b. *We are witnessing a new development.*
         c. *The destruction was awful to see.*

By contrast, complex event nouns derived from transitive verbs require the overt expression of the patient, while the agent may be optionally present, as seen in (11.47).[3]

---

[3] An asterisk before an expression in parentheses means that the expression cannot be left out.

(11.47) a. *The frequent examination *(of the evidence) (by the scientists) is necessary.*
   b. *The constant development *(of new inexpensive housing) (by the city) was applauded.*
   c. *The continuing destruction *(of rainforests) (by humans) will speed up desertification.*

In some languages, complex event nouns have an argument structure that is even more verblike in that the patient is coded as an accusative NP. An example comes from Modern Hebrew.

(11.48) ha-hafcaca   ha-tedira   šel   ha-cava   et   ha-ʕir
    the-bombing the-frequent of   the-army ACC the-city
    'the army's frequent bombing of the city'

(Siloni 1997: 170)

In English, only oblique arguments coded by a PP and clausal arguments may be retained in an action noun construction (e.g. *they rely on her* → *their reliance on her; they elected Maria as president* → *their election of Maria as president; I predict that it will rain* → *my prediction that it will rain*).

11.3.3 Agent nouns (V → N) and deverbal adjectives (V → A)

In English and in many other languages, agent nouns do not seem to inherit the verb's argument structure, in contrast to (complex) event nouns. Expressions such as **voter for Mitterrand, *thinker about deep problems* or **claimer that Armageddon is near* are systematically impossible. However, it is, of course, possible to have a possessive phrase that may correspond to a verbal argument: *explorer of Antarctica, founder of Lund University, Mitterrand's voters*, and so on. One could see this as evidence that to some extent the verbal argument structure may be inherited after all, but a simpler account is available: possessive phrases have a very general meaning, and often the precise interpretation is left to pragmatic inferences from the context, as in the case of compounds (see Section 11.2). Given the meaning of an agent carrying out some action, the interpretation of a possessive phrase as a patient of that action is readily available, so we do not need to say that it arises as a result of argument inheritance. This view is also confirmed by the fact that agent nouns, unlike complex event nouns, do not admit an agent-oriented adverbial such as a purpose clause:

(11.49) a. **an explorer of America in order to discover El Dorado*
   b. *the exploration of America in order to discover El Dorado*

Thus, the rule for deriving an agent noun of a transitive verb would be as in (11.50), where the derived noun lacks an argument structure.

$$(11.50) \begin{bmatrix} /X/_V \\ \text{SUBJ} \quad\text{---}\quad \text{OBJ} \\ \quad| \qquad\qquad | \\ \text{agent}_i \quad \text{patient}_j \\ \text{'A}_i \text{ acts}_x \text{ on B}_j\text{'} \end{bmatrix} \quad\leftrightarrow\quad \begin{bmatrix} /Xer/_N \\ \\ \\ \text{'person who acts}_x\text{'} \end{bmatrix}$$

If this is the right analysis, we have to revise what we said about synthetic compounds in Section 11.2.3. Since agent nouns do not have an argument structure, words like *truck-driver* would not strictly speaking be synthetic compounds. Perhaps we ought to say that the first approach to synthetic compounds outlined in that section is appropriate for agent nouns and other deverbal formations that lack an argument structure, whereas the third approach is appropriate for complex event nouns.

English deverbal adjectives in *-able* seem to be similar to agent nouns in that they do not generally inherit oblique or clausal arguments from the base verb (*convincible of the eventual success, *emptiable of water, *persuadable that I'm right*, but cf. *deductible from income tax*). However, for some deverbal adjectives that take an *of*-argument (*supportive of, indicative of*, etc.), one could contemplate an approach in terms of a valence change accompanying the transposition, similar to (11.43), because adjectives do not in general take *of*-modifiers (unlike nouns, which in general take *of*-modifiers), so that the explanation that we gave for *explorer of Antarctica* cannot be extended to *supportive of*.

11.3.4 Deadjectival transposition (A → N, A → V)

Adjectives are much less often associated with their own argument and function structure, but many languages have at least a few argument-taking adjectives (such as English *proud of, full of, similar to, obedient to, different from, responsible for, ready to do something*). In English, most of these oblique arguments are preserved in deadjectival quality nouns (*similarity to, obedience to, responsibility for, readiness to do something, ??difference from*), though in some cases we have idiosyncratic changes (*pride in*, not *pride of*).

In deadjectival verbs, the oblique argument may also be preserved. An example from English might be *differentiate from* ('make different from'). In Russian, deadjectival verbs are formed with the suffix *-i*, and the examples in (11.51)–(11.52) show that the adjectival argument structure is inherited. The adjective *gordyj* 'proud' takes an instrumental oblique argument, and the adjective *gotovyj* 'ready' takes an infinitival argument.

(11.51) a. *gordyj   svoimi   dostiženijami*
            proud   self's   achievements.INSTR
            'proud of one's achievements'

b. *On*   *gord-i-tsja*   *svoimi*   *dostiženijami*
   he   proud-VERB-3SG self's   achievements.INSTR
   'He prides himself on his achievements.'

(11.52) a. *gotovyj*   *vyexat'*   *iz*   *strany*
            read   to.leave   from   country
            'ready to leave the country'
         b. *On*   *gotov-i-tsja*   *vyexat'*   *iz*   *strany.*
            he   ready-VERB-3SG   to.leave   from   country
            'he is getting ready to leave the country.'

A counterexample would be English *fill*, which does not behave like *full* (cf. *full of, fill with*).

A difficulty in determining whether the adjectival argument structure is inherited is the fact that the choice of the preposition or oblique case that marks the adjectival argument is rarely completely arbitrary. In many cases, it could be argued that the choice of the preposition or case is determined semantically and is independent of the base adjective.

11.4 Transpositional inflection

A particular challenge for morphologists and syntacticians is the description of word-class-changing or transpositional inflection. In transpositional inflection, not just some, but all of the argument structure of the base is preserved, plus its other combinatory possibilities. An inflectional V → A transposition is called a **participle** in many languages (see (11.53) from German), and an inflectional V → N transposition is called a **masdar** in some languages (cf. example (see 11.54) from Lezgian).

(11.53) *der*   *im*   *Wald*   *laut*   *pfeif-end-e*   *Wanderer*
         the   in.the   forest   loud   whistle-PTCP-M.SG   hiker
         'the hiker who is whistling loud in the forest'

(11.54) *Wun*   *fad*   *qarağ-un-i*   *čun*   *tažub*   *iji-zwa.*
         you.ABS   early   get.up-MASD-ERG   we.ABS   surprise   do-IMPF
         'That you are getting up early surprises us.'
                                                      (Haspelmath 1993: 153)

A less well-known example of word-class-changing inflection is the Hungarian **proprietive** ('having', N → A):

(11.55) *rendkívül*   *nagy*   *hatalm-ú*   *uralkodó*
         extremely   great   power-PROPR   monarch
         'monarch with extremely great power'
                                                      (Kenesei 1995–96: 164)

The participle is similar to the deverbal adjective (Section 11.3.3), but note that it also inherits the possibility to combine with a locative modifier (*im Wald* 'in the forest') and a manner modifier (*laut* 'loud'). The masdar is similar to the action noun, but it preserves the verbal valence completely: in (11.54), the agent argument is in the absolutive case, and in this respect it is very different from a noun's modifier or argument. Moreover, (11.54) also shows that the masdar is like a verb, not like an action noun in that it can combine with an adverb (cf. the behaviour of English action nouns: **My perusal carefully of the article/my careful perusal of the article*). The Hungarian proprietive is similar to denominal adjectives like *powerful*, but, unlike such adjectives in English, Hungarian proprietives can take prenominal modifiers that only nouns can take.

This suggests that, if we want to describe the syntactic behaviour of participles, masdars and proprietives (and other inflectional transpositions not mentioned here), instead of invoking a mechanism of inheritance from the base lexeme, we should say that we do not have a new lexeme here at all but an inflected word-form of the same lexeme. Participles and masdars are verbs, and Hungarian proprietives are nouns. Combined with their dependents (i.e. their arguments and modifiers), they yield verb phrases and noun phrases:

(11.56) German

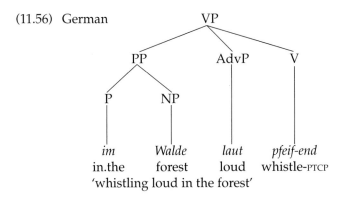

	im	Walde	laut	pfeif-end
	in.the	forest	loud	whistle-PTCP

'whistling loud in the forest'

(11.57) Lezgian

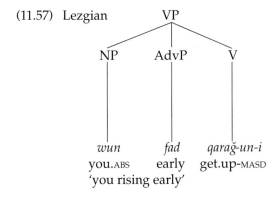

	wun	fad	qarağ-un-i
	you.ABS	early	get.up-MASD

'you rising early'

(11.58) Hungarian

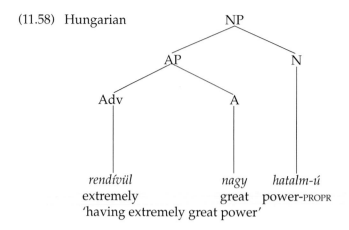

    rendívül   *nagy*   *hatalm-ú*
    extremely   great   power-PROPR
   'having extremely great power'

If we want to account for the behaviour with respect to their dependents, this description of these constructions is unexceptionable, but now we face a paradox: we have just said that participles, masdars and proprietives do not change the word-class of their base, although at the beginning of this section we said that they were examples of word-class-changing inflection. And, of course, there are good reasons for saying that a participle is an adjective. For instance, in German it shows exactly the same agreement inflection as adjectives, and it precedes the noun in an NP. There are also good reasons for saying that the Lezgian masdar is a noun: it shows nominal case inflection and occurs in the same syntactic environment as non-derived nouns. The Hungarian proprietive, too, is adjective-like with respect to its position and its pluralization.

A possible solution to this paradox is the following (see Haspelmath 1996). Participles, masdars and proprietives show dual behaviour – they act like verbs, verbs and nouns with respect to their dependents (= their **internal syntax**), but like adjectives, nouns and adjectives with respect to the other elements in the sentence (= their **external syntax**). We conclude from this dual behaviour that they have a dual nature: a **lexeme word-class** and a **word-form word-class**. As a lexeme, a participle is a verb, just like the other verb forms. But, as a word-form, a participle is an adjective. The internal syntax of a word is determined by its lexeme word-class, and the external syntax of a word is determined by its word-form word-class.

Let us now see how we could describe the external syntax of the phrases in (11.56)–(11.58). One possibility would be to assume a structure as in (11.59) for the German phrase in (11.53).

(11.59)

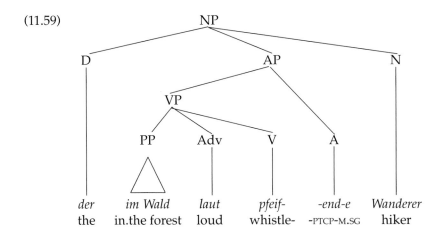

der	im Wald	laut	pfeif-	-end-e	Wanderer
the	in.the forest	loud	whistle-	-PTCP-M.SG	hiker

This representation has two disadvantages. First it makes the claim that the participle *pfeifende* belongs to two different syntactic constituents, although usually one assumes that a unitary word-form must also be a unitary syntactic constituent. Second, it works only for transpositional formations that are characterized by affixes. Participles such as Hebrew *šorek* 'whistling' behave just like German *pfeifend*, but they cannot be represented as in (11.59) because they have no participial affix – the participle is signalled by the vowel pattern *o-e* (cf. the past tense *šarak* of this verb).

An alternative proposal that does not have these disadvantages is to indicate the dual word-class membership in the syntactic trees. A participle can be represented as a word-syntactic tree as in (11.60a), contrasting with a derivational transpositional form such as an agent noun, given in (11.60b).

(11.60) a. *pfeifend* 'whistling'   b. *Pfeifer* 'whistler'

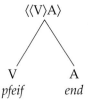

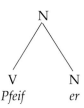

In (11.60a), the lexeme word-class is given in the inner angled brackets, and the word-form word-class is given in the outer angled brackets. Thus, in inflectional transposition, properties of the word-class of both constituents are preserved. By contrast, in derivational transposition, the derivative has primarily the head's word-class properties.

If such dual-word-class representations are admitted in the syntax, we get (11.61), where the phrasal node dominating *pfeifend* also has dual category membership. The notation '⟨⟨V⟩A⟩P' can be read as 'VP with respect to internal syntax, AP with respect to external syntax'.

(11.61)

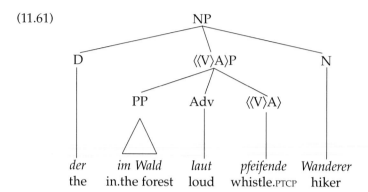

der	*im Wald*	*laut*	*pfeifende*	*Wanderer*
the	in.the forest	loud	whistle.PTCP	hiker

   The difference between transpositional inflection and transpositional derivation is interestingly similar to the difference between event-changing and function-changing operations that we saw in Section 11.1. Event-changing operations are generally derivational and involve a change in the argument structure of the base, like most transpositional derivation. Function-changing operations are generally inflectional and involve no change in the argument structure of the base, like transpositional inflection. The main difference is that function-changing operations of course change syntactic functions, whereas in prototypical transpositional inflection no functions are changed.
   Moreover, it should be recalled that the difference between event-changing and function-changing operations is not always clear-cut, and we often find intermediate cases. Transpositional operations are no different. Some inflectional forms do require some limited function changing – e.g. English masdar-like expressions of the type *Maria's criticizing Robert, the guest's arriving late*, where the verb's subject is coded not as a subject but as a prenominal possessor. On the other hand, derivational formations in some languages allow the expression of adverbials. Examples (11.62a–b) are from Spanish, and example (11.63) is from Modern Greek.

(11.62)   a. *la inauguración hoy en Barcelona del Congreso*
                'the inauguration today in Barcelona of Congress'
             b. *la caída de los precios todavía más*
                'the falling of the prices ever more'

                                                                      (Rainer 1993: 214)

(11.63)   *i katastrofí ton engráfon prosektiká*
             'the destruction of the documents carefully'

                                                                      (Alexiadou 1999: 19)

However, this blurring of the boundaries between word-class-changing inflection and derivation is not surprising if we remember what we said in Chapter 4 about the boundaries between inflection and derivation more generally.

Summary of Chapter 11

The most interesting inflectional categories and derivational meanings are those that affect the valence of the base: valence-changing operations, some types of compounding and transpositional derivation (in transpositional inflection, the base's valence remains unaffected). Valence-changing operations may be event changing (i.e. the event structure of the base and therefore its argument structure is modified) or function changing (i.e. only the function structure of the base is modified). The most important valence-changing operations are passive, reflexive, anticausative, resultative, antipassive, causative and applicative. In compounds, valence is potentially affected if at least one of the bases is a verb (as in incorporation and V–V compounding) or a deverbal derivative (as in synthetic nominal compounds). Transpositional derivatives such as action nouns and agent nouns inherit the base's valence to a greater or lesser extent. In transpositional inflection, the base's valence is completely preserved, but, in order to arive at a coherent description, one needs to differentiate between a word's lexeme word-class and word-form word-class.

Further reading

For syntactic theories that are deeply concerned with semantic valence (argument structure) and syntactic valence (function structure), see Dik (1997), Van Valin and LaPolla (1997) and Bresnan (2001).

Passive morphology is discussed in Haspelmath (1990). For antipassives, see Cooreman (1994), for resultatives, Nedjalkov (1988), and for causatives, Dixon (2000).

An overview of noun incorporation is given in Mithun (1984), and see Mithun and Corbett (1999) for noun incorporation and valence.

Japanese compound verbs are discussed in Matsumoto (1996); for Chinese compounds, see Packard (2000). Synthetic compounds are discussed lucidly in Oshita (1995). For action nouns, see Koptjevskaja-Tamm (1993) and Grimshaw (1990).

Transpositional inflection is discussed in Haspelmath (1996).

Exercises

1. Formulate the morphological rule for adjectives of the type *supportive of* (derived from *support*) (cf. Section 11.3.2), analogous to the rule in (11.43).

2. English has one kind of verbal valence-changing prefix that can be regarded as an applicative marker, the prefix *out-*, as in

run	*outrun*
play	*outplay*
shine	*outshine*

   Formulate the rule for *out-*, stating how the function structure, the argument structure and the meaning are affected.

3. The phrase *ruler over a large empire* is accepted by many speakers of English. Which generalization of this chapter is the phrase a counter-example to?

Frequency effects in morphology

In various ways, the frequency of use of linguistic units has a profound influence on language structure. In this chapter we will examine a number of cases in which this influence can be observed in morphology. The most striking effect of frequency differences on word structure is found in inflection, where frequency asymmetries result in asymmetrical structural behaviour of various kinds (Section 12.1). Frequency asymmetries also have an effect on the direction of language change (Section 12.2) and explain the patterns of irregularity in morphology (Section 12.3). In derivational morphology, frequency has an effect on the strength of synonymy blocking (Section 12.4).

All cases of frequency differences discussed in this chapter refer to token frequency – i.e. the number of times a given word-form is used. But type frequency – i.e. the number of existing lexemes with a given property – may also be important, as we saw in Chapter 6 and Section 7.5 in the discussion of productivity in derivation and inflection.

In psychological terms, the token frequency of an item has three main effects, all of which influence language structure in one way or another: (i) **predictability** (frequent expressions are more predictable because their occurrence is more likely), (ii) **memory strength** (frequent units are more easily remembered) and (iii) **fast retrieval** (in processing, frequent units are retrieved more easily and faster from memory than rare expressions). Frequency of use is therefore one of the most important sources for system-external explanation of language structure.

12.1 Asymmetries in inflectional categories

In inflectional systems, we often observe asymmetries in the behaviour of inflectional categories that belong to the same inflectional dimension. For instance, we find asymmetries in the dimensions of number (singular versus plural), case (nominative versus accusative), voice (active versus passive), and polarity (affirmative versus negative). These asymmetries have often been characterized in terms of an abstract notion of structural **markedness**: the singular is 'unmarked', the plural is 'marked'; the nominative is 'unmarked', the accusative is 'marked'; and so on. In this section we will see that the observed phenomena can be straightforwardly described and explained in terms of frequency differences, so that we do not need to make reference to abstract 'markedness'.

12.1.1 Frequent and rare categories

The most important inflectional dimensions and the frequency differences in their most important categories are summarized in Table 12.1, where '>' means 'is more frequent than'. It should be noted that these frequency asymmetries are assumed to be universal. Of course, not all languages have inflection for all these dimensions, but the claim is that, when a language has inflection for one of these dimensions and categories, it will conform to the generalization expressed in the table.

Dimension	Categories, ordered by frequency
number	singular > plural > dual
case	nominative > accusative > dative
person	3rd > non-3rd (1st/2nd)
degree	positive > comparative > superlative
voice	active > passive
mood	indicative > subjunctive
polarity	affirmative > negative
tense	present > future

Table 12.1 Frequent and rare categories

The correctness of the generalizations in Table 12.1 can be easily verified by examining a random text in a random language. Just for illustration, consider the results of one count of number categories in four languages:

(12.1)		Singular	Plural	Dual	Number of nouns
	Sanskrit	70.3%	25.1%	4.6%	93,277
	Latin	85.2%	14.8%		8,342
	Russian	77.7%	22.3%		8,194
	French	74.3%	25.7%		1,000

(Greenberg 1966: 32)

The differences between languages that we see here could be due to slight differences in the meanings of the number categories, or they might simply be due to the genre or style of the text chosen. Ideally, the token frequency of inflectional categories should be counted in a text that is representative of the everyday spoken language in the community, and finding such representative texts is not straightforward. But, fortunately, the asymmetries in Table 12.1 are so robust that the same result is generally obtained, no matter what texts we look at.

But why should there be such frequency asymmetries? In some cases, the asymmetry follows from general considerations. For example, the nominative can be expected to be more frequent than the accusative, at least in languages that do not allow unexpressed arguments, because all verbs require a nominative argument (i.e. a subject), but only transitive verbs also have an accusative. Similarly, the subjunctive must be rarer than the indicative because subjunctives are used primarily in subordinate clauses, and there is usually also an indicative verb in a sentence with a subjunctive verb.

The ultimate reason for the different frequencies of different inflectional categories is outside language. Some expressions are more frequent simply because humans (independently of factors such as culture, gender and age) find them more relevant: we all talk more about singular entities than about plural entities, more about third persons and things than about speech act participants (first/second person), more about present events than about future events, and so on. The linguist has no privileged skills for explaining these preferences, so we will not discuss them further. Instead, we will focus on structural properties that correlate with frequency.

12.1.2 The correlation between frequency and shortness

Quite generally, frequent expressions tend to be short in human languages. Frequent words are shorter than rare words. For example, in French the 10 most frequent words are *de, le, la, et, les, des, est, un, une, du*, and long words like *éléphant* or *questionnaire* are used rarely. Another instance of the same generalization is the fact that affixes are generally much shorter than roots, because affixes are relatively frequent in speech, whereas roots are relatively rare. And likewise among affixes, the more frequent affixes tend to be shorter than the rarer affixes. But even more strikingly, frequent inflectional categories are not expressed overtly at all but are left to be inferred from the context – i.e. they show **zero expression**. This is just one more manifestation of the correlation between frequency and shortness. As an example, consider the partial inflectional paradigm of regular nouns in Udmurt, given in (12.2).

(12.2)		SINGULAR	PLURAL	
	NOMINATIVE	*val*	*valjos*	'horse(s)'
	ACCUSATIVE	*valez*	*valjosty*	'horse(s) (dir. obj.)'
	ABLATIVE	*valleś*	*valjosleś*	'from the horse(s)'
	ABESSIVE	*valtek*	*valjostek*	'without the horse(s)'
				(Perevoščikov 1962: 86–7)

In this paradigm, the rarer cases ablative and abessive have a longer form than the more frequent accusative. The nominative and the singular are the shortest: They are both expressed by zero. This Udmurt paradigm is quite typical of inflectional systems. Zero expression is found in frequent categories, and when two contrasting categories are both overtly coded, typically the more frequent category has the shorter expression. Two more examples from verbal inflection are given in (12.3) and (12.4).

(12.3) Tzutujil	COMPLETIVE	INCOMPLETIVE	POTENTIAL
1SG	x-in-wari	n-in-wari	xk-in-wari
2SG	x-at-wari	n-at-wari	xk-at-wari
3SG	x-wari	n-wari	xti-wari
1PL	x-oq-wari	n-oq-wari	xq-oo-wari
2PL	x-ix-wari	n-ix-wari	xk-ix-wari
3PL	x-ee-wari	n-ee-wari	xk-ee-wari

(Dayley 1985: 87–8)

(12.4) Kobon	PRESENT	FUTURE	CONDITIONAL
1SG	ar-ab-in	ar-nab-in	ar-bnep
2SG	ar-ab-ön	ar-nab-ön	ar-bnap
3SG	ar-ab	ar-nab	ar-böp
1DU	ar-ab-ul	ar-nab-ul	ar-blop
2/3DU	ar-ab-il	ar-nab-il	ar-blep
1PL	ar-ab-un	ar-nab-un	ar-bnop
2PL	ar-ab-im	ar-nab-im	ar-bep
3PL	ar-ab-öl	ar-nab-öl	ar-blap

(Davies 1981: 166, 181)

Both these paradigms show zero expression in the third person singular. The Tzutujil paradigm shows that the non-indicative form (called 'potential') has a longer marker than the indicative forms, and the Kobon paradigm shows a longer marker for future tense than for present tense. The conditional mood in Kobon is marked by the two consonants b and p, so it is longer than the present indicative form, which has just a single consonant (this assumes that consonants are more important in counting length than vowels).

It is probably possible to extend the correlation to the nature of the segments that mark a category: more frequent categories tend to be expressed by phonetically simpler sounds (such as [t], [s], [n]), while rarer categories tend to be marked by phonetically less simple sounds (such as [k], [p], [m], [ŋ]). This question has not been studied systematically, but the generalization is clearly confirmed by (12.2)–(12.4). This means that the overall correlation is between frequency and simplicity of formal expression, of which shortness in terms of number of segments is just a special case.

This correlation is valid not only for inflection, but for derivation as well. Normally one thinks of derivational affixes as having a meaning of their own that is simply added to the meaning of the base. For example, in Wambaya the suffix -*ana* denotes an instrument (e.g. *ngarajag-ana* 'boomerang-shaping instrument', from the verb *ngarajag-* 'shape boomerangs') (Nordlinger 1998: 106), and it would not occur to anyone to say that the verb stem *ngarajag-* shows zero expression because the verb is more frequent than the instrument noun. However, in many cases it is not so clear that an affix is added because new meaning is added. For example, in many languages female person nouns are derived by a special affix from the corresponding male or general person noun – e.g. Dutch *handelaar* '(male) merchant', *handelaarster* 'female merchant', Hausa *àbookii* '(male) friend', *àbookìyaa* 'female friend'. From the point of view of the semantics, it would be equally possible to have a special affix that denotes male persons, but such affixes seem to be extremely rare. The reason for this asymmetry is probably that, in most societies, men tended to have more specialized roles, so that at least person nouns that denote professions and occupations are more frequently applied to men. Thus, the direction of derivation (from male/general to female) is determined by frequency of use.

Other cases of this are not so hard to find in derivational morphology. Action nouns such as *replace-ment* (from *replace*) and quality nouns such as *good-ness* (from *good*) do not really stand for different concepts from their bases. The main difference between base and derivative is a syntactic and pragmatic one: they can be used as referring expressions in noun-phrase slots, where verbs and adjectives are not appropriate. Now there is a general affinity between referring expressions and thing-denoting expressions, whereas property-denoting and event-denoting expressions are used primarily for predication and modification. Thus, again frequency comes into play: because the event-denoting concepts are used more often as verbs than as nouns, it is the noun (e.g. *replacement*) that carries the overt marker, not the verb. And, because property-denoting concepts are used more often as adjectives than as nouns, it is again the noun (e.g. *goodness*) that carries the overt marker, not the adjective (see Croft 1991: ch. 2).

12.1.3 The correlation between frequency and differentiation

In three different senses, frequent categories are more differentiated than rare categories. First, frequent categories show **less syncretism** than rare categories. Consider the partial paradigm of the Old English verb *bindan* 'bind' in (12.5).

(12.5)		PRESENT INDIC.	PRESENT SUBJ.	PAST INDIC.	PAST SUBJ.
1	SG	*binde*	*binde*	*band*	*bunde*
2	SG	*bintst*	*binde*	*bunde*	*bunde*
3	SG	*bint*	*binde*	*band*	*bunde*
1–3	PL	*bindaþ*	*binden*	*bundon*	*bunden*

This paradigm shows that there is more syncretism in the plural than in the singular (in fact, all plural forms of all verbs are syncretized in Old English), more syncretism in the subjunctive than in the indicative, and more syncretism in the past indicative than in the present indicative. The same tendency is found in Khanty possessive suffixes:

(12.6)

	SINGULAR	PLURAL	DUAL
1ST	-ēm	-ēw	-ēmən
2ND	-ēn	-lən	-lən
3RD	-l	-ēl	-lən

(Nikolaeva 1999: 14)

This paradigm shows that syncretism is found in the rarest of the three number categories, the dual, and in one of the rarer person categories, second person. (More syncretism in the dual can also be seen in Kobon (see (12.4)). More syncretism in the passive than in the active voice can be exemplified from Gothic (*niman* 'take').

(12.7)

	ACTIVE		PASSIVE	
	SINGULAR	PLURAL	SINGULAR	PLURAL
1ST	*nima*	*nimam*	*nimada*	*nimanda*
2ND	*nimis*	*nimiþ*	*nimaza*	*nimanda*
3RD	*nimiþ*	*nimand*	*nimada*	*nimanda*

The active has six different shapes, and the passive has only three.

The second sense in which frequent categories are more differentiated is that they show **more suppletive allomorphy** than rare categories. In other words, inflection classes differ primarily with respect to the frequent categories, less so with respect to rare categories. This can be seen in Russian noun inflection. The endings of the four most important Russian inflection classes are shown in (12.8) (the inflection classes are labelled I–IV, cf. exercise 5 of Chapter 7).

(12.8)

	SINGULAR					PLURAL			
	IV	I	III	II		IV	I	III	II
NOM	-o		Ø	-a		-a		-i	
ACC				-u					
GEN	-a		-i			Ø	-ov	-ej	Ø
DAT	-u		-i	-e		-am			
LOC	-e					-ax			
INSTR	-om		-ju	-oj		-ami			

The contrast between singular and plural is clear: In the singular, there are at least twelve distinct endings, while in the plural there are at most eight.

And, at least in the plural, the rarer cases (dative, locative, instrumental) show fewer allomorphs than the more frequent cases.

In Standard Arabic, transitive verbs belong to one of four inflection classes, characterized by different vowels before the final stem consonant. However, in the rarer passive voice the inflection is uniform and the difference between the inflection classes disappears (see (12.9)).

(12.9)

	ACTIVE			PASSIVE		
	PERFECT	IMPERFECT		PERFECT	IMPERFECT	
a-u:	*qatala*	*yaqtulu*	i-a:	*qutila*	*yuqtalu*	'kill'
a-i:	*ḍaraba*	*yaḍribu*	i-a:	*ḍuriba*	*yuḍrabu*	'hit'
i-a:	*ḥafiẓa*	*yaḥfaẓu*	i-a:	*ḥufiẓa*	*yuḥfaẓu*	'protect'
a-a:	*jamaʕa*	*yajmaʕu*	i-a:	*jumiʕa*	*yujmaʕu*	'gather'

The third sense in which frequent categories are more differentiated is that they tend to show **more cross-cutting categories**. For example, as we saw in Section 4.1, the Latin future tense lacks a subjunctive mood (or one could also say that the subjunctive mood lacks a future tense). In (12.10), we again see the third person singular of the verb *laudare* 'praise'.

(12.10)

	PRESENT TENSE	PAST TENSE	FUTURE TENSE
INDICATIVE	*laudat*	*laudabat*	*laudabit*
SUBJUNCTIVE	*laudet*	*laudaret*	—

Lack of cross-cutting categories is similar, but not identical to syncretism. In Latin, the distinction between indicative and subjunctive is not neutralized in the future tense. The form *laudabit* ('she will praise') expresses only the indicative, and future tense cannot be expressed directly in the subjunctive.

12.1.4 Local frequency reversals

Table 12.1 shows the frequency asymmetries that hold in general in languages. However, in particular lexemes, the frequency relations may be reversed. For instance, while most nouns (such as 'table', 'head' or 'doctor') occur more often in the singular than in the plural, a small group of nouns tend to occur more often in the plural in all languages. These are nouns referring to some paired or multiple body parts ('eyes', 'lips', 'hair(s)'), small animals ('ants', 'fish', 'mice'), small parts of plants ('beans', 'strawberries', 'leaves'), and some others ('sand grains', 'splinters', 'clothes').

In the case dimension, nouns that denote a place occur in the locative case more often than in the nominative, in contrast to other nouns. And, while the greater frequency of the nominative case is clearly true of animate nouns that may occur as subjects of transitive clauses, it is not so clear that inanimate nouns, which are typically patients, are also used more frequently in the nominative than in the accusative case.

Local frequency reversals may also be found in particular cross-cutting categories. While in general the third person is more frequent than the second person, in the imperative mood this relation is reversed: commands are more often addressed to the person who is supposed to carry them out, and indirect imperatives (with the subject in the third person) are rare in all languages.

Structural effects of these frequency reversals can be observed in many languages. In Welsh, plurals are normally marked by suffixes as in other Indo-European languages (see Section 7.5 for some examples), but in certain frequent-plural nouns, it is the singular that is marked by a special suffix:

(12.11) *dail*   'leaves'   *deilen*   'leaf'
        pysgod   'fish (PL)'   *pysgodyn*   'fish (SG)'
        ffa   'beans'   *ffäen*   'bean'
        cacwn   'wasps'   *cacynen*   'wasp'
        mefus   'strawberries'   *mefusen*   'strawberry'
        tywys   'corn'   *tywysen*   'ear of corn'
                                                  (King 1993: 67–9)

In case systems, splits between animate and inanimate nouns are common, especially splits between personal pronouns and other nouns. In English, at least in the pronouns *he/him* and *they/them*, we see that the direct-object case is formally marked by *-m*, whereas other nouns show no marking at all. There are also languages in which a marking contrast is found only in inanimate nouns (or non-personal pronouns), and here it is invariably the (transitive) subject case that is overtly marked, whereas the direct-object case is zero. Such a language is Godoberi.[1]

(12.12)   English   Godoberi
        (transitive) subject *he-Ø house-Ø* *den-Ø* 'I'   *hanqu-di* 'house'
        case
        direct-object case   *hi-m house-Ø* *den-Ø* 'me'   *hanqu-Ø* 'house'
                                                        (Kibrik 1996: 119, 36)

In the imperative, the second person form is often zero while the third person form is overtly marked (e.g. Latin second person imperative *lauda* 'praise!', third person imperative *laudato* 'let him/her praise!').

Local frequency reversals occur in derivational morphology as well. We saw earlier that male person nouns are generally more frequent than female person nouns. The frequency relations tend to be reversed with nouns like 'nurse' (because more women are nurses than men) and 'widow' (probably not because husbands die more often than wives, but because marital status has traditionally been considered more relevant for women than for men). As a result of the unusual frequency relations, we get unusual male forms with overt marking (*widow-er, male nurse*).

---

[1] Instead of the familiar terms 'nominative/accusative', the terms subject case/object case are used here, because overtly marked subject cases are usually called 'ergative' rather than 'nominative'.

12.1.5 Explaining the correlations

The correlation between frequency and shortness is clearly motivated by language users' preference for economical structures. Speakers can afford shorter expressions (or even zero expressions) when these are frequent, because frequent expressions are more predictable and are therefore those that are expected by default. The basic principle here is the same as in many other areas of human communication. For instance, in many countries local phone calls do not require an area code because most phone calls are local.

In language, such economical structures may arise when a new distinction is introduced that is coded only in one of the two contrasting categories. For instance, Spanish has a new nominative/accusative distinction, which is marked by the preposition *a* with animate NPs. This does not have morphological status yet, but if it becomes grammaticalized as an accusative case prefix, we will have a case system that conforms to the pattern in (12.12). The nominative was never marked overtly from the beginning of this change. Another way in which an economical case-marking system may arise is by selectively preserving older markers. For example, in the Old High German *n*-declension, animate and inanimate nouns alike had a distinction between nominative and accusative (see (12.13)).

(12.13)	Old High German		Modern German	
NOM.SG	*affo*	*knoto*	*Affe*	*Knoten*
ACC.SG	*affon*	*knoton*	*Affen*	*Knoten*
	'ape'	'knot'	'ape'	'knot'

Then the nominative/accusative distinction was lost in inanimate nouns, and in Modern German only animates preserve the zero marking in the nominative. Again, the resulting pattern conforms to (12.12), but it has come into existence via a different diachronic route.

The correlation between frequency and differentiation is due to the greater memory strength of frequent categories. When a category occurs rarely, it is more difficult to remember all the details of that category, so that syncretism is more common in rare categories, and various suppletive allomorphs are more easily kept apart in the frequent categories.

12.2 The direction of analogical levelling

A common type of morphological change eliminates morphophonological stem alternations by extending one stem alternant to word-forms of the paradigm that originally had a different alternant. For instance, many speakers of English have eliminated the alternation in *house/houses*, which in the traditional pronunciation has a voiced final stem consonant in the plural: [haʊs]/[haʊzəz]. Now crucially, it is the form of the singular stem that is extended by the innovating speakers ([haʊs]/[haʊsəz]), not the plural stem. There are no English speakers that pronounce the singular *house* as [haʊz].

This change is typical of analogical levelling in general: The form of the stem that is extended within the paradigm is the more frequent category. That frequency is the crucial factor is particularly clear from cases of local frequency reversals. A particularly striking case of this comes from West Frisian, where in the traditional language many nouns show a vowel alternation in singular–plural pairs. In innovative varieties of the language, this alternation is eliminated and the singular and plural stems are identical again, (see (12.14)).

(12.14)   conservative   innovative
   a. *hoer/hworren*   *hoer/hoeren*   'whore(s)'
      koal/kwallen   *koal/koalen*   'coal'
      miel/mjillen   *miel/mielen*   'meal, milking'
      poel/pwollen   *poel/poelen*   'pool(s)'
   b. *earm/jermen*   *jerm/jermen*   'arm(s)'
      kies/kjizzen   *kjizze/kjizzen*   'tooth/teeth'
      hoarn/hwarnen   *hwarne/hwarnen*   'horn(s)'
      trien/trjinnen   *trjin/trjinnen*   'tear(s)'
                                              (Tiersma 1982: 834)

In (12.14a), the singular stem form is extended in analogical levelling, but, in (12.14b), the plural stem form is extended. The choice of the form that is extended is by no means arbitrary: when the noun denotes a thing that tends to occur in groups and hence is more frequent in the plural, the plural stem wins out.

An example from case inflection is Latin *oleum* 'olive tree', which goes back to an earlier form *oleivum* (cf. *oleiva*, later *olīva*, 'fruit of the olive tree, olive'). Then three sound changes occurred: (i) the diphthong *ei* turned into *ē* and later into *ī*, (ii) the semivowel *v* [w] was dropped before *u* and (iii) long vowels were shortened before another vowel. As a result, the nominative/accusative form *oleivum* successively became *olēvum*, *olēum* and *oleum*, whereas the genitive and dative forms *oleivī/oleivō* became *olīvī/olīvō*. Then, analogical levelling extended the nominative/accusative stem to the other case forms (*oleiva* became *olīva* and retained the stem *olīv-*, because the *v* never dropped from its paradigm):

(12.15)   oldest form   later form   Classical Latin
   NOM/ACC.SG   *oleivum*   *oleum*   *oleum*
   GEN.SG   *oleivī*   *olīvī*   *oleī*
   DAT.SG   *oleivō*   *olīvō*   *oleō*

The greater stability of frequent stem forms can be explained either by memory strength or by fast retrieval, and it may well be that both factors play a role. The genitive singular *olīvī* is replaced by *oleī* because the stem *ole-* has a higher memory strength and may thus be used when a speaker (temporarily) forgets the old form *olīv-*, or because *ole-* can be retrieved more quickly from the lexicon and combined with the suffix *-ī* than the form *olīvī*, with its rarer stem form *olīv-*.

12.3 Frequency and irregularity

In language after language, if there are irregularities in inflection, these primarily affect the most frequent lexemes. Our first example comes from Koromfe, which has scores of regular verbs like those in (12.16a), and a few irregular verbs like those in (12.16b).

(12.16) a. HABITUAL PAST b. HABITUAL PAST

kam	kamɛ	'squeeze'	bɛ	bɛn-ɛ	'come'
tarı	tarɛ	'plaster'	bo	bol-e	'say'
leli	lele	'sing'	tɛ	tɛr-ɛ	'arrive'

(Rennison 1997: 271–5)

In Welsh, there are four irregular verbs whose past tense is totally unlike the past tense of a regular verb such as *gwel-* in (12.17a). Three of them are shown in (12.17b).

(12.17) a. *gwel-d* 'see' b. *myn-d* 'go' *gwneu-d* 'do' *do-d* 'come'

1SG	gwel-es i	es i	nes i	des i
2SG	gwel-est ti	est ti	nest ti	dest ti
3SG	gwel-odd e	aeth e	naeth e	daeth e

(King 1993: 183)

In Old English, grammars list just four verbs that are totally irregular and cannot be fitted into any of the inflectional classes. These are shown in (12.18b), and a regular verb is shown in (12.18a).

(12.18) a. 'bind' b. 'be' 'do' 'go' 'want'

1SG.PRES	binde	eom	dō	gā	wille
2SG.PRES	bintst	eart	dēst	gǣst	wilt
3SG.PRES	bint	is	dēþ	gǣþ	wille
1–3PL.PRES	bindaþ	sint	dōþ	gāþ	willaþ
1SG.PAST	band	wæs	dyde	ēode	wolde
PARTICIPLE	gebunden	—	gedōn	gegān	—

Thus, the verbs that tend to show irregularities are those that mean 'be', 'do', 'go', 'come', 'say', and so on – i.e. precisely those verbs that are used the most frequently in all languages.

In nouns, the situation is the same. For example, in Lango regular plural suffixes are *-ê*, *-nì* and *-í*. Some regular and most of the irregular nouns are listed in (12.19).

(12.19) a. *réc*   *réc-ê*   'fish(es)'   b. *dákô*   *món*   'woman/women'

      púnô *pùn-nì* 'pig(s)'   *ɲákô*   *àɲìrà* 'girl(s)'

      lɛ̀   *ley-í*   'axe(s)'   *ìcɔ̀*   *cɔ̀*   'man/men'

                               dánô   *jɔ̀*   'person/people'

                               dyàŋ   *dòk*   'cattle'

                               gìn   *gìgù* 'thing(s)'

                                            (Noonan 1992: 83–5)

Bulgarian has the irregular noun plurals *oko/oči* 'eye(s)', *uxo/uši* 'ear(s)', *dete/deca* 'child(ren)', and Italian has the three irregular nouns *uomo/uomini* 'man/men', *dio/dei* 'god(s)', *bue/buoi* 'ox(en)'. The appearance of words for 'cattle' and 'ox' on several of these lists may at first seem surprising – these are certainly not among the most frequent nouns in modern Italian and modern English. But in modern Lango they may well be (cattle herding is one of the main economic activity of Lango speakers), and in older Italian and older English the situation may have been similar.

There are two rather different ways in which frequency may cause irregularity in morphology. On the one hand, frequency leads to phonological reduction, because frequent expressions are relatively predictable, so that speakers can afford to articulate less clearly. This factor must be invoked to explain the irregularities in Koromfe verbs in (12.16). Examples from English are the verbs *have*, *say* and *make*, which were completely regular in older English, but became irregular because they were subjected to greater phonological reduction than comparable rarer verbs (e.g. *said* versus *played*, *had* versus *behaved*, *made* versus *faked*; and see the discussion of these changes at the end of Section 3.1).

On the other hand, frequency leads to memory strength and fast retrieval, so that frequent items are less susceptible to analogical levelling and other regularizations. So, while frequency causes faster phonological change, with respect to morphology it has a conserving, decelerating function. For example, the irregular Italian noun *uomo/uomini* 'man/men' preserves an old declension type inherited from Latin (*homo/homines*) that was otherwise eliminated by regularizing changes (cf. Latin *virgo/virgines* 'virgin(s)', Italian *vergine/vergini*). This conserving effect of frequency is also the cause of the Bulgarian irregular plurals *oči* 'eyes' and *uši* 'ears'. These were originally dual forms, and, because eyes and ears typically occur in pairs, these word-forms were probably the most frequent forms in the paradigm. Since eyes and ears are among the most frequently used paired body parts, it is not surprising that these forms survive.

From a diachronic point of view, the least well-understood type of irregularity is stem suppletion, as seen in Welsh *myn-/es-/aeth*, Old English *is/wæs*, *gæþ/ēode*, Lango *dákô/món*. It is difficult to understand why speakers would begin to associate roots that originally came from two different lexemes and integrate them as word-forms of the same lexeme. But, granted that speakers sometimes do that, the conserving effect of frequency will maintain the suppletion in the most frequent lexemes. It is also worth pointing out that affixal suppletion (suppletive allomorphy, which we discussed in Section 12.1.3) works in exactly the same way: suppletion can be maintained if the items affected are sufficiently frequent, whether owing to category frequency (as in Section 12.1.3) or to lexeme frequency (as in this section).

12.4 Blocking strength and frequency

We saw in Section 6.3.7 that the existence of a synonymous word often blocks the application of a derivational rule, but we also saw that this is not always the case. We return to synonymy blocking in this section because one factor that influences it is the token frequency of the blocking word: the more frequent the blocking word is, the greater is its blocking strength (Plank 1981: 182; Rainer 1988). Since the effect of frequency is relative, it is best to compare a range of cases that are structurally identical but differ in token frequency. We will look at quality nouns in Italian and German (Rainer 1988: 167–71).

The Italian quality noun suffix -*ità* is generally productive with adjectives ending in -*oso* such as *furioso* 'furious', *furiosità* 'furiousness'. However, when the adjective in -*oso* is itself derived from a non-derived quality noun, this noun has the same meaning as the (potential) derivative in -*ità*, and is thus potentially subject to synonymy blocking. For example, the adjective *bisognoso* 'needful' (derived from *bisogno* 'need') does not form a quality noun **bisognosità*, because this would have the same meaning as *bisogno* and is thus blocked by it. However, the blocking effect is not always observed. For instance, *malizioso* 'malicious' forms *maliziosità* 'maliciousness', although its base *malizia* 'malice' has the same meaning. When we look at the frequencies of a range of cases, we see that only the more frequent words have the blocking effect. In (12.20), the last column gives the frequency of the blocking word as determined by a frequency dictionary. (The frequency 0 means that the corpus is not large enough to contain a token of the word, not that the word does not exist.)

(12.20) base	potentially blocked word	blocking word		its frequency
coraggioso	**coraggiosità*	*coraggio*	'courage'	52.70
pietoso	**pietosità*	*pietà*	'pity'	34.04
desideroso	**desiderosità*	*desiderio*	'desire'	31.92
fiducioso	**fiduciosità*	*fiducia*	'confidence'	30.79
orgoglioso	**orgogliosità*	*orgoglio*	'pride'	10.64

armonioso	*armoniosità*	*armonia*	'harmony'	4.13
rigoroso	*rigorosità*	*rigore*	'rigor'	3.42
malizioso	*maliziosità*	*malizia*	'malice'	0
acrimonioso	*acrimoniosità*	*acrimonia*	'acrimony'	0
parsimonioso	*parsimoniosità*	*parsimonia*	'parsimony'	0
ignominioso	*ignominiosità*	*ignominia*	'ignominy'	0

The frequency effect on blocking strength can also be observed when a productive quality noun rule competes with unproductive quality noun formations. In German, the suffix *-heit* '-ness' has all monosyllabic adjectives in its domain, but it is blocked when a different quality noun is available, e.g. **Reichheit* 'richness' from *reich* 'rich' is blocked by *Reichtum* 'wealth', which uses the unproductive suffix *-tum*. Again, the frequency of the blocking word is decisive, as shown in (12.21).

(12.21)
base		potentially blocked word	blocking word		its frequency
alt	'old'	**Altheit*	*Alter*	'(old) age'	1400
groß	'big'	**Großheit*	*Größe*	'size'	1301
tief	'deep'	**Tiefheit'*	*Tiefe*	'depth'	613
warm	'warm'	**Warmheit*	*Wärme*	'warmth'	520
frisch	'fresh'	*Frischheit*	*Frische*	'freshness'	107
eng	'narrow'	*Engheit*	*Enge*	'narrowness'	67
blass	'pale'	*Blassheit*	*Blässe*	'paleness'	23
schnell	'quick'	*Schnellheit*	*Schnelle*	'quickness'	23

The explanation for the frequency effect on blocking strength is that frequent words are retrieved faster from memory than rare words. When a German speaker wants to say 'warmth', she has two options: applying the productive rule of *-heit* suffixation or retrieving an existing word with that meaning – i.e. *Wärme*. Since *Wärme* is very frequent and thus easy to retrieve, it will win out in this case. When the existing word is rare, the process of forming a new word may be faster, so that no blocking is observed (see Anshen and Aronoff 1988).

Summary of Chapter 12

Token frequency is relevant to morphology in a variety of ways, because frequent words are more predictable, more easily remembered and retrieved faster than rare words. Because speakers favour economical structures, the greater predictability of frequent categories typically results in zero expression (or otherwise short expression). Frequent categories are also more differentiated (they show less syncretism, more suppletive allomorphy and more cross-cutting categories). Because frequent words and categories are more easily remembered, they are less subject to analogical levelling, and this is also one of the reasons why irregularities exist mostly in frequent words. Another reason is that frequent words are subject to greater phonological reduction, again because of predictability. Finally, token frequency is relevant for synonymy blocking, in that frequent words have greater blocking strength because they are retrieved faster.

Further reading

Frequency differences between inflectional categories of the same dimension are discussed (under the name of 'markedness') by Greenberg (1966) and Croft (1990: ch. 4). The insight that frequency is the explanation for shortness was already emphasized by Zipf (1935). For local frequency reversals, see Tiersma (1982). For the relation between frequency and irregularity, see Mańczak (1980a, b), Werner (1989), Nübling (2000) and Corbett *et al.* (2001). Blocking and its relation to frequency is discussed by Rainer (1988) and Anshen and Aronoff (1988).

Exercises

1. The general correlation between frequency and shortness leads to certain expectations about inflectional paradigms. Consider the following (partial) paradigms and determine where these expectations are fulfilled, and where we should be surprised.

    a. Udmurt conjugation: past tense of *ućk-* 'look'

1SG	*ućki*	1PL	*ućkimy*
2SG	*ućkid*	2PL	*ućkidy*
3SG	*ućkiz*	3PL	*ućkizy*

    (Perevoščikov 1962: 203)

b. Even declension: *ǰuu* 'house'

	SG	PL
NOM	*ǰuu*	*ǰuul*
ACC	*ǰuuw*	*ǰuulbu*
DAT	*ǰuudu*	*ǰuuldu*
COM	*ǰuuñun*	*ǰuulñun*
ABL	*ǰuuduk*	*ǰuulduk*

(Malchukov 1995: 9)

c. Pipil possessive inflection: *nu-chi:l* 'my chilli pepper', etc.

1SG *nu-chi:l*   1PL *tu-chi:l*
2SG *mu-chi:l*   2PL *amu-chi:l*
3SG *i-chi:l*   3PL *in-chi:l*

(Campbell 1985: 43)

d. Tauya possessive inflection: *ya-potiyafo* 'my hand', etc.

1SG *ya-potiyafo*   1PL *sono-potiyafo*
2SG *na-potiyafo*   2PL *tono-potiyafo*
3SG *potiyafo*   3PL *nono-potiyafo*

(MacDonald 1990: 129–30)

2. With the same goal as in Exercise 1, examine the inflectional paradigms in (2.2), (2.7), (2.31), (2.32), (7.5), (7.13), (7.14).

3. Why is the change illustrated in (3.28) surprising after what we learned in this chapter?

4. Like German, English has a highly productive quality-noun suffix, *-ness*. Is this blocked to varying degrees, depending on the frequency of the blocking word? Compare a range of noun pairs such as *size/bigness, depth/deepness, warmth/warmness, height/highness, truth/trueness, reality/realness, readability/ readableness*. Establish their frequencies by means of a frequency dictionary (e.g. Francis and Kučera 1982), and establish their acceptability rate by asking 10 English speakers to 'grade' them. Is there a correlation between frequency of the blocking word and unacceptability of the derived word?

5. Go back to Chapter 10, where morphophonological alternations were discussed. Where did we make reference to frequency in that chapter? How did what we said there fit with the claims of this chapter?

References

Aikhenvald, Alexandra Y. and Dixon, R.M.W. 1998. Dependencies between grammatical systems. *Language* 74.1: 56–80.

Aldrich, R.I. 1966. The development of -scape. *American Speech* 41: 155–7.

Alexiadou, Artemis. 1999. *On the syntax of nominalization and possession: remarks on patterns of ergativity.* Unpublished. Habilschrift, Universität Potsdam.

Algeo, John (ed.) 1991. *Fifty years Among the new words: A dictionary of neologisms 1941–1991.* Cambridge: Cambridge University Press.

Allen, Barbara J., Frantz, Donald G., Gardiner, Donna B. and Perlmutter, David M. 1990. Verb agreement, possessor ascension, and multistratal representation in Southern Tiwa. In Postal, Paul M. and Joseph, Brian D. (eds) *Studies in Relational Grammar 3.* Chicago: University of Chicago Press, 321–83.

Anderson, Stephen R. 1988. Morphological change. In: Newmeyer, Frederick (ed.), *Linguistics: The Cambridge survey.* Vol. I. Cambridge: Cambridge University Press, 324–62.

—— 1992. *A-morphous morphology.* Cambridge: Cambridge University Press.

Annamalai, E. and Steever, Sanford B. 1998. Modern Tamil. In Steever, Sanford B. (ed.), *The Dravidian languages.* London: Routledge, 121–53.

Anshen, F. and Aronoff, Mark. 1988. Producing morphologically complex words. *Linguistics* 26: 641–55.

Arensen, Jon. 1982. *Murle grammar.* Juba: SIL Sudan.

Aronoff, Mark. 1976. *Word formation in generative grammar.* Cambridge/MA: MIT Press.

—— 1980. The relevance of productivity in a synchronic description of word formation. In Fisiak, J. (ed.), *Historical morphology.* The Hague: Mouton, 71–82.

—— (ed.) 1992. *Morphology now.* Albany, NY: SUNY Press.

—— 1994. *Morphology by itself: stems and inflectional classes.* Cambridge, MA: MIT Press.

Ashton, E. O. 1947. *Swahili grammar.* London: Longman.

Baayen, Harald. 1992. Quantitative aspects of morphological productivity. In Booij, Geert and van Marle, Jaap (eds), *Yearbook of Morphology 1991*. Dordrecht: Kluwer, 109–49.

—— and Lieber, Rochelle. 1991. Productivity and English derivation: a corpus-based study. *Linguistics* 29: 801–43.

Baker, Mark C. 1988. *Incorporation*. Chicago: University of Chicago Press.

Barker, Chris. 1998. Episodic -*ee* in English: a thematic role constraint on new word formation. *Language* 74.4: 695–727.

Baroni, Marco. 2001. The representation of prefixed forms in the Italian lexicon: evidence from the distribution of intervocalic [s] and [z] in Northern Italian. In Booij, Geert and van Marle, Jaap (eds), *Yearbook of Morphology 1999*. Dordrecht: Kluwer, 121–52.

Bauer, Laurie. 1988. *Introducing linguistic morphology*. Edinburgh: Edinburgh University Press.

—— 1990. Be-heading the word. *Journal of Linguistics* 26: 1–31.

—— 1992. Scalar productivity and -*lily* adverbs. In Booij, Geert and van Marle, Jaap (eds) *Yearbook of Morphology 1991*. Dordrecht: Kluwer, 185–91.

—— 1998. When is a sequence of two nouns a compound in English. *English Language and Linguistics* 2.1: 65–86.

—— 2001a. Compounding. In Haspelmath, Martin *et al.* (eds) *Language typology and language universals*. Vol. I. Berlin: Walter de Gruyter, 695–707.

—— 2001b. *Morphological productivity*. Cambridge: Cambridge University Press.

—— 2002. What you can do with derivational morphology. In Bendjaballah, Sabrina, Dressler, Wolfgang U., Pfeiffer, Oskar and Voeikova, Maria (eds), *Morphology 2000*. Amsterdam: Benjamins.

Beard, Robert. 1991. Decompositional composition: the semantics of scope ambiguities and 'bracketing paradoxes'. *Natural Language and Linguistic Theory* 9: 195–229.

—— and Szymanek, Bogdan. 1988. *Bibliography of morphology 1960–85*. Amsterdam: Benjamins.

Becker, Thomas. 1990. *Analogie und morphologische Theorie*. Munich: Fink.

—— 1993a. 'Back-formation, cross-formation, and 'bracketing paradoxes' in paradigmatic morphology. In Booij, Geert and van Marle, Jaap (eds), *Yearbook of Morphology 1993*. Dordrecht: Kluwer, 1–25.

—— 1993b. Morphologische Ersetzungsbildungen im Deutschen. *Zeitschrift für Sprachwissenschaft* 12.2: 185–217.

Berchem, Jörg. 1991. *Referenzgrammatik des Somali*. Cologne: Omimee.

Beyer, Stephan B. 1992. *The Classical Tibetan language*. Albany, NY: SUNY Press.

Bickel, Balthasar and Nichols, Johanna, forthcoming. Inflectional morphology. In: Shopen, Timothy (ed.), *Language typology and syntactic description*. 2nd edn. Cambridge: Cambridge University Press.

Bisetto, Antonietta and Scalise, Sergio. 1999. Compounding: morphology and/or syntax? In Mereu (ed.), 31–48.

Bloomfield, Leonard. 1933. *Language*. New York: Holt.

Bochner, Harry. 1993. *Simplicity in generative morphology.* Berlin: de Gruyter.

Booij, Geert. 1993. Against split morphology. In Booij, Geert and van Marle, Jaap (eds), *Yearbook of Morphology 1993.* Dordrecht: Kluwer, 27–49.

—— 1996. Inherent versus contextutal inflection and the split morphology hypothesis. In Booij, Geert and van Marle, Jaap (eds), *Yearbook of Morphology 1995.* Dordrecht: Kluwer, 1–16.

—— 1997 Autonomous morphology and paradigmatic relations. In: Booij, Geert and van Marle, Jaap (eds), *Yearbook of Morphology 1996.* Dordrecht: Kluwer, 35–53.

—— 1998. Phonological output constraints in morphology. In Kehrein, Wolfgang and Wiese, Richard (eds), *Phonology and morphology of the Germanic languages.* Tübingen: Niemeyer, 143–63.

—— Lehmann, Christian and Mugdan, Joachim (eds) 2000–2002. *Morphologie/ Morphology: Ein internationales Handbuch zur Flexion und Wortbildung/An international handbook on inflection and word-formation.* Vol. 1: 2000, Vol. 2: 2002. Berlin: de Gruyter.

Bresnan, Joan. 2001. *Lexical functional syntax.* Malden, MA: Blackwell.

—— and Mchombo, Sam M. 1995. The lexical integrity principle: evidence from Bantu. *Natural Language and Linguistic Theory* 13: 181–254.

Bubenik, Vit. 1999. *An introduction to the study of morphology.* (Lincom coursebooks in linguistics, 7.) Munich: Lincom Europa.

Buchholz, Oda and Fiedler, Wilfried. 1987. *Albanische Grammatik.* Leipzig: Enzyklopädie.

Bugenhagen, Robert D. 1995. *A grammar of Mangap-Mbula: An Austronesian language of Papua New Guinea.* (Pacific linguistics, C-101.) Canberra: Australian National University.

Bybee, Joan L. 1985. *Morphology: a study of the relation between meaning and form.* Amsterdam: Benjamins.

—— 1988. Morphology as lexical organization. In Hammond and Noonan (eds), 119–141.

—— 1995. Regular morphology and the lexicon. *Language and Cognitive Processes* 10.5: 425–55.

—— 2001. *Phonology and language use.* Cambridge: Cambridge University Press.

—— and Newman, Jean E. 1995. Are stem changes as natural as affixes? *Linguistics* 33: 633–54.

—— Perkins, Revere D. and Pagliuca, William. 1994. *The evolution of grammar.* Chicago: University of Chicago Press.

Campbell, Lyle. 1985. *The Pipil language of El Salvador.* Berlin: Mouton de Gruyter.

Carreira, María M. 1997. Spanish plural formation: it takes two (moras). *Chicago Linguistic Society* 33: 31–41.

Carstairs, Andrew. 1987. *Allomorphy in inflexion.* Beckenham: Croom Helm.

Carstairs-McCarthy, Andrew. 1991. *Current morphology.* London: Routledge.

—— 1993. Morphology without word-internal constituents: a review of

Stephen R. Anderson's *A-Morphous Morphology*. In Booij, Geert and van Marle, Jaap (eds), *Yearbook of Morphology 1992*. Dordrecht: Kluwer, 209–33.

Chang, Claire Hsun-huei. 1998. V-V compounds in Mandarin Chinese: Argument structure and semantics. In: Packard, Jerome (ed.), *New approaches to Chinese word-formation*. Berlin: Mouton de Gruyter, 77–101.

Chang, Suk-Jin. 1996. *Korean*. Amsterdam: Benjamins.

Chomsky, Noam A. and Halle, Morris. 1968. *The sound pattern of English*. New York: Harper & Row.

Coates, Richard. 1999. *Word structure*. (Language workbooks.) London: Routledge.

Comrie, Bernard. 1981. *The languages of the Soviet Union*. Cambridge: Cambridge University Press.

Cooreman, Ann. 1994. A functional typology of antipassives. In Fox, Barbara and Hopper, Paul (eds), *Voice: form and function*. Amsterdam: Benjamins, 49–88.

Corbett, Greville. 2000. *Number*. Cambridge: Cambridge University Press.

—— and Fraser, Norman M. 1993. Network morphology: A DATR account of Russian nominal inflection. *Journal of Linguistics* 29: 113–42.

—— and Hippisley, Andrew, and Brown, Dunstan and Marriott, Paul. 2001. Frequency, regularity and the paradigm: A perspective from Russian on a complex relation. In Bybee, Joan and Hopper, Paul (eds), *Frequency and the emergence of linguistic structure*. Amsterdam: Benjamins, 201–26.

Crocco-Galèas, Grazia. 1991. *Gli etnici italiani: studio di morfologia naturale*. Padova: Unipress.

Croft, William. 1990. *Typology and universals*. Cambridge: Cambridge University Press.

—— 1991. *Syntactic categories and grammatical relations: the cognitive organization of information*. Chicago: University of Chicago Press.

Dasgupta, Probal, Ford, Alan and Singh, Rajendra. 2000. *After etymology: towards a substantivist linguistics*. Munich: Lincom Europa.

Davies, John. 1981. *Kobon*. (Lingua Descriptive Studies, 3.) Amsterdam: North-Holland.

Dayley, Jon P. 1985. *Tzutujil grammar*. (University of California Publications in Linguistics, 107.) Berkeley: University of California Press.

—— 1989. *Tümpisa (Panamint) Shoshone grammar*. (University of California Publications in Linguistics, 115.) Berkeley: University of California Press.

Dench, Alan Charles. 1995. *Martuthunira: a language of the Pilbara region of Western Australia*. (Pacific Linguistics, C-125.) Canberra: Australian National University.

Dik, Simon. 1997. *The theory of Functional Grammar*. Parts 1–2. Berlin: Mouton de Gruyter.

Di Sciullo, Anne-Marie and Williams, Edwin. 1987. *On the definition of word*. Cambridge, MA: MIT Press.

Dixon, R.M.W. 1977. *A grammar of Yidiny*. (Cambridge Studies in Linguistics, 19.) Cambridge: Cambridge University Press.

—— 2000. A typology of causatives: form, syntax and meaning. In Dixon, R.M.W. and Aikhenvald, Alexandra Y. (eds), *Changing valency*. Cambridge: Cambridge University Press, 30-83.

Dressler, Wolfgang U. 1981. General principles of poetic license in word-formation. In *Logos semantikos: studia linguistica in honorem Eugenio Coseriu*. Vol. II. Tübingen: Narr, 423–31.

—— 1985. *Morphonology*. Ann Arbor: Karoma.

—— 1989. Prototypical differences between inflection and derivation. *Zeitschrift für Phonetik, Sprachwissenschaft und Kommunikationsforschung* 42: 3–10.

—— 1997. *On productivity and potentiality in inflectional morphology*. (CLAS-NET Working Papers, 7.) Montreal: University of Montreal.

—— and Ladányi, Mária. 2000. Productivity in word-formation: a morphological approach. *Acta Linguistica Hungarica* 47: 103–44.

—— and Mayerthaler, Willi and Panagl, Oswald and Wurzel, Wolfgang U. 1987. *Leitmotifs in Natural Morphology*. Amsterdam: Benjamins.

Dubinsky, Stanley and Simango, Silvester Ron. 1996. Passive and stative in Chichewa: Evidence for modular distinctions in grammar. *Language* 72.4: 749–81.

Dunn, John Asher. 1979. *A reference grammar for the Coast Tsimshian language*. (Canadian Ethnology Service Paper, 55.) Ottawa: National Museum of Canada.

Foley, William A. 1991. *The Yimas language of New Guinea*. Stanford, CA: Stanford University Press.

Ford, Alan and Singh, Rajendra. 1991. Propédeutique morphologique. *Folia Linguistica* 25.3–4: 549–75.

Fortescue, Michael. 1984. *West Greenlandic*. (Croom Helm descriptive grammars.) London: Croom Helm.

Fox, G.J. 1979. *Big Nambas grammar*. Canberra: Australian National University.

Francis, W. Nelson and Kučera, Henry 1982. *Frequency analysis of English usage*. Boston: Houghton Mifflin.

Gordon, Lynn. 1986. *Maricopa morphology and syntax*. (University of California Publications in Linguistics, 108.) Berkeley: University of California Press.

Greenberg, Joseph. 1959. A quantitative approach to the morphological typology of language. *International Journal of American Linguistics* 26: 178–94.

—— 1963. Some universals of grammar with particular reference to the order of meaningful elements. In: Greenberg, Joseph H. (ed.), *Universals of language*. Cambridge, MA: MIT Press, 73–113.

—— 1966. *Language universals, with special reference to feature hierarchies*. (Janua Linguarum, Series Minor, 59.) The Hague: Mouton.

Grimshaw, Jane. 1990. *Argument structure*. Cambridge, MA: MIT Press.

Groves, Terab'ata R., Groves, Gordon W. and Jacobs, Roderick. 1985. *Kiribatese: an outline description*. (Pacific Linguistics, Series D, No. 64.) Canberra: Australian National University.

Gussenhoven, Carlos and Jacobs, Haike. 1998. *Understanding phonology.* London: Arnold.

Hall, C.J. 1992. *Morphology and mind: a unified approach to explanation in linguistics.* London: Routledge.

Hammond, Michael and Noonan, Michael (eds) 1988. *Theoretical morphology: approaches in modern linguistics.* Orlando: Academic Press.

Hankamer, Jorge. 1989. Morphological parsing and the lexicon. In Marslen-Wilson, William (ed.), *Lexical representation and process.* Cambridge, MA: MIT Press, 392–408.

Haspelmath, Martin. 1990. The grammaticization of passive morphology. *Studies in Language* 14.1: 25–71.

—— 1992. Grammaticization theory and heads in morphology. In Aronoff, Mark (ed.), *Morphology now.* Albany, NY: SUNY Press, 69–82; 194–8.

—— 1993. *A grammar of Lezgian.* Berlin: Mouton de Gruyter.

—— 1995. The growth of affixes in morphological reanalysis. In Booij, Geert and van Marle, Jaap (eds), *Yearbook of Morphology 1994.* Dordrecht: Kluwer, 1–29.

—— 1996. Word-class-changing inflection and morphological theory. In Booij, Geert and van Marle, Jaap (eds), *Yearbook of Morphology 1995.* Dordrecht: Kluwer, 43–66.

—— 1998. The semantic development of old presents: new futures and subjunctives without grammaticalization. *Diachronica* 15.1: 29–62.

—— 1999. Why is grammaticalization irreversible? *Linguistics* 37.6: 1043–68.

—— 2000. Periphrasis. In: Booij, Geert, Lehmann, Christian and Mugdan, Joachim (eds), *Morphology: a handbook on inflection and word formation. vol. 1.* (Handbücher zur Sprach- und Kommunikationswissenschaft.) Berlin: de Gruyter, 654–64.

Heine, Bernd, Claudi, Ulrike and Hünnemeyer, Friederike. 1991. *Grammaticalization: a conceptual framework.* Chicago: University of Chicago Press.

Hooper, Joan B. 1976. *An introduction to Natural Generative Phonology.* New York: Academic Press.

Hopper, Paul and Traugott, Elizabeth C. 1993. *Grammaticalization.* Cambridge: Cambridge University Press.

Isaev, M.I. 1966. Osetinskij jazyk. In Vinogradov, V.V. *Jazyki narodov SSSR. Tom I: Indoevropejskie jazyki.* Moscow: Nauka, 237–56.

Jackendoff, Ray. 1990. *Semantic structures.* Cambridge, MA: MIT Press.

Jacobsen, Thorkild. 1974. Very ancient linguistics: Babylonian grammatical texts. In Hymes, Dell (ed.), *Studies in the history of linguistics: traditions and paradigms.* Bloomington: Indiana University Press, 41–62.

Kageyama, Taro. 1982. Word formation in Japanese. *Lingua* 57: 215–58.

Kaisse, E. and Shaw, Patricia A. 1985. On the theory of Lexical Phonology. *Phonology Yearbook* 2: 1–30.

Kanerva, J. 1987. Morphological integrity and syntax: the evidence from Finnish possessive suffixes. *Language* 63: 498–521.

Kastovsky, Dieter. 1986. The problem of productivity in word-formation. *Linguistics* 24: 585–600.

Keegan, John M. 1997. *A reference grammar of Mbay*. Munich: Lincom Europa.

Kemmer, Suzanne. 2002. Lexical blends. In Cuyckens, Hubert, Berg, Thomas, Dirven, Rene and Panther, Klaus-Uwe (eds), *Motivation in language*. Amsterdam: Benjamins.

Kenesei, István. 1995–6. Bracketing paradoxes in Hungarian. *Acta Linguistica Hungarica* 43: 153–73.

Kibrik, Aleksandr E. (ed.) 1996. *Godoberi*. Munich: Lincom Europa.

King, Gareth. 1993. *Modern Welsh: a comprehensive grammar*. London: Routledge.

Kiparsky, Paul. 1982. Lexical morphology and phonology. In Linguistic Society of Korea (ed.), *Linguistics in the morning calm: selected papers from SICOL-1981*. Seoul: Hanshin, 3–91.

—— 1985. Some consequences of Lexical Phonology. *Phonology Yearbook* 2: 85–138.

—— 1996. Allomorphy or morphophonology? In: Singh (ed.), 12–42.

Koptjevskaja-Tamm, Maria. 1993. *Nominalizations*. London: Routledge.

—— and Muravyova, Irina A. 1993. Alutor causatives, noun incorporation, and the Mirror Principle. In: Comrie, Bernard and Polinsky, Maria (eds), *Causatives and transitivity*. Amsterdam: Benjamins, 287–313.

Kozinceva, Natalija A. 1981. Refleksivnye glagoly v armjanskom jazyke. In Xrakovskij, V[iktor] S. (ed.), *Zalogovye konstrukcii v raznostrukturnyx jazykax*. Leningrad: Nauka, 81–98.

Lehmann, Christian. 1982. Directions for interlinear morphemic translations. *Folia Linguistica* 16: 193–224.

—— 1985. 'Grammaticalization: synchronic variation and diachronic change.' *Lingua e stile* 20: 308–18.

—— 1995. *Thoughts on grammaticalization*. Munich: Lincom Europa.

Lieber, Rochelle. 1992. *Deconstructing morphology*. Chicago: University of Chicago Press.

Macaulay, Monica. 1996. *A grammar of Chalcatongo Mixtec*. (University of California Publications in Linguistics, 127.) Berkeley: University of California Press.

MacDonald, Lorna. 1990. *A grammar of Tauya*. Berlin: Mouton de Gruyter.

McMahon, April M.S. 1994. *Understanding language change*. Cambridge: Cambridge University Press.

Mahootian, Shahrzad. 1997. *Persian*. London: Routledge.

Malchukov, Andrei L. 1995. *Even*. Munich: Lincom Europa.

Mańczak, Witold. 1980a. Frequenz und Sprachwandel. In Lüdtke, Helmut (ed.), *Kommunikationstheoretische Grundlagen des Sprachwandels*. Berlin/ New York: de Gruyter, 37–79.

Mańczak, Witold. 1980b. Laws of analogy. In Fisiak, Jacek (ed.), *Historical morphology*. The Hague: Mouton, 283–8.

Matsumoto, Yo. 1996. *Complex predicates in Japanese: a syntactic and semantic study of the notion 'word'*. Stanford, CA: CSLI Publications.

Matthews, Peter. 1991. *Morphology.* 2nd edn. Cambridge: Cambridge University Press.

Mayerthaler, Willi. 1981. *Morphologische Natürlichkeit*. Wiesbaden: Athenaion. (=Mayerthaler 1988)

Mayerthaler, Willi. 1988. *Naturalness in morphology.* Ann Arbor: Karoma.

Mel'čuk, Igor' A. 1991. Subtraction in natural language. In Weiss, Daniel and Grochowski, M. (eds), *Words are physicians for an ailing mind: Festschrift Andrzej Bogustawski.* Munich: Sagner, 279–293.

—— 1993–2000. *Cours de morphologie générale.* Vols. 1–5. Montreal: Presses universitaires de Montréal.

Mereu, Lunella (ed.) 1999. *Boundaries of morphology and syntax.* Amsterdam: Benjamins.

Merlan, Francesca. 1976. Noun incorporation and discourse reference in modern Nahuatl. *International Journal of American Linguistics* 42: 177–91.

Mithun, Marianne. 1984. The evolution of noun incorporation. *Language* 60: 847–94.

—— 1998. The sequencing of grammaticization effects: a twist from North America. In Schmid, Monika S., Austin, Jennifer R. and Stein, Dieter (eds), *Historical linguistics 1997.* Amsterdam: Benjamins, 291–314.

—— and Corbett, Greville G. 1999. The effect of noun incorporation on arguments structure. In Mereu (ed.), 49–71.

Mohanan, Tara. 1995. Wordhood and lexicality: noun incorporation in Hindi. *Natural Language and Linguistic Theory* 13: 75–134.

Nedjalkov, Vladimir P. (ed.) 1988. *Typology of resultative constructions.* (Typological Studies in Language, 12.) Amsterdam: Benjamins.

Newman, Paul. 2000. *The Hausa language: an encyclopedic reference grammar.* New Haven: Yale University Press.

Nguyen, Dinh-Hoa. 1997. Vietnamese. (London Oriental and African Language Library, 9.) Amsterdam: Benjamins.

Nikolaeva, Irina. 1999. *Ostyak.* Munich: Lincom Europa.

Noonan, Michael. 1992. *A grammar of Lango.* (Mouton Grammar Library, 8.) Berlin: Mouton de Gruyter.

Nordlinger, Rachel. 1998. *A Grammar of Wambaya, Northern Territory (Australia).* (Pacific Linguistics, Series C, No. 140). Canberra: Australian National University.

Nübling, Damaris. 2000. The development of 'junk': Irregularization strategies of HAVE and SAY in the Germanic languages. In Booij, Geert and van Marle, Jaap (eds), *Yearbook of Morphology 1999.* Dordrecht: Kluwer, 53–74.

Olsen, Susan. 2001. Copulative compounds: a closer look at the interface between syntax and morphology. In Booij, Geert and van Marle, Jaap (eds), *Yearbook of Morphology 2000.* Dordrecht: Kluwer, 279–320.

Oshita, Hiroyuki. 1995. Compounds: a view from suffixation and a-structure alteration.' In: Booij, Geert and van Marle, Jaap (eds), *Yearbook of Morphology 1994*. Dordrecht: Kluwer, 179–205.

Packard, Jerome L. 2000. *The morphology of Chinese*. Cambridge: Cambridge University Press.

Payne, Doris L. 1990. Morphological characteristics of Lowland South American Languages. In Payne, Doris L. (ed.), *Amazonian linguistics*. Austin, TX: University of Texas Press, 213–41.

Perevoščikov, P.N. (ed.) 1962. *Grammatika sovremennogo udmurtskogo jazyka: Fonetika i morfologija*. Iževsk: Udmurtskoe knižnoe izdatel'stvo.

Perlmutter, David. 1988. The split-morphology hypothesis: evidence from Yiddish. In Hammond and Noonan (eds), 79–100.

Pinker, Steven. 1999. *Words and rules: the ingredients of language*. New York: Basic Books.

—— and Prince, Alan. 1994. Regular and irregular morphology and the psychological status of rules of grammar. In Lima, Susan D., Corrigan, Roberta L. and Iverson, Gregory K. (eds), *The reality of linguistic rules*. Amsterdam: Benjamins, 321–51.

Plag, Ingo. 1999. *Morphological productivity: structural constraints in English derivation*. Berlin: Mouton de Gruyter.

Plank, Frans. 1981. *Morphologische (Ir-)Regularitäten*. Tübingen: Narr.

—— 1994. Inflection and derivation. In R.E. Asher (ed.), *The Encyclopedia of language and linguistics*, vol. 3. Oxford: Pergamon Press, 1671–78.

—— (ed.) 1991. *Paradigms: the economy of inflection*. Berlin: Mouton de Gruyter.

Plungian, Vladimir A. 2000. *Obščaja morfologija: Vvedenie v problematiku*. Moscow: Èditorial URSS.

Raffelsiefen, Renate. 1996. Gaps in word-formation. In Kleinhenz, Ursula (ed.), *Interfaces in phonology*. Berlin: Akademie Verlag, 194–209.

—— 1999a. Phonological constraints on English word-formation. In Booij, Geert and van Marle, Jaap (eds), *Yearbook of Morphology 1988*. Dordrecht: Foris, 225–87.

—— 1999b. Diagnostics for prosodic words revisited: the case of historically prefixed words in English. In Hall, T. Alan and Kleinhenz, Ursula (eds.) *Studies on the phonological word*. Amsterdam: Benjamins, 133–201.

Rainer, Franz. 1988. Towards a theory of blocking: Italian and German quality nouns. In Booij, Geert and van Marle, Jaap (eds), *Yearbook of Morphology 1988*. Dordrecht: Foris, 155–85.

—— 1993. *Spanische Wortbildungslehre*. Tübingen: Niemeyer.

Ravid, Dorit Diskin. 1995. *Language change in child and adult Hebrew*. New York: Oxford University Press.

Reh, Mechthild. 1985. *Die Krongo-Sprache (nìino mó-dì). Beschreibung, Texte, Wörterverzeichnis*. (Kölner Beiträge zur Afrikanistik, 12.) Berlin: Reimer.

Rehg, Kenneth L. 1981. *Ponapean reference grammar*. Honolulu: University of Hawaii Press.

Reis, Marga. 1983. Gegen die Kompositionstheorie der Affigierung. *Zeitschrift für Sprachwissenschaft* 2: 110–29.

Rennison, John R. 1997. *Koromfe*. (Descriptive grammars.) London: Routledge.

Rosen, Sara Thomas. 1989. Two types of noun incorporation: a lexical analysis. *Language* 65.2: 294–317.

Rowlands, E.C. 1969. *Yoruba*. (Teach Yourself Books.) Sevenoaks: Hodder & Stoughton.

Sadock, Jerrold M. 1991. *Autolexical syntax: a theory of parallel grammatical representations*. Chicago: The University of Chicago Press.

Sánchez Miret, Fernando, Koliadis, Antonios and Dressler, Wolfgang U. 1997. Connectionism vs. rules in diachronic morphology. *Folia Linguistica Historica* 18: 149–182.

Scalise, Sergio. 1988a. Inflection and derivation. *Linguistics* 26: 561–81.

——. 1988b. The notion of 'head' in morphology. In Booij, Geert and van Marle, Jaap (eds), *Yearbook of Morphology 1988*. Dordrecht: Kluwer, 229–45.

—— 1994. *Morfologia*. Bologna: Il Mulino.

Schachter, Paul and Otanes, Fe T. 1972. *Tagalog reference grammar*. Berkeley: University of California Press.

Schleicher, August. 1859. *Zur Morphologie der Sprache*. Ser. VII. Vol. I, No. 7. St Petersburg: Eggers.

Schultink, Henk. 1961. Produktiviteit als morfologisch fenomeen. *Forum der Letteren* 2: 110–25.

Selkirk, Elizabeth. 1982. *The syntax of words*. Cambridge, MA: MIT Press.

Shibatani, Masayoshi. 1990. *The languages of Japan*. Cambridge: Cambridge University Press.

Siloni, Tal. 1997. Event nominals and the construct state. In Haegeman, Liliana (ed.), *The new comparative syntax*. London: Longman, 165–88.

Singh, Rajendra (ed.) 1996. *Trubetzkoy's orphan*. Amsterdam: Benjamins.

Sneddon, James Neil. 1996. *Indonesian: a comprehensive grammar*. London: Routledge.

Sohn, Ho-min. 1994. *Korean*. (Descriptive grammars.) London: Routledge.

Spencer, Andrew. 1988. Bracketing paradoxes and the English lexicon. *Language* 64: 663–82.

—— 1991. *Morphological theory: an introduction to word structure in generative grammar*. Oxford: Blackwell.

—— Zwicky, Arnold M. (eds) 1998. *The handbook of morphology*. Oxford: Blackwell.

Sridhar, S.N. 1990. *Kannada*. (Descriptive grammars.) London: Routledge.

Štekauer, Pavol. 2000. Beheading the word? Please, stop the execution. *Folia Linguistica* 34: 333–55.

Stephany, Ursula. 1982. Inflectional and lexical morphology: a linguistic continuum. *Glossologia* 1: 27–55.

Stump, Gregory T. 1991. A paradigm-based theory of morphosemantic mismatches. *Language* 67: 675–725.

—— 2001a. *Inflectional morphology: a theory of paradigm structure*. Cambridge: Cambridge University Press.

—— 2001b. Default inheritance hierarchies and the evolution of inflectional classes. In Brinton, Laurel (ed.), *Historical linguistics 1999*. Amsterdam: Benjamins, 293–307.

Sullivan, Thelma D. 1988. *Compendium of Nahuatl grammar*. Salt Lake City: University of Utah Press.

Sutton-Spence, Rachel and Woll, Bencie. 1999. *The linguistics of British sign language: an introduction*. Cambridge: Cambridge University Press.

Švedova, N. Ju (ed.) 1980. *Russkaja grammatika. Tom I*. Moscow: Nauka.

Tiersma, Peter. 1982. Local and general markedness. *Language* 58: 832–49.

Topping, Donald M. 1973. *Chamorro reference grammar*. Honolulu: University Press of Hawaii.

van Marle, Jaap. 1985. *On the paradigmatic dimension of morphological creativity*. Dordrecht: Foris.

Vance, Timothy J. 1987. *An introduction to Japanese phonology*. Albany, NY: SUNY Press.

Van Valin, Robert D. and LaPolla, Randy. 1997. *Syntax: Structure, meaning and function*. Cambridge: Cambridge University Press.

Velázquez-Castillo, Maura. 1996. *The grammar of possession : inalienability, incorporation and possessor ascension in Guaraní*. Amsterdam: Benjamins.

Weber, David John. 1989. *A grammar of Huallaga (Huánuco) Quechua*. Berkeley: University of California Press.

Werner, Otmar. 1989. Sprachökonomie und Natürlichkeit im Bereich der Morphologie. *Zeitschrift für Phonetik, Sprachwissenschaft und Kommunikationsforschung* 42: 34–47.

Wilkins, David. 1989. Mparntwe Arrernte (Aranda): Studies in the structure and semantics of grammar. Ph.D. dissertation, Australian National University.

Williams, Edwin. 1981a. On the notions 'lexically related' and 'head of a word'. *Linguistic Inquiry* 12: 245–74.

—— 1981b. Argument structure and morphology. *Linguistic Review* 1: 81–114.

Wurzel, Wolfgang Ulrich. 1980. Ways of morphologizing phonological rules. In: Fisak, Jacek (ed.), *Historical morphology*. The Hague: Mouton, 43–62.

—— 1987. System-dependent morphological naturalness in inflection. In Dressler *et al.*, 59–96.

—— 1989. *Inflectional morphology and naturalness*. Dordrecht: Kluwer.

—— 1996. On similarities and differences between inflectional and derivational morphology. *Sprachtypologie und Universalienforschung* 49: 267–79.

Zepeda, Ofelia. 1983. *A Papago grammar*. Tucson: University of Arizona Press.

Ziervogel, D., Louw, J. A. and Taljaard, P. C. 1981. *A handbook of the Zulu language*. Pretoria: J. L. van Schaik.

Zipf, George Kingsley. 1935. *The psycho-biology of language: an introduction to dynamic philology*. Boston: Houghton Mifflin

Zwicky, Arnold. 1977. *On clitics*. Bloomington: Indiana University Linguistics Club.

—— 1985. Clitics and particles. *Language* 61: 283–305.

—— 1991. Systematic vs. accidental phonological identity. In Plank (ed.), 113–31.

—— and Pullum, Geoffrey. 1983. Cliticization vs. inflection: English *n't*. *Language* 59: 502–13.

Glossary of technical terms

ablative: an inflectional category of the dimension CASE: '(away) from' (e.g. Huallaga Quechua *mayu-pita* '(away) from the river').

accusative: an inflectional category of the dimension CASE that is used to mark the direct object (e.g. Latin *Marcus rosa-m* [rose-ACC] *vidit* 'Marcus saw a rose').

acronym: an abbreviation consisting of initial letters that are read like an ordinary word, e.g. *NATO* [neitoʊ] (as opposed to *alphabetism*).

action noun (or **event noun**): a deverbal noun that refers to the event or action itself (i.e. not to a participant of the event), e.g. English *replacement* (derived from *replace*) (Section 11.3.2).

actual word (= **usual word**): a lexeme that exists in the lexicon (Sections 3.1, 6.1).

affix: a short morpheme with an abstract meaning (Section 2.3).

affix compound: a morphological pattern that involves at least two stems and one affix (Section 5.1).

agent: a semantic role: the instigator of an action.

agent noun: a deverbal noun that refers to the agent participant of the action (Section 11.3.3).

agreement: a syntactic rule that requires related constituents to show identical marking for certain categories.

Akanie: a vowel-neutralizing alternation in Russian (Section 10.1).

allomorph (= **morpheme alternant**): two roots or morphological patterns are allomorphs (of the same abstract morpheme) if they express the same meaning and occur in complementary distribution (Section 2.5).

alphabetism: an abbreviation consisting of initial letters that are read with the letters' alphabet values, e.g. *CD* [siː diː] (Section 2.4).

analogy: the use of similar existing words as models in the modification and creation of words.

analytic language: a language that uses little morphology (Section 1.2).

anticausative: an event-changing operation signalling that there is no 'cause' element and no agent role in the derived event structure (Section 11.1.2).

antipassive: a function-changing operation that backgrounds the patient (Section 11.1.3).

applicative: a valence-changing operation that creates a new object argument (Section 11.1.5).

appositional compound: an exocentric compound denoting an entity that fulfils several descriptions simultaneouly (Section 5.1).

argument inheritance: the extent to which the argument structure (and function structure) of a deverbal derivative and its base are similar (Section 11.3.1).

argument structure: the set of semantic roles of a verb (= semantic valence) (Section 11.1.1).

aspect: an inflectional dimension of verbs that has to do with the internal temporal constituency of an event (categories: perfective, imperfective, habitual, etc.).

assibilation: the change of a stop to a sibilant ([s] or [ʃ]).

attenuative adjective: a deadjectival adjective that denotes a reduced degree of the base (e.g. *bluish* from *blue*).

augmentative noun: a denominal noun denoting a larger (or otherwise pragmatically special) version of the base noun.

automatic alternation: a sound alternation that has not lost the link to its phonetic motivation and that is purely phonological (Section 10.1).

back-formation: the formation of a shorter, simpler word from a longer word that is perceived as morphologically complex (Section 3.2.2).

base: the base of a morphologically complex word is the element to which a morphological operation applies (Section 2.4).

base modification: a formal operation that consists in a change of the pronunciation of part of the base.

blend: a lexeme whose stem was created by combining parts of two other lexeme stems – e.g. *smog* from *smoke* and *fog* (Section 2.4).

blocking: the application of a productive rule may be pre-empted by an existing word with the same meaning. This is called '(synonymy) blocking' (Section 6.3.7, 12.4).

bound form: an element (word-form or affix) that is prosodically dependent on its host and cannot stand on its own in a variety of ways (Section 8.2).

bound root (= combining form): a root that occurs only in compounds (Section 2.3).

bracketing paradox: a form that different criteria assign different hierarchical structures (or bracketings) to (Section 9.6).

case: an inflectional dimension of nouns that serves to code the noun phrase's semantic role.

category: see **inflectional category.**

causative verb: an event-changing operation referring to an event that is a caused version of the base event (Section 11.1.4).

circumfix: a discontinuous affix that occurs on both sides of the base (Section 2.3).

citation form: a word-form that is used by convention to refer to a lexeme – e.g. when listing a lexeme in a dictionary (Section 2.1).

clipping: (a method of forming) a shortened word that does not differ semantically from the longer version (Section 2.4).

clitic: a bound word-form – i.e. a word-form that is prosodically dependent on a host (Section 8.3).

coalescence: the diachronic change whereby two formerly free syntactic elements turn into a single word-form (Section 3.2.2).

combinatory potential: the information in a lexical entry about the surrounding elements with which a word or morpheme can or must combine (Section 3.2.1).

combining form (= bound root): a root that occurs only in compounds (Section 2.3).

comparative: an inflectional category of the dimension DEGREE ('having a higher degree').

competence: the speaker's knowledge of the linguistic system.

complex word: a word that is one of a group of words that show systematic covariation in their form and meaning – i.e. morphological structure (Section 1.1).

compound: a complex lexeme that is made up of more than one other lexeme stem (Section 2.1).

compounding: the formation of compounds (Sections 2.1, 5.1).

concatenative operation: an operation that consists of stringing morphemes together – i.e. affixation or compounding (as opposed to non-concatenative operations such as base modification or reduplication) (Section 2.4).

conceptual structure = event structure.

conjugation: (i) an inflection class of a verb; (ii) verb inflection in general.

constituent: a continuous part of a linguistic expression.

controller (of agreement): the constituent whose properties determine the properties of the agreeing constituent.

converb: an inflectional meaning of verbs: a verb-form that is used for adverbial subordination.

coordinative compound: an exocentric compound that refers to multiple referents corresponding to the compound members (Section 5.1).

conversion: a morphological rule in which the pronunciation of the base does not change (Section 2.4).

creativity: the creation of neologisms by unproductive patterns (Section 6.2).

cross-formation: the formation of a complex word from a base that is itself complex, by removing part of the base (Section 9.3).

cumulative expression: the expression of two morphological meanings simultaneously by a single unanalysable element (Section 2.5).

deadjectival: a formation whose base is an adjective is called *deadjectival*.

declension: (i) an inflection class of a noun; (ii) noun inflection in general.

default: a default rule is one that applies in the general case, but that may be overridden in special circumstances (Section 7.3).

defective: a lexeme is defective if some cells of its inflectional paradigm are not filled – i.e. if there are some inflectional meanings that it cannot express (Section 7.7).

degree: an inflectional dimension of adjectives having to do with comparison of gradable properties (categories: comparative, superlative).

denominal: a formation whose base is a noun is called *denominal*.

deponent: a lexeme that has a paradigm from a different category but not the meaning of that category (Section 7.7).

derivation$_1$ (= **derivational morphology**): a part of morphology that is characterized by relatively concrete morphological meanings, potential semantic irregularity, restrictions on applicability, etc. (see Section 4.3) (Note: *derivation$_1$* is closely related neither to *derive$_1$* nor to *derive$_2$*!).

derivation₂: the process of deriving₁ or deriving₂.

derivational phonology: an approach to (morpho-)phonology in which surface forms are derived₂ from underlying forms (Section 10.2).

derivative: a lexeme that is related to another lexeme by a rule of derivation₁.

derive₁ (A from B): build or form (a complex word) A on the basis of (a base) B (Section 2.4).

derive₂ (A from B): construct a (phonological) surface representation A by applying a series of modifying rules to an underlying representation B (Section 10.2).

dependent: in an endocentric construction, all non-heads are dependents.

desiderative: a deverbal derivational meaning ('want to do').

deverbal: a deverbal lexeme is one whose base is a verb.

devoicing: the loss of the feature 'voiced' of a phonological segment (e.g. Section 10.1).

dimension: see **inflectional dimension.**

diminutive noun: a denominal noun denoting a smaller (or otherwise pragmatically special) version of the base noun (diminutive adjectives, adverbs and verbs are also possible).

dual-processing model: a psycholinguistic model of inflection that assumes two completely separate modes of processing, rules and storage in an associative network (Section 7.5).

duplifix: an element attached to the base that consists of both copied segments and fixed segments (= a mixture of affix and reduplicant).

empty morpheme: a morpheme (generally an affix) that has no meaning but that must be posited for the sake of descriptive elegance (Sections 2.6, 7.4).

enclitic: a clitic that follows its host.

endocentric construction: a construction (syntactic phrase or compound pattern) that consists of a head and a dependent (or several dependents).

exocentric construction: a construction (syntactic phrase or compound pattern) that does not consist of a head and a dependent.

experiencer: a semantic role: the participant that experiences an experiential situation.

facilitative adjective: a deverbal derivational meaning ('able to undergo an action').

factitive verb: a deadjectival derivational meaning ('cause something to be Adj').

feature percolation: the sharing of (morpho)syntactic features by a head and its mother node.

female noun: a derivational meaning of nouns ('female') – e.g. English *poetess* (derived from *poet*).

free form: a word-form that is not bound (Section 8.2).

function structure: the set of syntactic functions of a verb's arguments (= syntactic valence) (Section 11.1.1).

future: an inflectional category of the dimension TENSE ('occurring later than the moment of speech').

gender: an inherent lexical property of nouns in some languages that determines their gender agreement (in adjectives, verbs and other agreement targets, gender is an inflectional dimension; typical categories are masculine, feminine, but sometimes simply gender 1, gender 2, etc.) (Section 7.1).

generic: an expression is generic if it refers to a whole class, rather than a particular item (Section 8.4).

genitive: an inflectional category of the dimension of CASE ('adnominal possessor').

global inflection class: an inflection class with many word-forms whose shape depends on the others in the paradigm (Sections 7.1–7.2).

grammaticalization: the coalescence of a full word and an auxiliary word to an affixed word (Section 3.3.2).

habitual: an inflectional category of the dimension of aspect ('an event that is repeated regularly').

head: the head of a compound or a syntactic phrase is the hyponym of the whole expression (Sections 5.1–5.2).

homonymous: two word-forms are homonymous if their pronunciation is identical (Section 7.6).

host: a clitic's host is the element that a clitic combines with to form a clitic group (Section 8.3).

hyponym: an expression is a hyponym of another expression if its meaning is compatible with it, but more specific.

imperative: an inflectional category of the dimension of MOOD ('speaker issues command to hearer').

imperfective: an inflectional category of the dimension of ASPECT ('an event seen from within or as not completed') (Section 4.1).

inchoative: a derivational meaning of deverbal verbs ('begin to do').

incorporation: N + V compounding, as found especially in polysynthetic languages (Sections 5.1, 11.2.1).

indicative: an inflectional category of the dimension of MOOD ('an event thought of as occurring in reality').

infinitive: an inflectional meaning of verbs: a nonfinite form used for clausal complements when the complement subject is identical to the matrix subject.

infix: an affix that occurs inside the base (Section 2.3).

inflection (or **inflectional morphology**): a part of morphology that is characterized by relatively abstract morphological meanings, semantic regularity, almost unlimited applicability, etc. (see Section 4.3).

inflect: When we say that a word INFLECTS (for some category) we mean that it has (inflectional) WORD-FORMS for that category – e.g. 'Russian verbs inflect for gender', i.e. Russian verbs distinguish different word-forms for different genders (of the subject argument).

inflectional category: a term from an inflectional dimension – e.g. FUTURE (from the dimension TENSE), ACCUSATIVE (from the dimension CASE), PASSIVE (from the dimension VOICE).

inflection class: a class of lexemes that inflect in the same way – i.e. that show the same SUPPLETIVE ALLOMORPHY in all word-forms of their PARADIGM.

inflectional dimension: a class of inflectional categories that share a semantic property and are mutually exclusive (Section 4.1), e.g. tense, case and voice.

inheritance₁: in a taxonomic hierarchy of increasingly general nodes, a lower node may inherit information from a higher node, so that it is possible to specify that information only once, on the higher node (Section 7.3).

inheritance₂: see **argument inheritance.**

interfix: a semantically empty affix that occurs between the two members of a N + N compound (especially in German and some other European languages) (Section 5.1).

intransitive: a verb that does not take a direct object is called *intransitive*.

isolating language: a language that makes only minimal use of morphology is called *isolating* (Section 1.2).

lexeme: a word in the sense of lexical entry; in other words, the set of all WORD-FORMS that are so closely related that they form a paradigm and are entered in a dictionary as a single entry (Section 2.1).

lexicon: the list of elements that speakers have to know in addition to the rules of grammar (Section 2.1).

markedness: of two contrasting categories (or meanings, or rules or constructions), one is said to be marked (and the other unmarked) if it is rarer, has a longer expression, a narrower distribution, etc. (Section 12.1).

masdar: an inflectional action noun (Section 11.4).

morph: a concrete primitive element of morphological analysis (Section 2.6).

morpheme: the smallest meaningful part of a linguistic expression that can be identified by segmentation (Sections 2.4, 2.6).

morpheme structure condition: a restriction on the co-occurrence of sounds within a morpheme (Section 9.7).

morphology: (the study of) systematic covariation in the form and meaning of words.

morphophonological alternation: a sound alternation that has lost the link to its original phonetic motivation and that is (at least in part) morphological in nature (Section 10.1).

morphophonology: the study of morphophonological alternations.

neologism: a new lexeme. A lexeme is a neologism in a language at time *t* if it was not an actual word immediately before *t* (Section 3.1).

nominative: an inflectional category of the dimension of CASE ('the case of the subject, the case-form that is used as citation form').

nonce formation = occasionalism.

number: an inflectional dimension of nouns, having to do with the number of items a noun refers to (categories: singular, plural, dual, etc.).

oblique: oblique cases are all cases apart from the most basic case(s) of a noun.

occasionalism (= nonce formation): a neologism that has not caught on and is restricted to occasional occurrences (Sections 3.1, 6.1).

paradigm: the structured set of word-forms of a lexeme (Section 2.1). (Often subsets that belong together (e.g. all past-tense forms of a verb) are also referred to as paradigms.)

paradigm rule: a word-based rule consisting of multiple correspondences between word-forms in an inflectional paradigm (Section 7.2).

paradigmatic relations: relations between units that could (potentially) occur in the same slot (Section 9.1).

participle: a verbal inflectional category signalling that the verb is used as an adjective.

passive: an inflectional category of the dimension of voice that signals that the patient is the subject.

past: an inflectional category of the dimension TENSE ('occurring earlier than the moment of speech').

patient: a semantic role: the participant that undergoes an action.

patient noun: a deverbal noun that refers to the verb's patient.

perfect: an inflectional category of the dimension of ASPECT ('an event that took place in the past but has current relevance').

perfective: an inflectional category of the dimension of ASPECT ('an event seen from the outside or as completed').

performance: use of language.

periphrasis: the use of a syntactic phrase to fill a cell of an inflectional paradigm (Section 7.7).

person: an inflectional agreement dimension of verbs (person of subject or object) and nouns (person of possessor) (categories: 1st, 2nd, 3rd).

phonological allomorph: two allomorphs are phonological if they can be related to each other by (morpho)phonological rules (Section 2.5).

plural: an inflectional category of the dimension of NUMBER ('more than one').

polysynthetic language: a language that makes very extensive use of morphology (§1.2).

portmanteau morph: an affix or stem that cumulatively expresses two meanings that would be expected to be expressed separately (Section 2.6).

possible word (= potential word): a lexeme that could be formed according to the word-formation rules (Sections 3.1, 6.1) (cf. *actual word*).

prefix: an affix that precedes the base (Section 2.3).

present: an inflectional category of the dimension TENSE ('occurring simultaneously with the moment of speech').

Priscianic formation: the formation of an inflected form on the basis of another inflected form (rather than an abstract stem) that is not closely related semantically (Section 7.4).

privative adjective: a denominal adjective signalling lack of possession of the base noun (N-PRIV 'lacking N').

productivity: a morphological pattern or rule is productive if it can be applied to new bases to create new words (Section 3.1, Chapter 6).

progressive: an inflectional category of the dimension of ASPECT ('an event that is in progress').

proprietive adjective: a denominal adjective signalling possession of the base noun (N-PROPR 'having N') (Section 11.4).

quality noun: a derivational meaning of deadjectival nouns (e.g. *goodness* from *good*).

reanalysis: a change by which a complex word comes to be regarded as matching a different word-schema from the one it was originally created by (Section 3.3.4).

reduplication: a formal operation whereby (part of) the base is copied and attached to the base (Section 2.4).

reduplicant: the copied element in a reduplication (Section 2.4).

referral: a rule of referral relates homonymous word-forms within a paradigm that exhibit unnatural syncretism (Section 7.6.4).

reflexive: a function-changing operation signalling that agent and patient are coreferential (Section 11.1.2).

relational adjective: a denominal adjective signalling some kind of relation to the base noun.

Rendaku: a consonant-voicing alternation in Japanese (Section 10.1).

repetitive: a derivational meaning of verbs: 'again' (e.g. English *rewrite*, derived from *write*, see Table 4.7).

resultative: an event-changing operation signalling that there is no 'cause' and 'become' element in the event structure (Section 11.1.2).

reversive: a derivational meaning of verbs: 'reverse or undo the effect of the base verb' (e.g. English *unfasten*, derived from *fasten*).

root: a base that cannot be analysed further – i.e. a base that consists of a single morpheme (Section 2.3).

rule schema: a schema that generalizes over several different morphological rules that exhibit similarities (Section 7.3).

secretion: a change whereby an element that used to be part of the root turns into an affix (Section 3.3.4).

singular: an inflectional category of the dimension of number ('one').

stem: the base of an inflected word-form (Section 2.3).

stimulus: a semantic role: the participant that represents the content of the experiencer's experience (Section 11.1.1).

structure preservation: the property of morphophonological alternations of not introducing new segments (Section 10.1).

subcategorization frame: see **combinatory potential.**

subjunctive: an inflectional category of the dimension of mood ('a non-realized event in a subordinate clause').

subtraction: a formal operation that consists in deleting a segment (or more than a segment) from the base (Section 9.2).

suffix: an affix that follows the base (Section 2.3).

superlative: an inflectional category of the dimension of COMPARISON ('highest degree').

suppletive allomorph: two allomorphs are suppletive (= show **suppletion**) if they cannot be related to each other by (morpho)phonological rules (Section 2.5).

syncretism: systematic homonymy of inflected words in a paradigm (Section 7.6).

syntagmatic relations: relations between units that (potentially) follow each other in speech (Section 9.1).

synthetic compound: a nominal compound whose dependent noun fills an argument position in the head's valence (Section 11.2.3).

synthetic language: a language that uses a fair amount of morphology (Section 1.2).

tense: an inflectional dimension of verbs that has to do with the temporal location of the verbal event, especially with respect to the speech event (categories: present, future, past, etc.) (Section 4.1).

theme$_1$: a semantic role: the participant that undergoes a movement or other change of state.

theme$_2$: an older term for 'stem'.

transfixation: interdigitation of vowel morphemes and consonant morphemes.

transitive: a verb that takes a direct object is called transitive.

transposition: change of word-class by a morphological operation (Sections 11.3–11.4).

type frequency (of a morphological pattern): the number of lexemes in the lexicon that were formed using that pattern, or that take inflected forms using that pattern.

Umlaut: a vowel-fronting alternation in German (Sections 10.1).

underlying representation: an abstract representation that is not actually used by speakers, but that linguists postulate to simplify the rule system; the rules of derivational phonology operate on underlying representations to produce actually pronounced surface representations.

univerbation: the coalescence of two full words into a compound (Sections 3.3.2).

Universal Grammar: the innate part of speakers' grammatical knowledge (Section 1.3).

usual word = actual word.

valence: information about the semantic roles and syntactic functions of a verb (or sometimes another word-class) (Chapter 11).

voice: an inflectional (and sometimes derivational) dimension of verbs that indicates a function-changing operation (categories: active, passive, reflexive, antipassive).

word: a word-form or a lexeme (Section 2.1, Chapter 8).

word family: a set of morphologically related lexemes (Section 2.1).

word-form: a 'text word' that can be isolated from surrounding elements because it is either prosodically independent (= a **free form**) or a **clitic** and not an **affix** (Section 2.1, Chapter 8).

word-formation (= **lexeme formation**): derivation and compounding (Section 2.1).

word-schema: a representation of a set of morphologically related words (Section 3.2.2).

zero expression: an inflectional category is said to be expressed by zero if there is nothing in the pronunciation that corresponds to the category, so that the presence of the category's meaning must be inferred from this absence of form. (In derivational morphology, morphologists usually talk about *conversion* rather than *zero expression*, though there is really no deep difference.)

Language index

Language	Family	Geographical area	Page numbers
Kiribatese	Malayo-Polynesian	Kiribati (Pacific)	106
Kobon	Trans-New Guinea, Adelbert Range	Papua New Guinea	240, 242
Korean	Isolate	Korea	26, 28–9, 67, 70, 89, 116
Koromfe	Niger-Congo, Gur	northern Burkina Faso	247–8
Krongo	Kordofanian	northern Sudan	32
Lakhota	Siouan	North and South Dakota	156–7
Lango	Nilo-Saharan, Nilotic	southern Sudan	155–7, 247–8
Latin	Indo-European, Italic	Italy	14–15, 17, 25, 29–30, 35–6, 52–3, 64, 72–3, 76, 78, 83, 108, 118, 120–5, 132, 142, 143, 146, 192, 205, 238, 243–4, 246, 248
Lezgian	Nakh-Daghestanian	southern Daghestan (Russia) and northern Azerbaijan (eastern Caucasus)	4, 5, 33, 34, 57, 84, 117, 131, 132, 133, 144, 199–202, 230–2
Lithuanian	Indo-European, Baltic	Lithuania	139, 140, 164
Malay	Austronesian	Malaysia, Indonesia	107
Mangap-Mbula	Austronesian, Oceanic	Papua New Guinea	24
Martuthunira	Pama-Nyungan	Western Australia	28, 30, 116, 121, 124
Mbay	Nilo-Saharan	Chad	37
Mixtec (Chalcatongo)	Oto-Manguean	Oaxaca (Mexico)	23
Murle	Nilo-Saharan	southern Sudan	24, 167
Nahuatl (Classical)	Uto-Aztecan	central Mexico	18, 19, 66, 84
Nahuatl (Huahtla)	Uto-Aztecan	Mexico	220
Old Church Slavonic	Slavic	used as liturgical language of various eastern European churches	52, 140–1
Old English	West Germanic	England	5, 9, 23, 52, 59, 115, 138, 241–2, 247, 248

Subject index

Page numbers in bold are pages where the term in question is in bold within the text.

113233